THE ASYLUM

THE ASYLUM

The Renegades Who Hijacked the World's Oil Market

Leah McGrath Goodman

WILLIAM MORROW

An Imprint of HarperCollins*Publishers*

Unless otherwise noted, the photographs are from the private collections of the author and members of the energy market, including Michel Marks, Sherry Collins Zabel, Zoltan Louis Guttman, Richard Schaeffer, and Jeffrey Sprecher.

HarperCollins books may be purchased for educational, business, or sales promotional use. For information please write: Special Markets Department, HarperCollins Publishers, 10 East 53rd Street, New York, NY 10022.

FIRST EDITION

Designed by Lisa Stokes

Library of Congress Cataloging-in-Publication Data

Goodman, Leah McGrath.

The asylum : the Renegades who hijacked the world's oil market / Leah McGrath Goodman. — 1st ed.

p. cm.

Includes bibliographical references and index.

ISBN 978-0-06-176627-5

1. New York Mercantile Exchange (N.Y.)—History. 2. Stockbrokers—United States. 3. Petroleum industry and trade—United States—History. 4. Petroleum products—Prices. I. Title.

HG6049.G66 2010

332.6092'27471—dc22

2010016641

11 12 13 14 15   OV/RRD   10 9 8 7 6 5 4 3 2 1

To John Cochrane Duncanson,
who, above all, believes in mankind

Losing money was no simple matter. It took months of hard work and careful misplanning. A person misplaced, disorganized, miscalculated, overlooked everything and opened every loophole and just when he thought he had it made, the government gave him a lake, or a forest or an oil field and spoiled everything.

—JOSEPH HELLER, *CATCH-22*

Contents

Part III | The Sellout

Author's Note

This book is the result of thousands of hours of interviews over the past seven years with what is very likely the only few hundred individuals on the planet who truly understand how the oil market works and why. For many of them, this will be the first time their words appear in print, as they did not realize—until recently—the significance of their actions and the impact they would have on the world.

Looking back now, many of the market's participants regret some of the things they did. They also recognize that by agreeing to be interviewed, they risked being seen as intending the far-flung effects. This would be the wrong conclusion to take. Those who willingly went on the record with their stories did so mainly to offer a greater awareness of what happened and how it happened, providing the first behind-the-scenes accounts of the events that eventually drove oil prices to nearly $150 a barrel.

They are looking to set the record straight, despite the fact that the record itself is often not pretty.

While the bulk of this book was put together by way of old-fashioned, shoe-leather reporting (read: obsessive interviews, phone calls, and face-to-face meetings), many of my sources provided original documentation of a highly confidential nature to tell their stories—transcripts, photographs, draft business plans, secret government filings, jottings from boardroom sessions, pay stubs, e-mails, legal records, cocktail napkin scribblings, and expense reports—in addition to innumerable hours painstakingly recollecting their conversations, some of which took place decades ago. These were corroborated and confirmed wherever possible with all parties involved, both living and dead (although in the cases of the dead, relatives, obviously, had to be interviewed).

For purposes of understanding much of the detail on which this book is based, the reader should not assume that the individual whose dialogue or specific emotion is recorded is necessarily the person who provided the information, though, in most instances, that is the case. At every opportunity, individuals are identified to preserve transparency, and information has been double-checked with witnesses—especially those being quoted—then vetted by secondary and tertiary sources where applicable.

While it is true groups of people will often diverge in the retelling of their versions of the facts, when enough people have weighed in, certain facts will prevail over others. Prevailing facts have been favored over outliers in my writings. For those who believe that too much has been revealed in some of the chapters, please bear in mind that many details have been omitted on the grounds that they were too sensitive, too personal, or just too plain bizarre. Moreover, some of the more recent events covered in this book have yet to reach their final conclusion, particularly legal actions against traders and other market participants who remain in administrative purgatory. In these situations, the latest information has been provided, although is clearly subject to change.

Finally, it should be stressed that one or two sources who openly began the interview process did not fully complete their sessions, as they felt the prevailing facts did not favor them, yet could not convincingly refute them. This is to be expected. Sources who do not wish to cooperate are well within their rights and have been respected. Conversely, a couple sources who did not wish to participate in the project at the outset changed their minds shortly before its publication. Under those circumstances, they were interviewed as much as possible before the book's final edit.

It is my belief that the accounts herein represent the best of the knowledge that's out there from those who personally witnessed the birth and the indisputably haphazard development of the modern-day oil market, culminating with record-breaking prices not seen before or since, as of this writing.

There is a misconception popular in the public discourse that Wall Street knows exactly what it's getting into when it endeavors to create a new market or financial product. But that is almost never the case. And I think this book proves it.

Cast of Characters

THE CHAIRMEN

Michel David Marks—Progenitor of the world's first free oil market who made headlines in 1978 for becoming the nation's youngest chairman at twenty-seven. He resigned, without ever having lost an election, in 1987.

William Bradt—Plywood trader who joined Nymex as a heating-oil pit trader in 1980 and was named Nymex chairman in 1987, succeeding Marks. Started the energy options market, but resigned after business dealings with another pit trader triggered a government inquiry.

Zoltan Louis Guttman—Hungarian émigré and Nymex chairman from 1988 to 1992, steering the oil exchange to global prosperity and launching the wildly popular natural-gas market. Forced to resign after a government inquiry found him culpable for the illegal trades of his business partner.

Martin Greenberg—Chairman of Comex, the global gold and silver market, from 1990 to 1992; legendary for an ego, fellow traders said, that was superseded only by his temper.

Daniel Rappaport—Former Park Avenue lawyer, pit trader, and Nymex chairman from 1993 to 2001. Merged Nymex with Comex in 1994. Earned the name "chairman of the bucks" for paying himself more than any other exchange chairman in the world.

Vincent Viola—Gasoline pit trader, West Point graduate, and erstwhile kung fu fighter. Chairman of Nymex from 2001 to 2004. Earned widespread accolades for reopening the oil market days after the September 11 attacks gutted the World Financial Center.

Mitchell Steinhause—Pit trader–turned–Nymex chairman, leading the oil market from 2004 to 2006. Handpicked by his predecessor, Viola, who continued to draw large consulting checks from the exchange.

Richard Schaeffer—The last of the oil chairmen who spent most of his tenure, from 2006 to 2008, selling off pieces of the energy market to the highest bidders—a private-equity firm, investors in a public stock offering, and the Chicago Mercantile Exchange, in that order.

THE TRADERS

Mark Bradley Fisher—Self-anointed czar of the oil market and one of the first Ivy League MBAs off Wall Street to make a name for himself in the Nymex pits. Started as a runner at the age of twelve in the wild metals markets of the 1970s, and hailed as a "brilliant" wunderkind by the *New York Times* by age twenty-eight.

Gary Glass—One of Guttman's first trading mentors who quit school at sixteen to take up an apprenticeship with New York options guru Herbert Filer in 1962. Later became a Nymex pit trader and, in 1995, a star witness at Guttman's trial.

Harold Jay Magid—Highly skilled options pit trader and New York University instructor whose business partnership with Guttman ended bitterly in the 1980s with a lengthy court battle, culminating with Guttman stepping down from the Nymex chairmanship.

Robert Ira Sahn—Third-generation member of a poultry family who traded at Nymex from the late 1970s until the first Gulf War. One of the oil market's richest and most powerful activists.

Randy Warsager—Pit trader and after-hours Nazi hunter who worked with the first and last of the oil market chairmen, both of whom confided in him but despised each other.

Bill Perkins—African-American pit trader forced to stand outside the entrance of the Nymex building for three days before being admitted in 1991. Went on to become one of the energy market's biggest success stories as a multimillionaire hedge fund trader in Houston.

Steve Karvellas—Natural-gas pit trader who pled guilty in 2008 to two counts of felony for illegal trading while heading the Nymex compliance committee responsible for making sure trading was fair. Fined $850,000 and sentenced to five years at the maximum-security Rikers Island prison in New York.

GREEK CHORUS (FROM THE PITS)

Ben Kaufman—Teenager who worked on the oil-trading floor during the second Gulf War after his father, a first–Gulf War trading veteran, introduced him to the pits in first grade.

Mark Lichtner—Self-described "scalper" and longtime pit trader who vociferously opposed many Nymex board members, executives, and chairmen over three decades.

Gary Lapayover—Witness to the "Great Potato Bust" of 1976 and vice chairman after Nymex transformed itself from a struggling potato exchange to a global energy monopoly.

Sherry Collins Zabel—The youngest known woman ever to have traded on the floor of a U.S. exchange, recruited by Marks to the Nymex pits in the 1970s. Appeared on the *Today* show and the front page of the *Wall Street Journal*.

Lenny Williams—Widower and father of two who finally blew the whistle on cheating in the Nymex pits in 2002—only to be tailed, threatened, and mistreated by law-enforcement officials, resulting in his being fired and permanently banished from the trading floor.

THE EXECUTIVES

Richard Leone—Ex–New Jersey state treasurer and Princeton University professor who worked as Nymex president under the Marks regime in the early 1980s for a stiff fee.

Rosemary Theresa McFadden—The nation's first female exchange president, appointed by Marks in the mid-1980s to much fanfare, outlasting two of three chairmen—including Marks.

David Greenberg—Metals pit trader, son of Martin Greenberg (former Comex chairman), and the only Nymex board member who dared oppose electronic trading in 2006.

Stuart Smith—Senior vice president of oil market operations and Kaufman's first boss; fired in 2004 after a criminal probe resulted in his pleading guilty to first-degree bribery.

J. Robert "Bo" Collins—Nymex president from 2001 to 2004 and a former options pit trader under Viola who sparked controversy over his seven-figure paycheck. Left to start a hedge fund that went under two years after its founding amid a gas market scandal.

John D'Agostino—Vice president of business strategy at Nymex during the second Gulf War, Harvard MBA, and one of the youngest executives ever to be appointed at the exchange.

GOVERNMENT OFFICIALS

Drs. Wendy and Phil Gramm—The free-market husband-and-wife team who helped pave the way for the infamous Enron loophole—Dr. Wendy Gramm as head of the Commodity Futures Trading Commission under Reagan and Phil Gramm as a prominent senator from Texas.

Brooksley Born—The Stanford-educated lawyer and head of the Commodity Futures Trading Commission under Clinton in 1996 who was credited with foreseeing the global banking crisis that would tear Wall Street asunder. Played a major role in ousting Guttman from his position as Nymex chairman.

Dr. James Newsome—Former strawberry and cattle farmer who, in 2001, was named head of the Commodity Futures Trading Commission, only to resign three years later to become Nymex president, CEO, and Schaeffer's right-hand man.

Greg Mocek—Head of the enforcement division at the Commodity Futures Trading Commission under Newsome, investigating Enron and the Nymex trading pits before resigning in 2008, just as global oil prices spiked to nearly $150 a barrel and plunged toward $30 days later.

KEY OUTSIDE PLAYERS

Francis Q. Marks—Produce merchant, businessman, and father of Michel Marks; affectionately dubbed "dean of the exchange" by the oil market traders.

J. R. Simplot—Idaho's famed "Potato King" and the farmer who
climactically ravaged Nymex in 1976.

Leo Melamed—Chairman of the Chicago Mercantile Exchange from
1969 to 1991 after narrowly escaping the KGB and the Nazis as
a child. Traded potatoes at Nymex, penned ribald science-fiction
novels, and masterminded the first global financial futures market.

Jeffrey Sprecher—Ex–race car driver, turbine salesman, and Beverly
Hills power-plant developer who, in 1997, founded the Atlanta
energy market ICE to compete with Nymex, funneling trades
through the United Kingdom to avoid U.S. regulation and
revolutionizing oil trading for good.

John Arnold—Ex–Enron gas trader and "boy genius" who became the
youngest person on the Forbes Richest 400 Americans list in 2007
after turning an $8 million bonus he received from Enron the year
of its bankruptcy into a multibillion-dollar hedge fund.

Brian Hunter—The Canadian trader for Amaranth Advisors who lost
over $6 billion in the gas market, annihilating his own hedge fund
and the hedge fund of Bo Collins in late 2006. Despite leaving
a paper trail, he repeatedly managed to thwart attempts by U.S.
authorities to bring him to justice, even after a judge found him
guilty of market manipulation, not in small part due to the Enron
loophole.

The Hazing

IT WAS DAWN when I received my first of many after-hours phone calls from Mark Bradley Fisher, otherwise known as the Fish. A self-made millionaire with a Napoleonic sense of his own destiny, Fisher prided himself on his work ethic, his intellectual prowess, and his ability to rise early in the morning and toil late into the night. As a result, he had a habit of calling me almost exclusively at inconvenient times.

It was February 2005, the year Wall Street began to realize something was wrong with the oil market. Fisher, however, was not particularly disturbed. After all, he was one of the wealthiest and most powerful energy traders in the world.

Fumbling in the darkness, I nearly fell out of bed trying to find my cell phone. As I flipped it open, Fisher sounded none too pleased at the five-ring wait.

"What are you doing?" he barked in his trader's rasp, the line crackling softly in the background.

The Fish never identified himself over the phone. You were just supposed to know it was him. Despite his coarseness and affinity for semi-sadistic pranks—often inflicted on the less fortunate of his many admiring acolytes—he was one of the few oil traders off Wall Street who boasted a fistful of Ivy League degrees. Traders in the multitrillion-dollar commodities market had long been aware of his indomitable presence—often acutely so—but, to the rest of the world, the Fish was a virtual unknown.

And he liked it that way.

He was already at work. Maybe he'd just arrived, or maybe he'd never left. Some traders swore the Fish never slept. That was how it was in the oil market, brimming with tall tales and conjecture. I could envision him sitting bolt-upright behind his desk, office shower to the right, views of the Hudson to the left, buried in a flotilla of computer screens and price charts, guzzling a can of soda in the dark, silent office building. Fisher had a penchant for sugar and his poison of choice was Pepsi, a can of which was by his side for much of the day.

"Nothing," I answered, struggling to wake up. "Sleeping."

I'd met Fisher before, but this was the first time he had contacted me at home.

He coughed, attempting to disguise the laugh that confirmed, at least to him, I was a slacker. "Come by my office today at eleven. I want you to see something." He paused before adding: "But you have to promise me I won't read about it tomorrow in the *Wall Street Journal*."

As a reporter for Dow Jones & Co., the financial news service that, along with the *Journal*, is owned by News Corp., my beat was the energy market. My duties included writing two wire stories a day, one in the morning and one in the evening, about where oil prices were heading and why. So far, it had not been a difficult job, because ever since the start of the Iraq War oil prices went mostly one way—up.

There was a small problem, though. With oil prices going up every day, I was beginning to run out of clever narrative devices and plot twists to keep my commentary interesting. Most of the time, I would just sit at my desk, trying to think of a new way of saying the same thing I'd said the day before—that there no longer appeared to be enough oil in the world to meet rising demand, that the rock on which modern industrial civilization had been built seemed to be slowly crumbling.

The strange term being tossed around by experts at the time was "peak oil." Dismissed by the opposing experts as a ridiculous doomsday scenario, it referred to the moment when the world's oil production would begin to decline until supply ran out. The feeling was that this would not be a good thing, since there was no decent alternative for oil and no reliable way of knowing exactly when the planet had reached its tipping point. In the meantime, guessing when peak oil would arrive had become somewhat like a parlor game to industry insiders, each trying the shout the others down. But behind the scenes, a much more terrifying question overshadowed the debate: had peak oil already arrived—and nobody wanted to admit it yet?

On one point the experts could agree. The world was not prepared for the catastrophic end of oil. Without question, its depletion would mean more wars, more political strife, and more awkward death matches between the West and the oil-rich Middle East.

Still, even as the United States fought wars in two Middle East nations and kept drilling for oil in ever more perilous depths of the ocean, nobody seemed especially alarmed at the thought of oil drying up. By all appearances, switching from oil to something less danger-ous was going to be gut-wrenching, no matter how high oil prices got. Americans remained bent on driving their monster SUVs while an end-less stream of upwardly mobile classes in increasingly populous nations such as China and India wanted nothing more than to drive monster SUVs of their own.

I arrived out of breath and a few minutes late for my appointment with the Fish after getting off the train at the World Trade Center pit. Dodging traffic on the West Side Highway, I passed a slew of trader hangouts: the Pussycat Lounge & Steakhouse, a seamy gentlemen's club and Wall Street institution; Cordato's Deli, the sub shop next door with the secret champagne room in back with an even more secret passage-way to the Pussycat; and Moran's, the church-turned-Irish-pub that remained, either way, a place of devout worship.

It was just after eleven A.M. when I reached the spot where Fisher plied his trade: the New York Mercantile Exchange, called Nymex, the biggest, most influential energy market in the world. Just beyond its doors, bets were placed on the future prices of the planet's most impor-tant commodities—crude oil, gasoline, heating oil, and natural gas, as well as gold and silver—in a football field–size room teeming with sweaty traders. A members-only club favoring the rich and well connected, this was the temple of the chosen few who stood as the final arbiters of what the world paid every day for a barrel of oil or a gallon of gas.

Power plants, gas stations, fuel distributors, and oil companies across the globe paid close attention to this rarefied casino, watching carefully for any price changes that would determine how much they would pay for fuel and what they'd charge their customers, the ordinary consumer. Newspapers and television networks trumpeted Nymex's prices as the holy gospel, beaming them throughout the continents for all to follow—banks, hedge funds, Wall Street investors, even the top-producing oil nations of Saudi Arabia, Iran, Russia, and Norway.

Yet nobody seemed to know who, exactly, these New York oil traders were or how they, of all people, got to wield such immense power. How did someone like, say, the Fish, a balding, middle-aged father of two from Long Island, come to dominate the market that decided what consumers would pay to drive their cars or heat their homes? Wasn't the Organization of Petroleum Exporting Countries—the mysterious oil cartel known as OPEC—supposed to be dictating the price of oil? What about Saudi Arabia, the country holding the world's largest proven oil reserves? Where was *its* energy market? And what really happened behind the tightly closed doors of Nymex's heavily guarded, sixteen-story building?

The answers, I soon found out, lay in the secrets of the pits, the clandestine trading arena where market speculators, mostly men in their thirties and forties, gathered every day to beat and berate one another in a money game so absurd that even they could scarcely believe they were being allowed to play it.

As I approached the building, I noticed what seemed like some sort of triumphal procession under way. Passersby were oblivious, just as they'd always been oblivious to the giant energy market in their midst. Nymex had camouflaged itself well among the high-rises of its upscale neighborhood.

What I didn't know then was that I was about to witness my first Mark Fisher signature event. This is what Fisher wanted to make sure I saw—one of his grandiose exhibitions of power. Hundreds of people poured out of the revolving doors of the skyscraper on the Hudson River: traders, executives, secretaries, compliance staff, technical personnel. I knew that the exchange was open and the oil market was trading, but *who* was trading it, I could not guess. It seemed as if all the market's members had dropped whatever they'd been doing to flock to the pier. Among the rabble, I even saw Mitchell Steinhause, the oil market's token chairman.

As I quickly learned, the Fisher event usually involved a boisterous horde, a smaller group of scapegoats, and some sort of ritual sacrifice. Today was no exception. At the center of the crowd stood Fisher's herd of sacrificial lambs, four or five men in their twenties, all rookie energy traders in various states of dress. They teetered at the edge of the ice-strewn Hudson, shivering in the subzero squalls. Beside them was the master of ceremonies himself, the Fish, who even looked a bit like Napoleon. A short, stout forty-four-year-old with a preternatural gift for fiery oratory, he addressed the throng from the comfort of his winter parka. Despite his height, Fisher seemed to tower menacingly over his captives.

These young men, he said, had been summoned to the river because they had bet they could win a round of Texas Hold'em, a poker game they'd unwisely proceeded to lose. Since the wager had indicated the losers would swim the freezing waters in sight of their colleagues, it was now time for them to pay up.

Some of Fisher's victims had come prepared. Two were wearing professional wet suits. One had his shirt off. Another had stubbornly opted to dress as if for a normal day, keeping on his Gucci loafers with the gold clasps, worn without socks, as was the style.

How you took your punishment said a lot about you. The traders who were wearing the wet suits were seen as cunning; the trader without his shirt on fearless; and the last, the one with the designer shoes, an admirable stoic. These were all excellent qualities to have if you were a trader in the pits, where how you took your medicine often determined how well you got paid.

Fisher had positioned emergency rescue workers along the marina to go in after anyone who didn't make it out, ambulances idling nearby. The market spectators tittered with eager anticipation. That is to say, the staff and attendant membership of the world's reigning oil market exhibited the basic characteristics of a lynch mob, heckling the traders and urging them to jump. A couple of the young men whose cardinal sin had been to play poker badly tried to laugh it off, but as Fisher began the final countdown to their plunge, there wasn't a person in the audience who didn't see the fear on their faces.

No one attempted to stop the brutish hazing. On the contrary, the bystanders were fully into it. Fisher, the market's ringleader, had everyone in his thrall. This was one time I was glad to be the reporter, observing but divorced from the events.

As I watched the scene unfold, I wondered just how long had the oil traders been acting this way? These were the chosen ones? The ones who called the shots on what we paid to drive our cars and heat our homes?

It was all too surreal.

If those who held the key to the global energy market could stand by while blithely throwing their own traders, their life blood, into the Hudson, then what would they be willing to do to us, the faceless public?

That day, oil prices topped $50 a barrel.

The pit traders just shrugged.

And that was only the beginning. Over the next three years, oil prices would slingshot to nearly $150 a barrel before crashing back toward $30 in a matter of days, roiling the global economy and raising suspicions that oil prices were rising and falling on little more than pixie dust. Against the backdrop of Washington politicians lamely suggesting that altering daylight savings hours or offering gasoline tax holidays might offer lasting relief, Fox News commentator Bill O'Reilly fumed at energy market executive John D'Agostino during an April 2008 interview on his television program, *The O'Reilly Factor*. What followed was a truly bizarre exchange, revealing what even supposedly informed individuals think about how the oil market works.

When O'Reilly is told that a group of traders in New York are responsible for the price of oil and gas in much the same way that traders of the New York Stock Exchange are responsible for the price of Microsoft stock, he simply cannot believe his ears. Instead, he concludes that it must be the sheikhs of the Middle East or Venezuela's ultra-leftist president, Hugo Chavez, who are arbitrarily slapping price stickers on barrels of oil. As the conversation gradually deteriorates, a member of O'Reilly's backstage crew is heard to say, "Oh shit, Bill's made an ass of himself again." But O'Reilly's confusion about the method behind the madness of the global energy market is typical—and worth hearing in full.

> **O'Reilly:** OK now, look, in my town out on Long Island, gasoline has gone up 75 cents a gallon in about a month, a month and a half. Why now? Why this point in time?
>
> **D'Agostino:** Well, a couple of things. One is oil has been high and has stayed high.
>
> **O'Reilly:** Now, who's driving that? Is that the greedy sheikhs and Hugo Chavez?
>
> **D'Agostino:** No, no, no, I don't know about that. What we know for a fact is that we have a weak dollar. We have global demand that's staying put, no matter how much the price has gone up. [A

weakened dollar means you need more dollars to buy the same amount of oil, hence a higher price.]

O'Reilly: We had that last year. The demand has gone up globally since last—but let's—wait a minute. Let's walk through it so everybody understands what we're talking about. The Organization of Petroleum Exporting Countries sets the price for a barrel of oil. And they keep raising it and raising it and raising it. Dick Cheney went over there and tried to say, "Hey, give us a break." They gave Cheney the middle digit. All right? So they can, they can charge whatever they want to charge, correct?

D'Agostino: No. OPEC only sets the oil *supply*. . . . The *price* of oil is actually set in New York. . . .

O'Reilly: Is there a guy who says $125 a barrel?

D'Agostino: No. There's a huge market. It's filled with hedgers. It's filled with speculators. It's filled with moms and dads, average Americans. It's a big market that sets the price.

O'Reilly: Somebody has to put the $125 on the barrel. Who does it?

D'Agostino: They're getting it from this market. . . .

O'Reilly: Who is "*they*"?

D'Agostino: The oil producers. They're looking at this, just like when you decide how much a share of IBM is worth. You look at the price on the New York Stock Exchange.

O'Reilly: The CEO of Shell or the CEO of ExxonMobil says, "We're going to pay $125 a barrel." Is that what they say? I thought it was the sheikhs and Hugo Chavez saying, "We're going to charge you $125 a barrel."

D'Agostino: No. They're all looking to the exchanges, the free markets, to set the price. . . . The free markets right now are saying the price of crude oil is about $120 a barrel. It's been going up. It continues to go up. And gasoline prices are directly related to crude oil prices.

O'Reilly: . . . But you still haven't explained, and I don't know if you can, Mr.—with all due respect, Mr. D'Agostino—who puts the $120 on—a human being has to do that. And somebody has to make a decision.

D'Agostino: It would be great if there was just *one* person who was doing that, because then we could go talk to him.

O'Reilly: But there has to be. Because just to get the word out, somebody has to say the word. So if you don't know, you don't know, because I certainly don't.

The viewers of the *O'Reilly Factor* also could not believe D'Agostino was telling the truth. After the program aired, they responded with dozens of furious e-mails.

And one death threat.

Contrary to popular opinion, oil prices were not being controlled by Arabs or leftist dictators. They were being controlled by the same bootstrapping traders who had embarked on an extraordinary experiment from the depths of a redbrick mansion in downtown Manhattan exactly thirty years earlier.

Individuals who, like the anonymous Wall Street professionals about to unleash a crippling financial crisis on the world, took the subway and ferry to work, earned unheard-of riches, gave to charity, and thought nothing of bringing the global economy to its knees.

Part I

The Gamble

1

Welcome to the Asylum

Some days, I would just stand there in the middle of the floor and say to myself, I can't believe this is really happening.

—BEN KAUFMAN

WELCOME TO THE ASYLUM. For those brave enough to venture down into the pits of the New York Mercantile Exchange, these were, more likely than not, the first words to greet them (often uttered conspiratorially by one of the market's self-described "inmates," as he juggled five telephones, three of them upside-down).

It wasn't so much that the oil business required you to be crazy. But it certainly helped.

Ben Kaufman, the teenage son of one of the biggest oil traders at the time of the first Persian Gulf War, grew up hearing all about his father's exploits minting millions in the pits. But nothing could have prepared him for his internship in the summer of 2003, just as the second Gulf War was heating up.

As he surveyed the windowless expanse of the twenty-five-thousand-square-foot trading floor, a wholly enclosed world of flashing price screens, live headline feeds, and hundreds of shouting traders trailing armies of minions, a primordial wave of emotion washed over him. "You go down there expecting just about anything," he says, "and it's *still* shocking. Every other word is a swear word. Traders yell because they don't have time to be polite. It is a world of super-assholes. They're all dicks, crude, manly men."

he traders Kaufman beheld were betting on something called the futures market. It was like the stock market, only faster and scarier. With most stocks, you bet that the price of a share of a particular company will go up, and in some cases down, but without any expiration date or time limit on the wager. The futures market was much more precise and, in a sense, more demanding. Energy traders bet on what they thought the price of oil or fuel might be for any of the separate twelve months of the year—or the next year, or the year after, for up to a decade—making and losing mammoth amounts of money in the process. Trading futures, you might correctly bet that prices would go up, but if you got the month wrong, you could still lose millions.

As a rule, the price of January crude oil was worlds away in dollars and cents from the price of April crude oil. And just about anything could happen in the intervening weeks and months due to multiple factors, like abrupt changes in weather (springtime was often called "the widow-maker," because so many traders got caught making the wrong bets on seasonal price swings) or international events (war, it seemed, couldn't help but break out wherever there was oil to be found).

While energy prices from month to month were intertwined, there was no guarantee they would follow one another in any kind of straightforward fashion. Sometimes the daily price of January crude oil and February crude oil would rise, while March crude would fall, or any combination of the three. Taking advantage of this, the traders would not only bet on outright price moves, but the differences *between* the prices of the months. Dubbed "spread trading," this required a very steady hand, as infinitesimal shifts in prices across the months could trigger all kinds of domino effects that could instantly gut a trader's bank account. If you could do it skillfully, though, you could cut your risk by finely balancing one set of transactions against another. This is what many traders called hedging.

There were many other types of maneuvers with all sorts of names. Condors, collars, strangles, boxes, butterflies, even the *iron* condor. And it only got more complicated from there. In short, getting caught up in the three-dimensional chess game that was the futures market meant predicting not just what prices would do but exactly when. This was how traders came to be such information junkies and why the world's richest trader, Warren Buffett, was perpetually glued to his newspaper.

As Kaufman quickly discovered, the money involved in the oil market was staggering. Because every crude-oil futures contract represented a thousand barrels of oil to be delivered at the start of the appointed trading month (July crude oil, for example, was delivered in July and so on), a single contract could put you at risk for some $100,000 or more whenever oil prices topped $100 a barrel. Yet few traders could bet on just *one*. First, it made you look yellow in front of the other traders. And second, why risk the cost of a single Bugatti when you could risk, say, ten? The more you risked, the more you stood to win. The traders tried not to think about what happened if they did not win.

The trading floor had no formal pay structure, no fixed jobs—or few that anyone cared to advertise—and no real hierarchy except the one bestowed by the tyranny of the majority. For those thick-skinned enough to cope with its constant turbulence, this was the only way to do business. In the stampede of buying and selling among market speculators who voluntarily wore jackets in hues that brought to mind the colors of bad bowling shoes, Darwinism ruled. And it was understood that to interfere with the market's natural selective forces was to risk millions, if not billions, of dollars. In this environment, it was inevitable that the bigger, louder, more physically dominant traders prevailed over lesser specimens, most of whom were forced out if not summarily trampled. But whether you made or lost money was almost immaterial compared with how the other traders assessed you. Your poise, political acumen, and overall fearsomeness under pressure were the true determinants of how long you lasted in the pits—assuming you even made it past the first day.

Kaufman bore witness to the vetting process firsthand. When a bank or a hedge fund needed to get rid of a thousand contracts of crude oil two minutes before the market closed for the day, it didn't want a shy, retiring type to do it. It wanted a major league athlete like Eric Bolling, known as "the Admiral," to ram it under the wire. Bolling, who, but for a rotator cuff injury back in 1984, would have had a long career as third baseman for the Pittsburgh Pirates instead of stuffing orders down other traders' throats. "Something you learned very quickly on the trading floor was that nice guys don't last," Kaufman says. "There were a lot of former sports stars, a lot of violence definitely. I still remember the guy who held the record for the fastest knockout. We called him Tiny. He was a three-hundred-some-odd-pound, ex–NFL linebacker. A huge black man, he was a phone clerk and one of the nicest guys you ever met. But you didn't want to ever get in his way. Once, someone tried to shove him. It was unbelievable. Shoving Tiny is like trying to move four people. He's all neck ligament and bulging muscle. His trading jacket size is extra extra *extra* large. Tiny took one look at him and just took him out. I personally got tackled by a floor broker once for nothing more than not checking on his trades fast enough. You'd think that tackling someone would not make the process go any faster, but common sense never got in the way of a senseless beating in that place."

Fortunately for Kaufman, he was a big, square-jawed kid. Standing well over six feet tall, he could take it. He was also whip-smart. He tutored math, devoured volumes of postmodern literature, and was the type of person who didn't think twice about ditching work to do things like hitchhike across Mongolia to sample the local delicacies, such as the horse, which he did. In other words, he was not your run-of-the-mill rookie. But Kaufman's first job didn't go very well, as his boss, Stuart Smith, was served with a search warrant right after Kaufman was hired and dragged into a probe by the Manhattan District Attorney's office over allegations that Smith accepted a bribe of $75,000 from a contractor working for Nymex. (Kaufman's reaction: "Seventy-five grand? That's *it*?")

Smith, who was fifty-seven years old, wasn't just Kaufman's boss; he was the oil market's senior vice president of operations, the person in charge of making sure all the trading floor functions ran smoothly. Smith's departure in February 2004 also surprised Oxford-educated John D'Agostino, who, at twenty-five, had just landed a job at the exchange as vice president of business strategy after graduating from Harvard Business School. "I came into the office that morning and my cubicle, along with Stuart's desk and just about everything else in the room, was covered in police tape," D'Agostino says. "I tried using my computer, and one of the staffers starts gesturing furiously, like, 'No crossing! Police tape!' I was like, 'How am I supposed to do my job?'"

The president of the exchange, J. Robert "Bo" Collins, finally convinced D'Agostino to take the day off. Smith's offices were padlocked, pending further investigation, and his leave of absence eventually turned into permanent termination. Smith pleaded guilty to first-degree bribery and was sentenced. No major newspaper covered it, although Smith was head of operations for the largest energy market in the world. Smith paid a fine of $124,100 for the cost of the probe and faded quietly into infamy. "At the exchange," Kaufman says, "you never really knew who was going to get nabbed for something on any given day."

Despite the misgivings of Wall Street and its CEOs, who looked down on the energy market from the confines of their stuffy board-rooms, Nymex was a well-oiled, if perpetually broken, machine—its chaos interpretable only to those who lorded over it. The fact of the matter was, Wall Street put up with it because it needed it.

Kaufman might have been a greenhorn, but he was also a quick study. Starting out in the crude-oil trading pit as a "runner," he got stomped on and spit on and, most crucially, rained on by thousands of pit cards on which orders were placed for oil and fuels that determined the daily trajectory of global energy prices. His job was to run and gather up great armloads of these cards to be thrown down a hole in the floor where all the trades and prices were logged onto a massive computer system and tracked electronically before being shot out to the world. The oil futures pit was the biggest and busiest of the Nymex trading pits and Kaufman would stand at the center of it all, in what the traders distastefully called "the soup," with another runner and a giant net tied around their waists, catching the falling cards that represented tens of billions of dollars in trades. "I was astounded that you could put a bunch of people from all walks of life in a room with almost no decent technology or training and over time create probably one of the most perfect forms of capitalism," says D'Agostino. "It was a thing of beauty. There would be cards flying through the air and only like five or six trade breaks a day."

The runners wore protective goggles. This was because the traders liked nothing more than to slice their pit cards in a runner's face. "You only had to do it for about an hour and a half a day before another runner would come in and take over, but it was brutal," Kaufman says. The trad-ers would get fined $100 for every card that didn't reach the pit within one minute of a trade, so they became experts at flicking the cards across the room, sometimes hundreds of feet in the air, with razor precision. "The traders standing at the edge of the pits were the most impressive," says D'Agostino. "They would shoot them like playing cards, so they would arch perfectly before landing."

The trading floor was only a few flights off the ground and two stories high, but to the traders it was a disembodied cosmos unto itself. With wall-to-wall data screens and no natural light, it was sealed off like a Las Vegas casino. TVs were mounted above the trading floor so that the traders could watch the news, but they paid little attention compared with what was happening in the pits. "The outer world was always secondary to the inner world," Kaufman says. "We'd watch the TV if there was a hurricane or a regularly scheduled news event, but that was about it. We didn't even really pay attention to the stock market. Our attitude was, why should *we* pay attention to *them*? Shouldn't it be the other way around? They're in the present. We're in the future." Standing outside the exchange, it was impossible to see the confluences of the pits. "Sometimes when we were out front, smoking cigarettes, we'd try to figure out where it was," Kaufman says. "You couldn't tell at all by looking at the exterior of the building. We'd be craning our necks, like, 'Where *is* it?' It was like a parallel universe. When you were outside it, you couldn't see it. And when you were inside it, you were dead to the world."

The floor was cut by large, circular trading rings with five descending stairs for the traders to perch on so that they could see one another in the crowd. Each ring was dedicated to a certain product—crude oil, gasoline, heating oil, and natural gas—the fuels that ran the world. Some traders also bet on price differences between two or more of the trading rings, running back and forth at high speeds, putting the trades together. For this reason, lounging anywhere near the corridors of the pits was verboten. And dangerous, since the traders would not hesitate to bodily run one another down in pursuit of a trade. In every ring, there was a human vortex that eddied like the eye of a hurricane. It was in these sweet spots that only the most aggressive traders gathered. "Traders were very picky about who stood near them," Kaufman says. "If a major trader let you stand next to him, that was a big deal, because you'd be hearing all the information he was getting."

It didn't take a genius to shuffle paper down a hole, but it did afford Kaufman a place at the bottom rung of a ladder that might one day lead to his becoming a bona fide trader. "I originally wanted to learn about trading to get closer to my dad," says Kaufman, whose father, Alan Kaufman, grabbed headlines in *BusinessWeek* and *Institutional Investor* for being a commodities all-star back in the 1990s. ("A leader in proselytizing among institutional investors!" proclaimed the latter in 1991.) Alan had originally gone to medical school to become a surgeon, leaving only when he decided he couldn't stand the fatality rate after performing experimental surgery on dogs. His mentor told him that if losing the dogs bothered him so much, losing his patients would be unbearable. "Growing up in my family was very intimidating, because everyone was an overachiever," Kaufman says. "Before my dad got into trading, he worked at Beth Israel on the *heart lung machine*."

When Kaufman was a kid, his father took him and his older brother down to the trading floor for a weekend of mock-trading with his brother's third-grade class. Kaufman's dad paid $10,000 out of his own pocket to have the exchange officials turn on the trading floor. Every kid received a gold trading badge, just like the real traders, before being shown how to trade pizza futures. Not that there was any such thing, but for a bunch of elementary school kids, it was easier to relate to than oil. "My dad taught us all the hand signals traders flash to one another in the pits to do trades," Kaufman says. "I was only in the first grade then, but I kept my trading badge as a souvenir, and, years later, when I came down to the floor as an adult, I found I could use it to get into the traders' dining room and all the other off-limits places that were supposed to be for members only. It turned out that instead of giving us fake trading badges, the exchange had actually given us real ones. Crazy, huh? I would flash mine and the guards would just let me in. They didn't care. As long as they saw some kind of badge, they let anybody in."

What Kaufman didn't count on once he'd entered the imposing granite halls of Nymex, was getting less of a trader's education than that of a market marauder. This fact did not escape the Wall Street traders who worked just one mile away from Nymex—specifically those of the NYSE. "I lived in an apartment building on 71 Broadway at the top of Wall Street next to the NYSE and it was full of traders, guys like me," Kaufman says. "We'd see each other going down on the elevator every day. They would all be wearing their NYSE badges and I would be wearing my gold Nymex badge and you would not believe all the evil glares. I knew what they were thinking, *you're not as good as us*. But I was thinking, no, I am better than you, because I am getting paid just as much if not more than you and I'm not on the hook for a bunch of Ivy League loans."

Kaufman had tried college and found it wanting. He felt more at home at Nymex, which didn't require a college education, let alone an Ivy League degree, a high school diploma, or even a résumé. In the oil market, you were limited only by the boundaries of your own hunger. And it just so happened that the primarily Jewish, Irish, and Italian men from the Bronx, Brooklyn, Queens, Staten Island, and beyond, who convened on the trading floor every day, had that in spades.

What typically got you a job in the pits was not your degree but your drive and whom you knew. This was true for John Scialdone, a local from the gasoline pit who started in 1993 and was hooked after one glimpse of the stadium-size boiler room that was the Nymex trading floor. Though still in college, Scialdone didn't need to see any more to know what he wanted to do. "At the time, I was a legal clerk, and the secretary for the firm was married to the owner of a midsize oil company, who arranged for me to go down there," he says. "Three weeks later, I called in sick, paid one of the Nymex security guards $100 to get on the trading floor, and met the owner of a large brokerage. He hired me on the spot."

There was just one catch: Scialdone was given three months to land his first big client or, just as quickly as he'd been hired, he'd be fired. It wasn't an easy feat in a market he barely understood, but in eight and a half weeks, he roped in bulge-bracket bank JPMorgan. "It was pure luck," he says. "But I'd rather be lucky than good."

Chris Adams, a college-dropout-turned-broker, ended up at the gold pit in the Nymex building after hearing about commodities trading from an infomercial. "A guy in a ten-gallon hat came on the TV selling a home commodities-trading kit and saying, 'You too can make millions in the market,'" he says. Adams did not buy the kit, but after learning about Nymex from the infomercial, he rode the subway down to the trading floor to see what more he could find out. He hit it off with some of the traders, who regularly stood outside the building chain-smoking and exchanging gossip, and one of them offered him a job. "Just like that," he says, "I went from hanging around outside the exchange to being right on the trading floor."

A number of Nymex traders actually got their jobs by simply working *near* the trading pits. Many of them were bartenders from popular venues like P. J. Clarke's or other watering holes at the neighboring World Financial Center. The Nymex traders recruiting them figured that juggling twelve-drink orders in a packed barroom wasn't entirely unlike filling a dozen market orders in a deafening trading pit. "You know how I know when someone's cut out to be a trader?" Mark Fisher remarked, hard at work at the time on an untitled screenplay about his concept of a dream trader. "If he can tell me, without looking, the exact time, what the temperature is outside, what I ate an hour ago, what I wore to work yesterday, and what the score to the ball game is on TV." Fisher loved whiz kids, which was why he once poached a young man driving an ice-cream truck in his hometown of Woodmere, New York. "True story," a former associate says. "Fish is hosting his son's birthday party on Long Island and orders a bunch of ice cream for it. The ice-cream guy comes and Fish watches him do all the math in his head for, like, $500 worth of orders. Right there, he pulls him out of the truck, teaches him how to trade, and puts him on the trading floor. And I understand that guy did very well."

Fisher, whose screenplay tells the fictional story of a natural-born trader who grew up in poverty before learning how to slay the markets, relished his role as talent scout. A former whiz kid himself, he was always on the lookout for his next big discovery. Aside from the MBA he got from Wharton, Fisher had two master's degrees—one in finance and one in accounting—also from the University of Pennsylvania. He'd worked for Drexel Burnham Lambert before it went under in the insider-trading scandals of the 1980s, and long before turning thirty, he was hailed by his fellow traders as a "genius." In his spare time, he had written a book called *The Logical Trader: Applying a Method to the Madness.* And when he said madness, he meant it. He kept about a hundred copies of it in his office.

Near-mythic multitasking abilities, however, weren't strictly necessary for admission to the oil market. Recalling long-held folklore, Kaufman says there was at least one homeless man panhandling outside the exchange who was offered a job there. "Everyone's heard some version of that story, but the way I heard it was that on a day when the market was completely out of control and the floor was understaffed, a trader was having a smoke outside, saw this bum, and said, 'Hey, you want a job?' The bum looked up from the ground and said, 'Okay.' And they went back inside."

The Nymex traders did not spurn those who had an education, but they were a lot more suspicious of them. Born in a rough patch of Jersey City, New Jersey, in 1969, Bill Perkins went to the University of Iowa to major in electrical engineering but was bored by his studies. "I barely graduated," he says. "I was too busy playing football and chasing girls." When he didn't receive his degree by twenty-one, his godfather called him and asked what he planned on doing with his life. "I said I didn't know, maybe trade stocks. My godfather said, 'How about commodities?' I didn't even know what that was." Perkins's godfather got him an entry-level position at Nymex, but when he reported for work the first day, the trader hiring him refused to let him in. Instead, he offered Perkins an endurance test he made up on the spot: stand outside the Nymex building. For *three* days.

"It was like that movie *Fight Club*, where you have to camp out on the porch before they let you in. I was never told how long I would be waiting there," Perkins says. "It's a funny story, but it just goes to show you how competitive the place is. It respects hustle and desire more than anything else. They assume if you're bright and you have the drive, you'll figure out the rest." Perkins, an African American who got his start at Nymex in 1991, went on to make millions in the oil town of Houston as a founding trader of Centaurus Energy Advisers, a multibillion-dollar energy hedge fund that remains one of the most successful in the world.

The NYSE traders were not incorrect in their assumptions about the Nymex traders, many of whom ended up working for the oil market because they didn't know what else they wanted to do. Before it became a refuge for New York's reluctant student population, Nymex had, indeed, been an asylum for its immigrants, many of whom could not get good jobs on Wall Street. The NYSE traders were also correct in their suspicions that the oil market was a hotbed of chicanery and cronyism. The Nymex traders were not wrought from Wall Street's blue-chip mold. While many had bypassed college, tens of dozens more had simply been born into families that for decades had been entrusted to run the global energy market, passing their high-earning jobs and insider knowledge down through the generations. The cradle-to-grave training made them thoroughbreds as far as oil traders go, but it also gave them a sense of entitlement. The floor's nepotism guaranteed that uncles, sons, cousins, nephews, and brothers would dominate the energy-trading landscape, with alliances and grudges going back for almost a century. As a result, the bonds and wars ran deep and thick. It wasn't unusual for two men who traded side-by-side all their lives to find their sons doing so twenty years later.

Stylistically, the Nymex traders fit the universal trader archetype: smooth-talking and utterly distractible. But many of the oil traders confessed to physical and mental ailments that made them completely incapable of holding down desk jobs. The most popular self-diagnosed condition seemed to be attention deficit hyperactivity disorder. Nymex traders openly bragged about the severity of their afflictions to a competitive degree. Says one pill-popping trader, "In the pits, psychostimulants were all the rage. You could always find someone with a batch of Ritalin or Adderall they were willing to sell you." ADHD seemed to be the disorder of choice in a young man's game where disorder reigned supreme.

By default, the Nymex traders wielded incalculable influence over the global markets, but they were by no means counted among its elite. Yet they welcomed their outsider status. They didn't care about being accepted. They *liked* being untouchables. Social climbing was for suits and suckers. Wearing a suit was considered emblematic of answering to somebody other than oneself. Sneakers (preferably untied), sweatshirts (preferably flapping outside the pants), and any other indicators of answering only to oneself were deemed important essentials of their far superior uniform. After all, they didn't need to dress up. Voluntary inconspicuousness was the true luxury of wealth. The oil traders' one sartorial concession was to wear brightly colored trading jackets, because it made it easier to see each other while screaming orders at one another in the pits. Otherwise, they dressed down, not just to disguise their riches but to renounce Wall Street in general. They didn't look rich. They didn't act rich. They didn't talk rich. And that's what made it all the more satisfying when they beat a highfalutin Goldman Sachs bank trader at his own game one minute before the market closed on a Friday. If the world ignored them, so be it. It only gave them a welcome excuse to ignore the world back.

Being reviled by Wall Street fed the traders' ferocity and gave them their edge. "You know what *really* pissed me off?" Kaufman says. "The New York Stock Exchange traders thinking that they were all *Boiler Room* and shit. These Ivy-League-having, broomstick-up-their-ass motherfuckers thought *they* were the chop-shop boys? *We* were the chop-shop boys. We weren't the ones whose daddies were building us trust funds. Their idea of a wild night out was being in a dive bar for five seconds. They couldn't survive any longer than that without a Cristal IV drip." The image of the blue-collar Nymex traders being at odds with the white-collar Wall Street traders made for a curious dichotomy. The rivalry between them, which had gone on for decades, amounted to the closest thing anyone had ever seen to a class war among millionaires.

The Nymex traders knew basic arithmetic, but that was about it. Still they were formidable at crunching numbers. Unlike the NYSE traders, few of them took an academic approach to the market. Some of them didn't even take a logical approach to it. They liked to trade from the gut. If you considered that on the floor your competition (read: all the other traders) didn't have much interest in applying advanced calculus to their transactions either, it wasn't necessarily a bad idea. Because trading had always been—and always would be—a zero-sum game with a clear winner and a clear loser for every trade, to not understand the thinking of the other pit traders, however superior or flawed it might be, was to work at a steep disadvantage. Since most of the Nymex traders didn't come from moneyed backgrounds, it was understood that an Ivy League education could get you only so far. (Unless you were Mark Fisher, who, being the market's undisputed deity, was above all stereotypes.)

In short, geeking up the trade was a dangerous proposition. Overthinking was bad. Raw instincts were good. Too many formulas or methodologies or Economics 101 classes could ruin your feel for the pits, your ability to psych out your fellow traders, and your response time. "In the pits, the few PhDs who actually turned up almost always flopped, because they suffered from the malaise of overassessment," Kaufman says. "They belonged at the NYSE. Stocks were for the Ivy League: 'Look at my charts, I've done all my homework, here's my ten-year back history.' In futures, we didn't have that. There wasn't enough time. Any model you might think of would get quashed, erased, changed, or reinvented in the time it took for you to measure the impact on your bottom line. It was all freestyle. In the pits, you didn't get formal training. Instead you were told, 'Go and sit in the middle of the pit and listen until you know the flow so well you can actually call a trade *before it happens*.' If you could do that—and some people can—you could make a shitload. The very best thing Nymex had going for it was its lack of education. The traders weren't book-smart. They were street-smart. That was the biggest difference between them and just about everybody else on Wall Street. And it's the biggest difference between the stock exchanges and the futures exchanges now. You want to trade stocks? Fine. While you're at it, why not also go watch some grass grow? With futures, you get action. Stocks are boring and slow. It's what you do for retirement, like playing golf."

Mark Lichtner, originally from Far Rockaway, Queens, remembers being in awe of the Nymex pit traders when he arrived in the 1980s. After working for months as a clerk, one day he realized he could suddenly do the fast math. "At first, you're watching and it's going a million miles a minute. But then, it slows down. It's like how a good hitter, like Ted Williams—I am not the Ted Williams of commodities, believe me—says, 'When the baseball's coming at me, it looks fast to most people. But I can see the seams as it's spinning toward me.' He said that. It took a while for me to see the seams on the baseball. You have an order and it's like two thousand lots to buy at the close and you have two minutes and you're grabbing at it from all sides, screaming, 'Buy ten—buy sixteen—buy twenty—buy twenty-two—buy a hundred—what's my count?' At work, I can do that. I can add it as I go. I know where I'm at. After work, forget about it. I'll miss by a mile. In the pits, it's different. It's six-nine-twelve-thirty-two—hike! You know, it's all checks and balances and your friends help you out. You're like, double-check my friggin' count! I was off by three. You take a deep breath. Those two minutes seem like an hour and a half. The first day I was on the floor, I remember how busy it was and how noisy it was. I saw a man standing by the phone, reading the paper, and I thought to myself, how is that person reading a god-damn newspaper in this place? How do you do that? Back to the seams on the baseball. How does a person do a crossword puzzle standing up in the middle of all this? And he still hears *everything*."

The pay at Nymex was highly attractive. And highly variable. Salaries were an art, not a science, and pit fights regularly broke out over who would extract the fattest pound of flesh. Warring factions among the groups of traders, often falling along ethnic and socioeco-nomic lines, was the norm. Some of the battles were needless, while others came with just cause. Either way, the victors almost always were rewarded. Above all, one rule stood out: *meum dictum pactum*—my word is my bond. If you broke your word, unless you had some friends in very high places, you risked permanent ostracism. "The trading floor is a very straightforward place," says John Morace, a retired Nymex member who traded in the pits for thirty years. "You come to appreciate that. You never have to read into anything anyone is ever doing or saying. It's all there. To even be brought down there, you have to be self-sufficient and completely self-aware. These people aren't afraid of saying or doing anything. There's a different DNA working down there. In the corpo-rate world, you have to be concerned about things like retaliation in the future. On the trading floor, retaliation doesn't happen in the future. It's immediate."

When Scialdone got fired by his brokerage boss right after his wife had a baby, he lost it. "I had just eaten a $10,000 trading error the day before to protect my brokerage firm's relationship with a customer," he says. "So when my boss fired me and let another guy take my business, I picked him up and threw him in the gasoline pit. I got fined $10,000—my second $10,000 debit in two days. But my boss was not a well-liked person and word spread about what I did. By the time I got home that afternoon, I had a half-dozen job offers on my answering machine." After swallowing their share of trading errors, some of the runners didn't make much more than $20,000 by the end of the year. But it was worth the rush. A large portion of the floor, especially its most talented traders, raked in salaries north of six, seven, or even eight figures. Deep-pocketed traders like Fisher were purportedly worth hundreds of millions of dollars. "There was no pay regime whatsoever," Kaufman says. "People just made it up as they went and threw their wages in the air. I once heard someone call the Nymex traders miserable millionaires. And most of them really are millionaires. But with everyone dressed in trading jackets and looking the same way, you can never tell who's making what for sure. There are lots of rumors. And there are lots of moments where you'll be talking to somebody, asking them how their day went, and they'll be saying something like, 'It sucked, I only made $10,000,' or 'I lost $10,000, whatever. I'm going for a drink.' Like it was *nothing.* That spoke volumes about what they were making." Whatever the salaries, since the trading day started at ten A.M. and ended around two thirty P.M., many of the Nymex traders considered their jobs among the best in the world.

As a sign of his lowly runner status, Kaufman wore a blue coat when he started, which meant that if anyone on the trading floor was having a bad day, they had automatic sanction to rip into him. "Most of us start at the bottom," he says. "And a major part of the job of being a bluecoat is to take abuse from others. The traders liked to break us, pull pranks on us, berate us. Some of the guys at my level would bow and scrape, but I would just dish it right back. And you know what? They *loved* it." One of the trading floor's most enduring jokes was to summon a new hire to find the key to the clearinghouse. "The clearinghouse is a group of market members, the traders and their companies, who financially back all the trades. They're the guarantors. It's basically a traders' bank. There's no actual *clearinghouse*. It's just a turn of a phrase. But no one ever knew that coming in, so the game was to see how long you could keep the new guy looking for the key to the clearinghouse until he either called your bluff or gave up. I'd heard about the trick from my dad, so I already knew about it when I came down. I would usually wait for a really busy day and then be like, 'Brad, quick! Go to the third floor and ask Joe for the key to the clearinghouse! It's an emergency. Run!' And he would run. And Joe would tell him, 'Bob has it. He's on the twelfth floor. Go—go—go!' Because everyone was in on it, we could keep it going all day."

Senior traders also got pranked. "One of the more excitable guys in the trading ring came in one morning all hungover and agitated," Kaufman says. "He could vaguely recall being with a girl the night before, but other than that, he couldn't remember anything." During a market lull, Kaufman snuck off the floor and ran into the nearest florist shop. He bought a bouquet, attached a note to it, and left instructions for the flowers to be delivered to the trader at lunchtime. "The note basically said, 'Last night was amazing. I've never had a man tell me he loved me before on the first night. Call you at home later. Looking forward to our trip!'" By the time the flowers came, word had spread across the pits of the stunt. "The trader sent his runner to pick up the flowers, and when they arrived, we could hear him freaking out," says Kaufman. "He was married, so he was on the phone right away, telling his wife, 'If somebody calls, don't believe anything she says!'"

A step up from the bluecoats were the yellowcoats, who stood in the pits and double-checked the prices being reported by the traders. Backed by the values on the bluecoats' pit cards, the prices were instantly transmitted to computers all over the world, letting the public know exactly where oil was trading, even if no one but the Nymex traders were technically allowed to do anything about it. And that was the rub. The Nymex traders alone were the stewards of the energy market and only they had the ability to do any of the buying and selling (or "bidding" and "offering," in traderspeak). As a result, many of the New York traders, also called locals, were able to build huge trading businesses around their exclusive access to the oil market. They were the human portals through which all energy trades were made. Any outsiders looking to trade on Nymex had to phone their orders down to the pits, including some of the world's best-capitalized players, such as traders from Wall

Street, London, Dubai, Singapore, and anywhere else, in addition to oil companies, Middle East royalty, and even ordinary farmers looking to manage price risks of petroleum for their farms. Outside traders turned to Nymex in droves, and they did so for only one reason: they badly needed to trade oil and they had virtually nowhere else to go.

For the privilege of standing in the pits, the Nymex traders paid dearly. They had to cough up a sizable chunk of change to buy one of the exchange's prized 816 seats, or get someone else to do it for them. That is, if any seats were even up for sale, which they often were not. (The term "seat" was a throwback to the early days of trading when buyers and sellers sat down to make deals. In the clamor of the pits, however, both feet were needed firmly on the ground.) Traders could also lease a Nymex seat from a market member, or a "seat holder," at an extortionate rate. In the oil market, the game was pay to play, and the barrier to entry was extraordinarily high.

The year Kaufman started, the price of a single seat reached $1.6 million, while seat leases hovered at $10,000 *a month*. Seat prices would keep rising throughout the Iraq War until they hit their all-time high in February 2007 at $11.2 million. Smith's ouster notwithstanding, Kaufman stuck it out after graduating from the George School, a private high school in Newtown, Pennsylvania, getting a job at nineteen with a Nymex oil trader as a screen clerk, a step up from a yellowcoat. He was officially out of boot camp. As a screen clerk, Kaufman's job was to eyeball his boss's trades from computers on the trading floor to make sure errors weren't being made or too much money lost in the confusion of the transactions. After a few months, Kaufman moved up to phone clerk, taking orders from customers to be executed in the pits. Kaufman's firm was one of many trader-run businesses at Nymex that offered services to outside clients who didn't own a seat at the exchange but wanted to trade there. He then became assistant booth manager, helping run his boss's trading operation, and, by twenty, Kaufman was named vice president of the firm.

Kaufman's rapid ascension had little to do with his getting along with his boss. "We butted heads, since he was at this late stage in his career where he was becoming lazy and ambivalent. He just didn't give a shit anymore. By the time I started working for him, everyone in the pits already knew that if you wanted to make easy money, you just traded the opposite of whatever my boss was doing. I used to put up HAPPY

RETIREMENT signs for him all the time, but he never got the hint." From time to time, Kaufman's boss would yell at him for his high jinks. Or they'd ignore each other. But Kaufman knew he couldn't be dynamited out of his position. "Whatever happened, I always got promoted," he says. "Not because my boss liked me, but because I could do the job." Goldman Sachs even tried to recruit him. "Because, you know, they like guys who are badass and I looked like a badass," he explains. "But I was too lackadaisical to follow up with them and if you work for Goldman, you have to wear a tie every day. There was no way I was doing that."

Kaufman and his boss eventually developed a grudgingly amicable existence conforming to the ebb and flow of the trading pits while honoring their firm's favorite brand of personal distraction. "We would start off each day by looking at the pinup girls in the local newspapers. That was our big thing. We not only went through the New York newspapers, we went through all the New Jersey newspapers too, including the Page Six girls from the *Trentonian*. We also subscribed to *Playboy*, and would have that mailed to our office, not somewhere else, but our actual *place of business*. We were nothing if not resourceful. One of my very first jobs was to get the latest *Playboy* and bring it down to the floor for inspection. Most people would keep their porn in their trading booths."

Like Kaufman's employer, most traders had enclosed booths stationed near the pits that effectively doubled as man caves. Here they would store their trading records, computer equipment, and anything else they needed to keep tabs on the market. The booths, worn by age, also had drugs and alcohol in them.

Porn was popular on the trading floor, as was, according to some, the occasional firearm. Exotic rumors made the rounds of traders stalking the pits carrying pearl-handled revolvers, some of them moonlighting as Nazi hunters. There was also more ordinary talk of garden-variety, gun-toting thugs. Such was the price of cultivating your inner trading beast. It got you paid, but it also came with its share of side effects. "For pretty much every kind of vice, there was a supplier in the pits. There were the booze guys, the coke dealers, the pot guys, the guys who knew all the prostitutes. Even one guy who ran what I can only call an adult video store," says Kaufman. "He would haul in this giant bag of DVDs every day like the Santa Claus of porn and set himself up. The traders would go over to his booth and pick out whatever they wanted and pay for it." Many of the more menial floor workers had their real job and their *other* job. The entrepreneurial spirit that had lured so many of New York's more ambitious drifters to the pits was a double-edged sword, stoking their darker impulses to nurture illicit side businesses.

At least one heavyweight trader did not hunt Nazis just for bravado. Randy Warsager, a soft-spoken, more serious sort, worked closely with high-profile human-rights activists tracking down war criminals across Manhattan and vociferously shaming Nazi prison guards who had the gall to list their names in the public phone book. One of his greatest coups was finding and confronting the son of the Romanian industrial-ist who funded the murderous Iron Guard fascist movement. (Warsager, whose other pastime was urban photography, also had a famous father, Hyman Warsager, a celebrated printmaker from Franklin D. Roosevelt's WPA, whose works can still be viewed at the Smithsonian and the Metropolitan Museum of Art.)

Many of the traders had their first serious brushes with substance abuse in the pits. "I never did any drugs in high school, but my first day there, one of the clerks gave me a tour, saying, 'That's your coke corner, this is your weed corner, and here's where your pills are,'" Kaufman says. Once a trader even tried to give Kaufman a bag of drugs as a paycheck. "He was out of cash, so he wanted to give me that instead. In a big, fat Ziploc bag. It was the dumbest, most wide-open drug-trading you've ever seen. It was absurd. At one point, it was said we held the record for the largest drug bust on the East Coast." According to a senior trader who preceded Kaufman, the floor was equally awash in drugs when he worked at Nymex in the 1980s. "People were actually making markets in cocaine right on the trading floor," he says. "There must have been like a dozen guys doing it."

So who, exactly, was caught dealing cocaine on the floor? No one at the New York offices of the Federal Bureau of Investigation, the Drug Enforcement Agency, or even the New York Police Department's First Precinct, where Nymex is located, seems to know. If you call them, none of them will confirm or deny the history of the drug busts that the traders say they remember. One admitted trader-cum-drug-dealer who served on Nymex's board throughout the 1980s (*and* 1990s) says there's a very good explanation for that. "Whenever there was a drug bust, the authorities would come down to our compliance department and we would work it out. The suspect would be discreetly called off the trading floor, not dragged out like an animal. If he needed to be arrested, he'd be taken off the premises and *then* handcuffed. That way, there'd be nothing to link him to the exchange, nothing to undermine the public trust. It happens on Wall Street all the time. The police are complicit because they have to be. What do they want to get caught up in a shit show like that for? You think they don't know there are drugs on Wall Street? They'd rather be busting Pablo in Harlem."

The police didn't bother much with Nymex, which gave generously to the New York City Police Foundation. Also, the oil market's heads of security mostly came from the city's police department itself. As a professional courtesy, the police did not like to interfere. They let their ex-colleagues at Nymex do their jobs as they saw fit.

Due to the extreme pressures of the market and the ready availability of mind-altering substances, it wasn't unusual for the floor traders to place their oil bets while under the influence. "The pits reeked of booze," Kaufman says. "Most of the traders were alcoholics. It was a very stressful place. They would drink, go to lunch, drink, go back to work, then go out and get hammered again. Have you seen some of them? They look like they're at the end of their lives."

Kaufman's preparation for the day was not complicated. Some traders got up at five A.M. and obsessively went over their price charts. They would look over the oil price highs and lows from the day before and check for any market trends, circling the numbers with colored markers. But most people, he says, came in cold and went by instinct alone. "You can't predict the market, so a lot of us didn't try. You just get used to it. After a while, you get to feeling like it's in your blood, that everything it does is attached to you in some way and that you're a part of it, that you have a *biological* connection. I know how that sounds, but it's true.

"My ritual was to wake up around eight thirty, go to the corner coffee shop, and get a really big cup of coffee. I'd pour half of it out and then replace it with some Jack. I'd save the rest of the bottle of Jack for later. I'd put the top back on the coffee and get to work by nine thirty. Most of the time, I'd be there before anybody else. I'd put my stuff in my locker, change into a trading jacket, pick up my trading sheets for the day, get my second cup of coffee—very important—and head into the pits. Nobody cared if I was drunk. As long as I got the job done, they didn't give a flying shit."

Although the trading day was just four and a half hours long, many of the traders had difficulty doing their jobs while staying sober. "The amount of money at stake in this market is so great, it's hard for people not to use something to take the edge off," Kaufman says. "Being on the floor is the adrenaline surge of your life. One of the requirements of the job that nobody ever tells you is that you have to love chaos and be truly, truly out of your mind. The days that I hated my job were the days that were quiet. The days I loved my job were the days I couldn't get off the phone. When prices are high and the market is moving, you get happy. If my customers were making money, I was on top of the world. Sometimes, I would even skip my Jack. It was like a drug. You'd get this incredible high during the day and pass out the second your head hit the pillow at night. It's the greatest job in the world. But you can't stay in it forever or it starts to kill you."

It was a far cry from the tight-knit circle of family farm businesses that founded Nymex as an egg, cheese, and butter market in 1872, before organized oil trading even existed. Back then, for a few hours a day, New York's dairy merchants would gather to exchange goods in a lei-surely fashion, recording their prices by hand with chalk on beat-up blackboards. Perhaps the only remnant of that time still honored by the Nymex traders was their insistence on sticking to farmers market hours. After all, who could argue with a four-and-a-half-hour workday?

Having narrowly and repeatedly escaped self-destruction, the oil market's evolution—or devolution—was probably inevitable. Over time, the merchants who didn't get pushed out became less leisurely and more aggressive. They brought in their sons. And each generation found itself more and more willing to take astonishing risks to protect their grow-ing global fiefdom. Slowly, the collective value of their trades began to rocket from the millions to the billions.

From debt and default to internal blood wars, countless run-ins with the law, and decades of sheer barbarism, how the humble traders of the New York Mercantile Exchange emerged victorious after more than 130 years of failure and skulduggery to become the biggest oil market on earth was anybody's guess. "The Nymex traders weren't supposed to be the ones who pulled this off," Kaufman says. "They didn't have the trust funds or the fancy college degrees or the connections or, to be honest, even the business acumen to do this. They were completely uncivilized. But that's what's so beautiful about it. They did it and they did it in their way."

By the time Kaufman had entered the pits, the oil market had long ago cemented its roughneck reputation, as well as its primacy as the world's leading energy emporium. It had succeeded in elevating the act of sidestepping disaster to high art. More than that, it *required* disaster to thrive. Had there been fewer hurricanes, heat waves, fuel bottlenecks, or wars in the Middle East, would things have turned out differently? In private, the Nymex traders often mulled this very question. It was one for which none had an answer.

What the traders were more certain about was the silent yet indelible code they observed when it came to outsiders in general and Wall Street in particular: us against them.

2

The Boy Who Would Be King

I was very naïve. That was an advantage.

—MICHEL MARKS

THE STORY OF the oil market began not with wildebeestial traders but with the rocky relationship between a father and son.

I first met Michel David Marks, the reluctant engineer of the modern-day oil market, in April 2004, after months of wheedling his assistant, Chris, for a face-to-face interview. For someone who personally laid the cornerstone to a global colossus, fifty-four-year-old Marks was not what I expected.

Marks liked publicity and hated publicity. He was lighthearted, yet intense. He coveted the finer things in life and, similarly, rejected them. He bought an enormous white house in one of the most sought-after shore towns of New Jersey, then got rid of it for a compact, two-bedroom apartment over a Starbucks. He had a taste for French wine, but dressed like a vagabond. He had a quietly confident, sagely air about him, but privately harbored grave doubts about being any kind of sage. Like a teenager, he listened to hip-hop music, drove a Jeep, and wore Patagonia sportswear. Like a classicist, he was given to spontaneously spouting quotes from Browning, Wordsworth, and Yeats, a well-thumbed copy of *Immortal Poems of the English Language* permanently tucked under his arm. He was a lifelong wanderer with an artist's eye and a stormy temperament. A sensitive man with an immense fear of intimacy, he would, without hesitation, cut friends and business partners off at the knees, leaving them apoplectic. Marks was a lone wolf, a dreamer, a congenital cult of personality—a Renaissance man without a Renaissance.

But when thrust into the position of playing unlikely savior to a dysfunctional farmers market, he boldly went where no man dared go.

Marks and I had spoken many times over the phone, but we'd never met. His interviews, when he felt like giving them, were thoughtful, strange, deliberative, and strategic. Dealing with him was akin to shadowboxing. He would bob and weave, call without warning, disappear without explanation. In 2004, the year we finally met, he traveled frequently to Manhattan for Nymex board meetings. He stayed at a woman's house in Greenwich Village. I was not allowed to visit him then. That, he said, would have been inconvenient. Instead, his assistant, Chris, suggested I take the train fifty miles south to Marks's hometown of Red Bank, New Jersey. I could never get out of the newsroom long enough to do that, so I put it off for months, thinking Marks would eventually relent. He didn't.

After unnecessarily elaborate negotiation, we settled on a time and place for the much-awaited summit. Chris kept me waiting by the phone until the final hour of the final day to confirm if Marks would, in fact, see me. He telephoned Thursday, saying, "Michel will decide tomorrow whether he will see you Saturday." He called Friday night, saying, "Michel will decide tomorrow whether he will see you tomorrow." At long last, when I got the word, I had to rush to the terminal in Newark to buy my train ticket before the day ended. Chris left me with detailed instructions as to where to get off the train, what vehicle Marks would be driving (the Jeep), and even what he would be wearing. "Oh, and by the way," he said before hanging up, "don't forget to bring your hiking boots."

I arrived at Red Bank on the afternoon train, at the appointed time and place, finding nobody. I waited in the dusty parking lot for twenty minutes, feeling foolish in my new hiking boots, hurriedly purchased that morning. The train station was deadly silent. I started to head back toward the platform to catch the next train out when a skinny, wan kid wearing reading glasses, slouched in the parking lot, caught my eye. He was alone, but there was no doubt in my mind who it was. Chris. After we introduced ourselves, he said, matter-of-factly, "Michel's decided to meet you at the Starbucks downtown" (the same Starbucks, I later learned, above which Michel lived). On the way into town, Chris held low-toned conversations with Marks on his cell phone while giving me a tour of the affluent suburb. We drove past the 1920s-era Count Basie Theatre, which he said Marks had helped restore, along with local celebrities like Patti Scialfa, the wife of Bruce Springsteen. "It took us a while, but we finally got it done," Chris said proudly. Whenever he referred to Marks, he never spoke in the singular. He always said "we."

At the coffee shop, I had another long wait. I was beginning to doubt there ever would be a Michel Marks, when a scruffy man with wind-ravaged hair loped distractedly in. Barely over five feet tall, the godfather of the oil market stood dressed in jeans and a sweatshirt. Chris excused himself like an obedient manservant, and Marks issued me a brief nod, making no apology for his lateness. I just stared. With his devil-may-care bearing and don't-give-a-damn attitude, he more resembled a surly teenager than an elder statesman of capitalism. Despite what appeared to be his concertedly casual appearance, I had to give him the benefit of the doubt. After all, I supposed if I were a reclusive multimillionaire who singlehandedly built the global oil market, I probably wouldn't think I had much left to prove either. Halfway through coffee, he got to his feet. "Okay, you can talk to me," he said. "But you'll have to do it while we hike."

I had given this some thought. On the one hand, I had no shortage of reservations about heading into unfamiliar territory with a stranger, not in the least a former oil trader. But on the other, I had to go where the source wanted me to go if I wanted to hear his story. I left word of my whereabouts back home and took a chance.

Gesturing to my foot gear, I indicated I was fully prepared. Marks barely glanced at it. "You call those hiking boots?"

We combed a series of local trails and Marks spoke about his life at length and with bracing honesty. Much like the oil market itself, he'd had a complex and disturbing past, filled with tragic events and surreal happenings. Born in Paris (the reason for the French spelling of his first name) and the eldest of four sons, he'd had a difficult childhood. He didn't get along well with his father and, from a young age, was reared without a mother. His memory of her suicide was piercingly fresh. He spoke of her without criticism, even as he touched on her emotional troubles, her depression, and her ultimate infidelity to his father, for whom he himself seemed to feel little tenderness. By all accounts, the loving father-son relationship that might have blossomed in the wake of his mother's death was supplanted by one of incurably conflicted competitors.

Francis Q. Marks was an entrepreneur of rare virtuosity and an unrepentantly repentant Jew. "He had some very odd views about being American and Jewish," recalls Gary Lapayover, a former Nymex trader and member of the board for ten years. "I remember talking to him over lunch about plans for my son's bar mitzvah and he went off. He said, 'Life is hard enough, especially in this country. Why burden the poor boy?' I really liked Francis. He was an astute and distinguished businessman, but sometimes he could be a very weird dude." Francis was neither short nor tall, had graying hair, a medium build, and always wore a suit. He used the middle initial Q for posterity's sake, as he did not have a middle name. Friends and colleagues described him as dignified and outspoken, a man who, although a bit of an autocrat, commanded admiration and respect. Michel's recollections of him were somewhat different. He recalled a father who never ceased to be overbearing, harsh, impenetrable.

Francis Marks was a restless soul. He'd studied English and the classics at the University of Virginia, the University of Pennsylvania, the University of Massachusetts at Amherst, *and* the University of Michigan, spending a year at each school before graduating. He'd liked them all, but was given to wanderlust. After receiving his degree, he lived and studied in Paris for a year and took a French wife, Myrna, a young woman who was impressed by his drive and self-possession. In World War II, he served in the U.S. Army, flying planes to China, India, and other parts of the Far East. He never spoke about the war afterward, except once. He was not a man to engage in nostalgia or regret. The one time he mentioned the war was during a Nymex marketing trip to Tokyo. The executives had brought him along as a witness to their junket to prove to the board that they weren't off gallivanting while pretending to be doing business. The pit traders had taken to joking that the office of the chairman doubled as the "Nymex Hunt & Fish Club."

While making small talk with some of the Japanese traders, Francis was asked if he'd ever been to Tokyo before. His response was met with stunned silence. "He said something to the effect of 'yes, but from a bomber,'" Lapayover says. "Hysterical, if none too tactful. He was, all over, a cold fish."

Settling with his wife in New Jersey, in the 1950s, Francis Marks started a fresh fruit and vegetable business in Camden with his brothers, called Paris Foods. Looking to support his growing family, Francis expanded the enterprise into one of the largest produce wholesalers in the nation. He would rise at four in the morning and go to the warehouses and docks, sometimes bringing his children along with him, to survey the day's deliveries. By the 1970s, he owned more seats on the New York commodities exchanges than any other known man or entity. Among these was the thriving metals market, the Commodity Exchange Inc., called Comex for short; the Coffee and Sugar Exchange; the New York Cotton Exchange; and the smallest and least consequential exchange of all, Nymex.

Francis had much greater ambitions than just vegetable vending. He launched Paris Securities and Paris Futures, trading arms that catered to Wall Street in addition to managing the finances of his produce business. (When asked why he named all his businesses after Paris, he told colleagues, "If I can't live there, I might as well work there.") His financial firms provided clearing services to dozens of New York traders, which meant Francis insured their trades for a fee on the city's stock and futures markets. Well-versed in the perks and loopholes of various trading strategies, Francis discovered that by bankrolling other traders, he could not only make extra money but also reduce his own trading fees. His interest in making money was rather more practical than material, says one of Francis's sons, Richard Marks, who now runs Paris Foods. "The word 'capitalist' is the last word I would ever use to describe my father. With my dad, it wasn't about the lofty goals or the endgame; it was just about the process, the act of building and of creating something. It's true he never bought a business that wasn't income-producing, but that was because he had a big family to support. He didn't want or need anything. He lived a simple life. He also was brutally honest and I think people appreciated that. His nature was always to be looking forward. He believed true intelligence was anticipatory."

Francis's brazenly holistic approach meant that when he tried energy trading years later, he would go ahead and buy a small oil refinery while he was at it, Lapayover says. Somehow, he'd found out there would be fewer restrictions on his trading if he could establish himself, however casually, as an oil man. With a stake in the petroleum business, Francis could be much more daring in the scope and complexity of his trades under U.S. trading rules than could market speculators, most of whom were seen as simple gamblers. As it turned out, Francis was equally dexterous with his taxes. His average annual income during his lifetime, according to Social Security records, came to just $27,485. "All the riches of the Marks family exist because of Francis's knowledge and foresight, period, end of story," says Richard Schaeffer, who started his trading career at Nymex in 1981. "He was tough as nails but fair. A key man in the history of New York and in the history of the market. A great man, with great vision."

The Marks family may have lacked for emotional nurturing, but it didn't lack for wealth. Francis Marks footed the expenses of supporting, educating, and even bailing out his children when they got into scrapes, while starting a new family with his new wife, Patricia. But wealth would not be the tonic to heal the wounds of the Marks brothers. As a result of their tragic history, they were less like kin than war buddies. Despite Michel Marks's strong artistic bent, his father pressured him to study economics at Princeton, which he dutifully did. This denial of Marks's underlying identity, his longing for artistic fulfillment—a fulfillment his father, given his own aesthetic leanings, should have been the first to recognize—only drove a deeper wedge between father and son. That and the circumstances surrounding the death of Michel's mother.

While accounts vary, people close to the Marks family tell of an argument between Francis and Myrna that rapidly escalated. Francis had found out Myrna had an affair with his brother. "Michel's mother climbed to the top of one of his father's warehouses at Paris Foods, which was several stories high," a family friend says. "Michel was standing there with his siblings. He was around ten. Michel's mother threatened to jump. Francis, who was angry and, I think, did not take her threat seriously, said, 'Go ahead, do it.' She did. Michel saw the whole thing. The worst part about it was Michel said his father had almost no reaction. He just said, 'Well, that's over with.' Which is a pretty fucked-up thing to say to your kid when he's just lost his mother."

Myrna had struggled to adjust to the squalid factory town of Camden after leaving Paris. "I don't think Francis ever realized the toll it was taking on her," says another family friend, noting that Camden remains a grim place. "Francis's philosophy was, 'This is *life*, take it or leave it.' He must not have thought she'd jump, or else he would have gotten the children out of the way. Francis was a man who was always in control. He thought he could talk her down."

Michel Marks never married or had any children. In 2006, he informally adopted four underprivileged kids whose mother was being airlifted to a hospital before she died from injuries suffered in a car wreck he chanced to drive past.

Shortly after graduating from college in 1972, Marks bought two seats at Nymex, apparently without the knowledge or involvement of his father. Meeting with friends at the Hunt Club inside the upscale Grand Summit Hotel in Summit, New Jersey, Marks discussed his plans to become a member of the exchange. He did not mention his father, who by that time had become one of Nymex's most esteemed members ("the dean of the exchange," as the pit traders affectionately called him). His friends were under the impression that Marks needed their help to get a membership there. "Michel gave no indication that his father had any connections in the market," says one of the friends in attendance. "We thought *we* were introducing *him* to our contacts on Wall Street to get his foot in the door."

During the meeting, Loree "Rip" Collins, a New Jersey Republican and Union County chairman, gingerly raised the question of how Marks planned to pay for his seats. "He started walking Michel through the financing process," the friend says. "And then Michel—I'll never forget this—looked kind of embarrassed and said, *very* unassumingly, 'That's okay. I am just going to pay cash.' It seemed he had some family money."

Marks started at twenty-three as a phone clerk for a New York brokerage firm called E. F. Hutton, pointedly avoiding his father. He was determined to carve his own path. "Michel was smart, but he wasn't just intelligent. He had ideas that were way ahead of their time," says the friend, a New Jersey superior court judge. "Even at that age, he had the ability to look into the future." By the time Marks arrived at Nymex, his father wielded no small amount of clout. He'd also gained a fanatical following among the younger generation of traders coming in from the city's outer boroughs, many of whom were in search of a successful male role model. Francis fit the bill and then some. Though failing to gain the adulation of his son, he became a towering father figure to many of the twenty- and thirtysomething boys of the pits. Once Francis remarried, Marks eventually had eleven brothers and sisters, so sharing his father with the entire floor community, in addition to a growing brood of siblings, could not have been an insignificant blow.

The young men of Nymex did not relate to Marks's paternal issues. No one knew his father the way he did. And no one wanted to.

If Francis's parenting skills were less than superb, he was, none-theless, a strong advocate for his son. Marks would later say his father played a minimal role in paving the way for him at the exchange, but his colleagues observed Francis fervently lobbying for him and, on occasion, even defending him. "Though my father introduced me, I went in independently," Marks says. "I was out there on my own every day learning the ropes. Painfully."

Marks climbed through the ranks quickly. Like his dad, he had an instinct for business and a fondness for the floor's warm fraternity. There was only one problem: the hundred-year-old exchange, unbeknownst to him, was unabashedly flirting with extinction.

When Michel first came to the pits, Nymex did not trade oil. It traded that other major commodity known for preserving the balance of world power—the Maine potato. But the Maine potato market was irreparably broken. Throughout the 1970s, trouble had been brewing as the older, more established commodities traders gleefully manipulated the price of potatoes, a market representing 80 percent of Nymex's business. So consumed were they by their games of brinkmanship, they hardly noticed that rampant inflation was lighting a fire under gold, silver, and oil prices, causing all three to rise more than tenfold in a decade. Political flare-ups between the West and the Middle East, leading to the Arab oil embargo of 1973 and mile-long lines at the gas pump, fueled the price surge and fed the public outrage. What would follow, in rapid succession, would not only be unprecedented for its time but touch off a series of events that would result in the strange and sprawling global empire that is today's oil market.

Marks and the roughly six dozen traders working at Nymex, which was located in a redbrick mansion at 6 Harrison Street in downtown New York, began to receive word of mysterious potato supply shortages. Maine's annual crop was *falling*, both as a percentage of national production and by absolute volume. Meanwhile, a new potato capital was emerging—Idaho.

As Maine lost market share, stories began to circulate of train cars coming from Maine filled with bags of potato-shaped rocks instead of real potatoes and some freight cars not showing up at all. The New York traders spoke of corrupt farmers, corrupt market officials, and potatoes passing inspection in Maine but showing up spoiled once they arrived at the Hunts Point rail yards in the Bronx. There was even the highly dis-quieting tale of a phantom cargo. "That old story was still going around when I arrived at the exchange," Kaufman says. "A train car supposedly full of potatoes was wax-sealed in Maine, but then arrived empty. That was the first time the traders began to suspect it wasn't just a robbery, but an inside job." The train, it seemed, had left the station with noth-ing in it. Someone, they deduced, was tinkering with supply with an eye toward influencing the prices. Worse, a national consensus was building: Maine potatoes were waxy and repugnant, but Idaho potatoes, grown in the West's light, volcanic soil, were delicious.

With Maine and Idaho crashing antlers over which state would claim potato primacy, prices went haywire, to the extreme satisfaction of the New York pit traders. As is the case today, the wilder the price swings in a market, the more opportunity for traders to buy low and sell high for maximum profit (or, in some cases, buy high and sell higher). It made no difference to the traders which way it went, so long as prices vacillated enough for them to snare a bonanza. Whether they bought at $4 and sold at $5, or bought at $5 and sold at $6, made no difference. They still made $1 profit. All they cared about were the spaces *between* the prices, and they were experts at working the gaps. As is well known to Wall Street, the trader's kiss of death comes not when prices are out of control but when they are calm, smooth, and stable.

The big month for trading potatoes was May. "Potatoes were grown in the summer, harvested in the autumn, and then stored until sup-ply ran out around May each year," says a longtime market executive. "That's when the supplies were the most uncertain and that's when prices got crazy. There were potato inspectors approving or rejecting the Maine cargoes and some of them were getting bribed and some of them were paid to say one thing when the other was true. The month of May was a period when a lot of the warehoused potatoes were also perishing. Remember, this was back before the days of frozen food, so potatoes were showing up rotten and wormy. They usually went bad after six months. So many things were wrong with the supply chain. It definitely made for an exciting, if corrupt, market."

Michel Marks watched with fascination as the drama played out. Every year, the Nymex traders would count down the days to May. "Each May, the biggest potato traders would choose up sides and face off," he says. "Usually, there were six large players. Three would bet potato prices would rise and three would bet potato prices would fall. They would bluster and cajole and you'd never know until the last moment where it would all end up." Traders from across the country would descend on the trading floor to have a crack at what, for one month only, was the planet's hottest market. There was no viewers' gallery back then, so everyone would just stand in the trading pits. Potato dealers, potato producers, speculators, even the Maine potato farmers would put on their Sunday best and make their yearly pilgrimage to New York to watch the sight.

Leo Melamed, the émigré son of anti-Communist Yiddish teachers from Bialystok, Poland, who would one day be known as the "Father of Financial Futures," was there. His family escaped the Nazis *and* the KGB by hiding in Asia before settling in Chicago. He graduated from law school, became a trader, and was later named chairman of the Chicago Mercantile Exchange, the largest futures market in the world. As far back as the 1960s, he would fly from Chicago to New York just to trade Maine potatoes. "There's an old warhorse trader saying: 'Trade wherever it's the loudest,'" Melamed says. "For those of us traders in the '60s, we listened to where the noise was. When I entered a trading floor, I would listen at the door and whichever pit was the loudest, that's where I'd go. In May, potatoes were the loudest. Each market had its own sort of time span. Before they could make chickens lay eggs all year round, eggs were the most active market in September, because that's when egg supplies fell as the bakers got ready for the Christmas season.

"I have a great fondness for Nymex. I was just a kid, in my early thirties, and a friend and I would rent an apartment in Manhattan each May and we'd trade potatoes for the whole month. I can remember sitting around and eating corned beef sandwiches in the Nymex pits. Potato prices were known to be squeezed and cornered left and right and that gave them a bad name, but them having a bad name was never sufficient reason not to trade them. The farmers would piss and moan, but they knew what they were doing. A farmer might not sound terribly sophisticated, but they played the game and they knew very well what was going on and how to benefit. It was the best time in the world to trade, because it was when prices were at their most volatile."

In Maine, the cultlike culture of farmers and merchants active in the potato market had materialized almost a hundred years before and had been going strong ever since. The state's breadbasket, Aroostook County, had crowned a Potato Blossom Queen since 1937, and its children were excused from school for three weeks every September to help with the potato harvest. Its success had made the county seat, Houlton, one of the ten richest towns in New England. The townspeople were so enamored of their potatoes they bragged that even the vistas of Provence couldn't compete with their vast fields of purple, pink, and white potato blossoms.

The potato trade was so enormous that Nymex had not one but *two* potato-trading pits. One pit was for the May potato futures contract only. The other was for the rest of the potato-trading months. On the side, the exchange also traded Australian boneless beef, butter, platinum, palladium, and even silver coin futures, but in smaller quantities. "It wasn't so much that these products were that exciting," the longtime market executive says. "It had more to do with their supply problems, their insane price swings, and the overall level of corruption present in those markets. Every one had a story. Take boneless beef. Why was a New York market trading *Australian hamburger?* That is a good question. We were trading it because the boneless beef prices were going nuts and there was a lot of tainted meat. The Australians were putting *kangaroo* meat in the beef supply. Who knows what other animals got in there. Listen to me, people will do anything to lower the cost of what they are selling by replacing it with something of lesser quality and continuing to charge the higher price."

The Nymex trading floor would swell every May with well-heeled politicians, bankers, traders' wives, and wealthy spectators, few of whom cared about potatoes. They just came to watch the show. The Nymex traders didn't care about potatoes either. They only came to cash in. But to do that, they had to bet on whether the potato supply would be bountiful in May, which would result in lower prices (since there would be more potatoes to go around), or lean, which would result in higher prices (since there would be less to go around). As can be imagined, the traders became obsessed with Maine gossip, Maine weather, Maine soil, Maine farming techniques, and all things Maine, as they plotted their moves. If you thought Maine potato prices would go up, you would buy potato contracts. This was called going "long." If you thought prices would go down, you would sell potato contracts. This was called going "short." Because potato futures contracts were tied to actual quantities of potatoes, you had to get in, make your money, and get out if you didn't want to end up with a pile of potatoes delivered to your front door.

Each contract represented fifty thousand pounds of potatoes. Most traders only wanted to make money, not buy or sell actual spuds, so they were careful to unwind their bets before the May contract expired near the start of the month. Unraveling the trades required that you buy a long contract for every short contract you owned, or vise versa. They would cancel each other out, leaving you "flat" in the market. Being flat meant you were safe, without any bets left on the table. If you were not in the market for the actual, physical potato supply, this was exactly where you wanted to be by expiration day. If not, the punishment was dire. If you were long and did not get out of your positions by expiration, as May arrived, you would receive thousands of pounds of potatoes with a large bill. If you were short, you would be on the hook to make a giant potato delivery in May to somebody else, which could destroy your credit. For this reason, expiration day has always been considered D-day for the futures trader. Even today, it is how the futures market works for physical products such as oil and gasoline. Until expiration, however, the market is a free-for-all, with the longs trying to push prices up and the shorts trying to push prices down in an endless war for maximum profit.

With the Maine potato crop dwindling and inflation overheating, Marks had a front-row seat to the jaw-dropping price gyrations. Nymex potatoes, the third most-traded commodity in the nation in 1976, soared from $5 a hundredweight to more than $19 a hundredweight. People shopping for potatoes were appalled. "You would have these incredible price moves on the last day of trading and the guys would play it down to the last five minutes, one minute, thirty seconds. Everyone from Maine would come down to the floor and there'd be a huge throng, waiting for the spectacle," Marks says.

The spectacle was made even more dramatic by the fact that on the final day of potato trading, there were absolutely no price limits, allowing traders to push prices up or down as far and fast as they could possibly go.

Both the longs and shorts in the market needed to get out by expiration, but until then, they would hold on for as long as they could to get the best prices. It was a contest of epic proportions where everyone would bluff. "The shorts would posture and say, 'We're going to *make* delivery on expiration day.' And the longs would say, 'We're going to *take* delivery,'" Marks says. Meaning neither side was going to get out, when both sides knew very well that wouldn't be the case. Standing in the pits before a riveted audience, the traders stared each other down like gladiators. "We would watch to see who'd blink first," Marks says. "We had a saying back then: 'The shorts didn't want what the longs didn't have.'"

Almost none of the traders had any real potatoes to buy or sell, just like most of today's oil traders don't have any oil to buy or sell. Most of them, instead, are just placing bets to make money. Technically, the traders are buying and selling pieces of paper, contracts, guarantees. Commodities traders don't need to hold the actual commodity they're trading. So long as they can get in and out of their futures contracts before expiration day, they don't need to make or take any deliveries. They only need to have the necessary cash or credit to participate in the betting process. Traders who bet solely for a profit are called speculators. They are the people who stand between the natural buyer and the natural seller of various products or commodities, whether it's potatoes or oil, taking positions and assuming the price risks that the potato farmers and oil-drillers don't want.

Futures traders, specifically speculators, make it possible for the ordinary farmer to sell not just this year's crop in advance, but *next* year's and the *following* year's and so on, before the crops are even grown, at an agreed-upon price *today*. This gives farmers financial stability and a chance to lock in profits in advance rather than take their chances on mercurial market forces that might otherwise ruin them. When price risks are transferred to the speculator, any fluctuations in prices automatically become the speculator's problem. By doing the trade, the speculator agrees to shoulder that burden, pocketing any profits or losses that might come his way. This is the underlying utility of the futures markets and why a non-farmer or non-oil-driller is allowed to go anywhere near them.

Dick Leeds, a Nymex executive who traveled the country educating people about futures, often used a Cadillac as an example of futures trading for those who couldn't understand it. "Suppose I told you that next year, I'll sell you a Cadillac for $3,000. And you think to yourself, well, that Cadillac's going to be worth $4,000 by then. So we make a deal. I sell it to you now for $3,000 and come next November, I deliver it to you for that price. If the market for a Cadillac by that time is $4,000, then you've just made $1,000. But if the market for a Cadillac is $2,500, then I've made $500 off you. That's futures trading."

Though its origins are hazy, the futures market traces back to the ancient Greeks and Phoenicians, but it didn't really take off until the early 1800s in Chicago, where hundreds of farmers across the Midwest gathered to sell their livestock and produce in a common marketplace. Over time, the farmers entered into contracts with each other to exchange goods for payment, but when one farmer couldn't hold up his end, nothing short of wielding a Colt Peacemaker could rectify it. The farmers eventually put down their firearms and organized themselves, forming members-only trading clubs guaranteeing mutual accountability—most prominently the Chicago Mercantile Exchange and the Chicago Board of Trade, which merged in 2007 after dueling for decades.

Nymex was not as organized. By the mid-1970s, Marks couldn't help but notice that the behavior of the New York traders was becoming highly erratic. In 1975, an electrical fire in the basement at Harrison Street disrupted futures trading. The lights shorted and the flames burned, but the traders, locked in heated negotiations, refused to evacuate. Nymex president Richard Levine finally stomped down to the floor and yelled, "This market is closed!" One trader, Mike Milano, looked up from his huddle, mid-trade, and hollered back, "This market is closed when I have sold my position!" The traders were a mixed bag of gangsters and gentlemen. They wore ties, but even back then also carried weapons. "In 1978, there was a sign at the entrance that said, PLEASE CHECK YOUR GUNS AT THE DESK. And there were people checking their guns. Let's just say there were a lot of personalities," says John Tafaro, who started trading there that year. "A gunshot never went off on the floor. That's where we drew the line."

As May approached, says Stanley Meierfeld, who arrived at Nymex in 1971, four of the biggest potato traders who were going long in the market locked themselves in a room in the Fifth Avenue Hotel the day before expiration to keep an eye on one another. "The longs would pressure the other longs not to give in to the shorts, and the shorts would do the same on their end," Marks says. How much money you made came down to how well you could bully both your allies *and* your opponents. If you had a large long position in the market and sold it, you would hurt the other traders on your side of the bet, because by selling, you would drive down the price. "Remember, this was still a small market back then," says another Nymex trader. "In a small pool, when you were buying or selling, it was easy to make big waves. People traded, what, a thousand lots [contracts] a day of potatoes? But on a thousand lots, people made hundreds of thousands of dollars if they were long and the prices were going up. In those days, a trader who made $100,000 a year was considered a fucking genius." A third trader says, "These guys all knew each other and they knew themselves to be less than honest. So, to make sure they didn't get screwed, they had to watch each other."

The all-nighter at the hotel didn't work. One of the traders who held a mess of long positions lost his nerve and jumped out the bathroom window. He inched along the window ledge and rushed off to sell his positions before the others could stop him. On Wall Street, keeping your friends close and your enemies closer was standard practice, but at Nymex, your friends often were your worst enemies. "You know how we spell 'trader'?" says one of the ex–potato traders. "*T-r-a-i-t-o-r.*"

Distracted by their hotel room antics and petty rivalries, the traders barely noticed the real threat on the horizon: an external enemy living thousands of miles away, who would be their ultimate undoing. Their far-off nemesis was an uneducated farmer from Boise, Idaho. But he was no ordinary farmer. Before being laid to rest in June 2008, at the age of ninety-nine, in an elaborate mausoleum redolent of Egypt's pharaohs, this farmer would be named the oldest person on the Forbes 400 Richest Americans list, reaping an estimated fortune of $3.6 billion off not just potato chips but also computer chips. He was J. R. Simplot, Idaho's famed "Potato King."

Simplot eschewed religion as "hocus-pocus," but was a devout flag-waving hawk. After leaving home at fourteen, because, like Marks, he didn't get along with his father, he got into pig farming. He shot and gutted his pigs after feeding them swill from potato peelings and wild horse meat and then sold them at market. He grew his own potatoes and killed the horses himself. From there, he got into vegetable farming, particularly onions. He made so much money off onions that he once likened onion powder to gold dust.

Onions, like many of the more dysfunctional commodities markets at the time, were considered a good market to be in because the prices were easy to manipulate, says Meierfeld. "It's illegal to trade onions now, because in the 1950s some guys pulled off this beautiful play. They drove the price up and then down so far that onions were worth less than the mesh bags they came in." Fed up, the U.S. government banned onion futures trading permanently in 1958, back when it still had the backbone to do such things. When oil prices went into a tailspin decades later, such measures were considered out of the question. "What happens when you can't trade futures on a product anymore? It means that you can't hedge your price risk," says a high-ranking futures exchange official who once worked for the CFTC. "Not being able to hedge means you just have to add the cost of your price risk to the cost of the onion or potato or whatever it is you're selling. Which isn't so bad. Sometimes, it is better than just letting it trade into the stratosphere."

Simplot parlayed his onion businesses into thirty thousand acres of land and started growing more potatoes, producing ten thousand freight wagons a year. During World War II, one-third of all potatoes consumed by American GIs came from his land. By the late 1960s, he'd become the largest supplier of potatoes to McDonald's. Off the farm, Simplot became a wise investor, swapping $1 million for a 40 percent stake in Boise start-up Micron Technology. The company went on to make billions of dollars manufacturing the semiconductors used to store data in memory cards and microchips in cameras and cell phones. A lifelong teetotaler, who didn't smoke but somehow became addicted to sleeping pills, Simplot was often chased by the IRS for tax fraud. He went around in his rattletrap Lincoln Town Car, cursing out "the goddamn parking spaces for cripples." His goal, he said, was to be successful at least 51 percent of the time. He beat that standard by a long shot. "Simplot developed and shipped some of the first frozen potatoes," Marks says. "He had all these supply contracts with big companies and drove a car with the license plate MR. SPUD." But in the 1970s, the potato potentate was discontented. Simplot wanted Idaho, not Maine, to be the epicenter of the potato universe.

The Nymex traders stood in his way. They stubbornly refused to accept Maine's decline. All appearances to the contrary, a potato, to them, was not just a potato. They were accustomed to trading potatoes from Maine. They liked Maine potatoes. All their connections went back to Maine farmers, bagmen, politicians, moles. The Nymex traders had no interest in starting over in Idaho. "Some of the potato traders I knew on the floor loved the fact that the Maine potato market was so easy to control," Marks says. Another trader who worked on the floor throughout the 1970s says, "If we'd accepted both Maine *and* Idaho potatoes, don't you think it would have been a lot harder for us to drive up the price on quote-unquote concerns of a supply shortage?" The other aspect to Maine that the traders liked, despite its plummeting potato production, was that it had more farmers contributing to its overall output than Idaho, which was ruled by Simplot with an iron fist. "There was a fear that Simplot and another major U.S. potato farmer, P. J. Taggares, would end up controlling the entire market," Marks says. "And nobody wants to trade in a market where the game is rigged in just one or two people's favor. We needed to know that if we extended the market, it would stay competitive." From the Nymex traders' perspective, Simplot and Peter J. Taggares already had too much power. They dug in their heels. They insisted on potatoes coming only from Maine. They underestimated Simplot. He was not the type of man to go quietly.

Lapayover came to Nymex the same year as Marks, and he was there on the day of reckoning. A self-proclaimed draft-dodger, he did not like gambling, playing cards, or betting on sports. He didn't even like trading that much, except for the part about making inordinate amounts of money. His father had been a tailor, but his family had gotten out of the garment business at the same time he was entering the job market. Before he came to the trading floor in 1973, his plan had been to find a job as a social studies teacher. "There aren't enough teachers in New York nowadays. But back then, teaching jobs were plums, they were cherries, because it was the only way you could get out of the draft." In his early twenties, Lapayover took a couple substitute-teaching stints, but was unable to get a full-time job. "I knew that if I got drafted, I wouldn't make it out alive. Look at me. I am six-foot-five, Jewish, a wise guy from Brooklyn. I was never going to get through basic training, let alone a war."

Without a teaching job, Lapayover focused all his efforts on getting rejected by the draft board, deluging it with X-rays and physicians' notes describing all types of ailments and physical afflictions, such as a bad knee. "I refused to get surgery to fix the cartilage on my knee. I was hoping that would be my ticket out. But, what do you know, whenever they checked, my knee seemed just fine. So I loaded up my file with everything bad that's ever happened to me. The doctor finally checked my back and that's what ended up saving me. I didn't even think of that. That's when my cousin, Stanley Levin, told me about the potato market."

Lapayover got a job as a runner at twenty-two. Three years into it, he became head clerk at brokerage firm Paul Mahler Inc., named for a New Yorker who got into trading commodities after marrying a woman whose family was in the potato business. Lapayover was getting good at brokering trades for a big-time clearing firm, Heinhold Commodities, when disaster struck. He remembers seeing it coming like a freight train from far off, but was powerless to stop it. The date was May 7, 1976, a day that would mark a staggering reversal of fortunes for Nymex and its traders, but one that none would fully appreciate for years to come. "It was your typical last day of trading in the May potato contract, which was to say the market was insane, but otherwise normal," Lapayover says. "Because my brokerage firm did so much business for Heinhold, we could see all the potato trades being put on. I saw an open position that wasn't getting closed out for a couple thousand potato contracts. It was huge. Whoever was behind it, they were massively short. It got to be later in the day, and I didn't see it going away. It wasn't getting sold out. I went to my boss. I was getting nervous. I knew we hadn't been asked to take care of that position and I didn't see anyone else being asked to do it. He told me not to worry about it, that probably one of the other big brokers was taking care of things. I went home, but in my gut I knew something was terribly wrong."

The next day, tension hung over them like a blade. "Back then, the minute the May contract expired, you could hear a pin drop. Traders lived for that day. It was like Mardi Gras. Immediately afterward, you would see trading companies downsizing their staff, traders going on vacation for weeks, people retiring. You didn't even have to worry about coming back to work the next morning, because it didn't matter. This time was different. People were anxious, hurrying in; the rumors started, and it just got worse and worse."

The traders looked up at the price board. The outstanding short position for a couple thousand potato contracts was still there. "We thought, 'Uh-oh, that's not right.' Then we saw the members of the board come in, which never happened after May expiration. That's when we got scared."

The Nymex traders had, as usual, attempted to run potato prices up at expiration. Simplot, betting against them, strong-armed the prices in the other direction, hammering them with the sheer size of his position. By selling millions of dollars of potato futures, he drove down the prices in the process. But he didn't unwind his short bets before expiration and he did not make good on them by delivering thousands of pounds of Maine potatoes. The noon deadline for contract delivery came and went. Simplot didn't have any Maine potatoes to deliver. But he did have plenty of Idaho potatoes. One floor trader's account:

> *Simplot went short. We still don't know why he did it. Maybe he was anticipating a good supply? . . . I do know that people screwed around with the potato deliveries again and again. I can't point any fingers, but from the stories I hear, the longs would pay off the inspectors who inspected the potatoes and have them say, "Oops, they're rotten, they're no good," which created a shortage in Maine and drove up prices. But there was no shortage of Idaho potatoes. Let's say I go long at $5 a hundredweight three months before delivery and the shorts go short at $5. Now the market is $5.50, now the market is $6. Now it's time to come make delivery and all of a sudden there're no potatoes in Maine to deliver, they are supposedly no good. The shorts have to buy some long positions back before expiration. And where's the price of potatoes going? To $6, $7, $8, $9, $10, $11. If I am a long, I can triple or quadruple my money by selling to the shorts. By creating a shortage, I am driving up the price. They were manipulating the price higher. The way you do it is to somehow get the farmers in Maine not to deliver. Or not grow. Simplot wanted to deliver Idaho potatoes, but our contract said the potatoes had to come from Maine. No exchanges. And Simplot was saying: "Hey, I got a fucking bunch of potatoes, all you want, and what, you're telling me you won't take my potatoes?"—"No, Mr. Simplot, they have to be grown in Maine, not in Idaho."—"You've got to be fucking kidding me, right? Fuck you."*

When Simplot's deliveries were not made, the market defaulted. Pandemonium ensued. And then came what traders dread most: crickets.

In all, over 50 million pounds of potatoes went undelivered. More than a thousand potato contracts were not honored and considered in default. The Nymex traders blamed Simplot for the brunt of the fallout. Taggares, Simplot's counterpart in Othello, Washington, also was suspected of having a role in the disaster *Time* magazine anointed "The Great Potato Bust." In an interview with *Time* in June 1976, Simplot seemed taken aback by all the fuss. He said he wasn't sure how many defaulted potato contracts were his, as he didn't keep track of such things. "There's nothing to get excited about," he said. "I think it will all work out." The total estimated damage came to between $3 million and $5 million.

Simplot was charged that year for attempting to manipulate the market and levied $50,000 in fines. It was found that the trajectory of Maine potato prices over the prior sixteen months had completely defied reason. By the time the May contract expired, it had taken a roller-coaster ride from a low of $5.92 a hundredweight in February 1975 to nearly $20 by early 1976, tanking at $8 and then shooting to $17 before falling back to $8.70 in the months that followed. "Isn't it amazing how the seeds of crookedness pervading the oil market began with something like a fucking potato?" one retired floor trader marvels. "Because we owned the place, we thought we could do whatever we wanted. We were the traders. It was part of our genetic makeup to be that way, something we could never change."

But owning the house had its limits. The traders hadn't bargained on anyone else, least of all an upstart farmer from Boise, being better at gaming their own market than them. The farmers in Maine, however, knew better. They'd seen the May potato contract get gamed so many times, they even had a name for it: "the Curse of the Potato." Herschel Smith, who grew two thousand acres of potatoes on his farm in Mars Hill, Maine, told the *Wall Street Journal* he'd finally thrown away his ticker-tape machine in disgust. He'd traded potatoes for years, but swore he was through. "The same old game is going on," he said. "I've watched since the 1940s and it's just been one mess after the other. I've had it." What was the point of buying a potato futures contract if it didn't allow for the delivery of actual potatoes? Even a trader who didn't want potatoes knew a futures contract had to be tied to the product it was representing or else it was useless. "When the potato market failed, there were headlines all over the world," Marks says. "There had never been a default anywhere in the entire 150-year history of the U.S. commodities market. Our exchange failed to prevent it from happening. The essence of an exchange is the sanctity of its contract, regardless of how it's managed. I don't think anything like that had ever happened before."

Simplot wouldn't be the only farmer to play a pivotal role in the foundation of what would eventually become the world's most unpredictable market. James Newsome, a kid from a strawberry farm in Plant City, Florida, also would have a major hand in shaping it. At the time of Simplot's default, the president of the Future Farmers of America was just about to graduate from high school, but he would soon be on a politically charged path leading straight to Washington.

Even in the disco era of fast-and-loose market regulation, the government felt it had to intervene in the potato crisis. Amid the subsequent rash of threatened lawsuits and allegations that potato trading had been overrun by robber barons and fraud for decades, the Commodity Futures Trading Commission, the newly created futures market watchdog, banned the trading of potato futures indefinitely. The move effectively wiped out Nymex's most prosperous business.

Already considered by Wall Street to be a dog market even in the best of times, Nymex immediately lost all legitimacy. The seventy-five-some-odd traders packing the floor each day thinned to less than twenty of only the most inept, inexperienced, and destitute of the speculators. For some of the potato traders, the effects were fatal. "We had one guy, an Irish trader in his fifties, who didn't come in one day," says one of the Nymex locals. "Everyone heard that he died, but what really happened is he blew his brains out." The price of a Nymex seat, which had leaped as high as $47,000 at the height of the potato-trading craze, plunged to $5,000, leaving Nymex's four hundred seat holders bereft and furious. Even the Maine potato farmers, whom the Nymex traders once defended, turned their backs on them. The New York traders were at a loss for what to do. Subsist off the boneless beef market?

Rumors soon began to make the rounds that, after 104 years of trading, Nymex would close its doors forever. The younger traders, frustrated at having only just entered a lucrative game already ending, blasted the older traders, many of whom were in their fifties and sixties, for running the market into the ground. The older traders blamed the Maine farmers and the state's market officials, who they believed had been regularly meddling with the potato supplies.

The subsequent battery of swipes and counterswipes between the junior and senior traders at Nymex snowballed into what Marks would call a "palace revolt," leading to an overhaul of the exchange's hierarchy. The older traders didn't want to give up betting on potatoes. They hoped the government's ban would be lifted and Nymex could go back to being a potato market. But the younger traders wanted a new leader, someone with a decent education and who, if it wasn't too much to ask, wasn't a total potato-trading psychopath. That's when Marks found himself running in and winning the election for vice chairman. The more reform-minded members of the exchange, many of whom knew his father, rallied around him and cast their votes. "Michel was young, but we knew he was intelligent and he had a father who was extremely worldly," says Lapayover. "Also, we didn't have much other choice."

Just like that, in 1977, Marks went from being a trading-floor drone to becoming the right-hand man to the chairman, Jack Stern. No matter that the cosseted son of Francis Marks had never been on a board before.

Or that his job was only part-time. Or that he did not get paid.

Two weeks into his new post, Marks got the phone call that would change his life. Stern, on the last leg of his final year as chairman, had suffered a heart attack. And just like that, Marks, at twenty-seven, became the youngest-ever chairman of the nation's most despised market.

3

From Wastrels to Wildcatters

Yea, I walk through the valley of the shadow of death but I fear no evil, because I am the meanest son of a bitch in this valley.

—MARTIN GREENBERG'S SLIGHTLY
MODIFIED VERSION OF PSALM 23:4

EVEN AS A child-prodigy chairman, Michel Marks still did not get paid. It wasn't long before he discovered that being top dog at a dog market didn't count for much. During the day, he slugged it out in the pits alongside the rest of the traders, attempting to squeeze some sort of livelihood out of the last gasps of a dying enterprise. Even as chairman, his job was still part-time. At night, he'd restlessly pace his $900-a-month apartment across the street from the exchange, trying desperately to come up with a way to turn the market around.

He was hamstrung. Only about fifteen traders bothered showing up for work anymore. "You could have fired a cannon across the trading floor and not have hit anyone," he says. It also was a not-for-profit market, so his annual budget was $1 million. His staff was a skeleton crew. Adding insult to injury, the CFTC, set up in 1974 to protect U.S. consumers from things like gargantuan potato kerfuffles, had forbidden Nymex to offer any new contracts on *anything*. The CFTC felt it had to be harsh. It couldn't afford to look like it was sleeping at the switch so soon in its infancy. There would be time for that later.

But Nymex couldn't afford to lose its top-grossing potato business either. The compromise hammered out between the two sides was that potato trading would continue to be banned, but Nymex could reintroduce old commodities contracts it had phased out in the past, if it wanted to. It wasn't much, but it was better than nothing for a down-trodden meat-and-potatoes market that should have gone under years earlier. Marks served the remainder of Stern's term while looking for his big break. His father was still a member of the exchange, but Marks found that he worked best when left to his own devices. He got up at six in the morning and put in eighty-hour weeks. He cherished his solitude. One of his colleagues asked him why he didn't find a girlfriend or get married. Marks's response: I don't have any time. Want to find me a girl?

When his term ended in 1978, Marks ran for chairman unopposed. He still didn't have any idea what he was doing, but he sensed that the world's worst job could only get better. Deep in his gut, he felt destiny was looking him straight in the eye and nobody else.

He pored over the fine print of forgotten Nymex futures contracts in hopes of resurrecting one that could become the market's saving grace. It wasn't a good plan, but it was his plan. "I worked for free for the next ten years. That's all I did. It consumed me," he says. "I was young, but felt I understood what I was doing instinctively. The first four to five years, no one cared what I did. I spent a great deal of time working alone. Jim Stone was appointed the new chairman of the CFTC. He was young, like me. In his early thirties. He'd been head of the Department of Insurance for Massachusetts and I supposed he had some connection to Massachusetts governor Michael Dukakis, who would eventually run for president. I figured that was the political connection that got him the job, though later he would tell me that Leo Melamed at the CME told him that he handpicked all the CFTC chairmen and commissioners. I picked up a copy of *BusinessWeek* magazine shortly after Jim's appointment, and there was a picture of him standing on a hill of potatoes! The new Sheriff Stone was going to make his mark, at our expense!"

Oddly enough, no one in Washington fully explained how Stone was going to make any mark on the futures market when he came from a background in insurance.

The political stakes were high, but the personal stakes, for Marks, were much higher. He didn't just fear for his reputation and fortune, he feared for his life. "The CFTC held a big hearing about what happened with the potato market in the heart of Maine potato country," he says. "I went and testified in front of four hundred angry farmers. I received threatening phone calls to New York, saying, 'Tell Marks if he comes to Maine, he'll never leave.' The state of Maine was up in arms. Senator Ed Muskie of Maine and Senator Frank Church of Idaho introduced a bill to ban potato futures trading permanently. There were headlines in the newspapers for months. I had to go to Washington to testify. I was petrified."

It didn't help that, with each passing day, his father's fortunes also became inextricably more entwined with those of Nymex. For Marks and his dad, it was not a minor matter. "You want to know what really happened? Michel took the crap for his dad," says a friend of the Marks family, who worked on the trading floor. "His dad didn't put him there to set him up for life. He put him there because the exchange was falling apart and he needed someone to look after his shit." If he was worried, Francis Marks didn't let on to the pit traders. To the young guns on the trading floor, he projected the image of the eternal optimist. Even as Nymex hemorrhaged business, he schmoozed with them and exhorted them not to lose faith or sell their seats. "I don't think Francis really knew how we were going to make it," says a trader well acquainted with him. "But he was always going around telling everyone, 'Do yourself a favor and buy a Nymex seat! Remember, Francis Marks told you! You won't regret it!' He was very gung ho, a big believer in hard work and determination and capitalism and the American way. He had a strong ethic about everything and was constantly broadcasting his views. I remember him insisting that the Dow was going to two thousand. We all thought he was bat-shit crazy."

Upstairs, his son was sweating the detail. Michel Marks wasn't a schmoozer. He was more interested in the nuts and bolts. Sifting through the yellowed pages of aged and discarded Nymex contracts, he found slim pickings. He dredged up a currency futures contract. Working the phones, he attempted to generate interest on Wall Street for it, but most people gave him the cold shoulder. With so much angst over the potato default, no one wanted to give him the time of day. He went at it again, going door-to-door to brokerage houses and trading shops. Those who didn't snub him to his face laughed at him behind his back. Melamed's CME had recently started a wildly successful currency-futures business, and there was nothing sadder than watching Marks at Nymex, the also-ran market, trying to scoop up his leftovers. "I went to see Henry Jarecki, one of the top traders in the business. He was founder and owner of Mocatta Metals, the largest bullion dealer in the world," Marks says.

"When I asked if he would trade our new foreign currency futures contracts, he said, 'I'll never trade anything on your exchange.'"

At the same time, Marks was trying to attract fresh blood. Among those he recruited to the pits was Sherry Collins, a fresh-faced nineteen-year-old he plucked out of Summit, New Jersey, who grabbed headlines for being the youngest female trader in the country. She was the eldest daughter of Loree "Rip" Collins, the New Jersey county chairman who had met with Marks years earlier at the Grand Summit Hotel when Marks was first planning to buy his Nymex seats. "To get on the trading floor, you had to take a ten-question written test and be approved by a committee," says Sherry Collins, who traded Marks's currency futures and commodities. "That was it. And they weren't even serious questions either. They asked you things like, 'What time does butter trade?' It turned out that it traded for only fifteen minutes on Thursday afternoons. The person who gave me the test didn't even know the answer. The test was really a formality, more than anything. I didn't understand the rules of the trading floor. I didn't know what I was doing. I did a little volume for myself and big-order volumes for my customers. You learned as you went."

Collins met Marks when she was in grade school after he was introduced to her father, who'd been a New Jersey state assemblyman. At the time, Marks was working for the Republican State Committee in Trenton and finishing up his studies at Princeton as president of the College Republicans. To the Republican committee, accustomed to receiving useless volunteers of the spoiled-rich-kid variety from well-connected families, Marks was "a breath of fresh air," says the superior court judge, who oversaw his labors. "From the day Michel walked in, he could run the place. He was quiet, but he was like a general with his troops. I've seen a lot of people in politics—I've been in the assembly and I've been in the cabinet—but I'd never seen anyone in my life like him. He was so intelligent, decent, and unique. Here was this young man who didn't have to work a day in his life if he didn't want to, but he worked very hard and he did great work. I think he had one of those minds that could never sit still." Marks worked so diligently as an organizer for the annual Republican conventions, he eventually moved in with the Collins family.

In Marks, Sherry Collins found a lasting friend. Marks drove her wherever she wanted to go, gave her advice, and treated her like a kid sister. Before dying of a heart attack shortly after Sherry left for college, her mother called Marks to her deathbed and begged him to look after her daughter. "I'd only been away three weeks at the University of Oregon when my mother passed away," Collins says. "My parents were divorced. My father just wasn't capable of taking care of my little sister. I had to quit college and come back to look after her. We moved in with my aunt and uncle and I started driving a cab in Summit. I was the only white teenager in an all-black cab company. I didn't mind, but a week into the job, Michel came to me and said, 'You're not going to be a cabbie the rest of your life. I am going to honor my word to your mother.' He made me the youngest trader at his exchange and he became its youngest chairman. We were the dynamic duo. I owe everything to him. The traders there treated the new guys like raw meat, but I was the baby and they all protected me. When I started, the trading floor was just like a family. We tried to make money together instead of against each other. It wasn't like it is now, where people are fighting for every penny. At first, I don't think anyone realized how young I was. That was Michel. He liked ruffling feathers and shaking things up. I guess somebody found out, because after that they moved the minimum trading age up to twenty-one."

Not all women felt so sheltered in the pits. From New York to Chicago to London to Sydney, many who withstood the lewdness and the dirt and the spitting of the commodities traders credited their success solely to their sense of humor. "Sexual harassment wasn't acknowledged at all in those days, so women had to kind of make the best of it," says one female pit trader. "You couldn't take it too seriously. And you always had to give it back. You had to be careful of where you kept your hands too. If you had them behind your back, the men would sometimes drop their trousers—and you know what—into them. But I found a way to deal with that. Grow nails!"

The publicity Marks attracted by bringing on board a teenager— a comely coed, no less—was priceless. He issued press releases highlighting Collins as the nation's youngest female pit trader and himself as the youngest exchange chairman. So youthful was Marks, with his handsome, unlined face and curly hair, that when he arrived for the first time at a meeting of the group of businessmen who oversaw the World Trade Center exchanges, no one recognized him. Seated at the table, he watched as the group's president handed out the printed agendas to all the other chairmen, most of whom were at least a generation older than him, skipping him over. "He just thought I was one of the staffers," Marks told a reporter later. "And it did make it difficult. The exchange had a credibility problem already and all of a sudden to have a kid of twenty-eight years . . . walk in, who didn't know anything about commodities, presented even more credibility problems."

Collins was featured on the front page of the *Wall Street Journal* and interviewed by *Cosmopolitan* magazine's editor in chief Helen Gurley Brown for her national bestseller *Having It All*. Her photos were splashed across the pages of *Working Woman* magazine and the *New York Post*. Collins appeared in 1977 on the *Today Show*, flashing her killer smile, tossing her golden locks, and dazzling the audiences with her girl-next-door appeal. But the ink spilled over "Miss Merc" and her white-knight chairman wasn't enough to save Marks's fledgling currency business. He was beginning to understand why the elderly traders had clung so desperately to potatoes. Introducing a new product was a near-Sisyphean task. The floor traders didn't object to test-driving his currency futures, but nobody else on Wall Street wanted to touch them without first seeing more activity in the pits. When it came to building a market from the ground up, nothing attracted a crowd like a crowd. But igniting the spark that would be its genesis was virtually impossible. Marks went back to the drawing board, hoping that somewhere in his heap of Nymex contracts he'd find his winning lottery ticket.

Mocking the Nymex traders in their impoverished state were the Comex traders, the market kingpins of the 1970s, who were betting on and winning big in the skyrocketing metals markets. Even Alan Greenspan, who later became the U.S. Federal Reserve chief, was seen roaming the metals futures pits. "It's true, I saw Alan down there sometimes," a trader says. "It's weird now, isn't it? He had a Comex membership. But we were all a lot younger back then."

In 1977, Nymex, along with Comex, the Coffee and Sugar Exchange, and the New York Cotton Exchange, decided to move their trading pits onto one common trading floor offering the traders more up-to-date technology. They opened an ultramodern facility on the eighth floor of 4 World Trade Center, where the traders would no longer be reduced to scrawling bids and offers on blackboards, but instead transmit their prices electronically to large screens posted above the pits. That same year, President Jimmy Carter founded the U.S. Department of Energy, a government agency housed in a penal-looking concrete fortress in Washington left over from the old Atomic Energy Commission, which would, over the course of the next three decades, burn through approximately $550 billion of the public purse with the express mission of ending America's dependence on oil, yet never actually come up with a plan for doing that. Along the way, the nation would be distracted by the Cold War, which would leave a mountain of nuclear weapons in its wake that would keep the DOE distracted permanently. In dealing with America's energy problems, this makes the DOE only marginally less useless than the CFTC. With 14,000 employees, 93,000 contract workers, and an annual budget of around $30 billion, the DOE is better known for being the place where taxpayer dollars go to die than a stepping stone to energy independence. To date, it is no closer to reaching its initial goal than the CFTC is to keeping bulge-bracket banks and designer hedge funds from committing fraud and trading abuses in the energy market.

Perhaps fittingly, the DOE's headquarters, previously part of the Department of Defense, are named after a distinguished serviceman with an equally bleak backstory. General James Forrestal, a former secretary of the navy who suffered greatly from depression, died in 1949 under unusual circumstances. Depending on whom you believe, he was either assassinated or committed suicide by tying the end of a bathrobe sash around his neck, the other to a radiator, and defenestrating himself. His body was found in an alley. The investigation into his death was marred by allegations of his being killed by Jews or Communists for political reasons, or by murderous government operatives for security reasons (due to his supposedly extensive knowledge of the nation's contact with UFOs).

After moving into the World Trade Center, the morale of the Nymex traders went downhill quickly. They had only to glance across the pits at the Comex traders to see the smorgasbord of riches they *weren't* getting. "This was the dot-com bubble of that era," Marks says. "With the metals traders, you didn't even have to be good to make a fortune. All you had to do was be there. Money was pouring out of the telephones." Until then, commodities had never been taken seriously by Wall Street. Even the commodities traders themselves called it "the Last Frontier." Suddenly, metals were all the rage. "I remember seeing a friend walk by looking like he wanted to jump out a window," Marks says. "I said, 'What happened?' He said he'd just lost $3 million in a day. He couldn't believe it. I saw him a few days later and he was ecstatic. I said, 'What now?' He said he'd just made $6 million. It might not seem like a lot of money to some, but to us, in our market back then, to go from a $3 million loss to a $6 million gain that quickly was outrageous."

Lenny Williams, a Comex clerk, remembers when the gold and silver pits got so busy that sometimes he couldn't leave for days. "I went to work one morning and didn't go home for two weeks! We would shower in nearby bathrooms and buy deodorant at the local department store, Century 21. We would sleep in the gold ring. In the beginning, there were no strict regulations and no compliance department. It was just gentlemen doing business with gentlemen. If someone needed help, we would work it out. If you ask me, people back then were a lot more honest than they are today. Some of the bigger players got crazy and ruined it for everyone. They forgot about the little things, the things that made this place great. Now it's all about the numbers and the shareholders and the prices. Back then, it was people helping people, with all of us making some money."

In the heavily trafficked sections of the new trading pits, the action was fast and dedicated. The floor was hard, the players were surly, and the smoke curling from the tips of their cigarettes hung thick in the air. While some of the traders were approachable, others looked like they'd just eaten their young. The milieu turned decidedly macho. The Comex traders strutted about in open displays of braggadocio, looking down their noses at the poorer Nymex traders.

Martin Greenberg first set foot in the Comex pits in 1976. His temper was the stuff of legend. Eventually, he became the market's chairman. "I was trading silver when men were men and sheep were nervous. Yeah, I could be mean. I once got mad at this guy. I was strangling him. I just put my hand on his face and he fell. Right in the middle of it, one of the compliance officers comes up and says, 'Hey, Marty, I'm going to have to write you up for $5,000 for this.' I was still going at it. I looked over my shoulder and said, 'Better make it $10,000, because I'm gonna kill him!'" Known for his pithy one-liners ("I'm an art collector—I like pictures on cash of dead presidents"), Greenberg cast a long shadow, even in a roomful of traders all searching for the inner heat. It didn't hurt that by the time he came to the floor, at thirty-six, Greenberg was already older than most of them. He'd never had a job he liked, but he had a family to provide for. "I worked for my dad's business, which was raincoats and sporting goods, for the first ten years of my adult life. I didn't get along with my dad, so I left. For the next five years, I was a stockbroker, liquidating companies. After that, I was in the ladies' sweater business. But I kept up my membership at this Long Island country club, Cold Spring. I thought it might be good for a connection or two. One day I was standing at the urinal with my buddy, who was a trader, and he asked, 'What are you doing these days, Marty?' I said, 'Nothing much, just odd jobs, trying to keep the money coming in.' He said, 'Why don't you come down to the floor?' I did, and that was it for me. After two years, I didn't have to worry about money anymore."

Although the four exchanges agreed to divide their twenty-five-thousand-square-foot trading floor into four equal-size quadrants, it wasn't long before they began squabbling over space. "Everyone thought we'd eventually merge, but instead we were like the roommates that went bad," says Daniel Rappaport, who quit being a lawyer in his early twenties to trade platinum, the only active market Nymex had left. "There were lots of petty jealousies among the traders. When I started, Comex was New York's premier exchange. We shared a cafeteria. But when we got in line for lunch, if there was a Comex trader behind us, the Nymex trader would usually be forced to step aside and let him go first, because the Comex trader had *real* business to do. Then there were the spats all over the floor. The exchanges had aisles running between them, so we could walk around. But when Comex wanted more space and Nymex, which had lots of it, didn't want to share, fights started breaking out."

It was in the testosterone-fueled cafeteria of the World Trade Center that Rappaport first ran afoul of Mark Fisher. A top-shelf Comex silver trader, Fisher made a habit of ignoring the Nymex traders. Watching them eat lunch one afternoon, though, his curiosity got the better of him. Fisher rose from his chair and swaggered up.

"How old are you?" he demanded of the trader nearest him.

"Twenty-nine," the trader spluttered, surprised.

Rappaport watched Fisher's reaction. "Mark just looked this guy up and down and decided that he, Mark Fisher, was making more money than him."

Fisher did not introduce himself. He knew they knew who he was. His trading badge was FSH. Everyone knew the Fish. While he'd gone to Wharton, he didn't have time for such pedestrian things as an Ivy

League education. That's what assistants were for. Instead of attending his classes, he had sent his friend Rhonda to take notes for him. While she was doing that, he was down in the pits trading.

Rhonda eventually graduated from the same MBA program as Fisher and joined his staff as one of his traders.

"Fisher went down the line, asking each of us our age. Every time, he'd size up whoever it was and once he'd decided he was making more money than them, he'd get a little bit more comfortable," Rappaport says. "It was rude. It was obnoxious. It was obviously meant to intimidate us."

Fisher finally arrived at Rappaport.

"How old are you?"

"Thirty," said Rappaport, gnawing on his ham sandwich.

"Well then," Fisher said, satisfied. He seated himself, uninvited, at their table. Leaning back in his chair, he smiled, his chest expanding with pride.

Rappaport decided that Fisher was probably of the peacock variety of trader. He also noticed Fisher was losing his hair.

"How old are *you*?" he asked.

"Twenty-three," Fisher said, still grinning.

"Oh yeah?" Rappaport said. "Well, you look like shit!"

Rappaport's lunch buddies laughed so hard, they spit up their meals—all over Fisher.

The smirk on Fisher's face instantly evaporated. Caught off guard, he windmilled around in his chair to see who else might be watching.

"He was completely taken aback," Rappaport says. "He didn't know what to do. After a minute or so, he just gave up and started laughing too. It was one of those rare moments where you don't end up killing each other. Years later, he told me, 'After that, I knew we'd be friends.' "

Like many traders, Fisher was too hypercompetitive to make friends the normal way. It was a common trait among the more megalomaniacal traders. "With Mark, it always came down to the dick-measuring," a colleague says. "But once you showed him what you were made of, you had his full respect."

Fish stories wafted through the trading floor like pit cards. Fisher was the bazillion-dollar man, the man who always won. Two of the most popular stories that went around about him told of how he got his start in the pits and how he persuaded his wife to marry him. In the first, he was in junior high, growing up in Long Island next door to one of the Brodskys, a household name in the commodities world. For years, Fisher badgered his neighbor for a job on the floor. The neighbor owned a large house and drove an expensive car and, even then, Fisher knew he wanted these things. After pleading for the job as if it was his birthright, the neighbor finally found him a low-level position as a runner. He figured Fisher would probably quit after a week.

Fisher never left.

The second story also showcased Fisher's tenacity. After falling hopelessly in love with a statuesque blonde, he earnestly proposed. She turned him down. He proposed again. She demurred. What followed was a series of propositions and rejections, which, again, found Fisher the victor. "You gotta hand it to him," says an admirer. "He knows what he wants and he doesn't stop until he either hits a wall or he gets it." Still married, Fisher and his wife have a daughter and a son, both of whom have followed in their father's footsteps. His daughter attended his alma mater, the University of Pennsylvania, and his son learned to trade well before he turned eighteen.

Rappaport also became friends with Richard Schaeffer, a pit trader with hyperbolic energy who would eventually become a key figure in the history of the exchange. Born in New York and reared in the prosperous town of Hewlett Harbor, Long Island, Schaeffer came from middle-class roots but possessed a fervent desire to one day become a wealthy man. "My ideal was to have $5 million to myself after taxes," he says. After graduating from the University of Maryland in 1974, an experience he described as "one giant fucking four-year party" (this he neglected to mention during his commencement speech at the school in 2006), he worked for his father's accounting firm for six years.

Schaeffer found the work unspeakable drudgery. He quit and took a series of odd jobs that included producing rock videos in the 1980s for Dolly Parton and Glenn Campbell, before going back to work for his father and then quitting again. "I gave accounting a good shot," he says, "but I hated every day." He cast about for a few more years before finding his calling—or the precursor to his calling—trading cattle futures at Nymex back when neither he nor pretty much anyone else had ever heard of the place. Randy Warsager, the soft-spoken Nazi hunter who happened to be Schaeffer's roommate when he moved to New York's East Village in the 1970s, persuaded him to try trading. Schaeffer began losing money almost immediately. But at least he was no longer bored.

He took out a trading account in 1976 at Merrill Lynch, where Warsager also kept an account. Schaeffer was not a natural risk-taker, so he bought one cattle contract and sat on it for ages. John Tafaro, who was their account executive at Merrill before joining Schaeffer and Warsager later in the pits, would tease Schaeffer mercilessly about his skittishness. "Schaeffer would call me up every day to ask where his one cattle contract was trading. One cattle contract represented forty thousand pounds of live cattle and traded in increments of tenths of a cent. If the price was up, Richie was ecstatic. If it was down, he would obsess over it. We finally got him out of that position, if for no other reason than to let him sleep at night. I sold it on a day when it was up."

When wrong-way cattle bets cleaned Schaeffer out, he took a loan from his father and lost that too on Treasury bonds. Even in a bull market, he couldn't get a break. To get by, he did tax returns for the floor traders. At thirty-one, he was too embarrassed to borrow any more money from his father or anybody else. "Those were really hard times," he says, "but I hung in there. After quitting twice, I couldn't go back to my dad."

To relieve the stress, Schaeffer wrote poetry, hundreds of verses. He also made up for his lack of trading skills with a more valuable gift: an uncanny knack for making friends and influencing people. Despite his poor trading performance, he survived by parlaying his political prowess and professional alliances into roles on the Nymex board, the executive committee, and the finance committee. He worked hard and soon became treasurer, remaining in that post for twelve years before rising still higher. An early backer of Schaeffer, besides Warsager, was Francis Marks. "Randy and Francis were extremely good to me," Schaeffer says. "Randy lent me an exchange seat so I didn't have to lease one. Even after I killed his bird, Mr. Finch, he still helped me out. I didn't mean to do it. When we were living together, I was trying to sleep one time and it wouldn't stop chirping. So I shook the cage. I guess I shook it too hard, because after that, it stopped moving."

THE FIGHTS WITH Comex did not end. It came to a head one day over an aisle. "The Comex traders wouldn't move back three feet so we could move forward three feet," Rappaport says. "The aisle got blocked.

Somebody called the fire department. The firemen tried to clear the trading floor, but the problem didn't get solved for weeks. Calling the police or the fire department was generally how we handled things back then." Rappaport took it in stride. Anything was better than being a bankruptcy lawyer. "I passed the bar exam and worked for a Park Avenue law firm for nearly two years. I couldn't remain in the legal profession, because I could never get comfortable selling my talent to represent people and issues I didn't believe in. I found it very demeaning."

Unable to extend their trading-floor space by fistfights, the Comex traders tried to buy Nymex wholesale. They didn't want the exchange; they just wanted the extra floor room. When Nymex seat prices caved in, they put in dozens of bids, but the Nymex traders fought back and Comex failed to clinch a full takeover. The Comex officials began hassling Marks to green-light a buyout deal. He refused, but agreed to convene a series of meetings to consider the option. During one of them, a Comex director suggested the Nymex traders should not be given any voting rights in the event of a takeover. "The implication being that they could hardly stand to associate with the Nymex traders, much less give them voting rights," says a bystander. "There was even one instance of someone getting personal with Marks about his height. A guy from Comex. I believe his exact words were, 'If you would get up on a chair, I'd punch you in the eye.'"

Marks didn't appreciate being treated shabbily. He also didn't like direct confrontation. "Michel asked the Comex guys, 'Do you mind if we step outside to caucus for a minute?' And the Comex officials said, 'Of course not, by all means.' And you know what Michel did? He took his group and left. It was a while before the Comex officials figured out he wasn't coming back."

Marks was torn. "The problem was that half of Nymex's board members were also Comex members, so it was hard for us to make a decision without conflicts of interest. Our committees met and, against my wishes, agreed to the buyout. We were going to swap five Nymex seats for one Comex seat. The Nymex board voted in favor, eight to seven. I was vehemently opposed. Three days later, the Comex officials changed their minds. They thought they were paying too much! They backed out. That's when I thought it was really over for us. The floor was dead. The potato stuff didn't bother me; I believed we'd made the right decision and were taking steps to clean the place up. But I really thought all was lost after the Comex vote. I walked out of that meeting with my head hanging down."

Marks's father only added to the anxiety, bursting in on his son's shoebox of an office to air his many views. "He would bark orders at Michel's staff like *he* was the chairman," says one high-level executive who worked alongside Marks. "It was contentious." Marks's quarters, just off the trading floor, barely held a desk and two chairs. He had room for his phone and his coat, but he wasn't equipped to receive city officials, visiting dignitaries, or an opinionated father. The intrusions annoyed him. "I felt like he was making things harder," Marks says. "And I deeply resented it."

At times, the relationship between Marks and his father was close, says one exchange official, who recalled them having "equally major-league egos" and "head sessions" in the chairman's office. Other times, it would completely break down, says a trader who knew them both. "You wondered how it was these two could pass each other in the hallway on some days and not even speak to each other."

By 1978, after he had spent a year working around the clock, Marks's knowledge of the market surpassed his father's. The diehard potato traders continued pushing for a revival of the potato contract. Exasperated, he brought it back briefly after getting a reprieve from the CFTC, but was forced to kill it again after another rash of trading problems and delivery scares. "No one under sixty was still trading potatoes, but these old codgers weren't adjusting very well, so we brought potatoes back, which I couldn't believe," says a Nymex staffer. "We even had our research department working on it, trying to find ways to bring this market back without it being such a nightmare, but it was unreal to me that we were even bothering. Here was the blackest mark on our market—and we're trying to revive it! Of course, the whole thing fell apart and we had to shut it down for good. We had a couple weeks where the traders were actually betting on potatoes *after* the season had ended and there wasn't any real, tangible supply anymore. The potato inspectors had all gone home and hadn't told anyone. So we were essentially trading on *nothing*. It was just the Nymex guys shouting in a room. When the traders found out, they pretty much went insane. Here Nymex is trying to establish itself as the global pricing center for the biggest trading houses in the world and we have these colossal assholes screaming at us for more potatoes. It would have been hilarious if it hadn't been so pathetic."

The CFTC imposed a permanent ban on potato trading. "The older potato traders, who still dominated the board of directors, weren't seeing the big picture," Rappaport says. "They didn't see the potential of the organization. They just saw potatoes as the No. 1 contract that needed to be resurrected." Harold Fisher was part of the potato-trading contingent. Trading potatoes had been his salvation. As a city kid who grew up poor, he'd drifted from a lifeguarding job on Coney Island to the air force in World War II. He was imprisoned in a POW camp after his plane was shot down over northern Germany, but made it back to New York, where he worked in the garment district and even drove a milk route in Brooklyn. He'd never been interested in any of his jobs until he'd joined Nymex in the 1960s and bought a membership for $1,000. The loss of the potato trade stung him badly. "The market was never the same after the problems, and I was out of a job," he said. "I had my membership, but no job."

Rifling through what was left of the exchange's dormant offerings, Marks rooted up a failed heating-oil contract and made some revisions. As originally written, the contract, devised by Emmett Whitlock, a sugar broker from Marks's former employer E. F. Hutton, stipulated heating-oil deliveries to Rotterdam in the Netherlands. That was obviously too far away. Marks crossed it out and changed the delivery point to the New York Harbor. He intended it only as a local contract for city merchants. He had no idea if offering heating oil would work, but after speaking with energy economist Arnold Safer he changed his mind.

Safer, a short, rotund man, had been an energy evangelist since the 1960s, preaching of a time when free market forces would dictate the price of oil, instead of the Middle East's global oil cartel, the Organization of Petroleum Exporting Countries. (Before that, the Texas Railroad Commission had ruled on oil prices along with the world's oil majors. Still earlier, it had been John D. Rockefeller of Standard Oil.) When Safer met Marks in the 1970s, Safer believed that a boost in global oil production from non-OPEC countries would destroy the cartel's stranglehold on prices by flooding the market with excess oil. He would live to see his predictions borne out, before dying at the age of fifty-nine in 1996. But in 1978, no one knew whether his ideas were anything other than outlandish theory.

Marks saw the wisdom in what Safer said. "Safer's idea was that you could only trade things that weren't regulated, because otherwise the prices would be fixed, so you wouldn't be able to bet on them going up or down. When the U.S. government deregulated heating oil, he drafted our contract." Safer would actually have to quit his full-time job at Irving Trust, which was later taken over by the Bank of New York, because his bosses disapproved of him working on an energy contract that might infuriate Big Oil. Nymex heating oil would be his and Marks's first experiment together.

Talking excitedly with Alan Lotterman, a Comex trader, about his plan, Marks received an unexpected warning. Taking on the Maine potato traders, Lotterman said, was one thing. But ambushing OPEC and the titans of Big Oil was another thing entirely. "Forget it," he said. "The government will never allow you to do it. They'll listen to OPEC and the oil companies and do everything they can to throw a wrench in the works."

Marks was stunned. "I really admired and respected Alan. When I heard that, I was afraid our heating-oil contract would never happen."

He also had another detractor. His father.

"Francis made it clear to Michel he did not think heating oil was the way to go," says a trader who knew them both. "He believed that heating oil was unproven and unsupported by the trade. He thought Michel should focus instead on metals."

But Marks didn't want to focus on metals. He wanted to do something no one had ever done before.

In the days leading up to heating oil's launch, he was on edge. Things got quiet. Too quiet. He didn't want any trouble, but neither had he expected radio silence. The avalanche of objections from the oil industry, against all odds, never came. Lotterman, who was almost always right, had somehow gotten it wrong. Sitting at his desk in his ill-lit, five-by-five-foot chairman's office with the single shaft of light pouring through the single window, Marks wondered why the oil companies weren't up in arms at what he was about to do. Where was the much-feared Leviathan that was OPEC? Where were the barbarians of Big Oil? "Then, it hit me. It seems we were not taken seriously enough to be seen as a threat. We were less than a flea on an elephant's back."

Marks launched heating-oil futures on November 14, 1978. That day, he stood virtually alone in the trading pit, trying to get the contract off the ground. A few other traders joined him, but most of them only traded one or two lots and then scampered off, as usual, to the bustling metals pits. Even with winter coming, trading volume in heating oil came to only twenty-two contracts on the first day. The rules of trading were finite: high volume begot more volume, low volume begot no volume. It was not a propitious beginning.

Marks kept trading heating oil for his personal account, but most of the other traders weren't hopeful. As the months passed, the contract barely scraped by. Some days, the trades Marks did represented half the market's activity. Howard Hazelcorn, a stock trader who came to the heating-oil pits that year, recalls money being so tight that the exchange hired professional excavators to see if a full set of U.S. coins from 1884 might be buried under the cornerstone at 6 Harrison Street, as was indicated in the building's master plans. "It was a tradition to bury a set of coins under a building the year it was built. If we had found them, it might have really helped us financially. Those coins would be worth millions today. I'm a huge collector, so I should know. The excavators came down with all their equipment and metal detectors, but found nothing. Who knows? The coins might still be there."

In those days, Nymex brimmed with fringe groups, people from all walks of life, united by little more than their zeal for trading and dreams of one day striking it rich. "The floor was a scene straight out of a Damon Runyon novel," Hazelcorn says. "It was picaresque; it was all the things you'd imagine it to be. We were a bunch of rough-and-tumble guys, tilting at windmills, not knowing what the future would bring." Even in New York, the Nymex demimonde was a habitat unlike any other.

Once more, Marks found himself trying to make something out of nothing. With great trepidation, he returned to Wall Street. This time, he brought with him three associates, all Nymex brokers about his age—Joel Faber, Jonathan Arginteanu, and Thomas McKiernan. Determined to make his heating-oil contract work, he waged a surgical strike. He and his entourage targeted the banks, the energy companies, and the big-name traders, banging on doors and muscling their way into conference rooms, speaking the only language that Wall Street understood: money. "No one thought there could ever be a free oil market," Marks says. "And no one wanted to try, because OPEC was so powerful. But we could afford to take the risk, because we had nothing to lose."

On the upside, Nymex's nonexistent standing in the oil community was actually a giant point in its favor. No one in the insular world of energy trading had ever heard of the wrecked potato market. On the downside, Marks still hadn't found somebody to replace the default-era president, Dick Levine. "Nobody wanted the job. For a full year, we couldn't get anyone to take it. Not that anyone cared. Our reputation was mud."

OPEC and the major oil companies had the power. Energy dealers and distributors worried so much about securing fuel supplies in the wake of the 1970s fuel crises that they'd pay whatever they were asked. "It was a take-it-or-leave-it pricing regime. OPEC and oil majors like Exxon would just stamp a price on the oil barrel and that was that," Marks says. "The dealers had no grounds for negotiation. They were told what they would *have* to pay for the supply contract if they wanted it. If a small-time heating-oil dealer in Vermont didn't take a contract at the price that was given, if he decided not to buy for whatever reason, then he would not only have no heating oil for his customers that winter, he would risk getting cut off by his supplier for good." Heating-oil dealers, which have always been mostly modest, family-owned operations, couldn't afford to take the risk. And they especially couldn't afford to risk the public-relations disaster of being caught shorthanded in the dead of winter without being able to bring enough heating oil to keep Aunt Nellie up on the mountain from freezing half to death. That was the sort of thing that woke dealers up in the middle of the night with the cold sweats. To them, their only choice was to keep suckling at the OPEC teat, grateful for any oil they could get at whatever price they were given.

Weirdly, even OPEC couldn't escape the wrath of its own pricing system. Its prices, set by its oil-producing member countries, often lagged regional changes in supply and demand within the United States, causing the cartel to charge either too much or too little for oil. Looking to exploit these price gaps were no fewer than eight thousand private oil-trading companies scattered across the nation, Marks says. The companies hoarded the OPEC oil contracts, hocking fuel at higher prices to the nation's distributors, dealers, and suppliers. Anyone in the oil or fuel business who couldn't get an OPEC contract had to swallow the trading companies' exorbitant fees or go out of business.

"From 1970 to 1980, the price of oil in the United States went straight up," Marks says, hitting what would be the equivalent of just over $100 a barrel today. "Anyone who could get a contract deal with OPEC could immediately turn around and sell that oil for about $10 a barrel more. It was crazy money."

Marks, being a contrarian, decided to do just the opposite. He offered heating oil at Nymex for less than the going price. He and his entourage used this outstanding fact as their key selling point. "We kept saying, 'It's $1.05 a gallon at Exxon, but only 85 cents here at Nymex'— you're giving away 20 cents," says Marks, whose first customers were small-time heating-oil dealers. "The standard response was, 'How can I be sure that your contract will work?' or 'Even if it does this time, what about next time? And what if Exxon finds out and punishes me?'"

Joel Faber, who, until then, had been a manager at the Bloomingdale's on Lexington Avenue, made the first breakthrough during a visit to Merrill Lynch. He dared one of its traders to buy a single heating-oil contract. "Just try *one*," he said. The trader was wary. He didn't want to buy anything from Nymex. But Faber's sales skills won out. The trader bought a single lot, just as a test case. When the contract worked, he came back for more. "Lo and behold, people started saying, 'I'm getting heating oil from someplace other than a major oil company—and for a lot less,'" Marks says. "Word got around on the street. The next year, the same trader took five contracts and the year after that twenty and so on. And that was how we got the oil market started."

Selling heating oil for less was no gimmick, but it did take some finagling. Many of the Nymex traders were dexterous market makers, people who made it their business to accommodate the needs of their customers for a fee. Their gift was finding an edge in almost any market, by hook or by crook, no matter what the price. "Guess what? We didn't care about prices!" says a trader who both undersold and oversold heating oil. "Who gives a shit about the prices? Nobody cared about them then and nobody cares about them now. As long as there are bids and offers, we can *always* find a way to work the gaps so the profits outweigh the losses. Maybe I'll lose a little bit here but I'll make it back there. Let me repeat: The. Price. Is. Irrelevant. Even the *product* you're trading is irrelevant, so long as you can make some money at it. Shit. If you want me to, I can make a market for you in broken dishes."

While Marks and his crew were busy drumming up business on Wall Street, an intense and ambitious young man seven years Marks's junior was also going door-to-door, trying to get financing for his first power plant in California. Jeffrey Sprecher, a twenty-six-year-old from

Madison, Wisconsin, who'd recently quit his job as a turbine salesman to seek his fortune, might have passed Michel Marks on the street. At any other time in history, they might have even been friends. But, without knowing it, both were on separate paths toward building global empires destined to go to war.

ONCE WORD GOT out about Nymex's cheap heating oil, the pits began attracting scores of traders and "commercial" players. Commercials were mostly corporate customers who drilled for, refined, stored, and shipped oil. William Bradt, a plywood trader who'd never bothered much with Nymex before, gave a start one morning as he looked over the *Wall Street Journal*. It was the heating-oil numbers that had caught his eye. Open interest, the number of long and short contracts held by the traders, had jumped sharply. "Initially, it just had a couple of hundred lots of open interest and it didn't seem that anyone was serious about it. But then I remember I looked and all of a sudden, the open interest was eight thousand. Weeks went by, maybe months, and the next thing I see it's at eleven thousand," he said. "I bought my Nymex seat in December of 1980. The open interest in heating oil at the time was around twelve thousand."

Bradt didn't even know how to trade heating oil, but the other traders showed him what to do. "Somebody said buy this month and sell this other month and it worked. It made me money and it was better and more reliable than Las Vegas and you could believe in it. There was no gasoline, there was no crude oil, there was no natural gas. Just the heating-oil pit and that was what Michel's whole hope was based on."

By tiptoeing into the energy market through the unlikely cover of heating oil, Marks literally snuck up on Big Oil. If oil was addictive, then heating oil was its gateway drug. For the first time ever, energy traders, dealers, distributors, and suppliers—anyone who cared to buy or sell oil or fuel—could look at the changing prices on the Nymex display boards and see exactly where heating oil was trading, minute by minute. As business took off, Nymex prices began to represent not just the knowledge of a handful of dealers, suppliers, and traders in New York, but innumerable dealers, suppliers, and traders across the country, making the exchange an invaluable source of information.

But serious obstacles remained. McKiernan says that when heating oil launched in 1978, few of Wall Street's traders had access to price quote machines, which were prohibitively expensive. "We had price terminals back then, but they cost $5,000 a month. So, for the outside trader calling his orders down to the Nymex pits, the question was, how do you trade when you can't see the price? Only the banks could really afford it. That all changed in the late 1970s when some guy named Lenny Elkins comes by my office and says, 'Let me have ten minutes of your time.' I didn't know who this guy was. I said, 'Okay, Lenny, you got ten minutes.' He pulls out an eight-inch-by-eight-inch black box with a screen and puts it down. Then he unpacks some suction cup thing with an antenna on it and sticks it on the outside window of my office on the twentieth floor. About ten minutes later, he turns it on and a bunch of green numbers pop up on the screen. Looking at it, I realize I am now getting real-time prices for heating oil over an FM network, or any other commodity I want, and it costs only $250 a month. And it's portable! He took his box to everyone, all the traders along the East Coast and Houston and Chicago. That was literally the beginning of the information revolution." Melamed, over in Chicago, was never seen without his black box. He walked around with it practically chained to him.

In the past, there had been no centralized pricing system for petroleum products, so the nation's energy traders had to go by word of mouth. With the advent of Nymex, they could suddenly check and challenge the prices they were being quoted against the wisdom of the crowd. More important, people felt they could trust the prices they were getting from Nymex, because the exchange was a public market and made money regardless of whether prices went up or down, unlike the oil-trading companies, which were only out to get the highest price. Nymex generated revenue from the fees it charged whenever trades passed through its pits. "In the grand scheme of things, Marks, at that moment, was like Robin Hood, because he was taking the power away from the oil companies and OPEC and turning it over to the masses," says John D'Agostino. "Marks put the spotlight on a corner of the market that had never seen the light of day. It was good for him and good for the traders, but most of all, it was good for the world. And nobody else had the nerve to do it."

Marks knew he was onto something when he arrived in Houston, the nation's oil capital, for a cocktail party and ran into a livid guest, Vito Bertolini, an energy broker. His name would remain forever seared in Marks's memory. Bertolini flew at Marks from across the room, hurling a stream of vitriol. "That fucking price screen!" he spat. "Everyone can see what is happening!"

The game was up. The oil companies could no longer bamboozle anyone into paying more than fair value for oil or fuel. "Even though we didn't start out as the most important player or the biggest, the accessibility of our prices made us the nation's main reference point," Marks says.

But the Nymex traders weren't used to success. As they began making more and more money, Marks gradually saw a change come over the pits. "It wasn't until the late seventies that I started to see the drug culture really emerge on the trading floor and in the men's room. We had full-time security detail and I knew the people I'd hired to be extremely professional, but you can't catch everyone. How do you manage and regulate a business when there's so much money involved? The truth is, if you put anyone in a situation where the cash is flowing freely, there are temptations, there are addictions. Trying to figure out how much to rein people in is very complicated. How do you get traders to do their jobs, do what they need to do, but not let things get out of hand? Sometimes it's hard to tell where that line is. It was never easy, achieving a balance. My view was to find the worst offenders and make sure that they were penalized severely."

The reality of the situation didn't come into sharp focus for him until the day he accidentally dropped cash on the trading floor.

"I remember going down into the pits to do a trade and realizing a $10 bill had fallen out of my pocket. I was shouting and trying to get my trade done and didn't pick it up right away. Out of the corner of my eye, I saw my friend Artie reach down, take the bill, and put it in his pocket. When I finished, I turned around and said, 'Artie, what are you doing? That's my $10!' Artie just blinked slowly and said, 'It was on the floor.' That was when the lightbulb went off. It was on the *floor*, so it was no longer mine. That's when I realized what we were becoming. It was a real lesson on ethics and our changing culture. I started to understand that what I wanted to accomplish and what we were turning into were two very different things. I'm not saying that I always knew how it should be. But I do know ultimately that a market can't be more than a reflection of its own members and constituents."

Bradt, who considered himself "very Catholic" before coming to the pits, felt pressured to leave his values behind. "If you worked out of the New York Mercantile Exchange it was impossible to live what one might call a religious life. There's all the money and the greed and also you can see what is happening."

An Orthodox Jewish boy recruited to the pits around that time put it another way. Showing up for his first day on the job wearing a yarmulke, he received a stern warning from an elderly trader who was also Jewish: leave religion at the door.

"You shouldn't be wearing that down here, son," he said. "You'll be disrespecting the faith doing what you're about to be doing."

What they were all doing would be tame by any standard compared with what was to come.

4

Deus Ex Machina

*The question wasn't, would you make money? You were going to
make money. It was how much money are you going to make?*

—GARY GLASS

FROM THE MOMENT he stepped into the trading pits, twenty-eight-
year-old Zoltan Louis Guttman knew there was no other place in the
world he wanted to be. And the day the global oil market was born, he
saw it happen.

The son of Jewish-Hungarian émigrés, Guttman arrived in New
York in 1956 with his younger sister, Magda, in the shambolic aftermath
of World War II. He didn't have any worldly possessions and he didn't
speak a word of English. "I was eight. We flew into Idlewild Airport and
rode through the streets to our hotel room in Brooklyn. I stared out
windows at the tall buildings in disbelief." Born in November 1949, in
the one-church town of Opalyi, Hungary, near the Romanian border,
Guttman may have been young in years, but he was old in experience.

"My mother's name was Aranka, which means 'gold.' She had five
brothers and four sisters. By the time the war ended, she'd lost her parents, three sisters, and two brothers. All of them killed at Auschwitz. She
was the only daughter who hadn't married before the war and it probably
saved her life. Let me tell you, if a mother showed up at Auschwitz with
a child, both mother and child were dead in twenty-four hours. If you
were single, though, they put you to work. That's what they did with my
mother. She was starving and had a week or two left to live when she

escaped on one of the last wagons out during the Russian liberation in January 1945. You think when the Russians freed everybody, they came with transportation and blankets and provisions? No. It was bedlam. Every man for himself. People had to walk on foot across Europe to get back to their homes. My mother barely got out of there alive. She was nineteen years old."

Aranka watched as her older sister Ilona was sent to the gas chambers at Auschwitz with her two babies, one on each arm. The last time she saw Ilona, she had stood beside her while holding one of the children. Ilona cradled the other. They were lined up with the other prisoners and a German soldier was picking them over. He saw Aranka take the child from her sister before stomping over.

"Whose child is this?" he demanded.

"My sister's," she said.

"Well, give it back!" The soldier grabbed the baby and returned it to the arms of its mother. For Aranka, it was a gift. For Ilona, it had been a death sentence.

The soldier thwacked Aranka on the head with his truncheon. The blow came down so hard, she saw stars. "That soldier noticing it wasn't her baby saved her life," Guttman says. "But she never saw her sister again."

Guttman's father, Herman, ran a dry-goods store, but in 1940 was forced to fight for the Germans in the Hungarian army. As if fighting for the enemy wasn't devastating enough, Herman was made to go unarmed, because Jews weren't allowed to carry weapons of any kind, even at war. Herman gave himself up as soon as the Hungarian army converged with the Russian battlefront, but he wasn't treated much better than the German prisoners. He was incarcerated in a Russian gulag until 1947 and remained there for two years after the liberation, one of many prisoners held in the wake of the war for political bartering purposes. He would later tell Guttman he watched dozens of men die alongside him in the death marches that took place at arctic temperatures. "People would sit down for a moment to rest and never get up," Guttman says. "If you stopped walking, you froze to death." Herman got a pair of fur shoes. They were several sizes too small and sliced into his feet with every step, but they saved his life. He never stopped walking, and, even when men fell, he never looked back. He did not know yet that his mother and two of his three sisters had already perished.

In 1948, after Herman's release, he took refuge in Opalyi, where he was met by Guttman's mother. The two married in a month. They'd known each other since childhood, when Herman, at fourteen, had boarded at Aranka's family homestead while he attended a nearby Hebrew school. Back then, she'd been only seven, tagging along behind him and sharing in the trinkets he received in the care packages sent by his family back home in Vaja. "Of the five thousand young Jewish men drafted from my father's district, only fifty lived," Guttman says. "That's a fact. After the war, everyone was already married or dead. My father's sister had married my mother's brother and everyone in our family who had nowhere to go ended up at my mother's in Opalyi, including my dad, who at the time was single. My mother did all the housework and took care of everybody. She was the glue. My dad used to joke that there was no one else left to marry. She would just wink at him and say, 'Oh, and you think you did so bad?' Parents who survived the Holocaust did not tell their kids about what they'd been through. They didn't want to burden them with the horrors, and it was absolute horror. But our parents wanted us to know. I felt sorry for them my whole life. It was probably why I tried so hard to be a good son."

For Guttman, finding Nymex was like finding a home after being lost all his life. "Nymex was a haven for me. It was for a lot of us. When I started, you couldn't be a Jew and work at a bank or an insurance company in New York. You couldn't work on a Saturday. Either that, or they wouldn't hire you. Nice Jewish boys became doctors or lawyers or accountants. I couldn't stand the sight of blood, so I couldn't be a doctor. I wasn't too hot on being a lawyer either. But with accounting, I thought you had versatility, so I'd studied that. I worked during the day and went to Baruch College for two years at night. I got good grades in high school and if you got good grades, you could go to college for free. I wanted to go to college so badly I didn't even wait for the fall after I graduated from high school in 1968. I went to summer school and got started."

Growing up in a blue-collar, Jewish-Italian neighborhood in Brooklyn, Guttman knew only too well the poor commercial value of a hard day's work. Though his parents had labored their entire lives, they never made more than what it took to barely make ends meet. His father was a knitting-machine mechanic back when knitting machines were the size of city blocks and demanded constant repair and attention.

He worked in Greenpoint, "between somewhere and the Bronx." His mother worked long hours as a seamstress. After witnessing their plight, Guttman vowed to make the best of his New World opportunities.

Looking at Guttman, the traders immediately sensed he was not like them. "Lou always looked and acted at least ten years older than the rest of us," Gary Lapayover says. Even as a young man, he was forceful, self-directed, and battle-ready. Guttman had a magnetic personality and strong powers of persuasion. He had a tough exterior, but was a person of depth. Those closest to Guttman were extremely protective of him, and those who weren't regarded him as a killer without a conscience. Throughout the oil market's history, he would be seen as one of its most polarizing figures.

After graduating from college, Guttman took a job at a New York accounting firm for a few months. Like Richard Schaeffer, he found it wholly unfulfilling. He left it for a stock brokerage shop on John Street called Commonwealth Securities, located between Wall Street and the World Trade Center. He toiled as a back-office grunt, living at home in Brooklyn with his parents and saving his money. He was still trying to figure out what he wanted to be. His stock-trading friends brought him up the street one day to the Nymex pits during his lunch break. Guttman was floored. "I'd never seen anything like it. Standing there, I was transfixed. There were people buying, selling, smoking, eating, sleeping, reading newspapers, arguing, whatever. I could see everything going on, who was doing what, all the hand gestures and how it moved. I couldn't tell what anybody was doing, but I knew I wanted to be a part of it." Guttman didn't think twice. He plunked down everything he had, including the $14,000 he'd gotten from his bar mitzvah. He received a membership and a bright gold trading badge. Printed neatly across it was his trading name, GUTT. He started just days later.

It was the siren call many had succumbed to long before Guttman showed up in March 1978, and would continue falling prey to long after he'd left. "The exchange needed warm bodies. They would take anybody they could get. You're alive, you're standing, you're breathing? Okay, come on down. You didn't have privileged guys down there. You had people like me who had just enough to buy a seat, one of the cheapest exchange seats around. Most of us were young and didn't fit in any-where else." As Guttman was shelling out for his $20,000 seat to trade at Nymex, seats on Comex shot to $200,000 apiece. Like everyone else, he planned to work at Nymex only until he could afford a Comex seat. In the outside world, Guttman was still a nobody. But on the trading floor, his aspirations counted for something. As he stepped nervously into the platinum-trading pit, the first place he ever traded, Guttman's heart pounded. He realized too late that stocks and commodities were completely different animals. "The day I started trading, I don't remember what the weather was or anything else," Guttman says. "All I remember is the fear."

The hardest part was getting used to the astronomical amounts of money he would be winning and losing daily. For a street-fighting kid who'd barely scraped together enough cash to buy his membership, trading many multiples of that was beyond daunting. "We're talking about thousands and thousands of dollars here," Guttman says. "I was smart, but it was very scary. I mean, in platinum, even when you were trading just ten contracts, for every $1 price move, you were winning or losing $500."

The year Guttman joined up was no ordinary year for the platinum market. Prices punched above $200 an ounce, rising and falling by as much as $20 a day. Eventually, the price swings would be as much as $40 a day.

From the start, there were many hardships. Guttman's parents didn't approve of him being a trader. Also, in the early days, when the other traders weren't mentally or physically abusing him, they were blatantly ignoring him. He was just another terrified stripling. "Most guys at least clerked for somebody before buying a seat and risking their own capital. Not me. I went in cold. It took me over a year to figure out how the markets worked and how to trade with my own money. The other traders would give you a rough time when you were trying to do a trade. They would yell at you that you weren't doing it right, or that you were out of line or that you'd missed the market. I came close to calling it quits a few times, I was losing my shirt so bad."

Watching Guttman take hit after hit, Gary Glass, a longtime inhabitant of the pits, staged an intercession. "Gary came up to me and said, 'Look, Lou'—by this time, everyone called me Lou, because no one could say or spell Zoltan—'You're doing it all wrong.' He saw me making a lot of rookie errors. I was like, 'What are you talking about?' He took me to lunch, we got a corner booth, and he sat me down."

Glass became Guttman's rabbi. He showed him that trading like a riverboat gambler was not strictly the wisest approach. Through him, Guttman learned a new art: how to find something close to a sure thing, or at least something vaguely approaching it. Like anybody else, the Nymex traders didn't like to lose money, so they looked for vulnerabilities in the market, unseen or overlooked loot waiting to be scooped up. With the help of Glass, Guttman learned how to improve his technique, identifying market opportunities, controlling his risks, and cherry-picking the low-hanging fruit where he could find it. Lucky for him, Glass was no two-bit trader, but a commodities all-arounder. With boundless enthusiasm for trading and a gambler's taste for self-enterprise, Glass showed Guttman how to keep his head above water. "Glass traded anything and everything, platinum, potatoes, silver coins, you name it," Guttman says. "A really intelligent guy who never took risks."

Glass tells a somewhat humbler story. "When I was sixteen, I read a book called *Understanding Put and Call Options*, by Herbert Filer," he says. "That was 1962. I read it, and the very next day I quit school and I went to see Herbert Filer. I walked into his office in New York and I told him, 'I'll work for you for free.'" Instead, Glass got paid $54 a week and received an in-the-trenches education from Filer and the other traders at Filer, Schmidt & Co., the largest stock-options dealer in the country. Glass was hooked. He eventually got his high school equivalency diploma in 1964, at the plaintive urgings of his mother. "In four years, I became a stockbroker specializing in puts and calls," he says. "I was one of the biggest in the city, in the top three next to Carl Icahn, who I still talk to sometimes. He was the largest one. Then I became a member of every exchange I could get into. It was hard transitioning from stocks to commodities at first. A lot of people can't do it. Commodities move much faster than stocks. It got so bad I even drove a cab for a while. But once I figured it out, it was amazing. Working at Nymex was like working at a casino where you owned the house. I used to hate the weekends. They were awful. I mean, I loved seeing my wife and kids, but I couldn't wait to get back to work. Nymex was like a dream. You never worried about losing. All you could ever think about was how you were going to win."

One of the things Glass taught Guttman was spread trading. He also was past master at something called arbitrage trading. Often referred to simply as "arbing" by its devout adherents, it allowed traders to profit off the price differences between two or more products of similar, if not identical, quality. This was done by buying a product when or where it was cheapest and then selling it when or where it would fetch a higher price. (Vendors at packed stadium concerts peddling bottles of Evian for $5 after buying them for a buck at the 7-Eleven are essentially arbing.) Glass's specialty was arbing silver coins. And it just so happened that Nymex had a contract for that. Silver coin futures, in fact, were one of the only contracts from Nymex's rash of awkward 1960s commodities experiments that had ever gained any traction (the failed ones being, among other things, such dubious offerings as futures on McIntosh apples and plywood). Meanwhile, Comex had its own silver bullion futures contract. With the two silver contracts readily available for arbing off each other on the same trading floor, it was only a matter of time before the traders fell on them like a pack of wolves.

A speculative boom in silver coin market began in 1967, when the U.S. Treasury halted the flow of silver bullion from its reserves to the market under the Coinage Act of 1965. Under the act, Congress brought an end to the age of the pure silver coin, replacing dimes with plain wafers of alloyed copper and nickel over a copper core. But that didn't stop scorching demand for silver coins. On the contrary, their growing scarcity meant that people suddenly wanted them more than ever.

The prices of the Nymex and Comex silver contracts loosely tracked each other but did not move in lockstep. As a result, one contract was almost always more expensive than the other. To traders like Glass, this was a market inefficiency just begging to be exploited. He and the other traders would profit off the price gaps by buying into the cheaper contract—whichever one it was—and selling the more expensive contract. Amid the flurry of activity there came another, less by-the-book way of playing the game, one that underscored the ingenuity of the Nymex traders, even as they struggled to stay in business. But the strategy came with risks. It required that the trader not fear the long arm of the law.

The method was straightforward enough. You'd buy up some Nymex silver coin futures contracts and take delivery of them. This was not illegal. Next, you'd go over to the Comex pit and sell an equivalent amount of silver futures contracts, which meant that you were agreeing to provide silver to the buyers. Also not illegal. But then, in a move most knew to be completely outlawed, you would pack up the stash of silver coins you'd taken delivery on, trundle them off to a smelter, and *melt them down.* You would then deliver that against the more expensive silver futures contracts to the buyers later, cashing in on the price difference. Done repeatedly and in enormous quantities, the maneuver translated into huge amounts of money. As a result, smelters were getting backed up melting coins around the clock. "If you did it right, you could make $30,000 to $100,000 *a contract*. It was like shooting fish in a barrel," says Glass. "A lot of people didn't understand how the market worked, but that's only because commodities traders are lazy." Glass had always had a thing for coins. Growing up, he even ran his own coin-operated candy-machine business.

Either in anticipation of, or, more likely, in response to, this kind of behavior, between 1967 and 1969 the U.S. Department of the Treasury banned the melting of silver coins, making it an offense punishable by a $10,000 fine or prison. The fine, obviously, was not enough to keep the traders from breaking the law. This is still the case in the commodities market. The Treasury believed it had very good reason for wanting to keep silver coins from being purchased and melted down. Melting coins, it argued, undermined the U.S. taxpayer. But to the New York traders, who made it their business to be experts on the finer points of valuation, unlocking the intrinsic worth of dimes by melting them into their more expensive form made perfect economic sense. Why leave them trapped in an inferior state? Wasn't the Treasury to blame for undermining the U.S. taxpayer by minting coins whose face value had fallen well below their melt value? To the traders' way of thinking, they were simply righting a wrong. Their attitude offers a rare glimpse into the mind of the trader, who, above all else, seeks to be a realist. Who was undermining whom often came down to one's vantage point. Still, in the final analysis, few of them claimed to have anything as lofty as the moral high ground at heart. "We used to call the silver coin pit at the Nymex the Suez Canal," says Glass. "Because every customer who placed an order there had to pay the *toll*." (The toll often being some form of overcharging the customer on a trade that had actually been conducted at a lower price. The trader or broker executing the transaction, or both, would pocket the difference.)

Silver coins became such a racket that Nymex once again drew the ire of CFTC, which revoked its right to trade the contract. "Whoever heard of a *futures* contract on something that's *not even being made anymore*? If the government was still minting silver coins, a futures contract might have made sense," Lapayover says. "But they were a thing of the past and now we're offering futures contracts on them? It was mind-blowing." A former CFTC official who helped fine and censure Nymex in 1980 recalls, "To my knowledge, Nymex was the only exchange to ever have its contract designations literally stripped from it, and it happened on more than one occasion. Any customer who traded there was molested, if not utterly raped. As far as we could see, the Nymex traders did nothing but run scams. In 1979, there was even a case of two traders forcing the price of palladium as high and as low as it would go, buying on the low end and selling on the high end and then splitting the profit between them. They made $82,000 off trading *just one lot.* They were acquitted, because the system called for them to be tried by a jury of their peers, and guess what all their trading buddies had to say? You cannot make this shit up." Even now, Glass talks about the silver coin trade with Stalinist fervor. "I stopped trading in the 1990s, but there's still billions in that market."

Guttman wasn't the only one grappling with the sharp edges of his trading losses early in his career. Daniel Rappaport also was getting bloodied. "You can only imagine coming to the floor and not knowing anything or anybody. When I first arrived, it was all brothers and cousins and uncles and nephews and there were absolutely no outsiders. I only found out about Nymex because I heard about it from someone I knew in college. I was attracted to the excitement, but I didn't have a relative to teach me. The exchange ran an introductory class on how to trade, but it wasn't very helpful. After the first year, I remember thinking about not going back." Noticing Rappaport looking especially dejected after a close call, Sherry Collins tried to cheer him up. "I remember Sherry saying, 'You can do this,' and throwing all these charts in my face. I'd never used them before, but I took the charts home and I studied them and now I am exclusively a market technician," Rappaport says. "I always say to Sherry, if it wasn't for you, I wouldn't have made it. She must have been in her late teens."

What Collins showed twenty-seven-year-old Rappaport was a way of reading the market called technical analysis, the scientific-sounding name for what, to most outsiders, would more appropriately be called market astrology. Its underlying assumption is that the market will repeat the same pricing patterns over and over again—therefore, it's reasonable to use the past as a predictor of the future (which might be laughable, except for the fact that it frequently works). With legions of traders analyzing and acting on similar price charts for similar products in similar ways, their collective assumptions, often acted out en masse, can become a self-fulfilling prophecy. In other words, the world's traders following the same rules of buying and selling at the same time *can actually bring about the very events they are fortune-telling.*

Superstition in large numbers breeds reality. Because technical analysis follows prices over time, marking them down on charts or graphs and connecting the dots sometimes forms pictures that look like constellations. Traders, throughout the years, have given these formations constellation-like names, such as the candlestick (first noted by a seventeenth-century Japanese rice broker), the shaven head (and, of course, the shaven bottom), the spinning top, the shooting star, the hanging man, the megaphone, the inverted hammer, the gravestone, and countless others. Chart patterns were one of many ways traders tried to get price guidance. Some of them even believed that the market switched course in direct correlation with phases of the moon. "One guy I knew always went long or short, I can't remember which, whenever the moon was full," Lapayover says. "He swore by it." Collins first learned technical analysis from Michel Marks, who also traded on what were called market fundamentals, such as supply, demand, seasonal trends, and more concrete economic factors not involving things like the moon or astrology.

On September 22, 1980, Guttman had been in the pits for almost three years. He didn't bet on heating oil, because platinum had become the busier market. But once in a while, he'd shuffle over to the heating-oil pit at the behest of Marks with the other traders to buy or sell a few lots. "Back then, the exchange was like a laboratory for all kinds of products and we were crazy enough to try just about anything," he says. "If something was available, we'd trade it. We didn't know anything was ever going to come of it." Heating oil was slowly gaining a following, but there was no sign that it—or any other energy product—would take off anytime soon. "Nobody wanted to touch oil in those days. I mean, this was a major global oil cartel we're talking about here, this was OPEC. We were Nymex, we were nothing. Everyone was still expecting the floor to get shut down one day. Platinum was the only thing really keeping us going. Marks would come down and ask the metals traders to push some volume through. I didn't know him back then. I doubt I even knew he was chairman. We didn't pay any attention to what was happening up in the chairman's office. There must have been about five of us loitering in the heating-oil pit the day the Iran-Iraq War broke out. It was way before any twenty-four-hour news networks, so we didn't have televisions on the floor like we do today. We didn't know what was going on. Suddenly, fifty to sixty traders come running into the heating-oil ring and the phones are ringing off the hook. That was the beginning."

It was, quite accidentally, the moment Nymex would stop being the nation's lowlife market and start becoming a global brand. On the other end of the ringing telephones were the banks, brokerage houses, and trading firms that had once wanted nothing to do with the former potato market—and they were all clamoring for heating oil. With two of the world's top oil nations at each other's throats and another 1970s-style energy crisis potentially at hand, no one was taking any chances. Better to do business with the devil you knew than be left twisting in the wind. If worse came to worst in the warring Middle East, at least Wall Street would be ready.

Over the next several days, Marks watched as the price of heating oil at Nymex more than doubled to nearly a dollar a gallon. But that was nothing compared with how fast it was climbing among the oil-trading companies. This was because Nymex, a regulated market, was forced to observe things like government-imposed price limits. The unregulated oil-trading companies, considered by the government to be advanced players trading with one another off the exchange, were not. In the Nymex pits, heating-oil futures weren't allowed to rise more than a cent or two a gallon per day. Higher-priced trades had to be forced underground into what the traders called the "over-the-counter" or "spot" market—the Wild West, to which only the most formidable traders belonged. Provided they could match private buyers and sellers, the over-the-counter traders could charge whatever they wanted.

"When the war started, spot prices in heating oil among the oil-trading companies took off and went as high as a dollar a gallon," Marks says. "But Nymex had limits, so our futures price was locked *limit up* at the highest point allowed and stayed there for more than twenty days. A price chart usually shows a slash mark indicating the lowest price of the day and a second slash mark showing the highest price of the day. When a market is locked limit up, the low and the high are the *same* thing. So all you see is one slash mark a day. That's what we call dotting the charts. It's what happens when there are all buyers and no sellers."

Transfixed by the heating-oil action, the floor traders hung around the pit as the war raged on, hoping to snap up a contract or two if any selling came in. Because heating oil's cost in the pit was so far below that of the over-the-counter price, they knew that any contracts they could snatch up would reap them hefty profits in the over-the-counter market. In short, it was risk-free money—and there was nothing a trader loved more than money that was risk-free. "Once the war began, some of the traders in the heating-oil pit stayed permanently," Marks says. "And the market kept building from there."

Trading in heating oil grew so quickly that even some of the bigger players had trouble keeping up with the zigzagging prices. Nymex barely avoided another breathtaking market default in 1981 involving a major oil company and Goldman Sachs. Marks knew he needed to swiftly assemble an executive team that could help him clean up Nymex before the rising tide of its own business swallowed it whole. The CFTC, for its part, was dubious. Its commissioners didn't think Marks could rid the exchange of its self-destructive tendencies in time. Looking to prove them wrong, Marks persuaded one of his former Princeton professors to take the open post of president. Richard Leone taught public finance at Princeton and had been New Jersey's state treasurer.

Leone drove a hard bargain: he wanted a share of Nymex's overall revenue. Marks was so desperate, he gave it to him. By the time Leone closed out his term two years later, the total number of heating-oil contracts being bought and sold at the exchange represented *more than three times the amount of heating oil actually available*. This wasn't seen as a problem, as nobody—or, to be exact, no more than 1 to 2 percent of those trading heating oil—wanted any. Like the traders of the much-maligned potato, heating oil's loyalists were in it only for the short-term cash.

Marks couldn't believe his eyes: the virtual market was dwarfing the real thing. Unbeknownst to him, the phenomenon would be only a simulacrum of what the global energy market would become over the next thirty years. A barrel of oil, by 2008, would trade roughly *forty-five times* before being delivered and consumed, making it one of the most overtraded products in the world.

Marks's foray into heating oil went so smoothly that he launched a second energy contract with Safer, in tandem with President Ronald Reagan's gradual lifting of oil-price controls imposed by President Richard Nixon during the runaway prices of the 1970s. (Reagan's motives for lifting Nixon's controls, to this day, are hotly debated, but likely stemmed from his enthusiasm for free markets, coupled with his desire to create an environment in which oil prices would be allowed to fall as a way of starving Russia of the oil money it needed to fund its arms race against the United States.)

Marks debuted futures on leaded gasoline in 1981. But progress at Nymex never came without an equal measure of defiance. Even after the United States had made the sale of leaded gasoline illegal and Marks offered a replacement unleaded gasoline contract, the Nymex traders continued buying, selling, and delivering *leaded* gasoline for up to two more years. Lead was bad, the government said, because it contaminated the nation's drinking water and poisoned children. But the traders would not stop trading it. "I couldn't *believe* they were still trafficking in leaded gasoline like that!" says one ex–CFTC official. "The CFTC has always been weak about coming in and putting its foot down. It was weak then and it is weak now. And there were the Nymex traders, as usual, taking nothing seriously."

Even having simple rules was a problem, says John Tafaro, one of the first heating-oil traders. "When people made a mistake with an order, you'd say, 'Are you on drugs?' And you would mean it. The traders would bring pizza into the ring. They would eat it in the pits and there'd be pizza lying around. Somebody came down and started saying, 'No more pizza in the pits.' The traders said, 'Well, then just fine us.' They would pay the $50 fine and bring the pizza back. We had the same problem with all the fighting. The fine for fighting in the ring was $100 in the 1980s. I remember one skirmish that I tried ignorantly to break up. Usually, the fights were over somebody's trading orders. We soon realized that the $100 fine wasn't a deterrent. They'd just say, 'Whatever,' and keep on punching. I was head of the floor committee at the time, so we raised the fine to $1,000. There were days when it was like Dodge City down there, but the orders got done. By nature, traders are not people who want to work in an office where there are lots of rules and decorum. They don't like to say 'sir' or 'mister.' Every step of the way, the traders defied the rules and defied change."

In 1983, Reagan removed the final energy barrier, resulting in what would be Marks's great white whale: a futures contract on light, sweet crude oil—the raw material from which the planet's major fuels are made. "I knew absolutely nothing about crude," Marks says. "I just kept on reading as many books as I could about it and taking excursions to places like London, which had a very active energy marketplace."

Privately, he had major reservations about going for the jugular of Big Oil. He couldn't banish from his mind Alan Lotterman's warning of oil being a powder keg that, once ignited, could never be brought back under control. "Marks certainly did not go about it balls-out," says a colleague. "Michel didn't want to piss off the industry's sleeping dragons. He worried that they might boycott his gasoline and heating-oil contracts and then he would lose everything."

But Marks didn't have the luxury of hesitation. The Chicago Board of Trade, a much larger, more politically connected exchange, also was thinking about a crude-oil futures contract. When Marks found out, he hastily submitted his proposal for crude to the CFTC, which had only recently agreed to let Marks offer new contracts in addition to old ones. The agency's approval policy was on a first-come, first-serve basis—yet, with oil up for grabs, all bets were off. "I was in Boca Raton, Florida, at the annual Futures Industry Association convention in February 1983 when I heard the commission was going to approve the Chicago Board of Trade's crude-oil contract first, even though we got our proposal in before them, and I went crazy," Marks says. "I could see our whole future going down the tubes. Nymex had gasoline and heating oil already, but this was the big one. This was for all the marbles. I was convinced that if we won this, we would own the franchise."

Marks arranged a breakfast meeting with then-CFTC chairman Philip Johnson, a Chicagoan and staunch ally of the city's enormously successful futures exchanges. Marks felt outclassed. In terms of political capital, he had nothing. That morning, seated across from Johnson, he could barely bring himself to eat. "I knew I was out of my league. Nymex had no political standing or special relationships in Washington, and Chicago held all the cards. As usual, Johnson was stone-faced. I begged and pleaded our case. He didn't give an inch."

Marks went back to his hotel room and paced. He dialed as many different people as he could think of. "Frankly, I didn't think any politicians or floor traders would care about us. Nymex total trading volume still wasn't much more than ten thousand contracts a day. I told everyone we had to get all the politicians we could on board, tell them it's New York versus Chicago, that this would hurt New York financially if we didn't get the approval first. I told everyone on the floor to send letters and telegrams to Johnson. Word spread and they got to the governors, the senators, the congressmen, and even the mayor of New York. All of them wrote." When Johnson returned to his office the following week, there were stacks of letters and telegrams on his desk. Three days later, his executive assistant called Marks. "You will get approval on the same day as the CBOT," he said.

It wasn't fair. And no one expected it to be otherwise.

The launch date was March 30, 1983. The subsequent clash between the exchanges, touted by Marks as a "battle royal," turned out to be more of a gimme, but not in the way anybody anticipated. Nymex debuted its futures contract on West Texas Intermediate light, sweet crude oil for delivery to Cushing, Oklahoma. (Cushing, a former Indian village in the flatlands of the Great Plains, had the greatest onshore oil storage facilities of nearly anywhere in the world—the result of repeated oil discoveries throughout the region in the early twentieth century. To this day, the town's graveyard markers outnumber its population, a testament to the plagues, deaths, and destruction wreaked by prospectors in their endless quest for oil.)

On the same day, the Chicago Board of Trade launched its futures contract on Louisiana light, sweet crude oil for delivery to St. James Parish, Louisiana—another oil stronghold. Having watched so many Nymex offerings crash and burn, Marks leaned heavily on Safer to produce a flawless contract design. Marks then asked twenty of the most gifted Nymex floor traders to meet him for dinner, where he did something extremely intelligent. He appealed to their greed. "Seats at the exchange are $50,000 each," he said. "They'll be half a million. Our trading volume can be in the hundreds of thousands of contracts a day, but it all hinges on making this crude-oil contract work."

For weeks, the New York traders stood in the crude-oil pit, pushing paper. At the Chicago Board of Trade, which had a much larger group of traders backing its contract, the orders piled in. A month passed. Chicago's oil contract hit a rut. There was, of all things, a delivery problem. Its energy contract, it seemed, had not been designed as well as Safer's. The Chicago traders recoiled in horror. Nearly overnight, Chicago's energy business was wiped out. Marks, who knew all about galactic delivery failures and how to avoid them, watched his crude contract go off without a hitch. The oil traders left Chicago and barnstormed Nymex, the only market left standing. Marks had stumbled onto his winning lottery ticket. In a year's time, Nymex crude oil became the most heavily traded commodity on earth.

The Nymex traders were clueless as to the full extent of how the big picture had played right into their hands. Oil production in the United States had topped out in 1970, inciting fears of an oil shortage without end. With domestic supplies sliding and prices rising, Americans began to cut their use of fuel drastically. Just as the recession started hammering the United States in the early 1980s, OPEC, the world's foremost oil supplier, jacked up its prices after realizing it had been lowballing itself for a decade. The major oil companies, also known as the Seven Sisters (Exxon, British Petroleum, Royal Dutch Shell, Chevron, Texaco, Mobil, and Gulf Oil), took a page from the cartel and also kept their prices propped up. Their timing was fantastically bad. The supply scare and the promise of increasingly higher prices had encouraged an explosion in oil-drilling, leading countries outside OPEC to douse the market with a tsunami of oil. The emergence of new energy supplies, combined with dropping consumer demand, caused oil prices to fall like a stone, putting OPEC in a bind that it had not expected.

The U.S. oil-trading companies suddenly found themselves stuck with fistfuls of overly expensive energy contracts they had expected to make a killing on. The Nymex traders, Marks says, had blindly injected themselves into the situation, just as an all-out war for market share among the oil companies, OPEC, and the non-OPEC nations started up. The battlefield left many crushed underfoot, but not Nymex, which found Wall Street's traders rushing to send panicky orders to the pits.

It was a period of fortunes made, fortunes lost, and mass confusion. During the first three years of the Nymex crude contract, oil prices catapulted to a record high of $31.75, then dropped to less than a third of that amount in the ensuing commotion. Hit by the upheaval, Wall Street traders found themselves needing to hedge their price risks more than ever. The Nymex traders benefited incalculably. "Before that, we had trouble convincing Wall Street that they needed to do *any* hedging. They used to say, 'What do we need to hedge for? Oil prices only go up,'" Leone says. The sudden outbreak of plummeting prices had proven Wall Street wrong.

Marks vividly recalls the shock of oil prices climbing 250 percent from 1978 to 1980, then tanking by the mid-1980s as oil flooded the market. "Once the oil-trading companies realized they were holding all this overpriced oil, they had to find a place to get rid of it. Many of them went out of business, because the only reason they ever did well was by taking advantage of the OPEC price gap that no longer existed. What happened to all that extra oil supply was that it was sold on Nymex, often at bargain-basement prices. The transition was fascinating. We basically became this huge liquidation center. When giant companies like Exxon, which refused to lower its posted prices, looked around two years later and wondered what had happened to all its customers, guess where they were going?"

For OPEC and the oil majors, the party really was over. With the influx of competition, they no longer had a corner on global oil prices. Much worse, a felled potato market run by a kid they'd never heard of was blatantly eating their lunch. And he wasn't based in any of the major oil towns, like Houston or Vienna or Riyadh, but in a rat-infested trading pit in downtown Manhattan inhabited by misfits and pranksters and gun-toting gangsters who had absolutely no knowledge of the oil business.

It was the very height of improbability.

"You have to remember, what we saw happening here was quite literally the global oil market following the U.S. oil market, and that's what's still happening today," Marks says. "Why would the rest of the world want to do that? Because our market has the most people doing the most business in one place. Not just a few big players who want to try and control everything. There's strength in those numbers. So our market, even with all its drawbacks, was seen as the best and the fairest. The reason why one market wins over another is that people need to see a critical mass to feel that a market is legitimate. From there, we became a natural monopoly. It fed on itself. And once that happens, it is almost impossible to establish a competing marketplace somewhere else."

Basing the global oil market in the United States at the time made sense, because it pumped the most oil of any nation in the world and consumed the most oil. As might be expected, Big Oil's cognoscenti did not take kindly to tectonic shifts in their market that they could not control. And they most definitely did not take kindly to a power grab by Marks and the traders of Nymex. Oil exploration and drilling demanded decades of planning and financing before execution and payoff. The logistics and infrastructure were infinitely complex, involving business partnerships and financial arrangements that took years to cultivate.

Who were Marks and a bunch of unknown traders from Manhattan's outer boroughs to go after the establishment?

As a peace offering, Marks rented out the biggest boat the Circle Line owned in the New York Harbor in 1983, throwing a lavishly catered party. The guest list had more than a thousand people on it, reading like a *Who's Who* of the planet's wealthiest industrial moguls. Most of them weren't people he'd ever met before and most didn't bother responding to his invite. The night of his coming-out party, he combed back his bristling mass of hair and put on a tuxedo. He was jittery as he strode across the yacht's waxed deck. Surveying the crowd, Marks couldn't help but notice that the scrappy Nymex traders outnumbered the oil industry executives by fifteen to one. He was crestfallen. As he was talking to some guests, his spirits suddenly lifted when he saw, just a few paces away, a group of men he instantly recognized. They, of course, did not recognize him. "It was Bob Black, president of Texaco, chatting with Harold Bernstein, owner of the Panama oil concession and the only pipeline connecting the East and West Coasts, and Pat Mazzarulli, owner of PVM in London, the largest oil brokerage in the world," Marks says. "Bob came out, glanced around, then looked at the others. There was an expression of complete bewilderment on his face. He asked, 'What *is* this Nymex?' I was thrilled. What could be better than getting the acknowledgment of these three men?"

Even the former CFTC official who was appalled by Nymex's dalliance with leaded gasoline noticed a change. "We started drawing reputable people into the market. That had never happened before. People who wore *ties*, had *real* customers, and *could actually trade*. We got rid of the piece-of-shit boneless beef contract, which was never anything but a total rip-off, and stopped trading crap. The velocity of the trading picked up, so that you couldn't just go into the pits and start stealing from everyone anymore. You needed to know what you were doing. It was a revelation."

Rappaport was glad about the turnaround. "After a few years of trading, it was clear that the exchange presented incredible opportunities. I like to say that the greatest thing about working at the exchange was that it seemed that every day you missed the opportunity of a lifetime. Michel Marks was really the first of the new generation."

Moonlight harbor cruises notwithstanding, the hatchet between Nymex, Wall Street, and Big Oil wouldn't be so easily buried. Marks did not fully grasp the far-reaching ramifications of his creation. He was too busy overseeing his energy-trading business, MercOil Inc., which he'd started in 1979 to compete with his father's brokerage, and managing his NYSE seat. He also was in the process of buying a vacation home that would become his reclusive woodland redoubt on Navesink River Road, a coveted piece of real estate that wound whimsically along the Jersey Shore.

No one had taught him or the other traders how to build the world's first free oil market.

And no one had left them with any idea of how to keep it from spinning out of control.

5

The Great Equalizer

When it comes to sex and money, I'll take the money. Also,
the sex.

—ROBERT IRA SAHN

BOBBY SAHN WAS one of the new breed of university-educated traders swarming the pits. The scion of a third-generation poultry family, he came to the job with an impressive working knowledge of Nymex's past life as an egg, cheese, and butter exchange. That is, before it became a potato exchange, a boneless beef exchange, a metals exchange, and an oil exchange.

Sahn showed up just as Marks was shepherding an explosion in trading volumes of 550 percent from 1979 to 1984. During that time, Sahn went from being a peon trader from Lawrence, Long Island, relying on his parents to help him make rent each month on his cramped Eighty-sixth Street apartment in Manhattan, to one of the trading pits' brightest stars. Initially earning $80 a week as a broker's apprentice, Sahn, by the mid-1980s, could make anywhere from $250,000 to $1 million a year. Nymex still had a terrible reputation, but salary appreciation being what it was, to even consider leaving it for the bond-crazed trading desks of Wall Street was unthinkable. "Every day you would go into the pits and see all your friends. Hundreds of people. Guys that, good or bad, you'd trade next to for years. It was like a high school that never ends. And it was a club, especially for the members, the people who owned a piece of the exchange. It was a place for us to go, to hang out, to see each other and make some outrageous money," Sahn says. He retired twenty years after arriving with a $100 million–plus fortune that trumped that of almost any other floor trader. His riches would redefine the kind of success that would put Nymex on the map.

Sahn invited me for a visit in February 2007 at New York's Hotel Plaza Athénée, the place he would call home for a year as he waited for a team of contractors to finish renovating his extravagant condo at the Plaza (or, as he called it, "the *real* plaza") overlooking Central Park. He also planned to knock down a house he'd bought in the Hamptons so he could build a better house on top of it. Originally, he'd been partial to a Philip Johnson–style glass abode, but now he was having second thoughts.

A jovial fellow with close-cropped hair, a perpetual tan, and a special affinity for the kind of bright salmon blazers not often seen outside retirement communities in Florida, Sahn was in high spirits. A man of many quirks, he brimmed with delightful, homespun wisdom about the market and women. In between issuing trading orders to his broker (retirement at Nymex never meant you actually stopped trading) through a souped-up, $5,000 cell phone that channeled the control board of a rocket ship, he sat down to share his pearls of wisdom over an egg brunch. I had expected we would be talking about trading, but Sahn, now a man of leisure, preferred to ease into the shop talk.

Avoid all long-term relationships with planes, boats, and women, he soberly advised. ("Never own anything that flies, floats, or fucks. It's better to lease.") Also, he told me, never let a woman who isn't good-looking set you up with a friend. ("You know why? Because hot women *know* hot women.") Sahn had a tendency to sidestep direct questions while moving seamlessly between the topics of money, sex, and sex. When asked about how energy traders had evolved throughout the years, he leaned back in his Chippendale chair and let loose with the following thoughts on the subject:

> It's nothing compared with what the newer guys in the market are doing now in terms of making money. I was at Hermès the other day looking for trophy wives. Just kidding. And I bumped into this guy, Mark Dickstein, who was a huge silver trader. He went to Wharton with Fisher. Great pit trader. When he came to Nymex, he stood in front of me, because I had the big business. Big locals are attracted to

*guys who have big orders. Sort of like women are attracted to guys
with big penises, or a lot of net worth. Or, hopefully, both. Then it's
sort of like the Daily Double, right? You get it coming and you get it
going. Money is an aphrodisiac. You don't think so? Mark was one
of the first guys to leave the floor and run a hedge fund, Dickstein &
Co. [sic]. And I invested with him. He was a really smart guy. We
were always up like 30 percent or 40 percent. Genius. Back then I
was 340 lbs. and he was really skinny. Good-looking guy. Now he's
gotten fat and I'm really skinny. We've got a lot of mutual friends.
So, the other day, I was like, "Mark, how you doing?" He bought
Hills Department Stores. When he was running his hedge fund, he
took a huge position in Hills and they stuffed him with the company.
You know, they were like, we're not going to take your greenmail.**
Fuck you. You own all this stock? You own the company now. And it
was a bad investment. He played chicken with the wrong guys. And
so he worked himself out of the company; he closed his hedge fund. He
plays poker professionally now. He's like the eightieth in the country
as a professional poker player. So I see him on TV playing World
Championship Poker. He would be the guy to talk to. You should call
him direct.*

Sahn came to the floor during its age of experimentation, when
young, eager traders were pushing the envelope financially, physically,
and legally. During the days of disco, the traders wore platform shoes to
increase their visibility in the pits. Now they just took a page from the
Comex traders and flattened their opponents with fisticuffs. Sahn ran one
of the largest brokerage outfits on the trading floor. One of his wealthiest
clients was the top gasoline supplier to the New York Harbor, a market
that controlled (and still controls) U.S. gasoline prices. The supplier had
a trick it liked to play. It would send Sahn down to the pits at the close of
the trading day with the following set of instructions: sell as few futures
contracts as possible for the sole purpose of driving *down* gasoline prices

---

* Greenmail is like blackmail, only it usually involves more money. Traditionally,
it consists of a trader buying up a large chunk of stock in a company hoping
the company will buy it back at a premium to avoid a hostile takeover. In
Dickstein's case, the move backfired.

as far as they could go. Because the Nymex closing price determined what a supplier would be asked to pay for gas in the over-the-counter market, where physical barrels traded, the cheaper the Nymex prices, the better off the supplier. The strategy could always be reversed later, when the supplier was looking to sell by goosing prices back up again.

"When all the other traders saw me coming, they would get out of the way," Sahn says. "They had to. I was, like, three hundred pounds! They wouldn't say anything, because they knew that I was going to sell the market down like 2 or 3 cents. It doesn't sound like a lot, but when your customer is moving huge volumes, it adds up. I would give one trade to one guy, one to the other. It was so stupid. It was ridiculous. The traders might want to buy my contracts at $1.34 a gallon and I would want to sell them at $1.30, so you know, just shut your mouth and let the damn thing settle at $1.30."

Easy money was low-hanging fruit for heavy-hitters like Sahn and his clients, many of whom had gargantuan credit lines. Even when Kaufman arrived twenty-five years later, he saw the same games going on during the U.S.-led invasion of Iraq in 2003, when oil began its steady rise toward $150 a barrel. "Slamming the close is a time-honored tradition," he says. "Where would we be without that? I can't tell you how many people I've known who've made their careers off it. It's not like it takes a rocket scientist."

It didn't help that the settlement committee at Nymex, which made the final rulings on each day's closing price, was run by *its own traders*. "That was the best part of it," a senior oil trader says. "We would make the call, which meant there was lots of room for wangling to square our books, if you know what I mean. Once, a newer trader, a Brit, objected. He was obstreperous. We voted to close the oil market at the same level as the day before and he was having none of it. 'That's bullshit!' he told us. 'I just traded the market down *50 cents* at the settlement!' The head of the committee ignored him and said, 'All in favor of settling at unchanged?' Everyone said, 'Aye.' Then the new trader stood up and threatened to file a formal complaint. The head of the committee said nothing. He was a black belt in karate. He just turned around and put his fist through the guy's solar plexus. The Brit went down like a ton of bricks. When he later tried to sue the committee head, all the members were questioned but, wouldn't you know, no one could remember having seen anything."

When it came to settling Nymex prices, it was best not to let the public see how the sausage was being made.

As the value of trades at Nymex leaped into the billions, it became prohibitively expensive for just one individual or even a small group of individuals to manhandle energy prices. Manipulating the settlement became the sacred preserve of only the world's largest banks, suppliers, trading houses, and hedge funds, those with the size and the money to do it. Smaller players could only follow—if they could keep up. "It was wild times," Sahn says. "People would try to fix the prices every day at settlement. They still do."

With business booming, many of the once solidly middle-class traders of Nymex were beginning to experience unimaginable riches. The rapid change to their financial status meant their lives were being dramatically altered, sometimes in ways for which they weren't fully prepared. As the older potato traders began dropping off—either because they couldn't compete or because they simply wanted to retire—the exchange's "family men" were giving way to a bumper crop of high-rollers with ample cash to burn. The lifestyle shift not only meant faster cars, harder drugs, and plenty of new vacation homes, but also a growing number of traders engaging in what one might call questionable personal activities. Topping the list of favorite risqué amusements was retaining women of equally questionable repute for steamy after-hours liaisons. It wasn't long before the Futures Industry Association's conference in Boca Raton became a mecca for jet-setting prostitutes who flew in annually from cities around the world, charging traders thousands of dollars a session. (As one underdressed, overpriced sex worker slyly told me while waiting outside an event, "This conference has been an international destination for call girls for *years.*" She had a slick business card that stated she was in "public relations.") Even Marks, who considered himself much more evolved than what he called the "simpletons" of the pits, was not above the occasional prurient pursuit. "I will never forget Michel telling me, in front of my wife, how he and another trader were orally serviced while quaffing champagne and discussing how great life is in one of those pink penthouse towers of the Boca Raton Resort & Club," a former associate recalls. "Whether you were the chairman of the Nymex or the lowest of the low, blow jobs were the one thing everybody could agree on. They were the great equalizer."

But for Marks, it was not about the sex. It was about the victory.

At a Nymex holiday party thrown at a split-level Manhattan lounge called the Underground, many of the traders invited both their wives *and* their mistresses. To keep them from running into each other, they separated the women between the first and second floors. "At first, I didn't know what was going on," says an attendee who was watching the traders running up and down the stairs all night. "But by the end, it was so obvious, I think even the wives knew. They didn't leave their assigned area though. In those days, you didn't confront things like that head-on. They just looked the other way.

"There was so much lying and cheating and gold-digging going on in the pits. You wouldn't believe the amount of beautiful women in this world who are drawn to that lifestyle, the money and the drugs. And I gotta say, it is fun for a while. I mean, it's *really* fun. Then it slowly starts to kill you. A lot of the women see us as predatory. But that's not the entire story. A lot of the women were too. They took jobs on the trading floor to catch a rich husband. They'd marry a trader, they'd break up a year later, and she'd walk off with his baby and half his net worth." Nymex, by and large, was becoming a get-rich-get-laid environment. Throughout its history, it was the standard for women in the pits to wear tube tops, short skirts, and high heels. "They would giggle and squeal when you pinched them and wiggle off," says a trading clerk who left in 2005. "I am not talking about the female traders. There were some of those and they were pretty respectable. I am talking about the traders' assistants. There was a constant stream of them that came through, so many we couldn't keep track of them. I remember these sisters from uptown who used to take the pit cards and throw them down the hole. They were nice. We used to fuck them."

Marks, who continued running MercOil under various trading badges, including MDM, his initials, and FUEL ("he was always changing his trading name," a colleague says), enjoyed the non-X-rated perks of the job as well. The film crew for the 1980s hit movie *Trading Places* asked him if it could shoot some scenes in the Nymex pits. "Apparently, they'd asked the Chicago Mercantile Exchange first, but the CME said no, because they thought a film about commodities hustlers might be bad for their image," Marks says. "When I heard that Dan Aykroyd, Eddie Murphy, and Jamie Lee Curtis would be in it, I said we'd take it. I never met them, but the pit scene was shot over the weekend using about 200 to 250 Nymex extras." Each extra was paid $50. Marks mingled with New York's models and business tycoons, frequenting yachts, townhouses, and the trendy Club 54 nightclub circuit, but he didn't really care for any of it. "I don't know how much of his heart was in those kinds of things," says his friend from the Hunt Club. "I think he mostly did it because he felt he had to."

The traders were constantly running into celebrities in the pits. "We had actors and actresses on the floor frequently," says John Tafaro, the heating-oil trader. "I even met Linda Gray from that 1980s soap opera *Dallas*. She was with some guy, *observing*. I didn't even realize who she was, because I was rushing through some orders like live hand grenades. I just said hello and kept running. My wife had to tell me later who Linda Gray was. If you went down there during the day, you didn't get treated special no matter who you were. It was all about the trading and you went down at your own risk. In the eighties, Robert Downey Jr. also came. He had hair with a purple tint in it. One of the traders walked up to him, shook his hand, and said, 'Nice to meet you. You look like a fucking faggot.'"

The Nymex trading floor also began to acquire its own set of rituals, often revolving around money. "We had so many of them, they're hard to remember now. Starting in the eighties, every Friday afternoon, at five minutes to two, everyone would start to clap," says Tafaro. "We'd pass around a hat and put a dollar bill in it with our badge name on it. At two on the button, a trading clerk, who was about twenty-five but looked around seventy-five and was huge, would do a dance that I can only call a standing worm, and everyone would applaud. Then he'd pick a name out of the hat to see who won the money." If the diversions didn't revolve around money, they revolved around money and food. "One clerk bet another clerk he couldn't eat twenty-four Hostess Twinkies in two minutes. We walked into the ring the next morning and there were twenty-four unwrapped Twinkies sitting on the rail of one of the trading pits. We timed the guy eating them, and he easily won."

Bill Bradt, a friend of Tafaro's in the heating-oil pit, ordered seventy-two Jameson Irish whiskey cakes for the traders every Christmas for twenty-four years. "I remember Billy Mainwald, one of the Jewish traders who didn't drink, ate a piece. I don't think he realized there was real whiskey in it. He got so dizzy he had to sit down."

Astonished by the rapid growth of the oil market, news outlets from London to New York to Chicago hailed Marks as a wunderkind, a "young Turk" who lit napalm under Big Oil and forced a revolution that had unexpectedly leveled the playing field. Even Daniel Yergin, author of *The Prize*, a book about the history of the oil market that won the Pulitzer Prize in 1992, remarked on Nymex. "If you want to take the temperature of the oil market," he said, "futures is the thermometer." Indeed, if oil was the blood of the world, then oil prices were the barometer of its every passing economic mood.

Hollywood's open embrace of the pits did nothing to silence the fears of Wall Street during the 1980s. While grudgingly accepting the ascent of Nymex, it worried that if oil was traded in a public market its transactions would be subject to public scrutiny. The oil companies were of the same mind. For a vampire industry that had never before seen the light of day, the idea of going from a secret society of gentlemen's agreements, unnoticed and unregulated by almost anyone, to openly posting trades and prices was morally repugnant. Yet repugnant wasn't as bad as missing out on golden opportunities to make money. One by one, Wall Street's prestigious trading houses and banks gave in and quietly began trading at Nymex. "They were extremely squeamish," Guttman says. "Traditionally, Wall Street was not at all interested in commodities markets. What's commodities? Pork bellies. We were the orphans of the financial community. It was very difficult for us to shake the pork bellies syndrome. And we didn't even trade them! That was Chicago. But after a while, more banks started realizing we would be useful for financial purposes. And suddenly it was, 'I can't live without you.' But they only traded at Nymex in secret. All the big firms moved their orders through smaller, third-party brokers on the trading floor, and we only knew who they were because they had to disclose their identities through the trading records. As for Joe Q. Public, he had no idea they were here. Our reputation was too tarnished for that. They kept it all under the radar. I doubt any of them liked having to deal with us. Our business is a business that the banks would rather have for themselves. Goldman and J.P. Morgan and some of the others were looking at us, going, 'Oh my God, we could have been doing all these trades. How is it that the clowns over at Nymex get to do that?' Hence, the ongoing war between us, Big Oil, and Wall Street."

The scorned backwoods of trading was now the only market in the world able to offer large players exactly what they wanted: a central marketplace with a clear pricing system for trading the world's most strategic commodity. As white-shoe firms burned up the phone lines issuing their orders to the pits, their presence there became one of Wall Streets's worst-kept secrets. By September 1984, the *Wall Street Journal* proclaimed Nymex the oil market's undisputed nerve center in an article bearing the headline "Crude Oil Futures Become Public Gauge of Prices Amid World Market Volatility." The piece, among other things, suggested that Sahn had artificially pushed up global oil prices for three days in a row by pelting the market with orders of five hundred to a thousand contracts at a time, even as OPEC doused the market with enough oil to send prices tumbling.

"Yeah, I was huge. The newspaper called, but I couldn't tell them anything. It was all confidential," Sahn says. The floor traders didn't mind squealing on him though. They said Phibro Energy, part of a $26 billion commodities conglomerate owned by Phibro-Salomon Inc., the holding company for Salomon Brothers, was behind Sahn's trades. "The way they went about it was definitely to scare the market up," one told the *Journal*. A second trader said Phibro was looking to groom the market ahead of selling millions of barrels of physical oil in the shadowy over-the-counter market trading alongside, but separate from, Nymex. By running futures prices up on Nymex, he said, Phibro had hoped to get a better rate on its oil in the over-the-counter market, which generally took its prices from Nymex. "Events in the crude-oil ring at the New York Mercantile Exchange are influencing oil prices in the spot market, which, in turn, set or influence the prices of millions of barrels of oil consumed by non-Communist nations," wrote the *Journal*'s Allanna Sullivan.

It would be the clarion call that would reverberate, unchallenged and unresolved, without end. Meddling with the Nymex prices had global impact—and it got you paid.

As repulsed as the Wall Street traders were by Nymex, they had to admit it was a brilliant game, running up the prices in the public, "paper" futures market as a way of controlling prices in the private, over-the-counter market where the real, physical, "wet" barrels of oil were being traded. Who could have imagined the Powers That Be would have allowed it? But allow it they did, and they would even come to encourage it.

 Without trying, Nymex and its traders had become the decoy market that disguised the activities of the much bigger oil traders in the over-the-counter market—also known as the "dark market"—where physical barrels of oil and fuel were exchanged for huge sums by unseen hands. The dark market grew so rapidly that it would soon come to represent many more billions of dollars of oil than Nymex itself. By 2009, a top financial consulting firm would discover that 85 percent of all global commodities trades were being conducted over the counter, with the rest taking place on exchanges like Nymex. When it came to oil trading—and pretty much everything else—the bias of Wall Street, and the rest of the world, was to keep as much as possible out of the spotlight. "If the big banks had their way, Nymex would only trade for ten minutes in the morning and ten minutes at the end of the day, just to establish the global 'open' and 'closing' prices, and the banks would take care of everything else," Guttman says. Wall Street needed Nymex for its open pricing system, but its largest traders didn't want any kind of public market as their primary hunting ground.

For most of the history of the oil market, nobody could say exactly how many trillions of dollars of oil and fuel were sloshing through the over-the-counter market, because almost nobody was watching it. Its purveyors worked anywhere from the gleaming office towers of Houston to the dingy backrooms of the nation's Chinatowns, conducting their trades face-to-face, by telephone, or over the Internet, but always in private. "That's not even the worst of it," says a high-level energy exchange executive. "Most people don't realize there's a guy out there with an Internet connection and a Rolodex putting together deals in his underwear. He's got six guys on the line and another thirty on hold." The over-the-counter traders brokering trades in their boxer briefs weren't doing small-size deals either. They were joining the ranks of the mastodons, assembling multibillion-dollar transactions for some of the largest energy-trading banks in the world, including Morgan Stanley and Goldman Sachs.

In 2005, the CFTC's director of clearing and intermediary oversight, James Carley, told a group of journalists that he wasn't even sure what the size of the over-the-counter market was anymore, but guessed that it was "very, very big." When asked for a better estimate of its size, he said he didn't really know but thought it probably had "a lot of zeroes in it." This from the watchdog agency assigned to look after the world's largest energy market.

The over-the-counter markets continued to flourish on the backs of ordinary energy consumers, without their knowledge, taking its cues from the prices posted on Nymex, which was only too happy to remain the tail that wagged the dog.

Up in the Nymex executive suite, which had more rodents than executives in it (some of the traders joked they couldn't tell the difference), the drawbacks of sudden success had proved hard to handle. If Marks found it burdensome starting the oil market from scratch, he found it all the more challenging holding it together. The decision-making and consensus-building process, which had always been hugely tedious for him, was made easier by an empathetic board that had granted him enormous latitude in steering the exchange. But as Nymex became more powerful, jealousies and internal politics grew thick and he was losing executive control. As one exchange member says, "There was a feeling that the board had only Michel yes-men. He usually picked who got elected and who did or did not stay in power. If you were running for the board and he didn't like you, he would get someone else to run against you. He was King Michel." With more people vying for a piece of the oil pie, Marks suddenly found himself having to defend his territory. He was not the pugnacious type. "The bigger it gets, the more political it gets," Marks told the *Financial Times* in July 1984. "There are different factions now. New groups to be satisfied. It's not my style."

Leone's tenure came to an abrupt halt. "Leone decided Nymex needed more of a brand name, putting things into place that would serve us well later," Guttman says. "The issue was that Francis and Michel Marks were envious of the reception he was getting. Francis said it was time to go. He had plans for Michel to become chairman, president, the whole works. Francis caused a revolt on the management committee, asking Leone, 'Why are we spending all this money? Why does the finance committee never meet?' Thirty or forty Nymex members were there. They'd never even heard of a finance committee, but they all nodded their heads in agreement, saying, 'Yeah! How come there's no finance committee?' Leone saw the writing on the wall and said, 'Screw you guys, I'm outta here.'" Leone, considered by many to be one of the smartest individuals to ever make it into the Nymex president's office, knew the oil market needed him more than he needed it. "Dick was not relating to them and he couldn't handle them very well. He was incredibly smart but also very thin-skinned," says a fellow executive. "After that, the Markses brought in their pretty boy, John Elting Treat," Guttman says. "He'd also come from Princeton. He was dressed for the kill and the model of corporate whatever. He was out of there in just months. That's when they brought in Rosemary."

Rosemary Theresa McFadden had everything Michel Marks thought he was looking for in a president. Born in Scotland of Irish parentage, she was a triple threat with a BA, an MBA, and a law degree. She was in her mid-thirties, experienced, and oozing self-confidence. Incidentally, McFadden was also extremely attractive. By naming her the first female president of any exchange in the nation, Marks stuck a thumb in the eye of the financial establishment—and there was nothing Marks liked better than sticking a thumb into an unsuspecting eye. Aware that his choice would impress the press, he dashed off a news release heralding the appointment, which led to reams of breathless media coverage. "McFadden excited the board. They thought that having a woman president would be a sensation," says an ex-officer privy to the deliberations.

The honeymoon, as honeymoons go, did not last. Instead of being Marks's obedient pet, the petite brunette in high heels had plans of her own. It seemed that two could aspire to the dual roles of chairman and president.

From the beginning, McFadden and Marks had difficulty understanding each other. But they also had a modicum of mutual respect. "I thought Michel was a good chairman, but he could be very hard to read. You would go to talk to him about something and he'd listen, but he wouldn't necessarily respond to you," she says. "You would walk away not knowing what he was thinking. Trying to read him was like trying to read the Sphinx."

Marks's leadership style was mysterious but effective. It consisted mostly of asking questions, listening, and waiting. He would remain silent while the other exchange executives went head-to-head over issues of the day and, only after sensing which way the consensus was building, would he weigh in on the winning side.

Intrigue surrounded McFadden from day one. Traders and board members alternately worshiped her as a sex symbol and called her "one of the boys." Lapayover met her in London in the plush, Art Deco lobby of Claridge's on the way to an industry event they were both attending. "She walked into the room dressed to the nines, pointed at me, and said, '*You*. Tonight, you will be my date,'" he says. "What was I going to do, say no? As soon as we got in there, she walks off. Drops me like a lead weight." The ex-officer credits much of McFadden's influence to her earthly charms. "She was short, Irish-cute, with bazooks way out of proportion. They were definitely natural. We didn't have all that silicone around back then. She was great if she didn't want your job. Instead of working with Michel, though, she started going after him. She was coming at him every which way, doing things that Michel didn't even know were going on. She wanted him out of there."

A New Jersey resident, McFadden, who was married, kept an apartment in New York and, not long after her arrival, became the focus of unwanted attention for her affairs with a Nymex board member and a deep-pocketed market client. One of them was Tommy McKiernan, who moved on from Nymex to start the institutional energy-trading desks of Merrill Lynch and Drexel Burnham Lambert. "What's the truth about Rosemary? Maybe I should be offended because she never tried to sleep with me," says one former Nymex executive. "She hired me and I always found her to be extremely professional. There were other women in support roles at the exchange who didn't hide how much they were sleeping with everybody. She wasn't one of them. Also, let's not even get into what all the men were up to. I know she could drink, she traveled around a lot, and she could hold her own. She was very charismatic and she was tough, but in the end, I don't think she was as tough as she thought she was."

A female executive who worked with McFadden portrayed her as a woman ahead of her time. "While members of the exchange and its executives slept with each other and their customers, the men had some kind of puritanical objection to the women at Nymex doing the same thing." (For her part, McFadden says she was separated from her husband, a high-profile real-estate lawyer, during her extramarital affairs, and eventually reunited with him.) Of the speculation around the exchange about her wanting to seize the chairmanship, she responds: "What would I have wanted that for? I was the president. I already had the C-suite."

As a newcomer, McFadden was no match for Marks's entrenched familial ties, but he did give her unparalleled authority to clean house. In addition to his father, Marks's brothers had started setting up businesses in the trading pits. The Marks clan had its share of arguments, but when it came to anyone whose last name wasn't Marks, they stuck together. Over the next few years, Marks would lay claim to running the fastest-growing market on the planet. After a decade of disasters, he'd finally reached the height of his powers. In the World Trade Center pits in the 1980s, the sound of the warring metals traders was now drowned out by the cacophony of traders screaming for oil. "Walking onto the floor in the morning was an exhilarating experience," says McFadden. "It was like being on the set of a movie."

The backward-roach-motel phenomenon of people defecting from Nymex to Comex promptly reversed itself. The enormity of Marks's success was such that some of the executives working beneath him began to think it was going to his head. "After oil's launch, Michel started getting very pushy and dictatorial," says Howard Hazelcorn, who, as head of Nymex's membership committee, interviewed prospective members. Marks threatened to strip him of his duties after an applicant who was sponsored by Francis waited a half hour to be vetted. "We did these interviews after the market closed, once a month, and it took us most of the night to complete them. Francis asked if they could get in front of the line," Hazelcorn says. "I said sure, fine. But when we were ready and they didn't show, we started with somebody else. They straggled in an hour or so later, and I guess I was supposed to just drop everything. Francis said something to Michel about it and Michel read me the riot act. After years of paying my dues to the committee and working my way up, he threatened to throw me off. I couldn't believe it. All because of his father."

So accustomed were the Markses to getting their way that a growing number of Nymex traders began to see their dynasty as a menace. "Michel once told me he considered Nymex to be his fiefdom," Lapayover says. "That's the word he used, 'fiefdom,' like he was some feudal lord or something. That pretty much set the bar for most of the rest of the chairmen to come." Many traders felt for Marks. "How else do you run a market full of little Napoleons than to be one yourself?" says one. "I never got the sense that Nymex could be run any other way."

Any delusions of grandeur Marks may or may not have had paled in comparison to the monstrosity he was attempting to commandeer. In November 1986, he launched what would be his swan song, a crude-oil futures options contract that, within months, would become the world's leading option on a physical commodity rivaling even options on the highly popular U.S. Treasury bond. More energy options would follow.

As more traders got interested in them, they began gathering in large, semicircular trading rings between the main pits to bet on options, or agreements that gave them the *option* to buy or sell a futures contract at a fixed price for a limited time. For instance, they could purchase an option to buy crude oil for $15 a barrel, which would lock them in at that price until the option expired at a preset date.

Oil prices fell below $10 a barrel that year, but trading volumes and open interest exploded. Marks was named "Oil Man of the Year," as the Nymex traders amassed record paydays on business from banks, oil companies, and trading firms all scrambling to manage the price freefall. As long as energy prices remained unpredictable, Marks predicted, people would keep coming to Nymex to manage them. "When the future is certain, then there's no need for this market," he said. "The more uncertainty there is, the more activity there is. The uncertainty now seems greater than it has ever been."

The uncertainty was at its greatest, just then, for him.

The same morning Marks launched crude-oil options, he got the bad news. His twenty-eight-year-old brother, Louis Marks, vice president of Paris Securities, had been accused of taking $1.8 million in funds from twenty-five customers, ten of them Nymex traders. While Marks had helped found Paris Securities with his father in 1974, and one of his other younger brothers, Jan Marks, was its president, he told the *Wall Street Journal* he no longer had any connection to the firm. He added that the company "is in my heart, and nothing more." The press, however, wasn't buying it. Marks, the media darling, suddenly became Marks, the hunted.

"Rosemary and Michel were increasingly at odds with each other even before the Paris Securities issue put the icing on the cake," Guttman says. "The Paris situation fell directly under Rosemary's oversight as president, and Michel had to remove himself from the proceedings. Rosemary had the ability to put the screws to the Markses and, from what I understand, she was merciless. To the credit of Francis, who was essentially the owner of the firm, he immediately wrote out a personal check for the entire amount of the missing funds. There was no grand confrontation between him, Michel, and Rosemary, but it was definitely the beginning of the end."

In the coming months, the CFTC brought embezzlement charges against Louis Marks, culminating with his being forced to resign from Paris Securities. The CFTC slapped Louis with a lifetime trading ban, a punishment that, for a trader, was like being handed the death penalty. Paris Securities paid a $175,000 fine and was ordered to temporarily cease operations. Neither Michel nor Francis nor Jan were ever implicated in the alleged theft. The case was briskly settled, as all such cases are settled, without anybody admitting to anything. The press never found its hoped-for smoking gun linking Michel Marks to the scandal, but it didn't have to. Marks, a dedicated introvert, had had enough. He could have run for another term and won, but the media grillings, the constant press of inquiring minds, and the recent breakup of his engagement to a woman he'd been courting in London had all taken their toll. "When we weren't making money, no one cared what I did. But as soon as we took off in 1986, it was a whole new ball game. Suddenly there were people underfoot, people in the way. I didn't want to share the power or the wealth with anybody who was putting themselves before the market. There were fights for control. I lost a few political battles. We were a club of potato traders. Then we were a club of oil traders. But the bottom line is, we have always been a club. And I felt that I was always fighting that culture. The mold I wanted to shape the oil market in, my ideal for what I thought it could be, became harder and harder to attain. I didn't care about the money. All I wanted for us was to be a successful and reliable market."

In March 1987, Marks tendered his resignation and, according to his colleagues, disappeared. Though he would sporadically return to the pits from time to time as chairman emeritus in the years to come, it would be a long time before they would find out what became of him. "To me, it was hands-down Michel who was the force that made Nymex what it is. He had great business acumen and presented himself well. There was nothing wishy-washy about him. You knew his feet were planted solid," says Bill Bradt. "He and his father were both strong characters. That cement was thick. You had these two strong personalities. The father created the son. Michel was the introvert and Francis was the extrovert. The Nymex needed that kind of dynamic to pull itself up."

"Michel had an aura about him," says Guttman. "But he had trouble keeping a stiff upper lip. When heating oil almost defaulted, he took off. When the Paris Securities fiasco took place, he took off. Other people had to take care of those things. Francis Marks was the backbone of Michel's chairmanship. Michel had the vision, but Francis had the strength. Francis was the weathered politician, the guiding force that propelled Michel forward. We wouldn't see Michel for a week, sometimes two weeks. His dad would come in and say things like 'You don't understand, the boy is very *ill*.' But as soon as the problem was solved, look who's back? That was the thing about Michel. When the going got tough, Michel got a cold."

Lapayover ran into Marks at a camping-supply store not long afterward. "He was in the middle of some sojourn or other and asked me, 'What are you doing here?' I was like, 'Never mind that. What are *you* doing here?' Even as chairman, he would take off for parts unknown, but instead of coming back looking rested, he would look worse than any of us."

In his final year as chairman, Marks received a bonus of $25,000, the first bonus ever paid by Nymex to a chairman. Though he'd managed to save the exchange, the payment immediately sparked debate and controversy. Because Nymex was a nonprofit organization, it was not supposed to be offering flashy incentives. Some of the traders complained piteously, and a few board members voted against it, but Marks, who came to the pits a virtual unknown, would never be unknown to them again.

An article in the *Journal* about the Marks brothers scandal, capped by the resignation of Michel Marks, concluded with a cruel postscript: "Mr. Marks said he plans to spend more time pursuing such hobbies as hiking and playing jazz piano, including his favorite tune, 'Don't Get Around Much Anymore.'"

As for Louis Marks, he became a salesman in Philadelphia.

Guttman also decided he'd had enough—of the trading pits. He was making a good living, but certain aspects of the job didn't sit well with him. A practicing modern Orthodox Jew, he fasted on holidays and attended weekly temple services, which required him to not work from sundown Friday to sundown Saturday ("Saturday night was when we'd let loose," he says). But the pits, given their tendency toward inside deals and corruption, weren't the most comfortable place for him to be. Until he was twenty-four, when his younger sister married, Guttman received strict warnings from his father to be on his best behavior at all times so as to keep the family's name in good standing, which weighed heavily on his sister's marriage prospects. For Guttman, it had been an upbringing rife with such warnings. "Parents who had survived the Holocaust were always worried about their kids," he says. "They would overfeed you, because they had starved. They were afraid to let you go outside to play, because they remembered all the people who went out and never came back. It was hard for them to stop being so afraid." Belonging to a deeply conservative Jewish community, his parents hoped that one day the local matchmaker might find someone whom Guttman, a proud bachelor, would want to marry. It hadn't happened yet.

On the floor, a group of senior traders, including Hazelcorn, urged Guttman to pursue an executive position at the exchange. They encouraged him to run for vice chairman in the next election. The same month Marks left, Guttman ran alongside Bill Bradt, who was campaigning for chairman. Both won by a landslide.

When he announced his candidacy, Guttman asked Marks for his support. The Nymex members and traders got to vote for all their officers, and Guttman knew Marks still had a great deal of sway in the pits.

Marks told Guttman he'd think about it.

"It was the first real conversation we'd ever had," Guttman says. "He never got back to me."

MARKS'S UNASSUMING, TWO-BEDROOM apartment above the Starbucks was narrow and orderly except for small bits of artistic clutter. It showed no sign of his past life at Nymex or on Wall Street. No trading badges or trading jackets or any other kind of trading paraphernalia lay anywhere. Even so, the decoration revealed much about the nature of the man who inhabited it. Crookedly thumbtacked to the living-room walls were sheets of acid-free sketch paper, splashed with bright reds and blues and yellows in gemstone designs. The paintings were large, abstract, and devoid of all self-consciousness. As if a child had drawn them.

"Who did these?" I asked.

"Who do you think did them?" Marks responded in his typical answer-that's-not-an-answer.

"Not an adult."

He smiled. He had done them.

His hallways were lined with many books. In the corner stood an untuned dreadnought guitar. I looked at one of the books. It was Bob Dylan's biopic, *Chronicles: Volume One*. It occurred to me that Marks was not unlike Dylan—proud, defiant, tight-lipped, moody.

Nearing the end of our hike, we scaled the last hill and looked out over the wintering valley below. "If you always wanted to paint," I said, "why don't you leave Nymex and do it?" Marks looked off into the distance, his eyes unfocused. He slowly shook his head. Not to me, but to himself. I tried to imagine what it would be like to know that the greatest thing you did with your life, the one thing you would be known for, wouldn't end up being something you cared about that much. Had Marks realized the implications of what he'd been doing while he'd been doing it? I supposed not. It seemed sad and yet inevitable that it was every man's fate to reach his apex and not know it. Marks hadn't known it. Maybe he still didn't.

"I don't know," Marks said. "I always tell myself I am going to leave, but somehow I keep coming back."

Part II
Black Fortune

6

The Rise of Zoltan

*I happen to be Hungarian. We Hungarians are known to be
very stubborn people.*

—ZOLTAN LOUIS GUTTMAN

EUPHORIC AT WINNING the race for vice chairman, Lou Guttman
went home to his family's brick apartment house in Brooklyn to tell his
parents. He had, in a word, arrived.

He did not get the response he was expecting.

Herman Guttman clapped his thirty-eight-year-old son on the back
and said, "This is not good."

"Dad," Guttman said, "I will be fine."

"Are you getting paid?"

"No. But I have my trading business. I'll make it work."

"See? You're not even getting paid," his father chided. "What if the
press drags your name through the mud? All a man has is his honor and
his name. Trust me, no good can come of this."

"This is not World War II Europe," Guttman said. "That is not
going to happen."

Guttman's early days as vice chairman were exciting, if perplexing.
Watching the interactions of the chairman, Bill Bradt; the president,
Rosemary McFadden; and the rest of the board, he was not sure what, if
anything, was going on. "I came in every day, but had no idea what we
were doing," he says. "I thought I was joining this omnipotent, powerful board. I went to the meetings and there's just paper shuffling and

shit. Nothing. This goes on for months on end." Guttman's first test as vice chairman came just before Thanksgiving that year. It would be an early lesson on how easily the politics of the pits could carry up into the boardroom to overturn the oil market's hierarchy.

"John Tafaro, who owns a floor operation that's probably even bigger than Bobby Sahn's at the time, comes into my office. Tafaro is loved by all. He is Mr. Squeaky Clean. And he is saying that Bill Bradt, our chairman, is trying to shake him down for floor-brokerage commissions. Bradt started out as a two-man operation, but in the six or seven months since he's been chairman, he suddenly has fifteen to twenty floor brokers executing trades. He's a guy with a lot of connections. I say, 'All right, you're making some major accusations here. Before you call for an investigation, you need documented proof, facts. Until you have that, please don't drag me into this, okay?'

"About five days later, I get a call from McFadden. She says, 'I have some business to discuss with you; can you come up to my office?' So I go, and she says, 'We have a problem with the chairman of our exchange. He may be trying to shake down one of our floor brokers. It has to be investigated.' Now *this* is a little different. When you have a bunch of traders bursting into your office every morning making a ruckus over whoever's on their shit list that day, you learn it's best to hold off until you have some proof of something. But when the president of the exchange decides she needs to address it in her official capacity, that's something else. We have an executive committee meeting to look into it. Tafaro is on the committee. Bradt is not invited. He is obviously like, 'What is going on?' How the shakedown worked exactly was never made very clear by Tafaro, but I say, 'Look, let's not play games, let's call Billy in here. We say, John, why don't you tell Billy what you're telling us?' He repeats it in front of Bill Bradt. And Bradt says, 'What, are you crazy? I never shook you down. It's a legitimate sharing of the customer commissions. This is my customer as well as yours. I just said you bill him and you give me half of it.' Long story short, Rosemary says we have to have a board meeting."

Sharing a customer was not unusual, since the pit traders had different specializations and sometimes one would refer a customer to another trader to execute a complex transaction that the first trader didn't know how to do. Guttman was flying to London for discussions with Britain's energy market, the International Petroleum Exchange, which wanted permission to offer and trade Nymex oil contracts. The board meeting would have to wait. Halfway through his trip, Guttman received a call from Vincent Viola, a young pit trader from Brooklyn and member of the board.

"You need to get your ass back here," Viola said. "They're changing their story." Guttman landed at the airport at 2:05 P.M. the next day. The board was meeting at four. He rushed in to find Bradt sitting dejectedly outside the boardroom. "Bradt comes up and says, 'Whatever happens, don't allow them to take a vote. Please don't let them do it.' I say, 'Billy, look, I don't know what the fuck is going on. The board will meet and we'll talk. Whatever happens, happens.'"

Earlier in the day, McFadden had gone down to the trading floor to tell Bradt that reporters from several major newspapers and television stations were asking about whether he might get thrown off the board. She said, "I have some bad news. We have been getting calls from lots of people because some son of a bitch is saying there might be a board vote to oust you." And sure enough, news cameras and journalists were already standing outside the boardroom and weren't going away. Someone, it seemed, had tipped off the media. McFadden called the tactic "vicious." Bradt thought Guttman did it. Guttman thought McFadden did it. "Bradt could never believe it was Rosemary, because she was Irish and he was Irish and, at the exchange, people kept close to their own," Guttman says. "I go into the meeting. Bill isn't allowed in. Out of deference to him, I do not sit in his chair. I'd only been on the board for six months and suddenly I am the second guy in command of this thing.

"As president, McFadden was not a member of the board, but she attended the meetings. Tafaro tells his story, but now he realizes the can of worms he's opened and he wants to put the kibosh on it. He says, 'I told Rosemary I thought Bill Bradt was shaking me down for floor commissions, but now I take it back. I think it was a legitimate business arrangement.' So now everybody's looking at me like, then why are we *here*? By saying this is a legit business arrangement, Tafaro is making me and the other executive committee members look like we're in a conspiracy against our own chairman. So I look over at Rosemary like, now what? And she goes, 'Sorry, John, did you or did you not ask for a meeting?' Yes. 'Did you or did you not say the chairman was shaking you down for commissions?' Yes. Well, come to think about it, he's worked it out with Bradt and he's changed his mind. So much for glasnost."

The board members were suspicious. Votes were taken and an investigation began, but it didn't lead anywhere until McFadden fired the head of compliance months later. The head of compliance was the one person at Nymex who was supposed to be making sure that everyone *else* was behaving. Instead, he was discussing starting a business with Bradt while investigating one of Bradt's clients. "It was considered a serious conflict of interest," says Guttman. "But when you fire the head of compliance, the CFTC suddenly comes in and wants to know what the heck is going on. Rosemary knew that. She was a lawyer. And, of course, this starts a whole new inquiry into Bradt by the CFTC over his involvement with the head of compliance. Just like with Michel, she's going to nail Billy's ass."

Most off-putting, Guttman says, was that the board voted *not* to read the findings of the investigation by a blue-ribbon panel of independent directors, which included Cathy Douglas, wife of former Supreme Court justice William O. Douglas, into the Bradt-Tafaro affair. "I thought that was strange," he says.

Sitting in his office in February 1988, hoping some of the excitement might be dying down, Guttman was taken aback when Tafaro sauntered in and told him that he, Tafaro, planned on running against him in March when Guttman was up for reelection. "I say to John, 'What, do you think I've done a bad job?'" says Guttman. "He says, 'No, I just think that you should have shoved the whole thing with Bradt and me under the rug.' And now it seems that Billy too wants to get rid of me." (Bradt, who still believed Guttman was responsible for the media leak at the board meeting, asked Rappaport to run against Guttman before lining up Tafaro to do it. Rappaport turned him down, saying, "Please leave me out of this shit.") "I said, 'John, let me understand: you come into my office in October and make all these allegations. Then you tell Rosemary McFadden and she makes it official. That's my fault? You come into the board meeting and take it all back. Now you and Bradt want to make me the fall guy for it? No, that's not the way it's going to happen. Here's the deal, unless you pull out of this race in the next week, I'm going to work on you and Bradt and I am going to make *dog meat* out of the both of you."

The next day, Tafaro resigned from the board and announced his candidacy for vice chairman. Guttman went into the pits loaded for bear. He told the floor brokers that if Tafaro and Bradt succeeded in taking control of the exchange, they would have free rein over the floor's brokerage business with the specific goal of lining their own pockets to the detriment of everyone else. Guttman then asked the board to unseal the findings of the blue-ribbon panel investigation into Bradt and Tafaro. "The CFTC is now looking at these findings, people are reading about them in the newspapers, and I think we, the board, should be able to see them," he says. "But they all say no. Then Bradt says he wouldn't mind taking a look. Well, the moment he says that, what's the rest of the board going to say? We start reading this crap and it is blatantly obvious all the back-scratching, double-crossing, and incestuousness going on at every level, including the board. No wonder no one wants to see it. I start telling anyone who will listen on the trading floor to go into the back and read this thing."

The move worked in Guttman's favor. Even the traders who didn't support him couldn't resist such tantalizing grist for the gossip mill. They read every word.

Nymex election politics being what they were, the showdown tested the bonds of the Italian, Irish, and Jewish factions of the boardroom and the pits. The ethnic infighting upset Guttman, who sensed a willful fanning of the flames of anti-Semitism coming from the opposition. "During my campaign, the word went out. There are too many of *them* on the board—Jews. It got turned into this whole Italian-Irish-Jewish thing. So I go to Rosemary McFadden, who would like to see more Irish on the board, and I say, 'Now you listen here. I am Hungarian, a Jewish-American Hungarian. If you do not stop what's going on on the floor about there's too many of *them* on the board, this whole campaign is going to be a blood war. I am going to blow this place up, and you'll be the first to go. You go out there and tell Billy Bradt, the Irish guy, and John Tafaro, the Italian guy, that we are a united group of people and while we are on the floor, we are going to conduct ourselves without that crap. When you leave this exchange at the end of the day, you believe what you want, it don't make a difference. *My mother survived Auschwitz and I am sure as hell going to survive all of you!*' I say this to her, and in twenty-four hours it stops."

In late March, the election results filtered in. Tafaro lost to Guttman by twelve votes in a photo finish. Bradt, who'd been depending on Tafaro's victory, was unable to hide his shock.

"Bradt, who is still chairman, goes white. The last thing on his mind is that his guy, Tafaro, is not going to beat the Hungarian. Bradt comes out and in front of everybody says, 'Congratulations, Lou, you were a true soldier! You fought this like a trooper.' I said, 'Billy, go fuck yourself. Whatever you did in the first year as chairman was fine. You run this board as you see fit. But if you get yourself tangled up again, next time around, I am not going to be so kind.'"

Bradt went back to running the board meetings and Guttman kept his head down. In August 1988, the CFTC's report on the Bradt-Tafaro situation arrived. "I'll never forget Rosemary saying, 'We have the CFTC report,' and my heart just about failed," Bradt says. "That year was a horror show. Immediately, all the political factions started circling the wagons. I didn't want to have to go through it all again."

The board called in its outside counsel to offer an expert opinion. "Bradt looks at the report and turns to us and says, 'I did nothing wrong and, as far as my deal with Tafaro, all I did was call in my chitz.' He leaves the board for us to talk, and this time, I make a big show of getting up and sitting in his chair," Guttman says. "I say to them, 'Ladies and gentlemen, I would like for our outside counsel to tell us what he thinks.' Our counsel doesn't mince words. 'The way I am reading this,' he says, 'is that the CFTC would prefer for Bradt not to be chairman anymore.' That's all that had to be said. So I said, 'Let's do this with some magnanimity. Let's treat him with respect.' We told him thank you for your services, had him resign, and eased him back into private life. We gave him a couple of bucks and he was gone. I never saw him eyeball-to-eyeball again."

Bradt had considered the chairmanship an honor. He never thought the experience, rather than enriching him, could hurt him. "It was absolutely wretched, because your name is just destroyed. It didn't matter that the CFTC came back later and said I hadn't broken any rules, that it was just 'bad judgment.' By that time, your name has been dragged through the mud and over what? Nothing. All these people you know, they are reading about you all over the world in the papers. An associate of mine even saw it going over the ticker tape in Paris. It was hard to believe that in a nonpaying job, a volunteering job, that this could take place."

Bradt and Tafaro returned to the pits. So far that year, Bradt had only made $56,000, embroiled as he was in all the political imbroglios. By December, he'd earned well over $1 million on heating-oil trades alone. The day after he resigned, he went blue fishing on Long Island

Sound. He decided to forget about it. "You know how I would sum up the whole Nymex chairmanship? It's like what they say about boats. The happiest day of a boater's life is when he buys his boat. And the other happiest day of his life is when he sells it."

The evening of Bradt's departure, Guttman became Nymex chairman by default. There was no need for an election. There was nobody else in line for the job. It was a Wednesday. The following Monday, Guttman was on a plane bound for Bürgenstock, Switzerland, with McFadden. The chairman's post was still an unpaid, part-time job, and Guttman didn't know what lay ahead of him, but he hoped it would offer the kind of opportunities a street kid from Brooklyn could only dream about. Being chairman also was good for business. It gave you automatic cachet when dealing with clients. "I was the accidental chairman," he says. "I was just months into my job and still getting my bearings when this happened. I never really saw myself as heading up a board. I was sorely unprepared. I couldn't even handle public speaking." By contrast, McFadden, who headed the exchange's operations and staff, fetched a six-figure salary and was past master at speaking in public. She had a raft of degrees and her office did not rely on her winning any votes.

She and Guttman had been shadowboxing each other for years. They'd always been extremely wary of each other, but now, with Bradt out of the way, there would be no more buffers. "I didn't know what this Bürgenstock thing was," Guttman says. "I was told it was an annual commodities industry event. There was a press conference at eight A.M. I'd never been to a press conference before. Vice chairmen didn't attend press conferences. I got up there thinking we were just going to do a question-and-answer session with the reporters when Rosemary throws me to the dogs, announcing that I'm going to give this big speech about the future of our exchange. She says nothing to me about this beforehand. She doesn't even prep me. She's just waiting for me to fall on my face."

Guttman got up, made a few statements, and muddled through it. He upbraided her afterward, but she offered no apology. She had only four words for him: "Welcome to the chairmanship."

Guttman was beginning to get the distinct impression that, far from insulating him from attacks, his new title was only going to make him more of a target. "I think Rosemary had a problem with all the chairmen. She would seek out the chairman's soft underbelly. She couldn't stomach the fact that the guy down the hall at our sister exchange, Comex, had the titles of both president and chairman and she did not. Her mission was to make every chairman's life miserable to the point where the board would somehow come to see that the president and chairman should be Rosemary. She tangoed with Michel Marks. She wore down Bill Bradt— although I took the brunt of the political fallout for that. And then, when she was done with them, she came after me."

The shot across the bow at Bürgenstock did not go unanswered. Guttman and McFadden began sparring openly, leaving the board helpless to do anything about it. They did not get along, and, from the start, it was clear the exchange wasn't big enough for the two of them. "Did Rosemary make the chairmen's lives miserable?" asks Anthony George Gero, one of the Nymex's longest-serving board members and a Guttman ally. "Yes. She wanted the job. But, let's be honest, the presidents and chairmen of Nymex were always trying to topple each other. If it wasn't that, it was the chairmen and vice chairmen trying to off each other. Also, women were treated like second-class citizens back then, so Rosemary was probably trying to protect herself. She was a hard worker. A much harder worker than many other Nymex presidents I could name."

The board knew the deal with the chairmen, presidents, and vice chairmen. It was a delicate dance where the rivals smiled as they shivved one another under the table.

Two weeks later, Guttman gave another, more serious speech during a dinner at New York's Waldorf-Astoria Hotel on Park Avenue. He was still nervous in front of crowds. A group of reporters nudged him encouragingly up to the podium. "They knew I was jittery, but they told me, 'Just get up there and do it, because we would if we could do it.' It took some time, but I realized that if you are running a good business and following a good business plan, you don't need to be a great orator. It's when you are spinning and double-talking that you get yourself tripped up. I kept track of the issues and was able to argue and debate something that made good business sense. And I found out you could not win with spin. That night, though, I sucked and it was obvious to all I had stage fright. I still have the videotape of it. It's painful to watch."

Guttman's goal in autumn of 1989 was to forge a deal with Leo Melamed, the chairman of the CME who wanted a piece of the Nymex energy complex. Guttman flew to Chicago with McFadden and Viola. In the sterile boardroom of the CME, he came face-to-face with Melamed, already a legend for creating the world's first commercially successful financial futures market. Melamed, who also penned science-fiction novels in his spare time, saw his groundbreaking financial inventions as just another extension of his visions for the future. Two years earlier, he'd published a book, *The Tenth Planet: When Human Equals Alien*, a first-edition copy of which he handed to me, inscribing the words "Science fiction is what I do!" The book contained many interesting passages, not excluding its opening:

> *"Where are you off to now, Dormah?"*
> *It was Rafflo. Dormah detested the little creep. Not for his neuter sex, nor his nasal whine (which was not unusual for neuters) but for his demeanor and sarcasm. Rafflo knew he was superior and made certain everyone was aware of it.*
> *"To pee—want to watch?"*
> *Rafflo gave her the finger and twirled around smartly, making certain his rear wiggled as only neuters can.*

Because of Melamed, traders who didn't feel like betting on Chicago's pork bellies anymore could now place bets on such diverse things as interest rates and stock indexes. "Leo wasn't just a legend to us, he was also a legend to himself," says one Nymex trader who knew him. "He loved Asian women. I remember he was considering dumping one of his mistresses, because he could only spend 10 percent of his free time with her. But then he changed his mind, because he decided that even 10 percent of his time was better than 100 percent of the time she could be spending with anyone else." Like Marks, Guttman was intimidated by the Chicago money machine. While the CME was throwing $5,000-a-plate dinners for Ronald Reagan, the Nymex traders were digging in their pockets for quarters to feed the parking meters outside the Chamber Maids strip club on Chambers Street just up the block from the pits.

Melamed wasted no time in showing Guttman he'd done his homework. Striding in with his cuff-linked entourage, he said, "Lou, I understand you and I are both immigrants and Holocaust survivors." Guttman had appreciated that. Likewise, Melamed appreciated Guttman's ability to understand his flowery, highly formalized Yiddish.

"Leo had a way of putting you at ease," Guttman says. "He was an elderly man, a giant of the futures industry, and he let you know exactly where you stood relative to him. I think when I was chairman he even called me 'kid.' But he was great at relating to people and my political position while running the market."

Melamed laid his proposal on the table. He wanted to offer Nymex energy contracts on the CME's new electronic-trading system, Globex, his latest futuristic invention. The mere mention of Globex made the New York traders break out in a sweat, because it meant trading on computer screens instead of the trading floor, their one true sanctuary. They didn't like the idea of technology creeping up on them. "In 1989, electronic trading became the new frontier. The technology was moving quickly and there were quarters within the industry that said, 'Why do we need all these people screaming and shouting at each other in a pit? We can transfer that onto a computer. You can save a lot of expense.' But nobody understood the implications of it. On a daily basis, the congregation of interests of the people in the trading pits actually creates the efficiency and the liquidity that the market enjoys. To outsiders, it seemed a little arcane, but it worked." After listening to the deal, which would have given the CME a generous share of Nymex's energy-trading revenue, Guttman kept his poker face. He knew very well that allowing even a small slice of his energy trades to be conducted electronically on Globex could lose him his chairmanship. McFadden was not as stoical. When Leo was finished talking, she thumped Guttman on the back and said, "Take the deal!" Guttman bristled. "This is not what we needed the CME to hear. It blew our cover. When we left, Vinnie was so livid, he could hardly speak. I'd never seen him that furious before." A West Point graduate and former infantry officer, Viola respected the chain of command above all else and couldn't stand seeing anyone break it.

Guttman and Melamed spoke again before coming to an arrangement, but the standoff between him and McFadden went on. "Those two couldn't tackle *anything* without sparks flying everywhere," says Joel Faber, who kept trading in the pits before retiring at fifty. The board, caught in the middle, jokingly called it "the Battle of Rosemary." There was a fire between Guttman and McFadden that nobody understood. And, like the relationship between Marks and his father, nobody wanted to.

While planning the world's first natural-gas futures contract, Guttman and McFadden crashed antlers again over where the natural-gas shipments should be delivered. "Rosemary wanted the delivery point to be Katy, Texas, but Katy wasn't ready yet. It would have taken months, if not years. My first order of business when I got to be chairman was, 'I'm getting tired of hearing about Katy, Texas! Is there any other place in this goddamn country that has an interchange where you can deliver natural gas?' One of Rosemary's staffers, a tall, nice guy in the research department, piped in with 'Erath, Louisiana.' Rosemary could have castrated him. We ultimately went with Erath, which is now known as the Henry Hub, the major delivery point for natural gas in North America. The guy in research did not even contradict her. He didn't say, 'I think it should be Erath.' He just answered my question, and he, in her view, should have not told me."

While running the exchange, Guttman avoided trading in the pits. He no longer considered himself a gambling man, though sometimes he bet on the currency market. He mostly supported himself through his own introducing brokerage firm, Harley Futures Inc., which played matchmaker between the Nymex traders and the various clearing firms. For making these introductions, Guttman received a generous commission from the clearing firms of $10,000 to $20,000 a month. It was the only reason he could afford to work for free at the exchange. One person he introduced to a clearing firm he worked with, Gerald Inc., was an especially skilled options trader named Harold Jay Magid. Guttman didn't know the first thing about options trading, but he did know a good trader when he saw one. Looking over Magid's books with a trained accountant's eye, he was struck by how much money Magid made without taking any big financial risks.

Magid came across as competent and precise, a savvy trader by day and an instructor who taught options-trading classes to New York University students by night. He and Guttman had met on the trading floor in 1987, becoming fast friends and business partners. Their objective had been simple: Guttman would share half his earnings with Magid from his introducing brokerage firm and Magid would share half his earnings with Guttman from his trading. They didn't commit to the deal on paper. No one ever signed written contracts at Nymex. They just agreed to it the usual way, with a handshake. "Though Magid earned roughly the same as I did, I didn't know if my business would grow faster than his, or vice versa, so I thought that this was a smart way for me to be hedged," Guttman says. "It seemed like a good idea at the time."

An FBI sting operation and multiple busts on the Chicago trading floors caught Guttman and the rest of the New York traders by surprise in 1989. Allegations of hidden crimes filled the newspapers for months, prompting a heavy-handed inquisition by Congress. The two stings, Operation Sourmash and Operation Hedgeclipper, resulted in charges being brought against traders at the CME and the Chicago Board of Trade for engaging in fraudulent acts, such as buying and selling ahead of customer orders, conducting fictitious trades, concealing profits from the Internal Revenue Service, and "trade-bucketing." (Trade-bucketing meant holding on to a customer's order without executing it immediately, usually for one's own gain. By law, traders were supposed to execute orders as quickly as possible.) In New York, one of the most talked-about examples of this kind of behavior was when Alvin Brodsky, a well-known Comex broker, deliberately threw out a sell order from the infamous Hunt brothers after the Hunts cornered the silver market in 1980. According to a Nymex trader, "He tossed the trade back to his assistant to buy time and said, 'This order's no good. Do it over.'" Of course, it was fine, but the Hunt brothers, who'd driven up the price of silver from $9 an ounce to over $52 in just a few months, were about to liquidate everything, which would crush the high price. "Before they could do that, Brodsky held their order off while he sold *his* silver contracts ahead of them at the top of the market." This was why, if you knew the right people, you didn't have to be a good trader to get rich.

The Chicago busts were a public relations disaster for not only the city's exchanges but also the CFTC, which was supposed to be making sure people weren't stealing with abandon across the nation's trading floors. To add insult to injury, the CFTC had been completely unaware that the FBI sting operation was under way. "I think the FBI did not really trust the CFTC," says a former CFTC official who left the agency in 1987. "The CFTC was called in at the last minute only for the FBI's press conference to announce the busts. It wasn't a good sign. It was not a happy development that the agency had been left out in the cold like that. Until then, there had been no prosecutions by the CFTC of anyone of *any* consequence."

Even the new prosecutions did not go as planned. Forty-eight indictments and twenty-two guilty pleas later, only thirteen convictions stuck, prompting the *Wall Street Journal* to lament, "Many lawyers are richer and many traders are poorer. Whether anyone is wiser is harder to answer." The example of the Hunt brothers, whose scheme led to their literally controlling half the world's deliverable supply of silver, seemed to answer that question. The rebellious progeny of Texas oil tycoon H. L. Hunt, the brothers had previously been booted from other markets, only to pack up and take their tricks to new territory. They eventually bankrupted themselves on silver bets and were convicted of conspiring to manipulate commodities prices.

The public didn't find out about Operation Sourmash or Operation Hedgeclipper until the FBI raided Chicago traders' homes in the middle of the night, armed with subpoenas and secret tape recordings of their alleged incriminating deeds. The first knock at a door came in January 1989 at the residence of Jimmy Sledz, a Japanese yen futures trader. More than two years earlier, the FBI had sent its moles, or special agents, to the Chicago pits to embed themselves in trading life while posing as traders. Chicago's politicians routinely complained about the number of agents trying to catch them taking bribes, but the infiltration of the city's trading pits had caught them completely off guard. While Nymex wasn't implicated in the bust, Guttman was summoned to Washington in early 1989 to testify before Congress, along with the chairmen of the Chicago futures exchanges.

Guttman was taken aback by all the flashbulbs and questions. He also was none too pleased at being sandwiched on a dais between Melamed and the Chicago Board of Trade's chairman Karsten "Cash" Mahlmann, big-time archrivals who weren't speaking to each other that week. "I was crapping my pants. The Chicago exchanges were in trouble. At the time, Nymex was not—yet, anyway. The *New York Times* comes and takes a picture of the Chicago chairmen on either side of me that makes it look like I'm at the center of this Mafia cabal," Guttman says. His impressions of the legislative proceedings on Capitol Hill going in were enormously different from what they were going out. He believed Congress was genuinely interested in hearing about how to fix flaws in the financial system. "I put in a lot of work and saw a lot of senators," Guttman says. "They were all nice, they were all great, but in the end they did whatever they wanted to do anyway. What we said didn't matter. And when they spoke, they didn't speak *to* us. They just talked facing all the cameras. They weren't bringing us out there to listen. They wanted us there for the charade, the three-ring media circus."

After testifying, Guttman hurried to London with McFadden for another commodities industry event. They took separate rooms at the Dorchester, a five-star hotel in Mayfair. Guttman picked up his bedside telephone to call New York when he heard McFadden's voice on the line. She was upset. "I heard her crying to this guy. She was saying, 'I miss you, I've got to see you.' They made a date to meet at the Concorde terminal at Heathrow airport. She was saying his name, which was a very distinctive name. I figured it was a crossed line and hung up."

A week later, a man by the same name came off a Concorde flight to New York to meet a member of the Nymex board. The man told the board member he'd just been to London, his visit overlapping with the time of the crossed phone lines with McFadden. The board member mentioned the meeting offhandedly to Guttman. Guttman recalled the name and put two and two together. He didn't care what McFadden did with her free time. The problem was, this person was a major bank trader from Texas who represented a large portion of Nymex's business. McFadden, as president, happened to be one of the only people in the world with extensive knowledge of which energy market players were doing what on a daily basis—information that was not publicly available but could be very useful to a favored client with active bets.

It was a conflict of interest Guttman wasn't sure he could ignore. "I called our outside counsel and we discussed it. I didn't know what I was going to do. I had an issue on my hands where our president was potentially disclosing inside information, but of course I didn't know. I mean, you never know with pillow talk. We already had a potato default and God knows how many other problems. I didn't want to think about us coming under threat of being shut down again if this came to light. The outside counsel said, 'Short of putting a tail on her or taping her, revealing it could be explosive.'" Guttman took the advice and, for the time being, decided to keep his eyes open and his mouth shut.

Running for reelection in March 1989, he stood unopposed. But that didn't mean he was lacking in opposition. At the spring futures conference in Boca Raton, a CNN reporter asked him about a stock market violation he'd had when he was younger. Guttman froze. "This is getting really dirty, isn't it?" he said. "I don't think I want to talk about it."

He knew exactly what the reporter was talking about. Back when he'd worked at the stock brokerage shop on John Street, his boss had given him and the other back-office employees an opportunity to buy into their first public stock offering. The company was called Beneficial

Labs. Guttman had thought of it as a privilege at the time. "I was just a kid. I asked our firm's lawyer, 'Is it okay?' He said, 'If it's not a hot issue, you can buy it,' which is to say, if it's not oversubscribed, you're not taking it away from anyone else." Guttman bought a thousand shares of the company. The firm's bookkeeper and a few others also bought a thousand shares each. "Come to find out there weren't enough subscribers for the stock offering, period, and Beneficial Labs should have never gone public except for us putting the stock purchases over the fifty-thousand-share mark," Guttman says. "My firm gets cited for breaking the law. I am named, our bookkeeper is named, and, after a hearing in the court, my boss goes to jail. I tell the judge our lawyer told me it was all right. He does not care. He just says, 'You should sue *him*, then.' I didn't have the money for that. I got an administrative slap on the wrist and paid a fine. The firm went under. It's 1973. I am twenty-one years old."

When Guttman joined Nymex, he disclosed the incident to its membership committee. "The exchange didn't have a problem with it," he says. "They asked, 'Did you steal money from customers?' No. 'Was it criminal?' No. 'No? Okay. You're in.' But now it was a problem, because now I was running for chairman."

The CNN reporter didn't go away. Guttman learned later that day he would be the subject of an exposé by Lou Dobbs, the famous television anchor. When the reporter called one more time for comment, Guttman again declined. He'd just finalized the deal with the CME and was about to be voted Nymex chairman of his own accord—not because the chairman got thrown out, like last time. He didn't need to contribute to his own bad press. "I called Leo Melamed and said, 'You're going to be hearing a story about me this afternoon on CNN. I don't know what they're going to say, but it's probably full of shit.' When the show aired, we all watched. CNN says I have been barred from trading stocks by the American Stock Exchange and that I've lost my registration with the CFTC. Then Lou Dobbs starts spouting off about how can people in corporate America have violations and still be chairmen? And so on and so forth. I sit there, stunned. First of all, I was never a member of the American Stock Exchange. I don't even know where they got that. And the CFTC registered me with full knowledge of my stock violation. All of it was wrong. Needless to say, the phone is off the hook and McFadden is circling the wagons at this meeting she's at in Houston, asking everyone, 'Have you heard about Lou?'" Guttman dialed up his counsel to ask if he could sue for libel. The short answer was no, because he was a public figure. Unless he could prove that CNN had the truth and then flagrantly ignored it, he didn't have a case.

Two hours later, Guttman received a call from CNN in Atlanta. "They were the ones who got the tip on me and now they realize they've fucked up. They need an out. They say they are going to do a retraction. I tell them, 'You're going to say two things about me: one, my license was never withdrawn by the CFTC. And two, I was never barred from the American Stock Exchange. Whatever you say after that, I don't give a fuck.' I was the lead story the night before. You would think I'd be the lead story that night. Nope. It's 7 P.M., 7:05, 7:15, 7:20, 7:25, then Lou Dobbs comes on and says, 'Last night we ran a story on Lou Guttman. Our story was in error and we'd like to apologize. Let this be a lesson to corporate America: we should keep our lines of communication more open. We called Mr. Guttman and he wouldn't talk to us. In the future, maybe we should all talk more.' Oh, what a victory. Such victory. At the butt end of the show. Then I get a call from this British guy on CNN, who did part of the piece the day before. Decent guy. He had nothing to do with it. He said, 'Look, Lou, I just read the teleprompter.' I said, 'I accept your apology, but you guys owe me. If you can tell me who set me up, who fed you this stuff, I would appreciate it.' He said, 'That's a lot to ask, but let me see what I can do.' Now this is a really big thing for a reporter, to disclose a confidential source, but it turns out that Atlanta was so fucking pissed that they got fed a line of bullshit, the next day they called back and said, 'Lou, this is very unofficial, but the person who gave us the information was Rosemary McFadden.' I said, 'Thank you very much.'"

Guttman got reelected. McFadden flew to Russia on a business trip. While there, she attended an energy conference covered by the Reuters news agency. Guttman and the board members read about it back in New York. So did the FBI, which was wondering what the president of the world's largest oil market was doing in Soviet Russia. The FBI sent agents to Nymex to find out. Guttman didn't have an answer. But he did know when to keep his own counsel and when to speak his mind. At the next monthly board meeting, Guttman made his power play. "In the middle of the meeting, I said, 'At this time I'd like for us to go into executive session. Ms. McFadden, if you and your staff would please leave?'" McFadden had never been dismissed before during a board meeting. She looked over at the directors for their reaction. Guttman, perturbed, repeated himself. "We are now going into executive session. You and your staff are excused. I am going to ask you one more time. Please leave." McFadden glared at him and walked out. Guttman cleared his throat. "Ladies and gentlemen, we've got to talk. This board is empowered to run the business of the exchange. I have CEO liability and I don't get paid for it. Not that the money makes any difference, I happen to like the job. But the leader of our staff feels she doesn't need to tell us what she's doing or why. FBI agents materialize at the exchange and want to know what our president is doing in Russia. I did not even know she was in Russia. The board did not know she was in Russia. And we're not really friendly with the Russians right now. I am telling this board that it's time for her to go. We need new blood and a new approach. Her approach is infectious, but infectious in the wrong way."

The board called McFadden back in. The directors handed down their decision. She and Guttman had thirty days to show they could get along. "The board knew it wasn't going to work," Guttman says. "But none of them wanted to be the ones to pull the trigger. I never let on that I knew she was sleeping with anyone. I really didn't want to use her personal life as a weapon, you know? What you do with your personal life, I don't give a shit. I have my standards, you got yours. I'm not going to tell you what to do, don't tell me what to do. But don't fuck around with my business."

McFadden says the trip to Russia came "after Perestroika" and was on her schedule in advance for anyone to see.

That summer, Guttman received a call from Melamed. He told Guttman he would be suspending their electronic-trading deal, because the CME and the Chicago Board of Trade were speaking to each other again. The Chicago exchanges were considering an exclusive partnership. (As Melamed once said of the Chicago Board of Trade's Mahlmann, "He's got a thick head, but give him time and he comes around.") The blow staggered Guttman. "I spent a lot of time on that deal. I mean, we'd finally got the floor and the board to vote for it and it was not easy. When the guys on the floor heard about electronic trading, they were ready to behead me. They were like, 'Trading on *computers*? What, are you kidding us?' They preferred trading eyeball to eyeball. Leo was not going to include me in the talks with the CBOT. He told me not to worry about it. He said, 'I will represent your interests.' I said, 'No one can represent my interests better than me.' I'd staked all my political capital on this. I begged, but he wouldn't budge." Once the go-between, Guttman was now the odd man out. He'd been the victim of a bait-and-switch. Melamed returned to him months later to revive the deal once the CBOT partnership fizzled, but by that time, Guttman had learned his lesson. The two men went their separate ways. Guttman put together his own electronic-trading system he called Access. The system would extend Nymex's trading day from five hours to twenty-two hours, allowing the pit traders to buy and sell energy futures overnight, which they did—obsessively. "Most of the guys were already psychotic about trading," says Mark Lichtner. "They couldn't stop talking about it, they couldn't stop doing it. Then you get the computers and it's even worse. You're looking at all the prices like, where is it now? Where is it *now*? With the computers, guys get bored, you know, maybe the wife won't wake up or something, and they go into their home offices and start trading and suddenly they realize they've been trading all night and it's morning." But even with Access, daytime activity remained strictly relegated to the pits, the traders' hallowed battleground.

In an effort to patch things up, McFadden invited Guttman to a function at New York's Russian consulate. At the last minute, she called to cancel. "She told me she wasn't feeling well and wouldn't be attending. Then I find out she went anyway," Guttman says. For him, it was the last straw. He pulled his trump card. "I never disclosed the crossed line in London to anyone on the board except Vinnie Viola. It just seemed that no matter what I did, Rosemary wouldn't play ball with me. She and I were always going mano a mano. You cannot run an exchange that way. I didn't start the chairmanship looking to get rid of her. She lived in my building at Gateway and would come up at night sometimes and we would have drinks. She told me about her upbringing, growing up in a cold-water flat. But she always seemed to think she had this supreme authority over the market that she did not have. I had Vinnie deliver the message to her in July. I trusted Vinnie and I think he realized she had to go. To this day, only two or three people know about the crossed telephone line."

When McFadden tendered her resignation hours later, most of the board assumed it was just another Nymex coup d'état. Considering the speed at which her predecessors had been pushed out, it had been a good run. "I was there for five years," says McFadden, who left at forty. "*That* is surviving." She was also tired of the Nymex politics. "You have to understand," says Rappaport, "petty spats like the one with the Lou Dobbs show weren't unusual for her and Lou Guttman. They were constantly digging up stuff on each other. It made the situation unworkable." Guttman was an elected official and McFadden was not, so it was understood she had to bow out.

McFadden's time at Nymex would be just a footnote in her career. Afterward, she made a habit of specializing in tough jobs, helping blue-chip companies on Wall Street expand into the former Soviet Union, the Middle East, and Asia, and working as a managing director for Credit Suisse. Even after retiring, she became deputy mayor of Jersey City, a post for which she accepted a salary of just $1 a year. The nation hasn't had a female exchange president since.

The Nymex directors argued until four A.M. over McFadden's resignation in a fourteen-hour marathon boardroom session, hammering out the terms of her severance pay. In the end, she received the usual consolation-prize consulting gig, and the media received the usual song and dance about how this wasn't another messy Nymex ouster but an amicable and orderly "reorganization." McFadden gamely backed the party line, denying that she had any rift with Guttman, although the press knew better. Privately, she had stronger words for the board. "I feel sorry for all of you," she told them before leaving. "I hope you stay in business. You have absolutely no idea what you are doing."

Guttman got a mysterious phone call after McFadden's departure. It was from a private number.

It was Michel Marks, who'd never initiated contact with him before.

"I heard about Rosemary," Marks said in his low, sonorous drawl. "And all I can say is that you're a better man than I."

7

The God Complex and
Other Minor Foibles

My attitude is, if I have two FBI agents on my floor,
so be it, stay there.

—ZOLTAN LOUIS GUTTMAN

FEMME FATALES WERE the least of Guttman's worries. The FBI was not just probing the Chicago trading floors and inquiring about business junkets to Russia. Now it was sending agents disguised as traders into the New York pits.

With oil prices sky-high in the 1970s, then diving into the single digits in the 1980s, commodities speculators were being demonized by the banks, the oil companies, Congress, and the press. "When prices are high, it's our fault. And when prices are low, it's our fault too," Rappaport says. "Never mind the wars and the recessions. I remember crude prices got so low there was even one restaurant in Houston that offered lunch at whatever the going price of a barrel of oil was that day. It would be like Nymex crude '$8.50.' They would post the price up on the wall."

In the pits, the traders were clueless as to the impact they were having on the world. Even as they unwittingly drew the planet's oil-producing nations and millions of energy consumers into their orbit, few of them paid attention to anything but the action on the floor. "No one down there fully understood the magnitude of what was going on," Guttman said. "Heck, I couldn't even get the directors to dress properly for a board meeting. The traders just saw an opportunity and went for it. It was very, very hard from the inside to see how we were affecting the great scheme of things. For a long time, we didn't even know the extent to which we'd gone global. But, look, we were the only game in town. There was no other place to go."

As always, the rumor mill on the trading floor was way ahead of the facts. Not that it meant the rumors weren't true. The pit traders had sussed out the infiltration of the FBI agents long before it was confirmed. They had a sixth sense about these things. They knew their kind—and at least two guys on the trading floor were decidedly *not* their kind. Robert Bruno first realized something was amiss when he felt wires under the clothing of a broker he'd shoved out of his way while leaving the crude pit one afternoon. His boss, Nymex board member Richard Saitta, brought it up with Guttman. Guttman, who was accustomed to alarmist chatter, took it with a grain of salt.

A few days later, a herd of Nymex traders suddenly recoiled when they found a second man with wires protruding from his trading jacket. The man narrowly escaped a mass drubbing. The traders, who barely trusted one another, began frisking each other in a floor-wide search for more spies and moles. As the witch hunt became more disruptive, Guttman put his foot down. "Whoever these spies are, they're getting in the way of trading in the oil ring. Nobody wants to stand near them. The whole floor is moving away, so you have these two guys standing there basically trying to do trades by themselves." He asked around and found out both men worked for Texas oil man and corporate raider Oscar Wyatt Jr.

Until being incarcerated in 2007 for sluicing kickbacks to Saddam Hussein's regime, Wyatt led a charmed life, running Coastal Corp., an oil company he sold to Texas competitor El Paso Corp. in 2001 for $24 billion, after repeatedly inflaming the U.S. Justice Department by inking foreign oil deals with countries like Libya. (About paying the Iraqi government for access to its lucrative oil deals after being sentenced to over a year in prison, Wyatt offered an extremely rare apology, blaming his actions on his personal politics. "My opinions in many ways probably caused me to skirt too close to the law. For that, I was wrong and for that, I am sorry.") A decorated World War II pilot at twenty-one, Wyatt got his start in the energy business working at a gas station. He spun off Coastal from an earlier enterprise, the ironically named Hardly Able Oil Company, which he financed in 1950 by mortgaging his Ford sedan.

Guttman wasn't sure what to do about having moles on the trading floor. He knew that sometimes big oil companies that ran afoul of the law were forced to cooperate in sting operations, but hadn't yet heard of spies infesting Coastal. His worry was that if he questioned the suspected agents, he might risk crossing the law himself. Once again, he decided to phone his outside counsel. Minutes later, he got a call back saying the U.S. attorney's office knew nothing about a Nymex sting and that he could proceed. Guttman rang Marianne Hughes, Coastal's representative on the board, and she cleared his inquiry. Monday afternoon, following the close, Guttman asked the two men to come to his office. He had their employer files sent over. All past work references for both men had led to dead ends. None of them checked out. Also, while both men purportedly came from opposite ends of the country, he noticed they had bank accounts at the *same* bank with sixteen-digit account numbers just one digit apart. Such things, in Guttman's experience, were not simply coincidences. Traders from the pits on the executive committee and senior staff filed in to watch the interrogation. At Nymex, everything was a spectator sport.

The first trader, who had a long ponytail and a single earring, became so emotional about being interrogated that some of the other traders began to think he was too much of a "whiny bitch" to be an FBI agent. "By the time he finishes his crying, everybody's convinced he and the other guy must not be with the FBI. We send them back to the trading floor," Guttman says. "Then we hear that Comex is dealing with a similar situation. They've hired someone in compliance who actually *recognizes* two of her former FBI colleagues on the floor and confirms that our suspects also are FBI agents."

When the truth finally came out, Guttman was on a business trip in Boca Raton with his new president, Patrick Thompson. "Pat gets on the phone and tells Marianne Hughes, 'You have to get those guys out of the ring, they're FBI agents! It's confirmed, they're FBI agents!' He gets off the phone and I say, 'What is going on?' He tells me. He says Comex is pulling its agents out of its ring and they are about to make a public statement about it and everything. I say, 'Are you fucking crazy? You're a lawyer! You call Marianne back and tell her to put our two guys back in the fucking ring! Ever hear of something called obstruction of justice? And what are you mixing in the Comex's business for? Not to mention, who ever heard of issuing a *press release* about it? Oh, wow, we booted two FBI agents from the floor, great thing!' So Pat calls Hughes and takes it all back."

After witnessing the brouhaha at Comex, the Nymex FBI agents decided to leave the Nymex floor of their own volition. They knew the pit traders wouldn't hesitate to deliver a much swifter kind of justice if they remained—one that would, more likely than not, involve a hospital bill.

Guttman did not know why the FBI had taken an interest in Nymex or Comex. Maybe it was just New York's turn, since the FBI was through with picking on Chicago. "There weren't just legal issues over whether our traders were walking the straight and narrow, but also what the oil companies were doing. Were they money-laundering? We don't know. There were all kinds of rumors. Maybe the New York Department of Justice was jealous of the Chicago Department of Justice and its midnight trading busts. They never tell you why they're going after you. They just go after you."

Guttman's legal pains in Boca did not go unpunished. In April 1991, a couple months after the scare, he received a subpoena from the Justice Department for obstruction of justice. "I handle my pressure fine, but I have to tell you, I went a little numb on this one. I said to my lawyer, 'Let me understand this. I don't get paid for *fucking sitting in this office* and now I'm going to be potentially brought up on criminal charges for obstruction of justice?'"

Guttman hired New York criminal lawyer Bernard Nussbaum. Nussbaum had been retained by the House Judiciary Committee back in the 1970s to impeach President Nixon and later became White House counsel under President Clinton. "Bernie glanced at the subpoena and said in his thick New York accent, 'Aw, don't worry about it, Lou. I'll take care of everything. Look here, they cited the wrong section of the code for obstruction of justice and everything. Don't you worry! We'll talk.'" Two weeks later, the charges were dropped, but Guttman was deeply shaken by even the fleeting prospect of going to jail for something he thought he'd gone out of his way *not* to do. "I should have taken it as a foreshadowing," he says. "The higher up you get, the more you come to realize that if the authorities really want to, they can indict a ham sandwich." A government official who later came to work for Nymex notes it was clear from the start that Guttman was under the gun. "If you are chairman, you've got to know that because you're in a high-profile position, people will be holding you up, looking to make an example of you and specifically trying to take you down. You're a lot easier to villainize. So was Lou targeted more than Joe Schmoe? Hell, yeah."

During his chairmanship, Guttman grew concerned enough about his villainization by both internal and external enemies to get his office scrubbed for wiretaps. "I was walking by Lou's office one day and there was someone inside combing the place," says a staffer who worked for Guttman. "I asked a coworker, 'What is going on?' And they said, 'Oh, it's nothing. Lou's just getting his monthly debugging.' I thought I was working for the oil market, not the CIA."

As Guttman dined with <u>Andre Suan, head of energy trading</u> at <u>Mobil</u> (which later merged with Exxon to become the multibillion-dollar oil conglomerate ExxonMobil), in a private room of Windows on the World, the luxe restaurant perched atop the north World Trade Center tower, the awkward subject of Guttman's salary came up. "As chairman of Nymex," Suan said, pouring the wine, "I would expect you are getting paid very well." Guttman almost choked on his Dover sole. "I said, 'Are you kidding me? I don't get paid at all.'"

Perhaps it was Guttman's willingness to work fourteen-hour days, six days a week, without salary, that won Suan over. Or perhaps it was the lasting friendship that slowly grew between the two men. But it also likely had to do with the fact that the oil companies and the banks were getting sick of pretending they weren't trading at Nymex when everyone knew they were there. Guttman wanted to globalize the exchange, but he knew he couldn't do it without the oil majors' stamp of approval. His relationship with Suan put an end to that impasse.

That night, Suan and the chairman of Mobil agreed to allow the oil company to become an exchange member, the first among the oil majors to do so. "It was huge. Mobil and Suan were enormous customers in our market and they had been trading under the radar for years," Guttman says. "Until then, no one wanted to be associated with the Nymex name. They didn't want to be blamed for trading there if oil prices got too high or too low. And they didn't want to be on our official membership list, lest anyone find out. That was the party line, anyway. I think they also put up so much of a fight because they did not like that *we* were pricing *their* oil. After Mobil joined, Texaco and a bunch of other oil companies did too. Then the rest of Wall Street followed." In a few years, Saudi Arabia's state-owned oil company, Saudi Aramco, the largest supplier of crude oil in the world, would be trading on Nymex. Even Henry Jarecki, who'd vowed he'd never trade there, changed his mind.

As chary as Wall Street was of the Nymex traders, no one felt like building an oil market from scratch to compete with them. Besides, for all anyone knew, oil would go back to being a dog market in another year or two.

White-knuckle politics, legal routs, and not getting paid were only some of the joys of being Nymex chairman. There was also the endless task of making the market bigger and better for its legions of ravenous traders who couldn't get enough of energy and were constantly demanding new and different combinations of products to bet on. In this respect, Guttman did not disappoint. By 1991, his natural-gas futures contract for delivery to Erath, Louisiana, had become the fastest-growing contract Nymex had ever seen. Even Michel Marks, who'd dropped by to see its launch on April 3, 1990, couldn't believe the magnitude of its success. As more than three thousand lots traded before his eyes, he confided to another local, "This is just a one-day phenomenon. This contract isn't going anywhere." The trader disagreed. Nymex seat prices were barreling toward $300,000 apiece, compared with their $50,000 price when Marks left back in 1987. Marks himself had predicted that the seats would one day be worth half a million. Actually, he would be wrong about that too. They would eventually be more than twenty times that amount.

Every year, the exchange was reporting record trading volumes, rising from 5 million contracts annually in 1987 to around 42 million under Guttman and gaining a steady following among commodities traders in the United Kingdom, Japan, Singapore, and the Middle East. Guttman's budget was now $20 million, compared with the measly $1 million Marks had had to work with. "It's true that Guttman was rough around the edges, but he was the best chairman we ever had," the trader says. "He would have been successful anywhere, in terms of his skill as a leader. I think maybe Marks, who was around the same age, might have been a little bit envious of that and regretful about having left. It was hard for him to accept that once he was gone, we didn't just fall apart. I think it was the reason why there was always so much tension between him and Lou."

Marks's feelings were understandable. During his first year as chairman, Guttman had been nothing more than one of the floor's anonymous minions.

Unbeknownst to any of them, the natural-gas market would become the $1,000 table at the energy casino, separating the men from the boys in creating overnight millionaires. The gas market attracted traders look-ing to get rich quick, because demand for gas often moved faster than available supply. A uniquely hard-to-handle substance, gas is compressed by about six hundred times into liquid for easy storage and shipping in large quantities. But because it's challenging to transport, facilities qualified to stockpile it are limited. As a result, when a sudden cold snap or demand surge occurs, gas shortages can strike quickly, driving the kind of rapid price changes that are the trader's bread and butter. For him, says ex-chairman Bill Bradt, the price changes came too swiftly. "I tiptoed into the natural-gas pit . . . and I tiptoed right out of there. The volatility is just too much, it's absolutely too much."

Guttman's natural-gas contract represented a much greater quantity of product than the oil contract, so trading it cost the traders much more money. Although they'd been warned about this before the launch, many of them forgot all about it in the excitement of opening day and traded it just like oil. "Shit, I lost $15,000 on gas," one of the traders confided in Guttman after the close. The clerk handed him his tally of the day's profits and losses. The trader did a double-take. "Correction. Make that $150,000!"

The riches of the natural-gas and power markets and the ease with which they could be won and lost would inspire Kenneth Lay to part-ner up with Jeff Skilling at Enron, which proceeded to make a fortune before bankrupting itself in 2001, bringing the fragile U.S. energy mar-ket to the brink. It also made the second career of T. Boone Pickens, the Dallas corporate raider–turned–hedge fund manager, and his second round of billions. And it allowed Enron's star gas trader, John Arnold, to become a self-made billionaire by the age of thirty-three, after founding a Houston hedge fund, Centaurus Energy Advisers, at just twenty-eight. Five years after starting his fund in 2002, Arnold became the youngest person on the Forbes Richest 400 Americans list, with an estimated net worth of $1.5 billion. By 2008, his wealth would jump to an estimated $2.5 billion, edging past $4 billion by 2010.

For his work, Guttman received his first bonus from the board in an eleven-to-seven vote. The sum, which came to $200,000, was less than what the other exchange chairmen were getting (in Chicago, Mahlmann received $240,000 a year while Melamed fetched $500,000) but more than the $8,000-a-month stipend Guttman had been subsisting off to cover the expenses of his high office. The old-guard board was still of the mind that a chairman should only serve altruistically and solely for the honor of the post. Being chairman was not supposed to be about the money but the power.

As trading volumes soared and Nymex outgrew its meager quadrant, Guttman hurriedly began laying the foundation for a new building that could contain the burgeoning oil market. "The floor traders couldn't fit in the World Trade Center anymore. It was a pigsty. Trading volumes were rising 15 to 20 percent a year. The traders were packed like sardines. It was much worse for us than it ever was for the Comex traders. We had five hundred to six hundred people crammed into 6,250 square feet of space. Once you accounted for everything else, it was about a foot a person. People were standing sideways just to fit in. There were more fistfights than ever. It was part of the reason why I insisted on a gym in the new building. The traders needed somewhere to get all their aggression out." Even the yellowcoats had run out of places to stand to record the prices. The not-so-popular solution was to construct spindly makeshift crow's nests one story off the trading floor, perching them on top.

Breaking away from the other commodities exchanges in the World Trade Center would be easier said than done. With all the money everyone was making, no one from any of the neighboring exchanges wanted to see Nymex go. The traders liked running back and forth among the different pits, working the price gaps between them. As some of the more reckless traders started to get into accidents outside work, Guttman arranged for life insurance, health insurance, and pension plans to be distributed to the floor traders. He also began the legal process of turning Nymex from a not-for-profit organization into a for-profit company. Then maybe he too could earn a normal paycheck.

The much-feared dry spell in the oil market would not come for a long time. The United States was on the verge of its first Persian Gulf War, which would see the CIA and National Security Agency setting up open lines to Guttman's rabbit hutch of an office, the same shrunken room Marks had labored in. Guttman received a seven-month warning before the United States declared war on Iraq. Economists around the world began to sound the alarm that wartime oil prices would surely top $100 a barrel. There was even talk that the oil market should be shut down to keep a price spike from happening. "Before the Gulf War came, the price of oil got up over $41," Guttman says. "And when the war actually started, it dropped more than $10 the very next day. If the exchange hadn't been open and somebody said the price of oil is fifty bucks, people would have paid fifty bucks. That was what we were there for. The biggest compliment I was ever paid came from Suan when he called me and said, 'My staff and I are sleeping well at night, because we know you aren't.' There was $3 billion in margin deposits representing the money people had down for trades in our market on the eve of the war. The Federal Reserve actually called *us* because they couldn't believe the massive amount of money coming in." Guttman received classified information and tips throughout the war from the U.S. Department of Energy. "We came in one morning and heard there were fires all over Kuwait. They called us and told us it was just a tanker that blew up. It was confidential but very useful in administering to the market."

The war attracted some of the energy market's biggest hedgers and hedge funds. Perhaps the simplest definition of hedging ever to make it to print comes from Ernest Hemingway's short story "Fifty Grand." In it, an aging champion boxer bets on his own opponent's victory in an upcoming match. The champion loses the fight and the prize money, but wins $50,000 on the bet. All in all, not a bad hedge. Traditionally, the purpose of hedging has been to guard against losses while boosting one's chances of making obscene amounts of money. But these days, what passes for a hedge fund is cryptic, often consisting of a large pool of rich people's money, run by soon-to-be-rich traders who get paid if they're wrong, paid *more* if they're right, and aren't hedged or don't know how to hedge. By contrast, the Nymex pit traders usually didn't make as much money as the hedge fund traders, because the money they won and lost was their own and they didn't get paid if they were wrong, unlike the hedge fund trader. Part of the reason why hedge funds are so profitable is because the traders are incentivized to risk their clients' money. If they win, they get richer, and if they lose, they aren't necessarily penalized for it. "The concept of hedging is not hard to understand," says McKiernan. "But there are lots of ways to make it complicated."

Some of the first hedge funds trading energy were Caxton Associates (founded by Bruce Kovner, an ex-cabbie); Tiger Management (run by former navy officer Julian Robertson), Moore Capital Management (started by the curmudgeonly Louis Bacon), and the Quantum Fund (run by George Soros, who, like Guttman, emigrated from Hungary). "The hedge funds and banks had been active in the energy market since before I joined the board," Guttman says. "We just didn't call them 'hedge funds' back then. We called them money managers. They were still engineering the whole hedge fund model, participating in active, liquid markets like gold, silver, soybeans, financial futures, and energy."

Banks trading energy at the time included Goldman Sachs, Morgan Stanley, and J.P. Morgan. While the hedge fund traders were engaged in hedging to make money for themselves and their investors, behemoth oil companies like Shell and Exxon—as well as the world's top oil-producing nations—were primarily engaged in hedging to protect themselves against unexpected price swings in the wet barrels they sold on the over-the-counter market. For them, the objective was to make a profit even when oil prices fell. In the dicey business of exploring and drilling for oil, managing price risk was paramount.

Guttman's successes did not change the fact he was working with embarrassingly limited resources. The Nymex offices were littered with scavenged furniture and its premises were slovenly. "I was interviewed by the exchange," recalls a former staffer. "I was excited about going to the World Trade Center to see the oil market, but when I saw the place, I couldn't believe it was real. The rooms were dirty and smelled like men's locker rooms. There were rats running down the hallways. I passed a doorway that looked like an open elevator shaft. It had boards nailed across it with a big sign that read KEEP OUT. Even after we got new offices years later, I would still sometimes go into the filing cabinets and find old rat droppings." Guttman expanded his office, knocking out a wall and putting in a couch for his visitors, but it wasn't much of an improvement. "We hadn't stopped being a not-for-profit organization," he says. "We hadn't really caught up to our own success yet." When he traveled, Guttman flew coach. "I was going down to Boca one year and Jon Arginteanu saw me walking past him in first class. He leaned back and said, 'Lou, what are you *doing* back there?' I said, 'Jon, I am saving you money.'" Arginteanu just shook his head.

Charging into the 1990s, their pockets bulging with cash, the Nymex traders acted almost intoxicated, bringing more drugs, weapons, and alcohol onto the trading floor, conducting business while inebriated and forming gangs that polarized the long-simmering turf wars of the exchange's Irish, Italian, and Jewish splinter groups. Off the floor, they were even more unruly. "Did you hear about the guy who got kicked out for doing dope while flying?" a Houston hedge fund trader who once worked at Nymex asked me. "I still remember seeing him on his last day before he went to jail. He was heading down south for a holiday with a couple of women, probably prostitutes. And he decided to freebase cocaine right on the plane. This was not a rented jet. We're talking about freebasing with *bent spoon and open flame* on a commercial airliner with, like, four hundred people on board. Of course, he was arrested as soon as they got to the tarmac. He had a good lawyer. He only did three years before he was back on the trading floor."

With no surveillance cameras anywhere in the pits and none to come for another fifteen years, the traders were free to collude with one another, sharing inside information about customers and trades in ways that allowed them to anticipate big price moves and profit off them. "Every last piece of information went through our floor," says one. "No one was safe. We didn't know just *some* of the big players. We knew *all* of the big players. We didn't know just *some* of what they were doing. We knew *all* of what they were doing. We often even knew *why* they were doing it, including, you know, when they were just fucking around with the prices. If a monster order was coming in from Goldman that might push prices up, we could get in front of that. You call that front-running. We'd profit off the price pop. You can also do it the other way when a large player sells. There are a million and one ways to play the market." Since time immemorial, another trader says, the rules of trading oil and fuel were made to be broken. "It's always been a flawed system and it always will be. No matter how they change it, there will always be ways to get around it. Not like Congress ever thinks about passing any rules that will actually fix anything."

Thimblerigging the market was such an accepted practice some traders were even taunted for *not stealing enough*. "In the pits, I remember they used to hold traders who stole *less* in contempt," says an executive who worked in Nymex's office of the president. "They used to say this one guy we all knew would miss the bank to pickpocket a toothbrush."

David Rousso, a heating-oil trader, told the same executive, "I know I'm in Disneyland. I'm just going to make the best of it while it lasts." Rousso never left Disneyland, even after being banned from trading for ten years by the CFTC. Now the sole proprietor of the exchange's Trading Places Concierge Service, he buys sports tickets, books events, and runs the dry cleaning for the other Nymex traders.

One of the chief problems was that the traders had their own personal trading accounts and, at the same time, managed their customers' accounts in a practice known as "dual trading." Originally justified as a way to build up healthy trading volumes between the traders and their customers back when Nymex didn't have much business, it had since gotten out of hand. "Obviously, this comes with all kinds of conflicts of interest. Yet somehow, Congress and the regulators still pretend it's not happening," says a trader. "Say I have a customer who wants to buy a hundred gasoline contracts. I buy them. Then, right after I do that, the price of gasoline goes up. Do I apply the contracts I just bought to my own account, knowing I can turn around and immediately sell them for a profit? Or do I give them to the customer, like I said I would? I could always give them to myself and buy more afterward for the customer at the higher price. The client doesn't know the difference. See what I mean? You have to be beyond impeccable in your principles to not give in to that temptation."

Back when Michel Marks ran his brokerage firm, he actually banned his staffers from dual trading. "Michel always had a lot of integrity like that," says one. "Rather than be banned, though, a lot of us quit."

After the market closed, many of the traders would continue trading on the seventh floor, just below the pits, but here they specialized in an entirely different type of precious commodity: drugs. According to those who frequented the "black-market drug den," untold quantities of cocaine, marijuana, and recreational pills, such as Quaaludes and MDMA, regularly exchanged hands. The traders threw in watches, cars, concert tickets, jewelry, and other sundries. They orchestrated elaborate sports bets. They also would call their booth clerks for a rate on an attractive female companion for the night. "You were dealing with a lot of people with a lot of extra money, so wherever there was a need, there was always a way to fulfill it," says Bill Perkins. "Everyone was trafficking in something. Everyone was a hustler."

Having exhausted all possibilities on the floor, the traders would organize unconventional games for the purpose of gambling and entertaining themselves. "One of our favorites was keeping track of how much money we spent on women before they'd sleep with us. We collected a lot of data. *A lot* of it. We included our mistresses, girlfriends, even one-night stands. And, of course, our wives. No one was spared. We took all that data and loaded it into an index of our own creation, like a stock index. Then we'd bet on where our future wives, mistresses, girlfriends, and one-night stands would fall within that framework. We called it the

CPFI—the Cost Per Fuck Index," says the trader who designed it while compiling other financial products, albeit less salacious, for clients on Wall Street. "Needless to say, the woman I married, had children with, and divorced scored very high on that particular index. In fact, I think she had the high score—and it's still rising." A few Nymex members got so caught up in the gaming, Perkins says, that they'd hardly ever trade. "I remember some of them would just sit in the cafeteria all day, playing backgammon. I even played backgammon with them sometimes. One guy, Old Bob, that's all he'd do."

Guttman did his best to contain the wilding, but found himself, like Marks, on terra incognita. He revamped Nymex's business-conduct committee and put together a regulatory-review task force of public governors to increase policing of the oil market. He also more than doubled the exchange's compliance budget. But the energy market's momentum easily outpaced any one man's ability to keep its populace in check while focusing on the broader duties of being chairman. "Our traders were not silver-spoon kids. I mean, I don't want to say it was a free-for-all, but it was not easy. We had hundreds of people from all kinds of backgrounds making unheard-of sums," Guttman says. "You do what you can do to keep everybody in line. I never got involved in the secondary or tertiary markets that sprang up around the trading floor. I did not join the drinking or the drugs crowd. I know there were members that went down to the Market Bar on the concourse at ten o'clock in the morning and came back at one in the afternoon, polluted. They would continue trading. They did well. Unfortunately, there were a lot of needs and issues that the traders had. There was even one guy who kept getting fined on his trading cards, because he didn't turn them in fast enough. He wrote them up too slowly. He brought in a letter from his neurologist that said he was dyslexic. About 90 percent of the board said, 'Fuck him.' I said, 'What about the Americans with Disabilities Act? Didn't that just pass Congress?' All of a sudden, a board member who had been silent raises his hand and says, 'I have dyslexia and it's tough.' Well, why didn't he say that before? What, we're picking on dyslexic traders now? I can't tell you how many times I had to embarrass the board into humanity."

Guttman closely guarded his privacy, but on his birthday, he received a knock at his door in Gateway Plaza. "I open it and a bunch of people from Nymex burst in. They bring booze and coke and women. They're like, 'Want a toke?'—meaning the cocaine. I say no. Then they all go into my bedroom. The door stays shut for four hours. I don't know what happened in there, but I sent the maid in the next day. I did not do the coke. My biggest vice was women and, uh . . . women."

As the trading strategies on the floor rapidly evolved, a handful of speculators began exhibiting distinct signs of genius. One of them was Robert Halper, an unassuming booth clerk who traded his way through the energy complex during the first Gulf War. A soft-spoken, understated man who always wore a plain shirt and khakis to work and avoided flashy status symbols, Halper drew a crowd of gawping onlookers whenever he stepped into the pits. His mind was like a steel trap. He never bragged or complained about wins or losses. He exemplified the trader cliché of having ice in his veins. He refrained from the rabble-rousing of the pits. And sometimes, he traded over ten thousand contracts a day. "Bobby was the best spread trader we'd ever seen, hands down," says one trader who knew him. "He was a human calculator, a machine. He was always twenty steps ahead of everybody else. He wasn't loud or pushy, like a lot of us. He was one of the few guys down there who was both successful *and* honest. He would put multiple legs of these intricate trades together and we'd just stop and stare, like, what's he doing *now?* He'd have it already worked out in his head. Then he'd set the whole thing off like clockwork. It was breathtaking. Like a Roman candle going up. His mind wasn't three-dimensional, it was *five*-dimensional. He left the trading floor to go to medical school, but eventually came back. I guess medicine wasn't as exciting as the pits. Whatever he did, he did it well and he made a hell of a lot of money at it."

Guttman held his business partner, Magid, five years his junior, in similar esteem. One of Magid's widely acknowledged talents was that he didn't require a computer, as most traders did, to calculate the theoretical values of his options trades. Sometimes, he even went so far as to boast to the other traders that his valuations were *superior* to those given by a computer. "He was an options junkie," Guttman says, "but an extremely consistent one. He never had abrupt drawdowns in his trading accounts, no big losses. He had lots of followers and held court in the pits every day. But after a while, he started liking the smell of his own bullshit."

As everyone at Nymex knew, a trader who became too successful ran the risk of getting a God complex. And once you got it, it was only a matter of time before you were met with a harsh comeuppance. As the pit traders began taking more risks in the oil market and leaning more heavily on credit instead of cash, Guttman saw a gradual change come over Magid. "When he was trading with his own money, he was very careful, very prudent. But when he started trading with other people's money, he got foolish."

In the winter of 1990, Magid pulled Guttman out of a board meeting in a panic. Magid's trades had fallen off a cliff. He'd miscalculated. They were looking at a potential debt of $7.5 million. Guttman was speechless. Options were generally a trading instrument used to control losses, not magnify them. Still, even conservative option trades, when mishandled, could go horribly awry. Magid's trades were no longer as conservative as they used to be. In this case, he had taken long positions on tens of thousands of options contracts representing more than 30 percent of the market in not oil but *sugar,* outstripping the holdings of even the largest trading houses. He'd executed his trades at the Coffee, Sugar & Cocoa Exchange, a market separate from Nymex but also based at the World Trade Center. "Magid was telling me that my net worth was being wiped out even as we spoke and we were *still* stuck in these bets. I was in a trauma. My biggest fear wasn't just going to zero. It was our going *well below* zero. With options, you can end up owing millions. If that happened, I knew that'd be it for me. I'd become an indentured servant. It was all our money. There was no bottom. And we had more to lose." Guttman returned to the board meeting looking like he'd seen a ghost. He'd scheduled a photo shoot that afternoon at the World Trade Center's Vista Hotel for the cover of the glossy Nymex annual report. He did his best to smile. "Needless to say, that shoot was not very pleasant."

Magid's trades were on high-risk, deep-in-the-money sugar options that required extensive financing, which meant that he and Guttman could end up in debt up to their eyeballs. Guttman insisted that Magid exit the trades immediately. Magid was not so enthusiastic. He'd hoped his trades would still make him and Guttman a fortune. In trader parlance, he was "wedded" to his bets. He'd already held on for so long, sacrificing his sanity and his bottom line—what if the trades finally made a comeback? "It was a bad situation," says a trader who worked with both Magid and Guttman. "You had these two people, Magid, the guy who supposedly knew everything and would never ever admit to being wrong, and Guttman, the guy who was never around and didn't understand a thing we were doing, but wouldn't admit it either. He was totally clueless as to the kind of trading that was going on in his name."

Guttman, on the hook to share in the gains or losses, fifty-fifty, had another reason for being furious. In mid-April 1989, he and Magid had agreed to wind down their business partnership after repeat arguments and scuffles. Guttman had allowed Magid to continue sharing his office as they disentangled their financial affairs, but the situation had dragged on for nearly two years. Realizing Magid might need many more months to get out of his complicated bets without losing huge chunks of their initial investment, Guttman agreed to a gradual liquidation of their shared accounts. He would have transferred his ownership if he could have, but U.S. trading rules wouldn't allow it. The only way to get out was to sell, and what Magid wanted to sell nobody was buying.

Making matters worse, Magid wanted to see his trades through to the end. They were at loggerheads. "Magid went to pieces. He was in a near-catatonic state. I hit the roof. My priorities were to contain the potential loss and liquidate our accounts. I didn't care anymore if we got paid or not. I just wanted to keep us from being exposed to more financial hell. I was going on pure adrenaline. Magid's dad came in from Long Island to make sure he didn't crack up. I was scared. I kept asking him every day, 'Are you still liquidating?' We met with Phibro to see if they would take it. They said no. I didn't know how to trade myself out of this stuff. It was like dealing with the toxic assets of the banking crisis. It takes the asshole who got you into the mess to get you out of it."

It took Magid three months to sell off the options contracts. He finally exited the positions at a loss of $500,000, a testament to his trading skills. Losing hundreds of thousands of dollars hurt, but it was a pain Guttman could live with. Anything was better than blowing through more than $7 million in just a few days. "Considering what we were up against," he says, "it was a gift from the gods."

Magid's downward spiral had begun when his sugar trades soured, racking up such astounding losses that even his clearing firm, Gerald Inc., told him it couldn't afford to cover them anymore. Gerald backed Magid's trades for as long as it could, agreeing to extend him $3 million in credit on top of an existing $2 million credit line, but had maxed out. In the past, Magid had found other ways to cover up the gaping holes in his accounts by arranging to have another Nymex trader shoulder the burden for a few days. Between March 31, 1989, and October 2, 1989, that trader was Gary Glass, who periodically bought Magid's trades in sugar options and held on to them before passing them back to Magid, at cost. They did this through trades the pit traders called strangles.* It was, more or less, a game of hot potato to conceal the magnitude of what Magid owed so he could keep trading. Glass was simply providing a service that Gerald could not. To the traders, it seemed harmless. Unfortunately, the CFTC did not agree. It accused Magid and Glass of muddying up the market with "non–bona fide" transactions, tainting otherwise competitive prices with what it deemed to be "fictitious," "wash," and "accommodation" trades. (Enron and Refco would be accused of similar cloak-and-dagger money-shuffling schemes in later years, only they would engage in trickery on a much grander scale before losses gutted them both.)

The CFTC's view was that these types of prearranged, anticompetitive trades weren't driven so much by the profit motive (read: the good kind of greed) as by the faulty instinct of an insolvent trader to undeservedly survive (read: the bad kind of greed). Prearranged trades were illegal because they did not involve the taking of any risk. And anyone who was anyone on Wall Street knew that taking risk was what you got paid for. Even when your bets went south on other people's money, you still got paid for going through all the stress. It was a little-known and underappreciated fact that it was hard work losing other people's money.

The Magid-Glass trades were technically a victimless crime, as they didn't involve stealing from anyone or ripping anyone off. All of which made it the regulatory equivalent of getting a ticket for driving five miles an hour over the speed limit. But for the CFTC, that was a major bust.

In the chairman's office, just off the trading floor, Guttman knew he and Magid were facing the occasional financing problem with their trades at certain times of the month. He was not, however, aware of the extent of Magid's trading schemes with Glass. "I wasn't watching him the way I should have. I was out of the country so much," Guttman says. "It was the mistake of my life. If I'd been getting paid by Nymex during my chairmanship, it might not have happened. I probably wouldn't have had to juggle running a market while trying to run

---

* A strangle is an option that lets a trader profit more off price *moves* than price *direction*.

a business. Until the shit hit the fan, I stand before you swearing I did not know he was doing it."

This also was unfortunate, since the CFTC was rather more partial to the juicier story line of a Nymex chairman cavalierly rubber-stamping the illicit trades of his business partner, even if neither of them had made any money off it. A little detail like that could really give teeth to something like a toothless parking ticket.

Once Magid had finished liquidating the toxic accounts in June 1990, he and Guttman were happy to part ways, but they did not part happily. Guttman had been repressing anger over having been forced into a financial quandary. Magid, likewise, was incensed at Guttman for forcing him to close out his trades while flying around the world playing chairman. (In the office of Harley Futures, a favorite joke among the traders was, "Where's Lou?"—"Lou who?") In the final days, the two men hurtled toward their bad ending. "I'd been kissing Magid's ass for months because I needed him to finish liquidating the accounts. I could tell that the danger had passed as soon as he stopped freaking out and began dishing out the attitude. I'd ask him a question, and, instead of getting a straight answer, I'd get a load of shit. Suddenly, Magid's virility had returned. 'You keep asking me if I've liquidated the accounts,' he shot back one day. 'Go fuck yourself!'

"I said, 'This is my office. *You go fuck yourself!*' "

At Nymex, there was no such thing as the clean breakup.

Yet Guttman was not that broken up. In the calm before the storm that would descend on him in July 1992, in the brief sliver of time after Magid's liquidation and before the CFTC's looming götterdämmerung, Guttman was thankful for his gift from the gods. Unaware of the calamity about to befall him, he felt nothing but grateful for having escaped yet another scrape. He did not yet know the hazards to which Magid and Glass had inadvertently exposed him.

And he did not yet know that someone, somewhere, had already dropped the dime.

8

The Futility of the Polygraph

Energy trading. It's a whore's game.

—ZOLTAN LOUIS GUTTMAN

LONG AFTER HE was jettisoned from Nymex and barred from ever trading there again, Guttman's name was heard up and down its halls. It continued to be on the lips of its traders and chairmen. Yet almost nobody ever saw him. He no longer liked to circulate. He didn't feel comfortable being out in the open anymore. Still, his influence was felt everywhere as he worked diligently behind the scenes, exerting considerable sway over the oil market and its rotating cast of extraordinary characters.

I'd wasted a good deal of time trying to find Guttman, but long before I ever started writing about Nymex, he had become the invisible man. It wasn't easy to find him if he didn't want to find you. I got a break one morning when a senior oil reporter took pity on me and tossed Guttman's home phone number across the news desk. "Try *this*," she said in a tone suggestive of a dare. "What's the worst that could happen? He hangs up on you?"

I dialed. It was a Manhattan landline. Guttman picked up on the second ring.

"Hello?" he said gruffly. He didn't speak, he projected.

I heard the unmistakable trader's rasp at the back of his throat. At least I knew I had the right place.

I introduced myself, launching into my well-rehearsed Nymex

Trader Spiel, which, to the untrained ear, is nauseating. With most people, you need only be polite and gently inquisitive when cold-calling them. But with the Nymex trader, that had little currency. Nymex traders were more responsive if you skipped the platitudes and went straight to the shameless ego-stroking.

To my surprise, Guttman was having none of it. He regarded my blandishments as if I were talking about somebody else. They had absolutely no effect on him. He didn't care what I thought, or what anyone else thought, for that matter. Before getting rid of me, he was distracted by another caller. "Hold!" he said, picking up the other line without bothering to hit mute. (Such openness was a hallmark of the Nymex trader, a species accustomed to handling calls by the dozen. To the pit trader, a phone was not a personal communication device but exclusively an instrument of commerce.) I heard a thin, male voice mewling distantly over the other line at Guttman. He listened for a few moments, then cut the caller short. "Get off my phone," he hissed. "You are a pest, and I don't need pests!" Less distantly, I heard the receiver slam and Guttman clearing his throat before coming back to me. "*Yes?*"

Fear erased my memory of the rest of that call. I found Guttman extremely intimidating. It wasn't hard to see how he'd clawed his way to the top in a market where claws, even on the secretaries, were mandatory. It took a while before he let his guard down long enough to talk to me frankly. Setting up interviews with him, given his preference for invisibility, also was challenging. A creature of habit, Guttman preferred to meet outside his usual stomping grounds. For years, we convened at dive bars, greasy spoons, parking lots, and other neglected corners of Manhattan. He would dress in sneakers, jeans, a sweatshirt, and a baseball cap, pacing the pavement and chain-smoking Capri Menthol Ultra Lites while parsing his war stories like rare coins. Tall, with ice-blue eyes that could go from kind to fierce in a heartbeat, he was still every bit the power broker the *Wall Street Journal* once described as "colorful, combative and controversial." He spoke without hesitancy and with a complete lack of concern for the impression made on the listener. He believed in letting the chips fall where they may. He had little interest in conversational delicacies and he didn't mind answering direct questions, so long as you didn't mind the direct answers. He was a gentleman by nature and a bone-crusher by necessity. A deeply closeted optimist, he reserved his greatest ire for those who had laid ruin to his ideals.

July 4, 1992, marked the turning point in his chairmanship. Over the holiday, Guttman's lawyer, Barry Bohrer of Morvillo, Abramowitz, Grand, Iason & Silberberg, received notice from the CFTC of its plans to file a regulatory complaint against Guttman in connection with the Magid-Glass trades of 1989. Until then, Guttman had believed that the agency was only going after Gerald, the clearing firm to which he'd introduced Magid some years earlier, after questions came up over Gerald's labyrinthine financial affairs. He'd believed he and Magid were just bit players in the wider probe. He also was under the impression that the worst of the damage from the investigation had already been done, as the CFTC had interrogated roughly forty traders with whom he and Magid had done business. "The regulators sent *subpoenas* to these guys, which scared the living daylights out of them," Guttman says. "No one knew exactly what the CFTC was supposed to be inquiring about. The CFTC only talked to each trader for about fifteen minutes and asked vague questions. It looked like a fishing expedition. That said, fifteen minutes was long enough for them to impress upon the traders that Lou Guttman was on their hit list, and let me tell you, once that gets started, it doesn't stop. It doesn't matter if you're innocent or not. You're tainted. They're going after you? They'll ruin you. There's an instant chilling effect. It undercut my chairmanship. It destroyed my authority on the board."

Guttman was repeatedly deposed that winter in connection with Gerald. During each encounter, a CFTC investigator and staffer worked on him as a team. "You walk into the offices of the CFTC at the World Trade Center with the American flag on it and the deposers and stenographers and, trust me, you're having a heart attack. They question you and it's a long, wearing-down process. Slow and repetitive and it takes all day."

The CFTC staffers wanted to know the nature and timing of Guttman's knowledge of the Magid-Glass trades. "They put printouts of the trades in front of me and said, 'What's this here?' and 'What's that there?' I did not know. It was indecipherable. I'd never traded options. I didn't know what I was looking at. I did have access to Magid's trading records for accounting purposes, but only Magid understood his actual strategies. He hadn't told me he was trading with Glass or doing these strangle trades or any of it. This was the first I'd heard about Glass being involved. I went nuts. I wasn't allowed to speak to Magid or Glass or anyone at Gerald, because we were all mid-interrogation. Each time

I returned, the first thing the CFTC investigator would ask me was, 'Have you spoken with anyone?' I'd always say no."

Guttman answered each question, assuming that would be the end of it. He had no useful information. He'd severed his relationship with Magid in the spring of 1989, which he also explained to the CFTC investigators. Magid, he said, had independently executed the strangle trades without his knowledge during a time frame in which he had been in Washington or out of the country more than 75 percent of the time. But the CFTC, a government agency whose reputation among government agencies was as rotten as Nymex's had once been among the U.S. exchanges, was not about to let Guttman go so easily.

In correspondence with Bohrer, the CFTC said it planned to charge Guttman not only with controlling Magid's actions at the time of the strangle trades with Glass, but also with being secondarily responsible for *all* the offending Magid-Glass trades, despite his lack of knowledge of them. The charges could be justified, it said, by the fact that Guttman had been Magid's business partner for at least part of the year in which the illicit trades had taken place and that Magid was still in the process of unwinding some of Guttman's cash from the toxic trading accounts at that time.

The only good news about the CFTC's notice to Guttman was that, before the agency could formally file charges against him, it would have to at least consider a written defense from him that could thwart the charges altogether. The bad news was that by contesting the allegations, Guttman would give the agency a blueprint of his defense strategy that could be used by its prosecution to try and nail him. "We decided to go ahead with the defense submission anyway, because I knew I was innocent and the facts were on my side," Guttman says. "My lawyer thought if we just made a strong case, we would hopefully avoid a lengthy legal battle." However, in the interim, deflecting any damage to Guttman's reputation would turn out to be impossible. In a nasty breach of protocol, the CFTC leaked word of the charges to be filed against Guttman to the press. The slip-up, which went curiously unexplained and unpunished, stripped Guttman of his rightful legal protections. Keeping the charges private until they were officially filed was considered key to shielding a defendant from public, irreparable harm in the event that he was innocent. In Guttman's case, he heard about the CFTC's allegations only *after* the press found out about them. When a journalist called making inquiries over the Fourth of July weekend, the Nymex press office immediately alerted him. "I rang Bohrer and asked, 'Is it true?' He said, 'Yeah, we just got it, but I didn't want to destroy your holiday.'"

The situation quickly snowballed. The CFTC gave Guttman several weeks to respond to its notice. Hit by a barrage of newspaper headlines, Guttman had no choice but to take a leave of absence from the oil market to put together his legal defense. He did not resign. In a letter to the pit traders, he wrote: "Recent press accounts regarding me have served as a distraction to this exchange. I emphatically deny any suggestions of wrongdoing on my part. However, because a purportedly non-public civil administrative proceeding has been made public, I must now devote my attention to personal matters entirely unrelated to the business of this exchange."

While Guttman had certainly been railroaded out of the executive suite, some of the traders wondered if he hadn't known more than he was letting on, or simply played too fast and loose with the market's gray areas. "Back then, gray areas were everywhere," says Glass. "And if you weren't careful, they were like quicksand." Danny Rappaport, who had become Guttman's vice chairman, took over as acting chairman.

"The press," Guttman says, sighing. "They build you up just to tear you down. My parents saw the news and they didn't know what to think. My mother was very upset. Had I robbed somebody? Was I going to jail? In the Jewish community, if you steal someone else's money, that's it, your name is blackened forever. Look at Bernie Madoff. A hundred years from now, his name among the Jews will still be synonymous with disgrace. Nobody understood what I was being accused of. So they assumed the worst. I tried to explain to my mother that no, I hadn't stolen any money, that the regulators were coming after me with this ginned-up legal concept. My father hadn't even told anybody in our neighborhood about his son being chairman of the oil market. He didn't think it was something to brag about. In his mind, it wasn't a job a nice Jewish boy did for a living. When the headlines hit and my parents were swamped with questions from friends and family, it hurt them real bad."

Guttman resolutely maintained his innocence in the defense he filed with the CFTC. "I ask you in all fairness not to increase the damage by charging me under doubtful and strained theories," he wrote in his letter to the agency. He and Bohrer hadn't been permitted to actually see the proposed complaint or any witness testimonies. Twenty-two pages of Guttman's sixty-page defense came from a man named Jerry Markham, associate professor of law at the University of North Carolina at Chapel Hill and author of two heavy-duty tomes on commodities regulation. He was also former chief counsel of the CFTC's enforcement division, the division that was now going after Guttman. "The division does not contend Mr. Guttman instigated, executed, or directly participated in these transactions or that he aided and abetted the violations," Markham wrote. "Instead, the division is recommending that Mr. Guttman be charged with secondary liability. . . . Such claims are wholly unprecedented and I do not believe that they can be sustained."

Along with the legal materials sent by Bohrer, Guttman took a voluntary polygraph test and included the results in his defense filing. The test was proctored by renowned expert forensic polygraphist Natale Laurendi. Hired as a criminal investigator for the New York Police Department in 1951, Laurendi went on to work as Manhattan district attorney Frank Hogan's "star lie detector," according to Laurendi's 1999 obituary in the *New York Times*. Hogan himself earned the nickname "Mr. Integrity" during his tenure as district attorney. Laurendi, at the behest of Robert Kennedy, testified before the Senate on racketeering in the Teamsters Union and even provided his services during the robbery trial of Patricia Hearst in San Francisco in 1976. Most important, he was one of the only lie detectors in the nation at the time whose findings were recognized by the U.S. court system. Guttman hoped that Laurendi's résumé would give credence to the results of his polygraph, persuading the CFTC to not file the charges against him. "Let me tell you," Guttman says, "taking a polygraph test is not a comfortable thing."

His session with Laurendi consisted of three central questions:

Laurendi: Did you know that Harold Magid was engaging in prearranged, noncompetitive trades during the period in question?
Guttman: No.
Laurendi: Did you ever have a discussion with Harold Magid and/or anyone else in which it was decided that Harold Magid would approach Gary Glass in order to conduct prearranged, noncompetitive trades?
Guttman: No.
Laurendi: Did you and Harold Magid agree in mid-April to terminate your partnership at the end of April 1989?
Guttman: Yes.

After unhooking Guttman's hands, arms, and chest from the wires attached to the polygraph machine, which resembled an electric chair without the headpiece, Laurendi made the following notation in his report and signed it: "Analysis of the psychological responses to the above pertinent test questions reveals no deception indicated. Based upon the material supplied, a pre-polygraph test interview and analysis of the physiological responses to the above pertinent test questions, it is my professional opinion that Mr. Guttman was not attempting deception and his answers were truthful." In his accompanying letter to the CFTC, Guttman said that while he believed Laurendi's questions specifically got to the heart of the matter, he would "gladly submit" to a second polygraph test of the CFTC's design at a time and place of its choosing.

Guttman's defense hit the mark, or at least seemed to. The CFTC held its silence for several months. Summer passed, then autumn. No advances came to the case. By December, Guttman, believing he was in the clear, approached the Nymex board with Bohrer and asked for permission to resume his chairmanship. Anthony George Gero stepped up to back Guttman first. The board voted ten to five in his favor, but he didn't exactly receive a hero's welcome. Since July 31, the day he took leave, the directors had been actively jousting over who was going to replace him. The next election for chairman was coming in March, and Rappaport had already begun campaigning for votes in the pits. Guttman's reentry to the fray meant that this would be a dogfight. "I remember coming in the first day I was back and one of the guys saying, 'You can't come back now. You *left.*' I said, 'Oh yeah? Watch me.'"

The CFTC had Guttman problems of its own by early 1993. It was in the middle of its changing of the guard from a Republican administration to a Democratic one with the departure of President George H. W. Bush and the inauguration of Bill Clinton. Yet the Guttman case was straggling into its fifth year. It had become a bit of an embarrassment. High-level staffers at the CFTC began to indicate to Guttman that their chairwoman, Dr. Wendy Gramm, did not find the evidence against him compelling and was inclined to let his case sink into the already considerable agency quagmire. Gramm, the Hawaiian-Korean wife of Senator Phil Gramm (R-Texas), had been running the CFTC since Ronald Reagan had appointed her its head in 1988. "Wendy did not want to bring the case, and, while she was there, she did not let it proceed any further. She thought the commission had better things to do," Guttman says. Except for bumping into Gramm a few times at business conferences in Washington and a few formal meetings, he had hardly ever talked to her. "Wendy did not want to get her fingerprints on either throwing out or pursuing the complaint against Guttman," says an ex–CFTC official. "She was just going to let it wither on the vine."

But as soon as Clinton took office in 1993, the partisan footwork commenced. The political climate swerved decidedly leftward. The facts of the Guttman case hadn't changed, but the incumbent political party had. Out of nowhere in February, the CFTC slammed Guttman, Magid, Glass, and Gerald with a formal seven-count complaint alleging various fraudulent trading practices. More headlines filled the newspapers. Just as Guttman was beginning to relax again, the salvo left him reeling. It was the first time the chairman of any major commodity market had been accused of violating the commodities laws. It was a death knell for his chairmanship and his career. He couldn't afford to be finished at forty-two, but neither could he go on as the hobbled chairman of the global oil market. In a surprising display of his trademark stubbornness, Guttman announced he would run for reelection as chairman. If he was going down, he wasn't going to go down without a fight. Seeing blood on the water, the Nymex board members moved in for the kill. "Everybody knew I was running, but there is no way I am going to win. The board asks for my resignation. I decline. Then they try to overrule me by a vote, but they can't get enough votes to suspend me."

Mitchell Steinhause, one of the newest members of the board and ordinarily not one to speak up, spoke up now. "This is ridiculous," he blurted out. "Why are we doing this? He's out of here in twenty-five days!" The Nymex press office was becoming extremely nervous about how all the internal brawling might look to the outside world. Its nervousness hit fever pitch when the board asked it to issue a press release describing the faceoff with Guttman in excruciating detail. "I was *so* embarrassed," says one staff member. "I begged them not to do it. What kind of reputable organization puts out a press release announcing that the board has asked the chairman to resign—and he *refused*?"

The Nymex directors ignored all objections. They wanted to officially be on the record as having attempted to throw Guttman out, even if they'd failed to do so. The press release was duly released, to the media's mirth and bemusement.

A week and a half later, a much more violent event rocked the exchange: the worst attack up to that time on U.S. soil, with Nymex at the center of the chaos. At midday on February 26, 1993, a 1,200-pound car bomb made of urea nitrate hydrogen exploded in the underground garage of the Vista Hotel. The aim had been to knock the north World Trade Center tower into the South Tower, bringing down both. The terrorist attack did not go as planned, but as the explosives detonated, the trading pits shook. The Nymex traders paused, looked at one another in astonishment, and then kept on trading. News reports claimed the noise had come from a malfunctioning gas generator in a nearby building. That sounded sensible to the Nymex traders. But the vice president of trading floor operations, Les Faison, recognized the sound as soon as he heard it. He was a Vietnam War vet. "It sounded to me like a mortar, a bomb." An hour later, smoke began filling the lower floors beneath the trading pits. Hearing fresh rumors that a transformer had exploded, Guttman called the local power company, Consolidated Edison, to see what was going on, but was told nothing was awry. Deeply unsettled, he announced to the traders that trading would close early, at one forty-five P.M. The traders were not happy. The building's landlord, Port Authority, assured Guttman he would receive timely dispatches in the event of an emergency and an hour's notice if the power was to be shut off. Guttman never heard back.

Around one P.M., the traders' wives began calling the pits. They were watching the news on television and saw smoke pouring out of the building. Was there a reason why the traders were still in there trading? Guttman rushed down the fire exit to take a look. On the third floor, he hit a wall of smoke. It was one fifteen. He rushed back to the pits, shouting to the traders that the market would close in a couple of minutes. The traders exploded. Hundreds of them were desperately trying to get out of their open positions in gasoline and heating-oil futures contracts that were expiring that day. "Cocksuckers!" one raged. "Make up your fucking minds!" At one thirty, trading abruptly halted.

At one thirty-one, without warning, the lights flickered out, plunging the traders into a sea of blackness. There were no windows and no natural light in the pits. The traders fumbled in the dark as they made their way down to street level. The smokers led the way, using their Bic pocket lighters to illuminate the stairwells. Six people died in the attack on the World Trade Center that city officials refused to acknowledge for hours, even as workers remained inside. "It wasn't until after three P.M. that they said it was a bomb," Guttman says.

Over a thousand more people were injured. More than fifty thousand workers were evacuated in all, many of them forced to walk down more than a hundred flights of stairs unable to see where they were going. Across the street from Nymex, an irate mob of traders gathered. Trades in progress had been left in the lurch, pit cards strewn on the floor. The last five to ten minutes of trades hadn't even been recorded. Rappaport, tipped to become the next chairman, was on vacation with his family in Key Biscayne, Florida. The mayor of New York, David Dinkins, was on a business trip in Tokyo. "No one could agree on what to do," Guttman says. "The board members were talking over one another. No one said boo to me. Who was I? Just the wounded chairman of Nymex."

An idea was floated that the traders should be cashed out automatically at whatever the going price was at the time of the market's emergency close. That did not go over well with the angry mob. The traders began hollering again. "C'mon!" Guttman said. "Does someone want to call Marianne Hughes at Coastal and ask her if she wants to do that? I doubt it."

Greg Boyd, a director and a Marine Corps graduate whose younger sister, Madeline, traded gasoline futures that were about to expire, whirled on him. He and Guttman had always been quick to get in each other's faces.

"Fine, if you're so smart, what do *you* think we should do then?" he said.

"Today is Friday," Guttman said. "We get the exchange reopened immediately. We move the expiration date to Monday."

"Wait," another director interjected. *"We can do that?"*

Moving expiration was like usurping the power of the gods.

"Yes," Guttman said. "We invoke emergency powers."

No one objected. Nobody had thought of that.

Guttman didn't get off the phone all weekend. He called Dinkins first. He knew Dinkins from when he'd brought him down to the trading floor to ring the opening bell back when he'd launched the natural-gas market. Dinkins was flying back to New York and no sooner arrived at the crumbling site of the terrorist attack than Guttman had him buttonholed on the corner of a blocked street. He pressed the mayor to give the all-clear for the traders to return to the bombed-out World Trade Center pits on Monday. Dinkins resisted. He said it was too risky. The building's electricity was back up, but not the alarm systems, air-conditioning, or plumbing. Guttman kept pushing. He promised to pay for off-duty firemen and security personnel to patrol the building's premises. He arranged for portable air-conditioners and trucks to pump pressure temporarily back into the water-supply system. And he made the ultimate concession, agreeing to a reduced, three-hour trading day. He had the Nymex trading software rewritten to delay expiration and data entry from Friday's unfinished trading session pieced back together to make sense. Computer hardware also had to be reconfigured. Guttman even found a moving contractor crazy enough to send fifteen burly men up several flights of stairs in the World Trade Center lugging eight-hundred-pound air-conditioning systems into the trading pits, just in case the elevators remained jammed (they didn't). Dinkins, realizing that reopening the market so quickly would make him look good, finally relented. By noon Sunday, Guttman had pulled it off. He scheduled a board meeting that afternoon to approve all the contingency measures. That's when Rappaport flew back from Key Biscayne. Guttman didn't hide his irritation at the delayed response. He couldn't understand why the bombing of one's place of business by terrorists wasn't a fantastic reason to cut short one's vacation.

Guttman walked into the meeting. Nine days after asking for his resignation, the board rose—and gave him a standing ovation. "Lou made a lot of enemies, because he got things done and never stopped to worry about what anybody else thought," says a long-standing member of the Nymex executive staff. "But he was the right man at the right time for the job."

When the market reopened on Monday, Guttman made national headlines yet again, refueling the debate over who would win the chairmanship. Steven Karvellas, a veteran pit trader, told the *Journal*, "In a crisis, nobody is better than Lou."

The praise felt good, but Guttman knew it wouldn't change a thing. "Whatever, my goose was cooked."

AS GUTTMAN FOUGHT for survival, thirty-two-year-old Mark Fisher was just hitting his stride. It hadn't been easy for him when he first arrived at the pits, but not for the usual reasons. His problem had been that he'd become too successful too fast. The other traders weren't buying it. "In the beginning, Mark was totally hated," an older colleague says, "because he was constantly making the correct calls on the market. No one could make sense of that. How could this kid be so right so often? How could he just come down to the floor and start buying, and, nine times out of ten, a ton of hedge funds and banks would suddenly show up and start buying too? People thought he had it rigged. Mark would make a pile of money and then the traders would accuse him of colluding. He kept insisting that he just knew all the formulas the Wall Street players were using."

David Greenberg, son of the former Comex chairman Marty Greenberg, had been tiptoeing into the metals market for weeks, trying to get his nerve up to do more than a five-lot trade. Just as he threw down his first trade ever for ten lots of gold, Fisher strode into the pit and killed it. "I bought ten contracts, the biggest bet I'd done yet, and I was feeling pretty good about it when Mark just shows up three minutes before the close and *sells* four hundred lots, which crushes the price on me. I am like, *what the hell?* Then one of the other traders says, 'Mark found out that Paul Tudor Jones was selling three thousand lots of gold at the close, so he got in front of it.'" Fisher and Jones, the famed billionaire hedge fund manager who once traded at the New York Cotton Exchange, were good friends. The Nymex traders had another term for what they were, but it wasn't fit to utter, let alone print.

Despite the traders' resentment of Fisher, he could not be denied. In a way, they needed him. He stood for something—a kind of excellence to which most of them could only aspire. It helped that he wasn't physically attractive. He didn't look like anybody special. He exemplified the possibility of the ordinary man. Once the traders decided to stop hating him, he became a kind of comfort to them, someone whose very existence seemed to prove the underlying truth of the superhero myth.

Fisher, however, was not wholly invincible. He'd gotten pulled into the same regulatory undertow as Guttman. After asking Rappaport to help him start a trading and clearing firm that took his initials, MBF, Fisher got caught in the rash of regulatory probes that ravaged New York and Chicago trading pits during the late 1980s. Postal inspectors had raided his offices and carted away boxes of pit cards and heaps of trading records. Five months before the CFTC charged Guttman, it slapped Fisher and nine of his closest trading buddies with a seven-count complaint. (When it came to charges, it appeared the CFTC's lucky number was seven.) Fisher, who traded just about everything—oil, silver, sugar, and other commodities—had gotten himself into hot water trading all three. The CFTC accused him of engaging in more than fifty different documented transactions between 1987 and 1989, including what it called "fictitious" trades, collusion schemes, and a slew of "wash trades" that enriched him at the expense of everyone else in the marketplace. In example after example of purported misconduct, it described how Fisher, behind Nymex's closed doors, engineered "highly suspicious" transactions with his cohorts in the pits that rippled across the global pricing system. Because the trading floor was not at all visible to the public—though, indeed, its prices were—this was not a difficult feat. It only required that one or more traders record trades at the wrong prices or change the terms of the trades after the fact to their distinct financial advantage.

The CFTC's complaint did not have its desired effect. Instead of buckling, Fisher threw his lawyers at it. Over time, even his friends in the pits who were charged began settling their cases and moving on with their lives. But not Fisher. His family, his livelihood, and his reputation were on the line. He was not going to be pushed out of his job like Guttman, or banned from trading for life like Marks's brother, only to become a salesman in Philadelphia.

Fisher's drawn-out battle would go on for over a decade. The Nymex traders weren't sure how Fisher would win, but they did know one thing: Mark Fisher never lost a fight.

Rappaport waited for the right moment, then made his graceful exit from Fisher's firm. With the election coming, he didn't want to take any chances. "Fisher was the heavyweight trader and they wanted him," he says. "For what seemed like a long time, I was meeting with lawyers every day trying to sort his case out. It was exhausting. I couldn't take it anymore."

Given the charges on Guttman's head, Rappaport should have won the chairmanship by a landslide. Instead, he won 386 to 213. "I shouldn't have gotten more than 40 percent of the vote," Guttman says. "After being run out, Danny should have clocked me. He didn't."

Still, the defeat stung. Guttman had never lost an election before. He couldn't blame Rappaport for grabbing hold of the brass ring. How could a trader begrudge another trader for being opportunistic? He put on a brave face. "The membership, whom I have served for the past six years with love and devotion, has voted," he said in his concession speech. "I am extremely proud of Nymex's growth and success under my administration. I wish my friend Danny equal success."

Rappaport, of all people, knew how much Guttman wanted to stay. "Nymex was Lou's life. It was in his blood. He loved that place. I don't think he will ever forgive me for running against him and winning."

Despite being a youthful thirty-nine years old, Rappaport looked every bit the part of a chairman. Easygoing, well-groomed, and matinee-idol handsome, he seemed almost too clean-cut to have come from the pits. He was used to people thinking he came from money, because that was how he carried himself. But he had not. He was a scrapper, like the rest of them. He'd put in his time as one of the exchange's longest-running board members, listening to the grousefests and backbiting for seven long years. He'd paid his dues. "I don't think Danny would have had the guts to run against Lou if not for all the regulatory charges," says the executive staffer. "But when you saw your boss on the ropes at Nymex, you didn't help him. You finished him off."

Guttman chafed. He saw Rappaport as a purely political animal, a man who didn't have the intestinal fortitude to be a market visionary. "Danny wasn't a strategic thinker. He was good at politics. He had the gift of gab. He was an attorney by trade. He laughed a lot, was very sociable and extremely perceptive." The Nymex staffer saw another side of it. "Who do you want to run your exchange? The tough guy with the Hungarian accent? Or the soft-spoken, meticulously tailored all-American? It was very hard on Lou."

Not that it made a difference. If Guttman didn't get cleared of the CFTC charges leveled against him, there'd be nothing left of his career to save. "The sniper rifle was pointed at my head and they pulled the trigger. There was absolutely nothing I could do about it. You know that scene with Clint Eastwood from *The Good, the Bad and the Ugly*? Where he's watching the guy dig a hole and the guy stops and says, 'Hey, why am I doing all of the digging and you're just standing there?' Clint slowly takes a drag of his cigarette, tosses the butt away, and says, 'You see, in this world, there are two kinds of people, my friend. Those with loaded guns, and those who dig. *You* dig.' I was a digger. I guess I should've loaded the gun. I told the board every last detail of what we were doing, to the point of them deciding they didn't really need me. I guess they were thinking, 'Why shouldn't one of us have Lou's job? We'll execute the plan.' Back when I ran unopposed for chairman, they were terrified of me. I guess I should have maintained my reign of terror. I didn't accept that what you need to do to stay in power is keep everybody else in the dark and shove the decisions down their throats. It's not the way it should be, but that's often what it takes."

Many questions troubled Guttman as he prepared for the CFTC administrative court hearing that would decide on his fate. Why had he been the target of a witch hunt? For twenty years, Nymex had been his raison d'être, his refuge, the home he'd never had. He hadn't been like the other chairmen at the time, carelessly burning up the first-class air miles and corporate expense accounts. He'd appreciated his office. He'd assumed everyone else would notice. He'd stuck out his neck to run things as smoothly as possible—admittedly, a near-impossible task in the oil market. Yet now he was being branded a crook. It was the worst kind of humiliation. He'd never even let the board members pass out their personal business cards while on exchange-related business trips, for fear it would be seen as a conflict of interest. Was that not aboveboard in the extreme? He couldn't fathom what he had done to deserve being ruined. "Lou was smart, but he was naïve," says one of his former colleagues. "He had no idea what he was getting into. He really was the last of the great chairmen. He didn't blow it all up his nose like so many of the others. When he came under attack, I didn't agree with the people who turned their backs on him. I didn't turn my back. But over there, everyone was always more interested in slicing each other up than doing anything good for anybody. Lou was less a slicer than a slicee. When the CFTC started going after him, he became like a lightning rod. The case against him involved options, and as soon as you bring that up, everyone's eyes glaze over. Whatever happened, it wasn't worth him being run out of there. It was a rotten shame."

Gero, who'd worked closely with Guttman, also was aggrieved. "Lou Guttman should have been the Leo Melamed of New York. But he was a terrible politician. Being chairman is a political job, and he never shied away from picking fights and making enemies. He was a target for the CFTC, he was a headline. In this business, it's easy to remove someone if you try hard enough."

Guttman may not have been good at politics, but those who worked with him said he had been a good manager. "He was focused on getting things done and he took the time to let you know that he appreciated your work," says a colleague. Guttman agrees he had no appetite for the political aspects of the job. "I *hated* the politics. All I ever wanted to do was keep things moving. By knocking me out of the box, the CFTC hurt the long-term interests of the energy market. It kills me that I did all the heavy lifting while the rest of them moved in for the sumptuous dinners." Howard Hazelcorn, one of Guttman's most ardent supporters, may have been the most disappointed of all. "The only chairman ever worth a damn was Lou. There was no question in the world he was innocent. I remember the shock on his face when he found out what his partner, that crumbum, was doing. You cannot fake that. I knew Lou from the first, when he started in the pits. He was straight as an arrow." The Guttman era marked the last time a chairman would lead Nymex unsalaried, much less nearly double the exchange's business while flying coach.

With Guttman out of the way, the market's politics grew increasingly ominous. The vicious cycle of power had become firmly established, with the most influential traders rising out of the pits to become chairmen and holding on to their power bases for as long as they could before getting toppled by another, stronger trader coming up behind them. With more money to go around, its leaders also began to get greedier. Guttman was given a bonus of $75,000 for his last seven months as chairman in 1992. It took nearly a year before Nymex even bothered to send it. Rappaport received $125,000 for the five months he filled in as acting chairman. Why Rappaport drew the larger paycheck when Guttman worked two months longer was never explained. With Guttman's departure, influence-peddling greased by appalling amounts of money became a dominant theme in the energy market. Under Rappaport, the chairman's pay scale took a gravity-defying leap, as did the salaries of almost everyone in the executive suite. Nymex officers previously paid token salaries started receiving generous paychecks and bonuses, particularly those on the executive committee responsible for green-lighting Rappaport's compensation package. As Nymex grew more prosperous, the ethos of its traders and directors changed. Money was piling up so quickly it was becoming an abstraction.

By the time Rappaport left office, he commanded a salary of $1.8 million—twenty-four times Guttman's parting paycheck—causing one

magazine to call him "chairman of the bucks." He was, by his own estimate, the highest-paid chairman in the world. When the board agreed to
Guttman's year-end bonus of $200,000 for his work in 1991, Rappaport
cast one of the few dissenting votes. "Danny said, 'I don't think *any*
chairman is worth $200,000,'" Guttman says. "I guess what he meant
was, 'No chairman is worth $200,000. I think a chairman should be
worth $1.8 million.'"

While Rappaport may have been less mindful of the budget, occasionally driving the exchange to a loss while he collected his hefty paycheck, his chairmanship brought a period of peace not seen since before
the previous three rocky chairmanships and their successive scandals. In
fact, Rappaport's mellow personality made him one of the least polarizing figures in the history of the oil market. It was a welcome departure
from the sturm und drang to which the traders had become accustomed.
"Danny was not much of a manager," says one trader who knew all of the
chairmen. "Most of the projects he tackled took too long and had a lot of
loopholes in them. But he was a very good front man. He had a nice smile
and was a good speaker." After observing Guttman's ouster, Rappaport
volunteered his time on various CFTC committees, working with no
fewer than five different agency chairmen, whose ranks switched at a
furious pace. He also took a milder approach to work than his predecessors. Though he was the planet's highest-paid chairman, he liked to take
Fridays off. Sometimes, in the summer, he would come in only three
days a week. "The traders used to complain about it, but I told them that
being chairman is a twenty-four-hour-a-day job. Just because I go home,
doesn't mean I stop being chairman. I said, 'The best thing you can hope
for is that while I'm on my day off, windsurfing, I'll think of a solution
to a problem I've been dealing with.'" The traders also ribbed Rappaport
for being a penny-pincher in spite of his millions. "We used to make fun
of Danny for being the cheapest man ever to walk the earth," says Marty
Greenberg. "I swear to God, he's still wearing the suit I met him in."

Rappaport was not as much a world traveler or marketer of Nymex
as Guttman and Marks were. He did not like crisscrossing continents or
staying in unfamiliar hotel rooms. He considered himself a family man.
"Remember, Lou and Michel were single," he says. "I was not." The oil
traders did not mind. Their attitude was that the world should come to
them. And the world did come to them. It had no other choice.

Those who didn't like Rappaport knew exactly where to go:

Guttman's office at Harley Futures in the World Trade Center, which effectively became the hangout of the opposition. Rappaport shrugged it off. "If it hadn't been Lou, it would have been somebody else. There were always forces of opposition. There were always *multiple* opposition forces. And there were always conspiracy theorists. None of it surprised me. I think anyone who expected Lou to go away didn't know Lou very well. He was always going to be a part of Nymex." That said, he and Guttman kept their distance.

Rappaport sat for a formal oil portrait of himself during his chairmanship. He also commissioned portraits of the rest of the Nymex chairmen, including Guttman, all the way back to the exchange's founding in 1872. Displaying oil paintings of the market's leaders, he felt, would give the traders a heightened sense of respect for the oil market's rich history. The bill for the portraits came to more than $100,000. When the paintings arrived, Rappaport hung his portrait near Guttman's.

Instead of admiring the paintings, however, the traders subjected them to vandalism and abuse reflective of their feelings toward the various chairmen. On the outs with Guttman after siding with Rappaport in the race for chairman, Lapayover, who still worked at the exchange, began swiping the nameplate off Guttman's portrait. "I am not confirming or denying I did that," Lapayover says. "It would be kind of embarrassing to have that in a book. But wouldn't you know, every time his nameplate was replaced, it vanished again!"

Exasperated, Stuart Smith bought a hidden camera to catch the pilferer. He installed the security camera on a Thursday. The following day, a different trader yanked Rappaport's portrait off the wall, dragging it into the men's room off the trading floor.

In front of the rest of the traders, the vandal ceremoniously urinated on Rappaport's face.

The painting was left desecrated on the tile. Smith captured the entire episode on film. It was not a good omen.

9

The Anatomy of the Takedown

I wanted to be a good guy, but I also wanted to make some money.

—DANNY RAPPAPORT

TEN YEARS AFTER Daniel Rappaport took office, I received my first anonymous e-mail from the trader who called himself "Deep Throat." He worked at Nymex and wanted to share his voluminous cache of top-secret information with me.

"I want to talk to you, but I can't tell you who I am," he wrote.

"I'd like to speak with you," I wrote back. "But I can't use anything you give me unless you tell me who you are."

He responded, "How do I know I can trust you?"

"Technically, you don't," I replied. "But I don't know I can trust you, either."

Five minutes later, my phone rang and I had my first encounter with the man who, from then on, would supply me with a fount of useful information about the oil market, much of it highly confidential, including the Nymex annual budgets with massive line items for such things as "board entertainment," "armed guards," and, at one point, a $250,000-a-year pack of "bomb [and drug] detection" dogs.

Like many of the other traders I'd met, Deep Throat (his e-mail literally was "deepthroatnymex@mac.com") became associated with Nymex under less than auspicious circumstances. A trading prodigy who'd attracted a great deal of attention on Wall Street in his day, he'd been invited by Rosemary McFadden to lunch for what he hoped would be a proposal of a joint business venture. "Imagine my surprise," he says, "when, after exchanging a few pleasantries, she leans over and says, 'We are going to *sue* you.' I don't think I even had the first piece of bread in my mouth."

The two sides later dropped the dispute and he went to work for the exchange.

A box of confidential documents arrived shortly after our first conversation. Others followed. The dossier revealed a long history of Nymex executives using the exchange as a sort of personal playground. Items regularly added to the budget, my source explained, funded some of the favorite recreational activities of the top brass masquerading as business functions. Even those who started out well-intentioned, it seemed, could not keep themselves from grasping at the oil wealth heaping before their eyes.

AHEAD OF RAPPAPORT stretched a period of plenty, untold fortunes, and early retirement. The divergence of paths between him and Guttman could not have been more pronounced. As Guttman worked from his home office at the Gateway Plaza on South End Avenue, his full-time job became extricating himself from his legal bind; caring for his sick mother, who was suffering from vascular disease; and preparing for the courtroom showdown that would rule on his fate.

Rappaport's reign saw the Nymex traders unapologetically defending their oil monopoly. He propounded the power of the pits, as their biggest players cemented their seats on the rapidly inflating board and built mini-empires below. Having come from the pits himself, like the other chairmen, Rappaport treated the exchange members for what they were—his power base, his voters, his constituents. From the start, he catered only to them. Not that he had a choice. "Imagine trying to run a company where you see your shareholders every day," he says. "Can you imagine it? This was what it was like to be Nymex chairman. Without warning, the traders would be coming through your door, into your office, into the boardroom, never knocking, never hesitating to tell you exactly what they thought of you. It is amazing anyone can run a business that way." Rappaport's party faithful included people like Harold Fisher, an ex-POW and former potato trader, who, by this time, had lifted himself from poverty by trading energy futures. The value of the $1,000 seat he'd bought in the 1960s had since jumped to $625,000. "I was a poor kid all my life," he says. "What I am telling you is like something out of a storybook."

Vincent Viola, who'd risen through the ranks since serving under Guttman, became Rappaport's vice chairman, and Richard Schaeffer shored up power on the board as well as the executive committee—the oil market's secretive inner sanctum that rubber-stamped Rappaport's paychecks.

Mark Fisher, witnessing Guttman's legal entanglements, gave a wide berth to elected office. Despite his growing popularity, he never ran for chairman or any other leadership post. For him, it would have been a step down. He was a man of action, not of board meetings. He didn't like turning the screws or applying the subtle pressures. He preferred blunt instruments. With his former business partner, Rappaport, in pole position, he didn't need to set foot in the boardroom to pull the reins on everybody else. It was he who held the chairmen in *his* pocket, not the other way around. At any rate, his place was in the pits. "Mark Fisher was the only guy at the entire exchange who could storm into a board meeting in the middle of a session screaming," says a departed executive. "Most of the time, he would already be in the middle of a sentence when he got there. He'd make these scene-stealing entrances, charging the door, one fat finger in the air, shouting, 'And another thing . . . !' You did not fuck with Mark Fisher. Mark could do no wrong. He was, more than anyone, the heart and soul of the oil market."

. In the pits, the larger trading firms, eager to groom the best of the prospective traders, became locked in heated rivalries over who would claim the choicest fresh meat. Fisher's firm, MBF, frequently vied for the same recruits as Viola's trading house, Pioneer Futures. Both were considered major feeders of top talent to the pits. The traders called Fisher's followers "Fisher's Boys," while Viola's trading army was dubbed "the Finance Mafia." Both Fisher and Viola made millions of dollars off their traders, so it was not unusual to seem them clashing over the same shark pool. "It definitely conjured up the *West Side Story* image of the two guys snapping their fingers, leaning toward each other," says Ben Kaufman. "Fisher and Viola had their own seats of power, but they were very different people. Each had his specialty. Fisher was into the big picture and the politics and the power. He also was the closest thing we had to an intellectual at the exchange. Viola was the street-smart Italian guy, always with a bunch of Brooklyn and Staten Island kids hanging around him. Vinnie had the influence and the intimidation factor going for him. Pioneer Futures *was* kind of like the Mafia. It was hard to get into, but once you were in, you were in. They would look out for you and insist on your loyalty. Vinnie would call you up, summon you, 'Come here, I need to see you . . .' He definitely played that up. He dressed and acted like a Mafioso don. It was all very pageant. There was this hush that came over the pits whenever he came down. People didn't talk shit about Vinnie. He took advantage of it, cloaked himself in the Godfather image, an image that is admittedly an American obsession. And he knew how to use it. We usually didn't see him come down to the pits unless he wanted to intimidate somebody. Once, when he came down, he said to a trader, 'Do that again and I'll *kill* you.' It took a long time before people stopped talking about that."

Always on the prowl for his dream trader, Fisher didn't need intimidation to win anybody over. His reputation preceded him. Every year, he'd take a small group of young men and women under his wing and deluge them with trading lessons, charts, books, homework, and curfews. "With Vinnie, you had an extended family, but with Fisher you got a real education," Kaufman says. "His trainees were usually in college or just out, and he'd make them come in earlier than everyone and get ready for the day. If he caught you out drinking the night before or heard about it, he'd take it out on you. He was ruthless, brilliant, a strict disciplinarian. And he expected you to be the same way. He had no respect for people who didn't have their shit together. He was infamous for pulling pranks. In the summertime, he never failed to find a way to get the traders to wear dresses and high heels to the pits. But if you said hi to him in the hall, he'd just give you this bored, self-important look like, 'What*ever.*' Fisher embodied Nymex both in style and attitude. Yet at the same time, he was better than that. It was a big deal to be one of Fisher's Boys. If you interned or traded for him, you could get a job anywhere in the pits."

Fisher's pranks included the one where he'd lined up rookie traders along the marina in the winter after they'd lost a game of Texas Hold'em. In addition to hiring ambulances, he'd even stationed EMTs by the water to fish the traders' bodies out in the event they didn't make it. Until the final moment, when he'd spared them, no one witnessing the hazing believed he wasn't about to throw them into the river. He sent them back indoors, handing them written reminders that they should never bet more than they could pay. "There was a balance between the pranks and the work," Kaufman says. "From the outside, it probably looked like chaos, but the pranks almost always made us learn faster and work harder."

Fisher's protégés were allowed to play with his money, but only in exchange for a fat slice of their trading profits. He negotiated his arrangements on an individual basis, so the percentage of earnings owed to him after expenses varied by trader. "The thing was, if you made money, he got some of it. But if you *lost* Fisher's money, that was now money you owed him. Until then, he *owned* you," Kaufman says. Perpetually a screamer, Fisher was known for ripping into traders at appalling decibels whenever they came back empty-handed from the pits asking for more. "What the fuck! Come back when you can *trade* something!" he'd bellow. But a successful trader who'd taken a rare hit would occasionally be forgiven, Kaufman says. "I remember one of Fisher's traders lost a huge amount, like in the millions. He was so shaken he couldn't concentrate on trading anymore. It happens to the best of them, when you take a major loss like that. Their fighting spirit is broken. Fisher wiped clean his debt and gave him more money to start over."

In the mid-1990s, the trading pits' fighting spirit was of particular interest to the U.S. Marine Corps. It sent more than a dozen generals, colonels, and other high-ranking officers to Nymex to conduct observations. They wanted to see how well the traders responded to changing information on price screens and the twenty-four-hour news networks, both of which had become indispensable moneymaking tools. The U.S. military was just beginning to move its combat functions onto computers and wanted to see how well people responded to digital information pelted at them under high stress. The oil market, they concluded, was the perfect place to do that. "In heavy combat situations, the stress lasts only a few seconds or minutes at most," says Gary Lapayover, who acted as ombudsman to the marines for Nymex (much to the annoyance of ex-military-man Viola, who knew Lapayover had been a draft-dodger). "I think a lot of them had never seen such sustained combat as in the trading pits. When the officers saw the intensity, the duration, the split-second decision-making and the money risks involved, it just blew them away."

Francis "Bing" West, former assistant secretary of defense for international security affairs in the Reagan administration, designer of computerized war games, and father of *Playboy* Cyber Girl Kaki West, came down to watch. "Most of the generals in the Marine Corps at one point or another observed the traders in the pits," he says. "With the military and trading, there are many similarities. Both are a tribal, male-bonding kind of thing. A lot of the Nymex traders would have made good marines, if you know what I mean. The marines and the oil traders had no trouble understanding each other.

"The whole purpose was to see how people make rapid decisions with incomplete data when they *have* to make a choice. When you are in a firefight, for example, you have to respond immediately, based on the limited information you have. You can't wait, and there are real consequences to that. That is exactly what traders do. We wanted to learn more about how the traders' minds worked. What we found was that when confronted with a number of options, they have an instant instinct for which one will have the biggest payoff."

The oil traders gave the marines trading badges and led them through simulated trading exercises, much like the Kaufmans had done with their pizza futures. Afterward, the marines invited twenty-five Nymex traders to the World War II aircraft carrier USS *Intrepid* to spar with marine and navy officers in a round of computerized war games devised by West. The traders and officers broke up into opposing teams. Each received a limited number of jets, troops, and scud missiles with which to destroy a certain amount of targets in a specific amount of time. "Each team had its munitions and troops and we had to order strikes," Lapayover says. "What we found was that the traders turned out to be far more bloodthirsty than the marines. We annihilated them. The traders were much more focused on the objectives. They also were more willing to sacrifice their troops than the marines in meeting their goals. If the traders lost fifty people, well, at least we got the job done. The marines were trying to preserve lives. They were going to tell us exactly how well we did, but then they decided not to, because we killed them so bad. They said it would be embarrassing to the higher-ups to reveal the results. We really weren't supposed to talk about it afterward. But we so slaughtered them."

West confirms the outcome of the games, but has a slightly different take. "It turned out the traders had a much more quantitative instinct for risk-reward when applying force on the battlefield. They focused on obliterating the enemy. The generals had to explain to them that the thing they were missing was that the payoff wasn't simply hurting the enemy, it was also that *the enemy did not hurt your troops.*"

The marines also invited the traders down to what Lapayover called "the military equivalent of Disneyland" at their high-security base in Quantico, Virginia. They picked the traders up at the airport in a C-130 Hercules turboprop aircraft without the seats. Eric Bolling, one of Fisher's Boys, and David Greenberg, the Nymex board-member son of the former Comex chairman Marty Greenberg, were among the two dozen traders from Nymex to be issued uniforms and forced to sleep in barracks until the marine officers woke them at four A.M. by banging garbage-can lids together and throwing them into freezing showers.

"A drill sergeant lined us up in our underwear and made us all stand at attention," Rappaport says. Scowling at one of the oil traders, the sergeant shouted, "What *are* those things? *Sideburns?*" When the trader said yes, they were sideburns, the sergeant spat on the ground. "Oh yeah? They look like shit!"

Staring at Greenberg, who'd been caught in the middle of changing, the sergeant hollered, "Put a shirt on! You are disgusting to look at!"

Rappaport was suppressing a laugh when the sergeant stepped up. He leaned against Rappaport until they were nearly nose-to-nose. "Did I tell you to say anything?" he asked, letting the spittle fly.

Rappaport, though repelled, leaned in even closer.

The sergeant started in abject amazement. "Boy, if this was the real thing," he said, "I'd have to beat the shit outta you!"

Lapayover decided not to sleep in the barracks that night. He never regretted avoiding the army, he told West, who called him a "real pistol." He got a hotel room. "They treated us just like recruits. We got the full experience. They drove us to the field and took us out in the helicopters. They had a mess tent set up where we had breakfast. Then they put us in all-terrain vehicles and we went across fields with live fire and explosives going off and then it was milk-and-cookies time. I am not kidding: they fired guns at us and then fed us milk and cookies. After that, we were given .45s, M-16s, grenade launchers, and 50-caliber machine guns. They even did a raffle for two Nymex guys to shoot *shoulder-fired missiles.* We got to shoot everything the marines get to shoot. At the end, there was a big going-away party for us. They presented me with a flight jacket at the dinner, and the commander was really pissed off because it was too short for me. He began waving his arms around and ordering someone to get to the bottom of it. It was all very impressive."

For years to come, the marines sent officers to the pits for observation until, according to Lapayover, Melamed's CME began inquiring why its market, the largest donor to Washington of all the exchanges, wasn't getting the same attention.

Lapayover succeeded Viola as vice chairman in 1996. The two-year post wasn't worth the contentiousness of his election. During the campaign, he intercepted an anonymous letter sent to his wife at their home. It detailed acts of infidelity done by him, disclosures clearly intended to disrupt his marriage and his family life. Lapayover, who eventually divorced, accused Guttman of sending the missive.

Guttman threw up his hands. "My motto is, if I'm coming to get you, I don't do anonymous letters," he says. "If I'm coming to get you, I'm going to let you know it!"

In 1996, Francis Marks died. It was also the year Arnold Safer, the man who had designed Michel Marks's energy contracts, passed away. The relationship between Michel and Francis, who lived to be eighty-two, softened as Francis's health began to wane. "All us children pitched in to buy Dad a parking space under the World Trade Center, so he wouldn't have to park up the street and walk to the exchange," Richard Marks says. "He was embarrassed, because he saw it as a luxury. But I think he appreciated it in the colder weather." Francis had never stopped trying to live his simple life.

Rappaport carried out Guttman's unfinished agenda, turning the exchange into a for-profit organization and finalizing the on-again, off-again merger of Nymex and Comex, which mimicked the love-hate relationship long ago mastered by the Chicago exchanges. Guttman had nearly clinched a Comex deal, but was blocked by Marty Greenberg when Greenberg was voted Comex chairman in 1990. Greenberg did not think Nymex was offering enough money for the metals market. In his day, he and Guttman didn't see eye to eye, but Greenberg always respected him. "A lot of guys at Nymex didn't care about anything but helping themselves," he says. "Lou had a problem in that he really cared about the job he did."

Nymex and Comex did not come together easily. They had never recovered from all the bad blood between them. It had always been green against gold—the gold badges of Nymex versus the green-badge traders of Comex. "There was uncharacteristic unanimity about the merger," Rappaport says. "The membership was unanimously *opposed*." But with gold prices stagnating and the metals markets cooling off, Comex was losing cash fast. It finally put itself up for sale. Rappaport, seizing the moment in 1994, rammed the merger through. "Danny Rappaport did an incredible job. We'd all tried to push for it many times before, but it never went anywhere. He did what we didn't do," says Henry Jarecki, the hedge fund trader who told Marks he'd never trade on Nymex. "Danny dealt with the details of it. He dealt with the nitty-gritty in a highly intelligent way and thought about what the different players wanted. That's why it finally worked." Nymex, which had once been scorned by Comex, now owned it. At forty, Rappaport was chairman of the two most important strategic resources in the world—oil and gold.

He wasted no time in moving the exchanges from the embattled World Trade Center to a custom-built skyscraper at the World Financial Center on the Hudson in Battery Park City. He envisioned a new head-quarters projecting an air of respectability. "The architect, David Childs, wanted a modern statement building. I wanted it to blend in with the other buildings at the World Financial Center. I just didn't want us to look like the flashy asshole commodities traders." Located across the marina from Guttman's place, the building would stand as a totem to the oil market in every way, its tasteful, pale veneer belying the controversy that surrounded it.

The traders spoke of kickbacks and sweetheart deals funneling through the building's construction to the exchange's executives, rumors that were substantiated when Stuart Smith pleaded guilty to taking a bribe from one of the contractors working on the project. Rappaport couldn't believe Smith had brokered a side deal without his knowing about it. "On the other hand, I really tried not to know these things. You never know when you're going to be under oath. I didn't want to have to lie later and say I didn't know about something when I did. I never wanted to know those stories. Being chairman was such a high-profile position and so many people wanted your head." In other words, it was in the best interest of the oil market chairmen to look the other way. In the eyes of the world, ignorance was vastly more forgivable than complicity.

The building took years to construct. The traders, as was their wont, began to grow impatient. Fisher made a bet with Rappaport that he couldn't get the job done on schedule. "Fisher said if he lost the bet, he would pay $60,000 to the charity of my choice," Rappaport says. "If I lost the bet, I would have to walk from the World Trade Center to the site of the new building wearing high-heeled shoes in my underwear with a marching band behind me." Fisher never made a bet that didn't call for some blatant form of humiliation, preferably involving women's trappings. Their bet was the only wager anyone could remember Fisher ever losing. The traders moved into the building in 1997. The oil paintings of the chairmen promptly went up on the tenth floor in a long, carpeted hallway leading to the boardroom. The interior's country club furnishings and pre–Revolutionary War color scheme had been carefully selected by Viola. No one knew who suggested putting in the terraced lounge with the jukebox bar and stunning views of the Hudson. But the traders soon found it and began drinking there as soon as the oil market opened on weekday mornings.

With the exception of the first Gulf War, oil prices didn't go much higher than $20 a barrel for most of the 1990s. They even fell below $10 during the second half of that decade. But Nymex trading volumes kept on growing, as did the over-the-counter commodities market, which was seen creeping toward the trillion-dollar mark, led by the bulge-bracket banks, hedge funds, and Big Oil. While the government was certainly aware of the dark market's existence, its true value still remained unknown, as nobody in a position of power—including the CFTC—bothered to find out much about it.

My conversations with traders in the over-the-counter market generally read like Sanskrit. Their realm was one of rumors and hearsay, of secreted transactions and inside information. Everything worth knowing came by word of mouth via telephone or Yahoo! instant messages. Though the physical energy traders followed the Nymex prices religiously as part of their day, their shadow-land operated by a different set of rules and used a completely different language. Their job was to put together elaborate fuel deals in time frames that boiled down to months, weeks, sometimes even less than twenty-four hours for refineries or distributors in need of immediate energy supplies.

Because time was of the essence, their communiqués to other traders were heavily abbreviated. Light, sweet, distillate fuels were LSD. A specific period in time was referred to as F6. Explaining M4 was hopeless. Prices were expressed in terms of how much higher or lower they were in dollars and cents than the Nymex prices, depending on the types of fuels for sale, shipping rates, and regional demand across the country. The Nymex price was the lodestar, but the over-the-counter traders overlaid it with their own ornate calculations. Aside from talking about which fuels were trading at which prices, the traders endlessly swapped stories about which refineries were blowing up or on fire—a common occurrence in the United States, where a new refinery hasn't been built since 1976 and most fuel plants barely chug along even with constant repair and attention. Whenever something went up in smoke, the prices jumped. And that was basically all the time.

An excerpt from a typical conversation I'd have with one of these traders:

Me: F6 M4-75 trades sweet.
Trader: Do you have any NY numbers that show ratable March *anything*?
Me: Not yet. . . .
Trader: Anything trading B6?
Me: Uh-uh. . . .
Trader: Watching the clock. Gonna start guitar lessons. . . . I hate this job. The money here is the only incentive.
Me: Poor lamb. Horrific to be trapped by money.
Trader: I just get sick of the same conversations all day long, you know? This whole year seems like one giant day.
Me: Hydrotreater shut down. Lots of LSD buying. Just heard LSD B5 +80 done, did you?
Trader: F6 A4/M4 done 1.05 . . . reoffered 1.10. Hydrotreater down where?
Me: Trying to find out . . . thanks for the regrade! . . . Hey, not a hydrotreater. . . . It's a transformer fire. Happening at Garyville, Louisiana, refinery run by Marathon Ashland. . . . Is it possible for a refinery not to constantly break down or spontaneously combust?
Trader: Nope, but they've been a good buyer today. . . . Good info. You brought that first.
Me: So MAP's been buying?
Trader: I'll answer that if my name stays out.
Me: Deal.
Trader: Yup, buying 74.

Me: Is it dominating, though?

Trader: No, the West Coast thing is. It adds to the melee, but not as significantly.

Me: Is it fair to say there's a squeeze on the LSD values?

Trader: BIG squeeze . . . uh, what do you mean by squeeze?

Me: Now you're trying to start trouble again.

Trader: Did the trouble ever end?

In the early 1990s, a major event took place that would forever change the oil market for the worse. Strangely, at the time it happened, almost nobody knew about it. Since the Great Depression, Congress had recognized that a healthy market had to be carefully balanced between the speculators, who were essentially gambling on prices, and the commercial hedgers, like oil companies and refineries, which were in the market specifically to protect themselves from price pops and drops. It was understood that if speculators, who liked prices to be volatile, outnumbered the commercial hedgers, who liked prices to be stable, the market would come off its hinges, with prices being controlled by something other than supply and demand, which was not seen to be a good thing.

Limits were put on the size of the bets of certain market players, so that nobody could control too much oil at once. The system could still be abused and manipulated, but overall prices became a lot harder to bully. Because commercial hedgers actually wanted oil and needed it to run their businesses, they were given more leeway to take large market positions than speculators, who were seen as not wanting oil and just trying to turn a quick profit.

Then, in 1991, a group of traders at Goldman Sachs decided to challenge those rules. They wrote a letter to the CFTC, saying that because they also had big bets on the market, they needed to hedge their price risk too. They didn't see why they should have to buy an oil refinery, like Francis Marks, to get the same privileges as commercial traders. The CFTC, forgetting all about why speculators had been separated from the commercial hedgers in the first place, thought that sounded like a perfectly logical idea. The commissioners signed off on an *exemption* so that the Goldman traders could trade freely without the same limitations as the other for-profit traders. The CFTC proudly christened it the "Bona Fide Hedging" exemption, and as soon as it gave one to Goldman Sachs, every other bank and hedge fund on Wall Street wanted one.

To the trading community, it was a masterstroke. If you could get the CFTC to agree to look the other way—which, after all, wasn't so difficult—it meant that certain rules and regulations did not apply to you. Of course, this was already true for the over-the-counter market, but now titanic traders at the banks and hedge funds could declare open season on the public market as well.

Before long, exemptions were being passed out like ribbon candy, allowing speculators to bet on ever-larger slices of the market, creating a rapidly expanding casino that would eventually make it impossible for the CFTC to tell who was doing what. Not being able to tell the difference between a speculator and a commercial hedger was why the CFTC could repeatedly tell Congress speculators *weren't* driving up the price of oil, even as gasoline topped $4 a gallon and oil approached $150 a barrel in 2008. The CFTC wasn't trying to obfuscate the facts so much as it was refusing to accept that it had passed out too much candy. It no longer knew what was going on anymore. Worse, the CFTC had given Nymex the express authority to pass out ribbon candy too, which meant energy speculators were being reclassified as commercial hedgers and handed exemptions without the CFTC knowing about it or having any centralized authority over what was happening.

A lawyer with Nymex's compliance department, who once worked at the CFTC, saw what was afoot, and he did not like it. "I wrote exemptions at Nymex for years. I don't know what happened with the Goldman exemption. We didn't do that one. But you know what? You have to be a real prick to do that job. The object is to make people squirm to get an exemption. It was never supposed to be *easy*. It used to be that a bank or a hedge fund or whoever had to come in and personally make a case for why you should be giving it to them. There is something about being forced to put on a suit and tie and doing things face-to-face that makes people behave themselves. Nymex held up the stop sign and that's how it should be. But then the exchange was holding up the stop sign and it was smoking; then it was smoking and driving; then you're naked in the car . . . you see what I mean. It got so that nobody wanted to come in and ask for an exemption anymore. They said it would disrupt *the flow of business*. That's what they always love to say. They wanted you to meet them at the 21 Club after work over drinks to ask for something they didn't deserve, that you had no business giving them. I'd come, drink my drink, and tell them to fuck off. Going to the 21 Club to talk about exemptions! You've got to be fucking kidding me."

To this day, banks and hedge funds regard the exemption as unadulterated genius. In the 1990s, however, the CFTC passed them out very quietly along Wall Street, neglecting to publicize what it was up to. In fact, the next CFTC chairwoman wasn't even told about the existence of the exemption. She only stumbled onto it accidentally, after discovering her staff was industriously doling them out. Today, the Goldman exemption, the touchstone for all the others, remains a top-secret document at the CFTC, the release of which, the agency claims, would be "a felony."

BACK AT HIS office, Guttman felt like he was navigating a burning ship. His mounting legal bills were draining his life savings, and his acrimonious relationship with Magid was getting worse. "I was on the balls of my ass with Magid and the CFTC coming after me. I still don't want to think about it." Even with the CFTC pitting Guttman and Magid against each other, Magid decided to file a separate breach-of-contract lawsuit against Guttman in Manhattan State Supreme Court. He asked to be compensated $3.3 million for Guttman's decision to pull out of their trading partnership and remove money from their shared accounts. Guttman countersued. They eventually settled out of court. In March 1995, just ahead of Guttman's hearing with the CFTC, Magid also settled his charges with the agency. It was a major win for the CFTC, as it desperately needed incriminating testimony from Magid to make its case against Guttman. Gary Glass, it turned out, had not been so cooperative. He stood by his original account of the events, maintaining that Guttman had played no role in the planning or the execution of Magid's illegal trades. Glass would pay a steep price for sticking to his story.

Guttman once said that Magid, a well-respected options trader, had become more careless as the amount of money he was given to bet with rose. In a sworn affidavit filed with the CFTC in 1991, Glass confirmed that assessment, giving a damning account of Magid's conduct and reputation in the pits. In it, he wrote, "It was common knowledge among the traders that they could dependably profit by selling their options to Magid at an inflated or depressed price near the close. In options markets that were highly illiquid and thinly traded, Magid could significantly affect the price of options through his bidding, and it was widespread knowledge that he did so consciously, deliberately, and regularly." Glass's statement was meant to lampoon Magid as a market manipulator. The CFTC did not disagree but, in its own court documents, called Magid a "credible" witness, even as it characterized his trades as "egregious."

Guttman's hearing went from October 24 to October 27 of that year. George Painter, the administrative law judge assigned to hear the case, presided over the court at the CFTC's chambers in the North Tower of the World Trade Center. Barry Bohrer represented Guttman, while Lenel Hickson, the lawyer with the CFTC's enforcement division, represented Magid. Painter was considered a rather volatile judge, known to both Wall Street and Washington for being unpredictable. Hickson, on the other hand, was one of the CFTC's good soldiers and remained with the agency for the rest of his career.

During the witness testimony, much attention was paid to what, if anything, Guttman might have known about the nature of Magid's trades. The CFTC did not present any hard evidence of wrongdoing by Guttman, but it did have Magid's full cooperation. As an indicator of the level of Guttman's knowledge of his illegal bets, Magid told the CFTC interrogators he'd phoned Guttman in the chairman's office to get approval for one of them. When the timing of the phone call was checked against Guttman's schedule, it was shown that Guttman had not been in the country but in Bürgenstock, Switzerland, for the annual commodities conference. Reminded of this, Magid, according to the CFTC's transcript, then changed his account to reflect the new facts, explaining he now remembered calling Guttman in Switzerland.

Magid also testified that he, Guttman, and an officer at Gerald met in the winter of 1989 to discuss the trading schemes they might conduct with Glass to hide Magid's losses. Magid could not remember when the meeting took place, and the officer, Julian Raber, had trouble corroborating his testimony. In the transcript of an earlier interrogation, Magid denied having any knowledge of the meetings or conversations about the trades in question. In the courtroom, however, he changed his mind, stating clearly that a meeting had occurred. Magid said that during the meeting, he, Raber, and Guttman had decided that Guttman would reach out to Glass about doing the illegal trades. Glass denied Magid's account, saying that while he had personally spoken with Magid and Raber about the trades, he had never spoken with Guttman. Guttman said that because he'd been out of the office traveling most of that time, he hadn't even seen or spoken with Glass for months. Guttman, Glass, and Magid, to this day, all stand by their courtroom testimonies.

Hickson tried to highlight Guttman's alleged role in getting Glass to take the opposite end of Magid's illegal trades. Guttman's lawyer tried to focus on the CFTC's struggle to prove that Guttman had even attended a meeting to discuss any illegal trading schemes, let alone personally initiating them. There also seemed to be some doubt as to whether such a meeting had ever taken place. Part of the problem was that the men met and spoke, mostly informally, all the time.

Then there was the issue of the polygraph test. The CFTC said it could not accept Guttman's test results, because it hadn't received any notice of his test in advance, it wasn't present at the time it was proctored, and it didn't have time to replicate the results with its own polygraph test. All reasonable objections, it seemed, until one read the fine print. The CFTC's claim was that it didn't have time to counter with a test of its own, because Guttman hadn't notified it of his polygraph results until just a few weeks before Painter's hearing in October 1995. That turned out to not be true. Guttman *had* submitted the results to the CFTC in the summer of 1992 as part of his initial defense. All of which meant that the agency had more than *three years* to take Guttman up on his offer to undergo a second polygraph test with a CFTC-appointed expert, but had decided not to. Yet according to the CFTC, this was somehow Guttman's fault.

The hearing, which was essentially Guttman's trial, would have appeared highly unusual in any normal court of law. But this was not a normal court of law; it was the court of the CFTC, a no-man's-land fit for no man. With one judge and no jury, it was a little-known offshoot of the government's executive branch, a Kafkaesque mutation of the U.S. legal system put together in the wake of the Great Depression by Congress to handle the regulatory proceedings of federal watchdog agencies so that the rest of the court system didn't have to deal with them (read: end up with their dockets overrun with white-collar offenders and their armies of top-paid, happy-to-shuffle-paper lawyers ready to do battle for decades).

Painter generously gave the CFTC's enforcement division three of the four days of the hearing to make its case against Guttman. Bohrer was allowed only the time left over to make his defense. "We listened to them throw the book at me all week," Guttman says. "Judge Painter knew Bohrer had to leave for London the following Monday, so we had to wrap it up. But when they finally gave him the floor, they wouldn't let him finish a sentence without shutting him down."

During Bohrer's cross-examination of Magid, a critical part of the proceeding, Painter repeatedly barred Bohrer from asking questions on the grounds that he did not consider them relevant to the earlier testimony. When Magid's attorney offered his objections, Painter mostly sustained them. On the rare occasion that Magid's attorney did not raise an objection, the judge actually turned to Hickson to ask *if he would like to.* Painter even once objected himself when Magid's own attorney would not. As a result of what appeared to be a concerted gang-up, it was difficult for Bohrer to even speak for more than a few seconds before being interrupted. The transcript of the hearing beggared belief. When it became obvious that Bohrer wouldn't be permitted to advance any line of questioning he'd prepared, Painter began to cruelly scold him for not making progress sooner. Most disturbing was the judge's disparaging tone when he addressed Bohrer, which, at one point, included the issuance of an implicit threat:

> *Mr. Bohrer, you know how to cross-examine a witness—don't you?*
> *. . . Mr. Bohrer, if you can't understand me, I'm not going to try*
> *and educate you. . . . You're going to have to get on to the cross-*
> *examination, or I'm going to deem that it's concluded. . . . I don't*
> *know where you're going with this, but we're sure not going to make*
> *it by five thirty. . . . If you can't get there, we're going to be finished*
> *before you know it. . . . I have just about reached the end of my string*
> *with you. . . . I am going to have a five-minute break. I want you*
> *to think about whether you have anything to ask this witness. . . .*
> *Mr. Bohrer, please. This is your last shot. . . . That concludes your*
> *examination, Mr. Bohrer. . . . I'm going to consider other matters*
> *concerning your conduct in this. I request you to take your seat and let's*
> *hear no more. . . . [At this point, Bohrer pleads to make use of his last*
> *half hour of time, to which the judge responds:] . . . You may discuss*
> *anything you wish with Mr. Hickson here. I'm finished for the day.*

After reminding Bohrer repeatedly that he had only until five thirty P.M. to conclude the cross-examination, Painter adjourned the hearing at five. As a judge with a lifetime seat on the bench, Painter was supposed to hear both sides of the case, impartially weigh the facts, and then hand down a ruling. Yet Painter shared offices in Washington with Hickson, the CFTC attorney representing Magid, and was on the same U.S. government payroll. The Nymex members attending the hearing in support of Guttman filed out, ashen-faced. "That was worse than the Nazi Gestapo," Lapayover's cousin, Stanley Levin, told him. Another trader, Billy Mainwald, confronted Magid about his testimony when they returned to the pits.

"Are all the things you said about Lou really true?" he asked.

"No," Magid said. "But he deserved it anyway."

Painter took more than a year to make his final ruling. The decision, laden with punctuation, spelling, and grammatical errors, veered between calling Guttman responsible for Magid's offending trades and not responsible for Magid's offending trades. In twelve pages of legalese, Guttman was found guilty as charged for what was seen as his arm's-length involvement in the illegal trades, but Painter dismissed Guttman on a separate charge of being the "controlling person" who had directed Magid's actions. This, the judge reasoned, was taking it too far.

Even to seasoned Wall Street lawyers, the September 11, 1996, decision proved an onerous read. For example, on page 7, Painter wrote, "Guttman, as the equal partner in the enterprise, is vicariously liable for the misconduct of Magid," while, on page 8, he explained: "This court finds that Guttman did not control Magid and is not vicariously liable for Magid's acts." The statements, on the face of it, would appear to directly contradict each other.

In his own convoluted way, Painter was simply trying to say that he did not agree with the facts as presented by the CFTC's enforcement division or by Guttman. "The people apprehending Guttman couldn't figure out what they were going after," says a former CFTC lawyer familiar with the decision. "They tried to get him on one thing and, when that didn't work out, they tried to get him on another." Painter wrote that the enforcement division "failed to prove by a preponderance of the evidence that Guttman controlled Magid." He added: "The record reveals that Guttman never possessed the power to direct Magid's trades. To the contrary, the record reveals that Guttman did not understand options trading while Magid was considered a genius in this field."

No one disputed Guttman's assertion that he knew nothing about trading options. Painter had agreed with that finding, noting, "Guttman never traded for the accounts, nor interfered with Magid's trading strategies. . . . The trading scheme was the brainchild of Magid, and was implemented by Magid and Glass. It is this fact—that Magid was the sole decision-maker over all trading—that makes it impossible for Guttman to be the controlling person of Magid regarding these trades. Accordingly, this court finds that Guttman did not control Magid and is not vicariously liable for Magid's acts."

Painter, in addition, voiced his reservations, as Professor Jerry Markham had, about the piece of law used by the CFTC to go after Guttman—an ellipses-addled portion of the Commodity Exchange Act, section 2(a)(1)(A)(iii), written as follows:

> *The act . . . of any . . . agent or other person acting for any individual . . . within the scope of his employment or office shall be deemed the act . . . of such individual . . . as well as of such . . . agent or other person.*[*]

The law, Painter said, had no historical precedent in cases such as Guttman's and no legislative standing whatsoever. "It is generally known that this section is grounded in the theory of common law *respondeat superior*," he said, acknowledging the law's absence from the U.S. legal code. "Guttman and Magid were partners, a group not traditionally covered by *respondeat superior* theory. The plain language of the section, however, allows for the inclusion of copartner liability, provided the division successfully proves that Magid was acting for Guttman." The CFTC had never bothered to define the criteria for proving when one person was, in fact, acting for another. This gray area worked to its advantage. It was, in truth, the only reason Painter could charge Guttman with *anything*. A second former CFTC attorney remarked, "The CFTC started at point A, couldn't make its case, then went to B and C and pretty much ended up at point X. It's a pretty damn aggressive interpretation of the law. It's really on the outer reaches. But you can stretch the law any way you want to if you try hard enough."

In finding Guttman guilty of the unreadable 2(a)(1)(A)(iii), Painter then shifted his language in the decision to address Magid's trades as if

---

[*] Ellipses inserted by the CFTC.

Guttman had done them, although he'd just finished saying Guttman had not played a role. "That Guttman, chairman of a major exchange during the relevant time period, would engage in such a smoke-and-mirrors operation is nothing short of shocking. If there is a saving grace to be found, it is that Guttman elected to pull off this scheme on the Coffee, Sugar & Cocoa Exchange and not on the Nymex," Painter wrote. "As the chairman of Nymex throughout the relevant time period, Guttman was bound by the highest ethical standards, yet permitted his partner to subvert the free market system through prearranged trades. . . . Guttman's gross violations of the Act over a period of six months, especially in light of the fact that he was chairman of the Nymex, directly taint the integrity of the futures market and warrant serious sanctions."

Painter ordered Guttman to pay a fine of $500,000 and issued a five-year trading ban. Glass, whom Painter also found liable for assisting Magid in the illegal trading scheme, was fined $150,000 and banned from futures trading for life following previous infractions. Magid, who was described by Painter as the engineer and executor of the illegal trades, paid $25,000 and was allowed to return to the trading pits in just thirty days.

Magid's trades were offensive enough to warrant the removal of a chairman from office, but not offensive enough to call for the removal of the trader who'd done them. Magid continued trading in the pits until he retired in 2009.

In the aftermath of the Guttman case, the CFTC argued that it had the right to issue lopsided fines and punishments to offenders that were not consistent with the lopsided fines and punishments imposed on other, similar offenders. How the CFTC chose to assign its penalties, it said, was "not a matter of law." The trader who worked with Guttman and Magid learned a lot from that. "Perfect, we have a government agency randomly enforcing the law in whatever way they see fit."

Glass, who was devastated, retired with his family to Palm Beach, Florida. "I get to live in paradise, but otherwise retirement sucks. I'd give it all up if I could go back to the pits. I didn't think I'd get kicked out like that permanently. We were wise guys. No one ever got banned for life trading before that. It was all winks and nods and you just paid your fine and went home and before you knew it, you were back in the ring."

Before settling with Magid, the CFTC had offered Glass the $25,000 fine and thirty-day suspension if he would cooperate in the prosecution of both Magid and Guttman. "I think the 25k and thirty days was the CFTC's standard settlement," Glass says. "They wanted Lou real bad, because he was the chairman. They made it clear that if I wanted to stay in commodities, all I had to do was lie about Lou. I didn't have any problem with throwing Magid under the bus. But Lou, I couldn't do that to him. I didn't know I'd be banned from trading for life. If I'd known that, you know, telling the truth might have been a lot harder to do. I might have taken the settlement."

Magid maintains the CFTC did not pressure him to bend the facts. He recalls Glass was so blasé about the hearing, "he pretended he was broke and used a court-appointed attorney instead of hiring one." As for Guttman, Magid calls him "very charming" and a "pathological liar." To this day, his overarching assessment of Guttman is harsh. "The punishment didn't fit the crime, but it fit the criminal."

Guttman filed an appeal. He and Bohrer argued that, among other things, Painter's obstruction of the cross-examination of Magid violated Guttman's right to due process and a fair trial. "I believe in the justice system," Guttman says. "I believed that justice would prevail." The CFTC's enforcement division filed a cross-appeal. It also asked for an increase in the severity of Guttman's punishment.

Guttman wasn't the only one rattled by the Painter decision. The entire futures industry was up in arms. In the next thirty days, the CME, the Chicago Board of Trade, and the Coffee, Sugar & Cocoa Exchange filed an amicus curiae, a "friend of the court" brief, denouncing Painter's findings. Due to a "fundamental misunderstanding" of the law, they argued, Painter "improperly created a sweeping principle of vicarious, quasi-criminal liability for individuals" who relied on others to do their trading for them. He'd imposed "draconian penalties upon [Guttman], despite his lack of knowledge and participation" in the Magid-Glass trades and without any consideration of whether Guttman "knew of, participated in, or approved of the illegal activity, and without regard to his good faith." New York's Commodity Floor Brokers and Traders Association were in complete agreement. If Painter's decision was upheld, it said in its brief, all investors placing their trust in a trader would be subject to guilt by association:

> *For example, a trader in cotton futures who gives a sum of money to a successful trader in the crude oil ring will be liable for wrongful*

trading by the crude oil trader, even though he does not know
anything about the trading activity by the crude oil trader other than
what is reported in the monthly statements. Such a holding would
extend secondary liability in an unprecedented way in an enforcement
proceeding without need, fairness or logic.

The court was unconcerned. The CFTC wasn't especially concerned either. It didn't have to be. Under a quirk of administrative law, the CFTC would be the final judge of Guttman's appeal *and* the cross-appeal filed by its *own enforcement division*. Again, the fact that everyone was on the same government payroll and worked for the same agency in Washington didn't really seem to be an issue. Three days before Guttman filed his appeal, the CFTC abruptly rearranged its long-standing rules to let its commissioners—those who heard the appeals—throw out any decisions of judges like Painter in favor of entirely new rulings and punishments of their own design. This move effectively put the CFTC's inner circle in the driver's seat in conducting fresh trials and issuing new decisions overruling its own judges in courts of law. In the new "trial," there would be no judge or jury and no lawyers or appearances by those being tried. All deliberations and decisions would be made within the confines of the CFTC's stone-and-glass offices. Guttman's case was one of the first on which it would flex its newfound authoritative muscles.

THE SAME YEAR Painter handed down his ruling, President Clinton named Brooksley Born the new head of the CFTC. A friend of Hillary Clinton, Born came from the Washington law firm Arnold & Porter, which helped represent White House counsel Bernard Nussbaum, Guttman's ex-lawyer, during the Whitewater investigations into the Clintons' real-estate dealings in Arkansas.

Born was the polar opposite of former CFTC chairwoman Wendy Gramm in nearly every respect. Where Gramm was pro-market, Born was pro-regulation. The pro-market and pro-regulation camps were seen in Washington and on Wall Street as diametrically opposed. Too many pro-market policies seemed to undercut the protections of the ordinary citizen, but too many market regulations seemed to kill off both negative *and* positive revolutionary forces in the market. ("Innovation is a by-product of excess," one of my market-purist sources liked to say. "You don't get innovation without getting the Frankenstein.") The argument for strong regulation was a persuasive one. Consumers, clearly, needed to be protected. But protecting them frequently gave the oft-confused babysitters in Washington the upper hand, which was not deemed to be good for business. There were also lamentable conflicts of interest, not in the least because many of the market's regulators were more or less people who didn't have the credentials for top-paying jobs on Wall Street but were still trying to cross over. (This problem, by the way, did not exclude financial journalists, many of whom took plush jobs working for Wall Street firms, or big oil companies, or trade organizations after becoming too chummy with industry officials who offered to pay them far more than any news organization ever could.)

Born, a Stanford law graduate admitted to the university's under-graduate program at just sixteen, was not one of these people. A top lawyer, she was accomplished enough to work for nearly any law firm she desired, but believed in public service and hoped to one day become a federal judge. "She hired me and I worked very closely with her," says a former CFTC director. "She was very impressive, very professional, extremely savvy on the realities of the market, and a truly dynamic leader. She was absolutely incorruptible, which frustrated a lot of people." Detractors, some also from the CFTC, described her as aggressive and principled, sometimes to a fault. One colleague went so far as to say her regulatory style approached scorched-earth, which had made her enemies. "Brooksley made a cottage industry of always saying, 'I am right and everybody else is wrong,'" he says. "So much so that when she *was* right, nobody listened." This was true when Born famously took on Federal Reserve chairman Alan Greenspan in the 1990s, warning of the stark dangers of unregulated financial derivatives in the dark market, which had started long ago with commodities and had since branched out into complex debt instruments.

Of course, she'd been right. Less than two decades later, in 2008, she was branded a market Cassandra during the 360-degree disembow-eling that shredded banking citadels Bear Stearns, Lehman Brothers, and Merrill Lynch, as unregulated credit-default swaps—bets on the creditworthiness of a company or product, such as mortgages—hurled the global financial system into its death spiral. Having specialized in obscure financial instruments at Arnold & Porter, Born easily grasped the inner workings of the market in ways that went right over Congress's head. She had no qualms about shouting down a room full of stuffy men (including successive Treasury secretaries Robert Rubin and Lawrence Summers) when it came to the realities of their old-guard ideas about the newfangled markets, and she certainly wasn't about to back off Guttman at a time when it was absolutely crucial she make her mark.

Given Born's impeccable credentials, the only blemish on her record was her relationship with the person who helped her get her job. Washington pundits and politicians—in particular, Republicans—did not care for her cozy friendship with the first lady, with whom she shared intimate lunches. But it wasn't the intimate lunches that were raising eyebrows. Before Born's appointment, Clinton had become embroiled in a Nymex-style commodities-trading scandal that came to light just as the Whitewater hearings were getting under way in Congress. The timing was inopportune, as the Beltway was still reeling from the suicide of Vincent Foster, Nussbaum's deputy, who died James Forrestal–like, in the forest in 1993, triggering a storm of conspiracy theories.

In March 1994, there was an uproar when it was discovered that the first lady had made $98,000 off a paltry $1,000 investment in just ten months, through a Refco trading account (the same Refco of ill repute that went under in 2005 in another commodities flap). With no prior trading experience, Clinton scored a bonanza that confounded the experts by betting on cattle futures in the bull market of the late 1970s. Richard Schaeffer would have liked to have done so well when he'd bet on cattle futures and gone to zero in the same market. Clinton's trading coup had only surfaced now because she was entering the White House and the press was arduously combing through her tax records. Robert L. "Red" Bone, a former World Series of Poker semifinalist and the broker of Clinton's trades, didn't exactly inspire confidence, as he'd previously been suspended for trading offenses.

Even after a *New York Times* article suggested that the Hillary-as-trading-dynamo story seemed highly suspect, the issue was swept under the rug. At a live White House press conference in the State Dining Room, broadcast by the major news networks, positioned under a portrait of Abraham Lincoln, Clinton calmly explained that she had achieved her trading success by reading the newspaper. Leo Melamed at the CME, where the cattle futures were traded, confirmed finding discrepancies in the Clinton trading records, but said he didn't see any evidence—or lack of evidence—of any explicit wrongdoing. All of which left the public more mystified than ever. "Mrs. Clinton violated no rules in the course of her transactions," he said at the time. Years later, he spoke to me with more candor. "Hillary was a customer of Refco and she was the client of Red Bone. And we know Refco did everything you could imagine for violating the rules for their customers. Hillary wasn't even seen as a major client; she was a pipsqueak. I saw Hillary's violations as meaningless. Was she being paid off? Anything is possible, but I am not going to play psychologist."

Independent studies of Clinton's trading records found the circumstances surrounding her bets to be improbable in the extreme and her winning streak nothing short of miraculous. Yet, with Born at the helm of the CFTC, Clinton was never investigated or charged.

When Hillary Clinton visited the Nymex trading floor years later to ring the opening bell, the traders, recalling the scandal, unreservedly booed her. "After we booed, the exchange executives yelled at us and brought her back a *second* time and made us clap," Kaufman says. "It wasn't because the traders hated Democrats. A lot of the traders *are* Democrats. They just hated *her*." A Wall Street lawyer with high-level connections in Washington and ties to the CFTC says Born's selective battle-ax approach was part of the reason her contract at the CFTC was not renewed. "That Brooksley was incorruptible is a joke. Look at how she ignored the Hillary Clinton fiasco. She didn't resign. She was told to resign or she'd be forced out. You want to know the truth about Hillary? No one wanted to touch that thing. It was radioactive."

When Guttman's appeal of the Painter decision crossed Born's desk, she did not hesitate to use her new super-legal powers. She sided with the CFTC's enforcement division, finding Guttman guilty of being the "controlling person" behind Magid's illegal trades—the charge Painter had specifically dismissed—and scuttled Guttman's five-year trading ban, replacing it with a lifetime trading ban. Guttman had considered he might lose his appeal, but he didn't think he might be *retried on a charge that had already been dropped* with the penalty increased to a *life sentence*. "I was punished for filing an appeal," he says. "I never met Brooksley Born, but in the comfort of her own office, without hearing any of the testimony, she simply decided I was guilty." Three other commissioners at the CFTC signed her decree, issued in April 1998.

Born says she cannot discuss the ruling, but Melamed, who knew both Guttman and Born, summed it up. "First of all, I liked Brooksley Born. She was well-intentioned, a good lawyer, and I respected her. She didn't have a good name in our industry, but we got along and I think she liked me. But the credibility of the CFTC has always been in question, and, because of that, the CFTC is painfully conscious of trying to find ways to raise its credibility. Here, they had the Nymex chairman in their crosshairs, wow. Frankly, I think Lou Guttman was telling the truth, that he didn't know what was going on. He was the victim of an agenda. He got a raw deal."

Guttman also still owed his $500,000 fine. He had no idea how he was going to pay it. He wasn't allowed to trade commodities or be an exchange chairman, the only two things he knew how to do. And he needed to make a living, not just pay off his fine. He had aging parents to support. With no other choice, he decided to appeal his case yet again, this time to a court outside the CFTC. Federal appeals courts did not like to tinker with the affairs of the government's administrative courts, but he figured it was worth a shot. He and Bohrer took his case up the next rung of the legal ladder, to the U.S. Court of Appeals for the Second Circuit. "They can rumor-monger you to death," Guttman told the news reporters still trying to keep up with the twists and turns of the case, "but facts are facts and they will ultimately bear out."

Guttman and Bohrer pleaded their case before the court's three judges, who Guttman thought asked probing, intelligent questions. It went so well that the opposing attorney actually told Guttman on the way out, "Lou, you had a good day today."

The appeals court took more than a year to make its decision. As Guttman waited, trade publications such as *Securities Week* gave him excellent odds of having his charges dropped, as evidenced, it said, by "the length of time the court has contemplated the issues involved, as well as a widespread view among commodities attorneys that the case is flawed in Guttman's favor." In the meantime, many of the charges piled onto the New York and Chicago traders in the 1980s sting operations were beginning to fall through due to double-jeopardy issues. A whiff of vindication was in the air.

On November 16, 1999, the court handed down a simply written seven-page document denying Guttman's petition. "We hold that the weight of the evidence supports the commission's findings," it said. It did not explain the reasons behind its decision aside from parroting the findings of the CFTC, which immediately shot out a press release announcing its win against Guttman. As always, a torrent of newspaper headlines followed. Bohrer called Guttman as soon as he found out. "Don't worry," he said. "We can appeal this to the U.S. Supreme Court."

Guttman's shoulders sagged. He'd spent tens of thousands of dollars on his defense, thinking he would eventually be exonerated. The chairmanship had delivered its death blow.

For the first time since embarking on his legal battle, Guttman felt nothing. He hung up the phone. He'd been bogged down in courts for a decade. One of the questionnaires he'd received from the CFTC had contained over 3,200 questions, each requiring a lengthy answer. "Psychologically, more than anything, they kill you," he says.

He couldn't go through it again. Even Glass had given up and settled years ago.

Guttman took a long walk along the marina, circling back to his home at the Gateway Plaza, his office with the cracked paint, the beaten parquet floor, and the halogen lamps on either side of his desk, leaning inward like dead trees in dead water.

His father's prophecy, foretold when Guttman returned home exuberant after winning the vice chairmanship, had come true.

"My parents were street-smart. They were Old World Hungarians. I was a New World kid. They were right. I was wrong."

Guttman sat on the narrow felt couch. "I put my foot up on the table," he says. "I gave up."

10

Dark Days

Lemme tell you something—you know how our market might be better? If we had a war or a hurricane. People pray for that shit.

—MARK LICHTNER

DANNY RAPPAPORT SHOULD have known better than to bring a former race car driver into the boardroom to try and do a deal with the pit traders.

Jeffrey Sprecher, a tanned, forty-five-year-old chemical engineer and power-plant developer from Beverly Hills, was a virtual unknown to the oil market, but he was an entrepreneur of formidable talent. Physically broad and mentally unflappable, he cut an intimidating figure. He was bald, but bald in that well-scrubbed, authoritative way, not in the scruffy way of the pit trader. A self-described workaholic, Sprecher admitted to thinking about work "even while I'm watching the TV." He grew up in a middle-class family in Madison, Wisconsin, went to business school at Pepperdine University, and raised $50 million for his first power plant by age twenty-seven, even as he struggled to get approved for the $100,000 mortgage on his first condo. Such were the ironies of raising money on Wall Street.

Approaching Nymex for the first time in 2000, at the height of the dot-com bubble, he floated an unorthodox proposal: why not move the energy market from the trading pits onto the Internet, where it could be accessible to traders around the world twenty-four hours a day?

In the back of their minds, the Nymex directors had known this moment was coming. For years, they'd been hearing about how electronic trading was the wave of the future, how it would revolutionize the business, how they should just embrace it and stop fighting it. But ever since Guttman and Melamed began discussing it in the 1980s, a sense of dread had gripped the pits whenever the topic came up. With the hype over the Internet reaching fever pitch, it seemed that everyone, save the Nymex traders, wanted to ditch the pits for online trading. The overseas oil traders, who phoned in their orders down to the pits every day from Asia, Europe, and the Middle East, were tired of planning their days around when the New York traders felt like coming in. The Nymex traders still only worked four and a half hours a day, beginning at ten A.M. and closing at two thirty P.M. For the traders in other time zones, it was beyond inconvenient. Wall Street's banks, oil companies, and hedge funds were in perfect agreement. They'd always disliked the Nymex oil monopoly. This was their chance to establish something more modern, more accessible, and, if possible, much more secretive. The Nymex traders, once again, stood in everybody's way. The pit traders had taken great pains to corner their oil market. If the pits closed, what would happen to them? And who would control the energy market in their place?

The board members had known this moment was coming and they had thought long and hard about it. After Sprecher was finished speaking, they gave their unequivocal answer. Richie Schaeffer, the board's de facto mouthpiece, was the first to speak up.

"You know what? This is a shit deal!" He called for a vote to get the proposal off the table—immediately.

The other traders seconded it.

The meeting did not go well for Sprecher. He was literally bodily thrown out of the exchange roughly five minutes into his pitch.

"We didn't know who he was or where he came from or what he really wanted, but we did *not* like what he was saying and we wanted him outta there," says one of the traders who heard Sprecher's presentation. "We're thinking, who *is* this guy to walk into our exchange and ask us point-blank to give our market away?" To the Nymex members, it was nothing short of madness.

Sprecher's professional background was one of a capitalist's capitalist. His personal background, like Leo Melamed's, was that of a bad boy. He'd earned a reputation for being adept at juggling women. During an interview, when I asked him about how he'd managed to pursue so many deals at once, he crisply responded that a deal was like a woman. "I've learned over the years that deals have a pace and a timing that you develop an instinct for. It's kind of like the process of dating. There is the process of meeting someone, going through the courtship, and ultimately getting married. We've all done that, had that process where there's so many people you meet, and you think it's going to be great up front, and over time, you know, you change your mind. Getting to the end is a complicated thing. But the earlier you can recognize the pace, the easier it is to have multiple things going on." (In one of the more well-circulated stories about Sprecher's multiple goings-on, he arranged for two dates on the night of an industry cocktail party, making trips back and forth between the two, Underground-style, throughout the evening.) He eventually settled down with a sharp Midwestern farm girl, also a naturalized Californian, hired by his company as a vice president. His highest-paid female employee, she is now also his wife.

Building power plants in California for seventeen years, Sprecher became frustrated with the archaic ways of power trading. He wanted to make it easier for power plants, specifically *his* power plants, to buy and sell their electricity. In 1997, he purchased an exchange in Atlanta from Warren Buffett, gutting it and assembling a global electronic-trading platform that could handle a wide array of futures and over-the-counter trades. He'd only intended it to be a side project, but it ended up consuming him. He left his full-time job as president of the power-plant development firm he'd started with some business-school friends to give it his full attention.

His project soon piqued the interest of Enron, which, by 1992, was North America's largest merchant of natural gas, the lifeblood of power plants. Pretending to contemplate a partnership with Sprecher, Enron's executives listened intently to his ideas about how he planned to start an online power-trading company. They told him thank you very much, but they weren't interested. Then they turned around and created EnronOnline, beating him to the punch. (An executive close to Sprecher says, "Jeff knew something was up when the Enron guys started asking things like, 'So when you get to the customer firewall, how do you get around it?'")

Sprecher continued with his toils. In 2001, he bought London's International Petroleum Exchange, the same European energy market Guttman had considered doing a deal with decades earlier. Sprecher didn't just plan to build a trading platform for electricity—he wanted to trade the full spectrum of energy markets, including oil. Whether by calculation or serendipity, his purchase of the London oil market gave him tremendous advantage over Nymex. Sprecher was building his business off a *foreign* exchange and putting it onto the *Internet,* so he wouldn't have to follow the same U.S. trading rules as Nymex. That meant energy traders using his electronic-trading system could bet on much larger quantities of oil and fuel than on Nymex, without having to report to the CFTC what they were doing. Wall Street liked that. It also liked that it wouldn't have to call in any more orders to the Nymex trading pits, where the locals might try to rip them off.

Sprecher's system let traders make bets at any time of the day from anywhere in the world, not just during the four and a half hours Nymex was open. All they had to do was log on to their computers. Best of all, using Sprecher's system let them conceal the totality of their trading activities, since electronic trades were conducted anonymously through automated trade-matching engines in milliseconds. By contrast, trades in the Nymex pits were mostly done by human hands. In short, Sprecher's company, which he called IntercontinentalExchange and soon became known around the world as ICE, was the solution energy traders had been praying for. It was like Nymex, only without all the rules or the headaches.

Sprecher wisely suspected it wouldn't be easy to get the world's energy traders to change their ways. After all, Nymex was the monopoly. But he also knew that the Wall Street traders loathed the fact that Nymex had a hammerlock on oil. So he did what he did best: he made them a deal. In exchange for test-driving ICE, he would give away all but 5 percent of his business to thirteen of the world's largest energy-trading companies and banks. They included Goldman Sachs, arguably the most powerful bank on earth; Morgan Stanley; Duke Energy; Deutsche Bank; Reliant Energy; Shell; Total; and BP, among others. It was a shrewd move. In amassing a team of cash-heavy behemoths who, in exchange for their grubstakes in ICE, would begin channeling millions of trades through his system, Sprecher instantly became Nymex's worst nightmare. In short order, ICE would become the eBay of the energy market.

But the Nymex traders didn't know it yet.

When the Nymex board members discovered that Rappaport had been in confidential talks with Goldman Sachs and Morgan Stanley about doing a deal with Sprecher, they went into hysterics. They saw it as a blatant betrayal. The banks were some of their best customers—but they were also their worst enemies. Goldman's bad reputation at Nymex had started under Guttman's chairmanship, when the bank began backing pit traders who were running for the board. "The idea was that Goldman wanted a board member on every exchange in the world. Typical Goldman, they had to have their tentacles on everything," Guttman says. "When we had a guy on the board from Goldman, he couldn't help but be all the way up our ass. He would try to bully the board into voting against things that made perfect sense to the members or else he would make sure Goldman took away their business in the trading pits. It could really undermine your agenda as chairman. After that thing with Sprecher, we never took any more chances on the Goldman guys, because we never knew if they were trying to help us or put us out of business."

Rappaport continued unfazed. Even if Sprecher failed, it was only a matter of time before somebody else put around-the-clock energy trading on a computer screen and started gorging itself on Nymex's business the same way that Marks had fed on OPEC and the oil majors more than twenty years earlier. What did OPEC's oil prices mean to the world today? Virtually nothing. OPEC's oil-price basket was a joke, a political tool, a symbol of what OPEC *thought oil prices should be,* not what they really were. Whenever prices got out of hand, OPEC would just blithely point to its price basket, based on the valuations and assessments of its member countries—many of which did *not* have free markets—as proof that it had nothing to do with the wild markets of the West. "This day and age, even the OPEC officials don't think they have any control over oil prices anymore," says a well-connected academic, citing private conversations with OPEC officials.

Yet OPEC's ministers plowed bravely on, attempting to maintain their rock-star status, relishing the media attention every time they held a meeting at their headquarters in Vienna, rushing through conference rooms often chased by roving bands of journalists waving notebooks and microphones at them. The journalists themselves regarded the ritual as farcical. "The oil ministers love the attention and all the cameras," a close friend told me while covering an OPEC meeting for the *Financial Times.* "They never get that level of attention anywhere else. Vienna is kind of like a Disneyland for them compared to places like Doha, Jeddah, and Tehran."

Whenever OPEC announces to the world how much oil it plans to pump, what it doesn't mention is that its decisions are unenforceable and its members almost always cheat the plan, pumping more than agreed upon. In actuality, OPEC doesn't even meet the definition of a real "cartel," because it has no control over its own members' actions. Just as the world can't stop itself from overconsuming oil, the oil nations can't stop themselves from overproducing it.

Rappaport had been witness to Nymex snatching OPEC's power away, and he didn't want to see it taken again by ICE. But he was having trouble getting the Nymex members to listen. "Gary Cohn, who once traded in the Comex pits, was our Goldman representative on the board," Rappaport recounts. "He was by far the most powerful bank executive we'd ever had, but because he was from *Goldman,* the other traders hated him. Gary would be the first to admit he's outspoken and extremely arrogant, but what he was saying absolutely needed to be said. He thought we should do the deal with ICE. The Nymex guys couldn't stand him. They rejected the idea outright. He's now the No. 2 guy at Goldman." (The No. 1 guy at Goldman, the Bronx-born Lloyd Blankfein, also came from a hardscrabble commodities-trading background after being rejected when he first applied for a job at Goldman. As fate would have it, his trading shop was later bought by the bank and the rest is history.)

Cohn and Neal Shear, a managing director at Morgan Stanley, introduced Rappaport to Sprecher. "That's when I first found out some of Nymex's biggest customers were going to do this deal and start trading on ICE, whether we were going to get involved or not," Rappaport says. "Sprecher wasn't targeting our business directly, but he was filling in the gaps. He was offering all kinds of things that Nymex wouldn't offer because we were trying to protect our trading pits. So did I feel threatened by that? Yeah, I felt threatened."

The floor traders felt threatened too, but not enough to do anything about it. They believed that time was on their side. Trading behind closed doors day in and day out, they didn't realize they were trapped in a self-sustaining bubble, unable to see that the big picture was rapidly changing. All they could think about was what was happening in the pits.

What had once been a new generation of traders storming the stodgy dinosaurs of Big Oil and forcing a new world order had become a league of dinosaurs themselves. And worse, they'd lost all humility.

They were now an overindulgent generation of egomaniacs stuck in their ways. Exemplars of a bygone age, the traders were incompatible with the dot-com era. They didn't want to trade on the screen any more than the potato traders had wanted to give up trading potatoes for oil. They liked their carefree lifestyle in the pits. They liked going to work every day and seeing hundreds of friends. So long as the status quo remained even remotely profitable, they didn't want to change anything. "Looking back, it seems ridiculous how much in denial everybody was. But they stayed in denial for a long time, because not being in denial meant not making seven figures a year while you worked a few hours a day," says a former Nymex executive. "You'd be in denial too. But they hung on way too long. The executives simply locked themselves in a room and kept telling each other how they were giving the traders of the world what they wanted, even as the floor lost all value to anyone but the people trading on it."

From that day forward, to speak Sprecher's name was to emit poison. He became persona non grata, an enemy of the state. And for the time being, few spoke of him. In fact, in the months ahead, the board would conveniently forget all about the man who'd come to them with a proposition that would have made them more money than God. By the time they realized the error of their ways, it would be too late.

Meanwhile, the traders were more focused on another market—the unauthorized market in college basketball.

The futures market based on NCAA basketball teams materialized spontaneously one afternoon between the Nymex heating-oil and natural-gas options pits. "People deserted the crude-oil pit and the other pits, and, one by one, before you knew it, you had three hundred people trading basketball futures and no one in the other trading rings," says Bill Perkins from Centaurus. "Even people on Wall Street would be calling down to place bets. It would usually happen right before March Madness, before the exchange executives banned it. It went on for like two or three years. They *had* to stop it, because it kept defaulting and no one would trade any of the other markets as long as it was going on."

The basketball futures market grew to more than $2 million in value before it was finally shut down, says one of the Nymex executives. The ban happened only after a trader who didn't get paid on a bet threatened to tell the IRS about it. The lack of a clearinghouse to back up the basketball futures market also made it extremely risky, says Conrad Goerl, one of Perkins's colleagues and a former pit trader. "Without a clearing-house, the trades weren't insured or guaranteed by anyone, so it wasn't always easy to collect on your bets. You had sixty-four teams, so the guy who bet on a winning team got $64 and everyone else got zero. But people wouldn't trade just one. They'd find a team that wasn't ranking and then short a hundred or a thousand lots. Sell each lot, for example, at 25 cents. Or the other way around. After a while, people were trad-ing enough of them that they would try to trade arbitrage. It started up small and then evolved and the clerks got involved. You had people who were buying lots and others who were selling them and there's no clearinghouse for any of this, right? You could basically buy or sell as much of anything as you wanted. There was no limit. For a while there, it got really crazy. People outside the market were getting involved, and Nymex and over-the-counter brokers were even brokering the bets. But the credit risks were too big. In a situation like that, technically, you should only be trading with people who you know can pay up, but it didn't always work out that way. When you have clerks making only $35,000 a year and trading thousands of lots of basketball futures, what do you do when they can't pay and default? In the end, I think that's what killed it, more than the executives banning it."[*]

Rappaport, as chairman, found the basketball futures market very amusing. "I so enjoyed that creative aspect of the market," he says. "Nymex was still this immature organization growing at an extraordi-nary rate and gaining global acceptance, and sometimes we just couldn't keep up. We didn't have the staff or technology or any of the pieces in place to be totally efficient. I remember you could short a certain team and go long on another team. There was a major flaw in it though. It was something like if you shorted every team, you would always win, because only one team can win in the end, right? People from off the trading floor would call in their bets on the NCAA tournament. The Morgan Stanleys, the J.P. Morgans, the Goldmans, anyone trading energy would call down. They'd even take positions on behalf of their clients."

Guttman did not much like the "creative aspect" of the market. He

---

[*] Years later, Goerl would reflect on how the downfall of the basketball futures market was not unlike the 2008 banking crisis that would take place on Wall Street.

still owned three seats on Nymex he considered to be among his most important assets. Since he leased the seats to floor traders for several thousand dollars a month each, they were his primary financial life-line. After the CFTC decimated his life savings, it was all he had. "My mother was sick. I didn't have the money to take care of her and pay the CFTC's fine of $500,000. The fine was the highest ever in a case where money wasn't stolen and customers weren't ripped off. Even the federal judges were shocked. The CFTC said I couldn't pay the fine in install-ments. Then they turned the bill over to the U.S. attorney, who went after me. I was in the poorhouse. My life was a shambles. I borrowed the money from friends. In all, I paid $90,000 in interest. I only started feeling okay again after I'd taken care of my debts. It took me years to get reestablished. In the meantime, I was living in the Twilight Zone."

While caring for his mother, who died of vascular disease in November 2000, Guttman kept in close touch with the Nymex traders. He continued to support or oppose board members and took on proj-ects under contract for the exchange working on new financial products, from which he earned a couple hundred thousand dollars a year. With his livelihood inextricably linked to that of the exchange, he remained highly engaged in the politics of the boardroom and the pits. He also started putting out a newsletter, the *Nymex Advocate*, e-mailing it to four hundred or so Nymex members and journalists. On it, he posted news stories and offered commentary whenever Nymex's leadership appeared to be running off the rails. In doing so, he became a force to be reckoned with. Guttman couldn't be chairman, but he would have a say in who could. He became the oil market's kingmaker.

"I used the *Advocate* to keep the members informed of what the chairman and the board members were doing and what they weren't doing. Because I campaigned for certain members, when a board meet-ing was over, they'd all call me to tell me what was going on. That was my information flow. Basically, I wasn't doing much while taking care of my mother, so I dedicated my hours and days to Nymex."

With the energy market becoming more and more emboldened, Guttman effectively became the watchdog where the CFTC was not.

Rappaport's eight-year chairmanship grew increasingly rocky as he kept trying to nudge Nymex in the direction of electronic trading. The board members weren't willing to enter such perilous waters, lest the pit traders kick them off the board. Politically, it was just too risky. But

Rappaport plunged ahead anyway, spending tens of millions of dollars on an electronic-trading system that he called eNymex. It went nowhere. After his meeting with Sprecher, the tide began to turn against him. The Nymex membership, spooked by the specter of electronic trading, wanted Rappaport out and a new chairman in, one who would be a sworn protector of the pits. Vinnie Viola, who'd remained in close contact with Guttman, started openly challenging Rappaport, a telltale sign he was testing his upward mobility. Privately, he was even more forceful. Viola asked Rappaport to build eNymex off his own fly-by-night Internet trading company using cash from the Nymex coffers. Rappaport refused. He did not trust Viola because of his loyalty to Guttman. Viola's company foundered. It did not bode well for the relationship.

Guttman took Viola on one of his marina walks. "Vinnie was the only guy who could take Rappaport out, but at first he didn't care; he had other business interests," Guttman says. "He told me, 'If I run in the next election, it's going to be a bloodbath.' I said, 'Trust me, if you put your name in, Danny will drop out.'" Viola was skeptical, but days after announcing his candidacy, Rappaport withdrew. When Schaeffer, Rappaport's good friend, pulled Rappaport aside to tell him he would be backing Viola, Rappaport knew it was over. Schaeffer never backed the guy who didn't win. "Throughout my career, I was always the guy behind the guy," Schaeffer says. "That's how I survived." Viola won four-fifths of the vote. Rappaport went on to coach Little League, do landscaping around his house in Westport, Connecticut, and help his wife raise their three kids—a daughter and two sons. He also continued to trade.

There was just one catch. Viola didn't really want the chairmanship. He'd only agreed to it to appease Guttman. Nymex was still the laughingstock of Wall Street, even as it practically printed its own money. At best, he saw the chairmanship as a garnish for his résumé; at worst, a career-ending cul-de-sac, as it had been for Guttman. He did not sentimentalize Nymex as chairman by hanging expensive oil paintings on the walls. He declined to sit for his portrait. From the outset, he made it abundantly clear to the traders that he didn't plan on staying chairman for any longer than a couple of years. As far as he could tell, *they* were lucky to have *him*.

Viola was perhaps the handsomest of all the exchange chairmen, but beneath the spit and polish he was still a tough guy from Brooklyn. Growing up, he'd attended a vocational technical high school and graduated from the military academy at West Point in 1972. He'd gone on to the Army Ranger school, served as an infantry officer in the 101st Airborne Division, and transferred to the Army Reserve in 1982. Viola left the Army Reserve as a major in 1993. Returning to civilian life was an enormous adjustment for him. He hadn't planned on having a career outside the army and didn't like to discuss the reason he left. After becoming a local in the Nymex gasoline pit, he finally found his niche. He compared trading to being in an army platoon. "You have all this information coming at you and you have to focus, to pick out what's significant and make decisions in real time." He started out with just $5,000, which took him five years to save up as an infantry officer. He founded Pioneer Futures in 1985, gaining fast footing among the traders, who, like him, were all diamonds in the rough. "Vinnie had a way of appealing to you by making you believe you could have the same salary as the guy at Goldman with the C-suite without his shitty lifestyle," says a former associate. "I wanted to make real money, but I didn't want to end up neglecting my family or leaving close friends behind while I got fat and grew old. I didn't want to work around the clock, eat at my desk, and lose my identity. Vinnie made it seem like that was possible."

After becoming a Nymex trader, Viola also dabbled in other businesses, running some community banks in Dallas and starting up proprietary trading shops active in the New York and London energy markets. After taking the chairmanship, he even invested in the Nets basketball team alongside real-estate developer Bruce Ratner, who'd worked on the construction of the Nymex building that had generated so much controversy. The two men moved the team from New Jersey to Viola's hometown of Brooklyn, with Viola bringing in other investors from Nymex—most notably, bestselling mystery romance novelist Mary Higgins Clark, whose daughter Patty Clark Derenzo was Viola's secretary. (Mary Higgins Clark's third husband was John Conheeney, a Nymex board member and the retired CEO of Merrill Lynch Futures.)

When it came to running his businesses, Viola was a complicated man. His modus operandi, according to those closest to him, was to engage in swift takeoffs followed by hard landings. "Vinnie was great at finding partners to look after his financial affairs and he would show up when it came time to collect," says a former associate, who worked with him, but not as a direct partner. He watched a number of Viola's cohorts come and go. "His trick was to treat you like a million bucks

98 percent of the time and really badly only 2 percent of the time. He'd pay you incredibly well, so you always felt like you owed him. People would watch his back. But his partnerships often ended in lawsuits or fights with Vinnie screaming vulgarities." Viola had a nasty temper, but Guttman says he didn't lose control of his emotions easily. "He exuded leadership. His personality was amazing. He drew people in. He was a phenomenal speaker. Even if he didn't know what he was talking about, he *sounded* like he knew what he was saying. He was an astute business-man and an extreme opportunist." The only Nymex chairman to have an established entrepreneurial background, Viola made short work of almost every project he tackled. "Vinnie was more of a builder than a taker," Guttman says. "Most of the other chairmen didn't know how to build. They only knew how to pork-barrel to the point where they drained the market of all its value."

The year Viola got elected, 2001, was the year Michel Marks emerged from his decade of reclusion. During the course of his lengthy absence, he'd embarked on what he described as a "Jack Kerouac jour-ney," commencing with a three-month trip to South Africa to watch the breakup of apartheid. He took a detour in Florida's South Beach, where he bought some property before heading to Russia, where he observed the Communist regime in its final death throes. The KGB was "following me around," he said in filings with the Securities and Exchange Commission, so he left. Marks also invested in a handful of semi-futuristic businesses, including a pre-Internet startup that failed because it was too far ahead of its time. Marks went out west and painted in Berkeley, California. He washed dishes at Esalen on the island of Big Sur. A private adult bohemia offering courses for thousands of dollars each, such as "Soul Motion" and "Being with Your Self," Esalen billed itself as a utopia for serious intellectuals looking to swap "revolution-ary ideas" in clothing-optional environments while sunbathing, hot-tubbing, and enjoying nude massage.

Marks traveled cross-country to Utah and Wyoming, hiking and exploring with local guides, rock-climbing, mountain-biking, practicing yoga, and, according to the SEC filings, "drinking a lot of good wine." He kept one foot in the oil patch, joining the board of Petroleum Argus Inc., a global energy pricing and news agency. He disclosed all this to the Nymex members, and they promptly voted him back on the board in March of that year. Marks opted to keep a low profile until the right moment.

Two weeks into his chairmanship, Viola summoned Guttman for a private meeting. "Vinnie gave me the greatest compliment. He said, 'Louie, in the ten years since you left, all we've been doing is executing your strategic agenda. There was nothing you wanted to do that we did not do. You said we needed to merge with Comex, we merged with Comex. You said we needed a new building, we got a new building. You said we needed to become a for-profit organization and we became a for-profit organization. You said we needed to expand our trading business and we are doing that.' Then he leaned in and said, 'I'm the chairman now, so you can shut down the *Nymex Advocate*.' Obviously, he didn't want my newsletter to have any influence over the members. I said, 'Vinnie, I wanted Rappaport out of there, but let me tell you one thing: as long as you stick to fucking business, you don't have to be afraid of the *Advocate*. Once you start hurting my business, I'm going to blow you out of the water, just like him. My friendship has *nothing* to do with the future of this exchange, so if you're asking me to shut it down, my answer to you is no. Any further questions?' Then I got up and walked out. I was pissed. Two days later, he took it back. He said, 'Lou, I didn't mean it.' I told him, 'You're getting this all wrong. You think I blew Rappaport out because I hated Rappaport? Because he succeeded me? That had nothing to do with it. My time has come and gone. But he was not good for the business.'"

Guttman didn't realize how quickly the oil market would resume its slide into the same sinkhole of patronage and gluttony he had been hoping it would avoid. Titanic struggles erupted as the board turned into a microcosm of the pits, engaging in many of the same backhanded maneuvers and character assassinations. It seemed that no one could get near the oil money machine without being tainted by it. Not even Viola, whose riches were estimated to be in the hundreds of millions—less than those of Mark Fisher but more than those of almost any other trader at Nymex. Marty Greenberg, who ran the trading firm Sterling Commodities with his son, David, and was a member of Nymex, backed Viola, but soon changed his mind. "The one thing almost all of them had in common at Nymex was they were only interested in the smash and grab. Nymex liked to compare itself to the Chicago Mercantile Exchange, but the difference between them and Chicago was that the CME was full of really bright guys doing some really great things. The Nymex was just a bunch of pygmies asking, 'What's in it for me?'"

Viola's chairmanship was, to many, one of the most cold-blooded and cannibalistic in the oil market's history. While Viola and Guttman had discussed in confidence the need to tear down and rebuild the exchange from the ground up with "no sacred cows," Viola ousted valuable senior staff members and colonized the executive suite with a slate of handpicked sycophants whom he paid far more exorbitantly than any chairman had ever paid his staff before. In an environment where money bred loyalty, humongous paychecks to key staff members ensured not only obeisance but all-out servility. Chief among the payees was J. Robert "Bo" Collins, a former options trader from Pioneer Futures. A native Texan, Collins had been recruited from the pits after working for Viola at Pioneer to head up El Paso's over-the-counter energy-trading desk in his home state. A year later, El Paso became embroiled in the Enron fallout, for which it was ultimately forced to disgorge millions of dollars in trading profits. Collins got out just in time, being hired back by Viola as Nymex president. Despite his lack of executive experience, Collins earned a yearly salary of over $1 million as Viola's right-hand man. Guttman was baffled.

"Did you even *read* Bo's contract?" he asked Viola. "We've never paid a president over a million before. What the hell is that?"

Viola didn't think it was such a big deal. "C'mon, Lou, you know I don't read that shit."

Collins replaced Nymex's longtime president, Pat Thompson, who'd died on the eve of his daughter's wedding. Guttman felt very badly about it, but, he had to admit, a weight had been lifted. He'd never stopped wondering if Thompson, a former CFTC official he had not always gotten along with, had set him up for his fall. "I guess now I will never know," he says. "But let's just say when he died, I went to the funeral just to make sure he was in the box."

Given the rise of the tough-guy mentality in the pits, it only made sense that Nymex should have a tough-guy chairman. The traders liked Viola, because he was someone their egos could handle following. He was a triple threat, with looks, smarts, and brawn. Tall, with a chiseled jaw and dark, wavy hair, he had excellent political skills and a sharp intellect. "Vinnie was the all-in-one package. He attended museums and plays, but he wasn't above letting you know he could also break your legs," said a former associate. "He was no goombah, but he had a way of leaving you with the impression that he was well connected on Wall Street and on *the* streets. Which meant that if you fucked him, he could fuck you back harder."

The irony was that Viola probably was a more refined person than he let on. But at Nymex, the pit traders weren't into intellectuals. They responded to raw power and brute force. "He put the act on really hard," says Marty Greenberg. "He threw the tough-guy thing around a little too much, if you ask me. It may not have been real, but he definitely let the actor become the essence."

Viola's plainspoken talk of reward and punishment, rule of order, and overall willingness to get in people's faces when necessary appealed to the traders. "Vinnie used to have a huge bodybuilder goon he went around with," says the executive who worked with him. "He made the guy rich, but they had a falling-out. I saw the goon somewhere afterward and he told me he was going to kill Vinnie. When I told Vinnie, he got this crazy look on his face and said, 'Oh, yeah? He's gonna kill *me*? I'll kill *him*!'"

So dedicated was Viola to the art of war, he even set up a dojo in his office to study kung fu under a martial-arts master who would later become head of Nymex security. "We would hold attack poses for an hour or more," Viola says. "It taught us discipline and clarity." While devoting himself to a practice called Yi Chuan, he would hold all his phone calls.

The son of a truck driver, Viola transcended the chairman's mold. He could mix with society pagers and pit traders with equal aplomb. He gave the traders who didn't make it on the floor jobs in the executive suite and made it known that he'd take care of them if they took care of him. A man of grand gestures, he contributed large sums of money to philanthropic causes and attended dinners at the White House with his wife of three decades, Teresa, including one hosted in 2008 by President Bush for Italian prime minister Silvio Berlusconi. When in New York, he also ate at Rao's, the famed mob dive in East Harlem known for its gangster violence. Viola's fondest wish, says the former associate, was to be ambassador to Italy or the Vatican, but "he acted way too shady for that."

While some of the Nymex staffers resented Viola's habit of disappearing for hours a day to study in his dojo, it turned out that learning the art of war would not be entirely irrelevant to the job he'd soon be called on to do. War was about to come right to his doorstep. Just a few months after settling into the oil market's highest office, Viola was faced with something for which no chairman on Wall Street could ever be prepared. It was, as he later called it, a devastating "discontinuous nonlinear event."

To everyone else, it was the terrorist attacks of September 11.

David Greenberg got up early that morning. He hurried to Windows on the World, the swank restaurant on the 107th floor of the North Tower. He'd been invited to sit in on a breakfast meeting with the pit traders from Carr Futures, one of his most important clients. Carr, the financial firm that later became Calyon, was considering putting a ban on dual trading, the controversial practice by which the oil traders could trade for themselves alongside their clients through separate trading accounts. Dual trading, which Marks had once banned at his own trading firm, was getting to be very unpopular among the Nymex customers on Wall Street, as many of them felt they were being bilked of profits by pit traders trying to front-run them. If the folklore was true that Alvin Brodsky had sold his silver futures ahead of the Hunt brothers' massive sell order in the 1980s, then that would have qualified as front-running. It was illegal, but it was also very hard to prove. The pit traders were aware that their clients were crying foul, but they didn't want to give up one of their easiest inroads to undeserved riches. The Windows on the World meeting was a chance for them to make their final case.

That morning, Greenberg's driver brought him to the World Trade Center shortly after eight A.M. He walked to the wide bank of elevators to catch the express lift, but it was broken. Instead of riding directly to the top, he'd have to switch elevators midway before continuing. Greenberg opted out. He liked to ride express. If he couldn't ride express, he didn't want to ride at all. After arriving at his office at the Nymex building, which stood directly in the shadow of the Twin Towers, he got a call from his father. "A plane just hit the World Trade Center," Marty Greenberg said. "They think it was a Cessna."

"Oh yeah?" His son riffled through the papers on his desk. He barely glanced out the window. New Yorkers were always wringing their hands over planes flying too low. He stayed on the line, going over the day's business with his dad. After they hung up, Marty Greenberg saw on TV the second jetliner streaking toward the second tower. He also noticed the plane seemed far too large to be a Cessna. He tried to reach David, but was unable to before impact and the downing of all of Lower Manhattan's telephone lines. He sent his son an e-mail—the fastest e-mail of his life. GET THE FUCK OUT OF THERE. I LOVE YOU. GO NORTH.

"My father is a man who never panics. But at that moment, he freaked out. Nobody knew what was going on. He just saw the second plane on the TV and, like everyone else, realized the first plane was no accident." David Greenberg ran into a crush of other evacuees on his way out, but hit a slow-moving crowd once he reached the veranda outside Nymex where everyone was smoking. The traders and brokers were standing there, dumbstruck, their cigarettes hanging out of their mouths. Two immense plumes of smoke were rising up over the Twin Towers. Greenberg followed their gaze. Unfolding before him were some of the most nightmarish scenes in American history. He did not run. His feet were fused to the ground. "We watched person after person jump out of the windows of those towers. We just couldn't accept that what we were seeing was real. We could see their faces. They were choosing to die. We knew they had to be jumping because whatever was happening inside was far worse than falling hundreds of floors to their death. We all knew people in there. The Carr traders I knew were there. I could have been there with them. That broken express elevator saved my life.

"When the first tower, the South Tower, fell, it didn't just collapse. It wasn't like the footage everyone saw of the North Tower falling. No one ever captured the South Tower on film, because its falling was so unexpected. But we watched it crack right down the middle, where the plane had hit it, and literally saw the roof turn in, toward us, from horizontal to vertical, so we could see the entire face of it. Then the whole top half of the building slid sideways off the base and came crashing down." People stranded on the roof of the building had placed 911 calls. They'd reached the roof safely. When the calls were received, they were told they'd be all right. But nobody came. As the South Tower fell, those on the North Tower witnessed the fate that, in twenty-nine minutes, would be theirs.

Workers and residents abandoning the financial district raced on foot toward the Brooklyn Bridge. As they crossed, the South Tower came down in a wall of steel and ash. The bridge evacuees found themselves downwind of the hazardous debris, says gold broker Chris Adams, who also stood outside Nymex that day. "A lot of us thought we should make a run south for the bridge, but when the first building came down and we saw what happened, we were glad we didn't. The bridge was packed, I mean shoulder-to-shoulder people. And they were cramming it, trying to run to the end, but there were too many of them. When the tower fell, the whole thing just blew into them. I don't know how they made it, or if they did. We just turned and ran the other way. Everybody at the exchange was running for their lives, going uptown." Just before he fled, Greenberg took one final look back. He saw boats backing out of the marina on the Hudson. People were jumping off the pier into the river. "I turned, and I'll never forget it. All the yachts were pulling away as fast as they could. It was as if time had stopped. I remember seeing that and thinking, the world will never be the same."

The oil traders sprinted north, up the West Side Highway toward Fourteenth Street, black smoke and remnants of the South Tower billowing up behind them.

Richie Schaeffer and Stuart Smith were the first to go back inside the Nymex building that night. Schaeffer passed a triage center set up beside the marina. "It was supposed to be for the survivors, but it just ended up being a temporary morgue instead," he says. "It was gruesome. I guess it wasn't really a good idea, going back inside the building so soon. But I'm not afraid of dying either."

Oil prices immediately crashed, heading below $20 a barrel. With the exception of sixteen Nymex members and staffers, six additional members of Comex, and the nine people from the Carr Futures meeting, most of the oil traders escaped alive. Nymex had a backup facility a few blocks from the World Trade Center, but that too had been annihilated by the towers' collapse. (Wisely, Nymex later chose to build its next backup facility on Long Island.) On the day of the attacks, Viola relocated the exchange's senior staff to his home in Chatham, New Jersey. He set up a war room the next day at the Dorchester-owned Palace Hotel on Madison Avenue in New York, where the board and staff worked around the clock to get the market opened again. Viola, the exchange's first Italian-American chairman who was Catholic, went back to his hotel room that night and looked out the window. He was just above the nave of St. Patrick's Cathedral.

He got down on his knees.

"I was overwhelmed. It was an impossible task we were facing. We were literally *laying microwave wires by hand* around the exchange, trying to set up cellular relay points so we could rebuild our entire telecommunications system. I was trained for combat, but I didn't know if I could do it. I got down on the floor and I prayed. I prayed to God that we might be able to get the oil market back up and running."

Despite the floor traders' trauma of having witnessed unspeakable carnage, Viola managed to reopen the exchange the following Monday for a short trading session. He also donated his chairman's salary of $1.3

million to found the Counter-Terrorism Center at West Point. Hours after fleeing for their lives, the traders marched right back into the pits to resume the all-important business of oil trading.

Nymex turned out to be the first business to open west of Ground Zero, and its oil traders were some of the first people to venture downtown after the attacks. With all other means of transportation cut off or destroyed, Viola hired private ferries to bring the traders in from New Jersey, Staten Island, and all points above Fourteenth Street. Police and security guards escorted them through the smoking ruins.

The charred landscape seemed post-apocalyptic to Adams. The smell of burned things, the sight of abandoned restaurants, stores, and office buildings that only a few days before had been filled with people, repelled him. Through the haze, the traders could just make out the mass of molten steel hulking in the distance, nearly twenty stories high, that had once been the World Trade Center. Its profile was dark and monolithic. "Other than us, no one was allowed down there," Adams says. "It went on like that for a long time. But we started trading a couple days afterward like the attacks never happened."

The neighboring World Financial Center and its Winter Garden were gutted. Gateway Plaza had been rained on by plane parts, asbestos, and human remains. The smell had been overpowering, driving out all inhabitants, including Guttman. Yet the Nymex building and its trading floor sustained only minimal damage. "One thing I've always thought about this exchange, and I've told others about it. For whatever reason, and I don't know what it is, we are somehow blessed," Lapayover says. The traders did not take grief counseling or time off. They'd dealt with a terrorist attack before.

A moment of silence was observed before going back to trading, in honor of the ones who didn't make it. The exchange issued a press release listing the people connected with the market who lost their lives. One man missing from the list was Joshua A. Rosenthal, a forty-four-year-old who died on the ninety-seventh floor of the South Tower. He'd been senior vice president at Fiduciary Trust and was unknown to most of the oil traders. But in the early 1980s, after graduating from Princeton, he'd been brought in by then-president Richard Leone and became the star researcher behind Nymex's crude-oil contract. Even on a day of senseless death, his death had been particularly senseless. The fire command center at the World Trade Center had told him and his staff to stay put after the first jet hit the North Tower. The miscalculation proved fatal. Rosenthal and his colleagues had exactly sixteen and a half minutes to flee to safety before the second airliner slammed into floors seventy-eight through eighty-four of their tower, effectively trapping them.

Just three months after the terrorist attacks, Enron filed for bankruptcy. Its demise put a public spotlight on the corruption that had long been afoot in the energy market. From the start, the Nymex traders hadn't liked Enron, because the Houston energy giant had stolen their business doing the very thing Sprecher had suggested they do. In 1999, when Enron launched an Internet trading platform called EnronOnline, it had feasted on the orders of the locals in the pits. Enron had an edge over Nymex in that it was a member of the shadowy, over-the-counter energy market nobody seemed to be watching. Not only that, but Congress had gone so far as to approve special legislation in 2000 promising *not to watch it*, as part of its infamous measure called the Commodity Futures Modernization Act. Modernizing energy trading, it seemed, meant not keeping an eye on it. Lawmakers on Capitol Hill rammed the legislation through as an attachment to an enormous, unrelated budget bill during a lame-duck session the day before their holiday recess, on the same night that Democratic presidential candidate Al Gore conceded the election recount to George W. Bush.

The strategic timing had not been a coincidence, and no one on Capitol Hill pretended otherwise.

Buried in the bill's legal jargon lay the even more notorious "Enron loophole," a piece of legislation that specifically exempted over-the-counter energy traders from *any* regulation. The text of the loophole, drafted in consultation with lawyers hired by Enron, left over-the-counter traders free to behave exactly as they pleased in buying and selling financial products pivotal to the health of the United States and the global economy. The loophole was so potent it took the liberty of making clear that if regulators did happen to uncover fraud in the over-the-counter market, they were *still forbidden to do anything about it*. The bill was unanimously passed by the Senate and approved by the House in a sweeping vote of 292 to 60. The Senate wanted the bill so badly, says one witness, it approved a draft of it before it was even reported to the Senate floor.

The public was told virtually nothing of the loophole. Nymex, the regulated energy market, continued publishing its prices as before, using its clearinghouse and maintaining a proper paper trail—unlike many of its over-the-counter competitors.

The Enron loophole had worked like an enchanted tonic. After it was approved, U.S. crude-oil and natural-gas futures volumes leaped 90 percent in just five years, with the number of traders betting on the market more than doubling, according to the U.S. Government Accountability Office. But the real victory was off-exchange, in the over-the-counter market, where Wall Street traders drove commodities volumes up *850 percent* to an estimated *$3.2 trillion* in the same five-year period, according to the Bank for International Settlements. The real figures, as always, went unreported and were impossible for anyone to know.

Despite the spirited rivalry between Enron and Nymex, the need for energy traders to hedge their complex trading positions in one market by venturing into the other greased the businesses of both. The ascendancy of Enron and the era of the energy-trader-as-cowboy briskly commenced and rubbed off quickly on the Nymex traders. The New York locals sometimes even outdid their counterparts in Houston. When John Scialdone, the gasoline pit trader, flew to Texas with some brokers from Nymex to court new business, they made appointments with the city's energy royalty—Duke Energy, Dynegy, Enron, El Paso—in a junket they'd been planning for weeks. Being floor scourge, none of them owned a suit, so they bought new clothes for the trip. Still, they had plenty of cash and traveled in style, booking rooms at the Four Seasons Hotel and renting luxury cars.

They got as far as Highway 610, the loop outside Houston. Stuck in traffic, two of the traders grew cranky after hours of sweating in their starched shirts and jackets. They began arguing. "We didn't even think about what we were doing," Scialdone said. "We just pulled the car over in the middle of the highway and got out. I don't remember who started the fight or why we even did it."

When it was all over, nobody was fit to go to any meeting. The traders were covered in dirt and blood, their shoes scuffed, their suits ripped, lapels torn and hanging at their knees. There wasn't enough time to drive back to the Four Seasons to change. They were forced to attend their high-profile sessions as they were.

"As soon as we walked in, the corporate guys were like, 'What the hell happened to you?'" Scialdone said. "We're like, 'Uh, we got into a fistfight on the way over here.' They were like, 'No *way*.' We got so much business that day. Enron and Dynegy, especially."

Enron and Dynegy, incidentally, would soon be finding themselves sliding toward the slick precipice of bankruptcy.

The Enron effect also captured the imagination of Congress—Democrats as well as Republicans. Before Enron filed for bankruptcy, Barack Obama and Hillary Clinton both accepted campaign donations from it. "Everyone was in love with Enron, it was the new religion," says Jay Hakes, head of the U.S. Department of Energy's statistics branch during much of the 1990s. "I hate to say it, but Kenneth Lay had much greater access to the White House than we did. We used to go in to testify before Congress, and Ken would come with his boys and they would all look at us like, *You're just not smart enough to understand what we're doing.* Come to find out, this is a Fortune 500 company with no underlying wealth! I think Jeff Skilling knew better, but Lay, Lay was the son of a Methodist preacher and was a true believer. He was the holy roller preacher of trading. He thought that trading solved all problems. It's a myth that's still prevalent today."

Lay, who'd been friendly with George W. Bush, died of a heart attack in July 2006 while awaiting sentencing for committing corporate fraud at the company he'd founded. Some thought that seeing his life's work torn apart had killed him. Others said he wasn't really dead at all but had conspired with the president to stage a cremation-cum-disappearing act. He was sixty-four.

Skilling, Enron's ex-CEO, was sentenced later in 2006 to twenty-four years and four months in a federal prison. From jail in Waseca, Minnesota, he appealed.

It was partly Enron's edge over Nymex that undid Enron in the end. While Nymex always had regulators breathing down its neck, Enron was not watched carefully enough. Like the traders of the Nymex basketball futures, Enron hadn't relied so much on a clearinghouse or a paper trail to back up its bets. It had, however, managed to find itself a fraudulent accountant, Arthur Andersen, to help it hide its mountains of debt and shred its documents. It also had duped Wall Street analysts with such things as a fake trading room in Houston, filled with seemingly busy traders making fake phone calls meant to create the impression that business was booming. Its employees laughed about it, calling it a Hollywood set. Enron's financial liabilities, the result of a number of bad investments, eventually caught up with it. Even the best and brightest traders with billions of dollars at their disposal could not out-run the company's terminal losing streak. Enron filed for bankruptcy in December 2001. More than five thousand people lost their jobs, and $1 billion in employee pensions was wiped out. As shock waves from the meltdown wracked the nation, the same lawmakers in Washington who'd approved the Enron loophole only eleven months earlier shook their heads in disbelief. *Yet the Enron loophole stayed open.*

Few in Washington were prepared to take on the captains of indus-try to regulate a seemingly unregulatable market lost long ago to the monsters of finance. Even if a handful of legislators were willing to go on a kamikaze mission to address the issue—and, for the record, they were not—they didn't see how they could win against the Wall Street money machine and its cavalcade of private interests.

The progenitor of the Enron loophole was none other than the Republican senator from Texas, Phil Gramm, husband of Wendy Gramm, the ex–CFTC chairwoman. The senator took great pains to make clear he did not *write* the text of the Enron loophole, but those familiar with the situation credit Gramm with stuffing the Enron loop-hole into the bill just before it went to the Senate floor for the vote that would overwhelmingly pass it.

"That bill did *not* have the Enron loophole in it when it left commit-tee for the Senate floor," says one well-placed government official who was there at the time. "But when it got there, the loophole had suddenly appeared. When Phil stresses he did not *write* it, he is being awfully clever about it."

A prominent Wall Street executive who worked for Enron and knew about Gramm's efforts to advance the loophole says it is highly unlikely that many of the senators knew the loophole was in the bill. "That bill was cooked long before Gramm ever got his hands on it," he says.

Whenever he caught flak for pushing his free-market ideologies onto other people, Gramm, a former investment banker with a PhD in economics and, most notably, one of the largest benefactors of Enron campaign funds, liked to tell the story of his cash-strapped mother, who once took out a high-risk loan to buy his family's first home in Columbus, Georgia. Because of his mother, he said, he had come to believe that a deregulated marketplace worked just as well, if not better, than one hidebound by regulatory red tape. If not for the home loan received by his mother, a nurse who'd worked double shifts to support him, his two siblings, and his disabled father, she would not have been able to shelter her family, he said.

Gramm brought up the "mother" story again in 2008, when the Enron loophole was blamed for the credit crisis that rivaled the Great Depression. The loophole, which applied to complex financial instruments as well as the over-the-counter energy market, had allowed trillions of dollars of credit-default swaps to go completely unregulated, causing global banks to fall in on themselves like dying stars. (The credit-default swap, as it happened, was perfected by a group of J.P. Morgan bankers in 1994 on the exact site where the Nymex traders met every year for their wine-soaked futures conferences—the Boca Raton Resort & Club.)

Gramm had initially wanted *looser* regulation, which would have opened up additional loopholes, causing Alan Greenspan and even Enron itself to object. They urged Gramm to settle for something less radical, lest the "modernization" act not pass at all. The result had been the Enron loophole, the Pandora's box that unleashed the 2008 credit crisis and recession that shook the world. "Which idiot in Congress decided *not to regulate credit-default swaps*?" a blogger wailed on one of the many Web sites chronicling the mushrooming events. Gramm indicated that he didn't think he should be blamed for it. He had no regrets, he told the *New York Times,* explaining again that the home loan received by his mother had been similar to the devastating subprime loans tied to the credit crunch. "There is this idea afloat that if you had more regulation, you would have fewer mistakes," he told the *Times.* "I don't see any evidence in our history or anyone else's able to substantiate it."

Also not substantiated was why Wendy Gramm, just before leaving the CFTC, decided to issue a special exemption to Enron to conduct unregulated, over-the-counter energy trades—before she joined Enron's board. Later Enron made a donation to the George Mason University Mercatus Center, a free-market think tank that hired Wendy Gramm as a distinguished senior scholar after Enron's bankruptcy. Her biography on the Mercatus Center's Web site conveniently fails to mention her time at Enron.

Viola, surveying the events, realized that Nymex finally had a shot at seizing much of the over-the-counter market's energy business that had been abandoned by Enron. When a brute force that had once been the nation's seventh-largest company couldn't keep its crown as the overlord of the underworld, *someone* had to step in. That man, Viola thought, could be him. He ditched Rappaport's dead-on-arrival electronic-trading system and formed his own online trading platform. The result, ClearPort, provided financial clearing for billions of dollars of over-the-counter trades that might have otherwise threatened the nation's financial stability. Collins, intimately familiar with the elusive ways of the over-the-counter energy market after trading for El Paso, helped spearhead the project. With so many traders left in the lurch by Enron's downfall, their timing couldn't have been better.

There was just one flaw in Viola's plan. Sprecher was way ahead of him.

FOR MARK FISHER, the tragedy of September 11 held an ironic twist. The trading records that had been carted away from his office by postal inspectors nearly ten years before, resulting in the charges brought against him by the CFTC, had been stored at the agency's offices on the thirty-seventh floor of the North Tower of the World Trade Center. When that tower collapsed, his records were incinerated. It happened five years to the day that Guttman had been found guilty in the kangaroo court of the CFTC. "Had it happened anywhere else, it would have been completely unbelievable," a trader says. "But at Nymex, weird things like that happened all the time."

The incident, once again, reinforced Fisher's standing as a god among men.

"Of *course* the World Trade Center towers came down," says another Nymex trader. "What could be more natural? The World Trade Center towers had to come down so that Mark Fisher's files could be lost."

11

The Beauty of the
"Self-Regulatory Organization"

We thought we had something different with Vinnie Viola.
He was good for the first year. Then he got the disease.

—MARTIN GREENBERG

IT WAS A uniquely blistering March morning in Boca Raton, Florida, home to some of the most expensive gated communities in the nation and, not coincidentally, the chosen sanctuary of the retired Nymex trader.

The pink stucco, Spanish-style Boca Raton Resort & Club was abuzz with gossip over the Enron furor. Much of the talk at the Futures Industry Association's annual conference concentrated on who was to blame (no one would say), who was going to jail (almost nobody), and who might get away with it (almost everyone).

As exchange CEOs, presidents, and chairmen rubbed elbows with bank traders and hedge fund managers over canapés, fresh fruit, and Camembert—the pit traders were too obsessed with trading to attend such boondoggles, and the call girls would not arrive until nightfall—journalists from the major newspapers huddled outside, awaiting the introductory remarks of the CFTC's chairman, James Newsome, Future Farmer of America.

Seated at the perimeter of the hotel's garden, sipping from free bottles of spring water doled out by Jeff Sprecher, with ICE's ice-block logo on them, we listened to Newsome give a speech that in no way reflected the industry's dire straits. This was typical. When it came to speech-giving, the CFTC had two strategies: if the market was not melting down, it would assume a self-congratulatory posture, taking credit for the fact that the market was not melting down. If the market was melting down, it would take a different tack, patting itself on the back for how well the meltdown was going compared with how bad it could have been. It was a good approach and always very reliable. Newsome, at this time, was indulging in the latter.

What was atypical was the reaction of a certain *Chicago Tribune* reporter when Newsome let slip a term most of us had already heard. He glibly referred to U.S. exchanges, including Nymex and the CME, as "self-regulatory organizations."

Susan Diesenhouse, new to the *Tribune* after leaving the *New York Times*, let out an involuntary gasp. The room stirred. We were not used to involuntary gasping at press conferences. Newsome and the exchange officials looked at one another in befuddlement. What was so odd about a self-regulatory organization? The reporters also looked at one another. But we all laughed. Each of us could remember the first time we'd heard the term and what we'd thought of it. Who could believe that Congress, in its infinite wisdom, had once agreed to sign off on allowing the foxes to guard the henhouse, in effect letting the exchanges *keep an eye on themselves*? A gaffe like that, once done, could not easily be undone.

When Newsome's speech had ended, Diesenhouse stood up, cheeks blazing, utterly incredulous. Several journalists gathered around her. We attempted to offer comfort, support, ice water. One person in the group tried to explain the hall of mirrors she'd stumbled into, that the "regulators" were, for the most part, regulators in name only.

Diesenhouse shook her head. She'd spent years writing about real estate and health care, and thought she'd seen it all. She *had* seen it all, but she could not conceive of this. "They honestly let these exchanges regulate *themselves*?" she asked us. "But how can that be?"

Will Acworth, a former journalist who'd since become editor of the Futures Industry Association's in-house trade publication, *FI Magazine*, chuckled and said, "It's been that way for a long time, Susan."

Being a self-regulatory organization wasn't quite a get-out-of-jail-free card, but it did afford the exchanges a great deal of latitude in policing themselves unmolested by uniform federal standards, auditing, or oversight. What it specifically meant was the exchanges could conduct their businesses unfettered, so long as they stuck to the basic trading rules, groveled once in a while before their masters in Washington, and tried to refrain from openly flouting the law. As a result, they had a grievously poor track record when it came to preventing or punishing wrongdoing in their own markets, though they liked to argue otherwise. One top CFTC official who worked in the enforcement division during Enron's bankruptcy says that in his ten years on the job, he never once saw an exchange bring a case against *any* of its traders, no matter how outrageous their behavior. "Sometimes, we'd hear about Nymex or the CME strong-arming somebody after they got caught doing something stupid, but we'd only hear about it in a roundabout way. They never took formal action and it always smelled of more than what they were saying it was."

Because the traders were the exchanges' primary source of income, the exchanges had no interest in cracking down on them. Some markets, such as the CME, even went out of their way to block government investigations, the official says. "The executives would try to talk down to you, like you didn't know what you were doing, and you'd eventually have to throw it down, like, 'Listen to me; you're going to do *exactly as I say*, not the other way around, *get it?*' These guys don't appreciate that you don't interfere with federal investigations or you can get your ass into some serious trouble."

When Congress granted exchanges their self-regulatory status back in 1934, it was a different time. A more trusting time. A time when narcotics and contraband weren't to be found on the nation's trading floors and oil prices weren't pushing the limit. Ironically, the so-called SRO designation once represented the exchange's hallowed compact with regulators and consumers to balance the traders' interests with the interests of the public. Somehow, along the way, it had become a smokescreen for Congress and the regulators both to deflect blame, so that when something went wrong—and it always did—no one could say it was Washington's fault. As a result, traders are not infrequently rewarded for manhandling prices, while consumers are left on the hook. On Wall Street, there's even a name for it: the "reverse Robin Hood" system, a term propagated not by the angry consumer groups but by the traders and bankers of Wall Street themselves. It refers to taking from the poor and giving to the rich.

Newsome ably handled the CFTC's diplomacy drive in the wake of the Enron scandal. How market regulators had managed to overlook such flagrantly deceptive trading practices as "Fat Boy," "Load Shift," "Get

Shorty," "Ricochet," and "Death Star"*—to name just a few of the Enron traders' better-known code-named maneuvers—was beyond Congress's grasp. Never mind that Congress had *chosen* for it to be beyond its grasp by agreeing to the Enron loophole in the first place.

Though mostly unknown outside Washington, by 2002 Newsome was a major behind-the-scenes player in the energy world, paving the way for "freer" markets. Every decision he made mattered, because it had global ramifications. Newsome made it clear to Congress, when asked, that he had no objections to the Enron loophole, although he knew very well it would render his own agency useless in regulating the over-the-counter energy and financial markets. Before passing the legislation, Newsome says, lawmakers on Capitol Hill conducted *no* due diligence on the potential side effects of their actions.

Newsome also signed off on a "no-action" letter to Jeff Sprecher, allowing the ICE trading platform to avoid crucial U.S. trading rules, such as the submission of the commitment of traders reports that Newsome called "the heart and soul" of his agency's regulatory authority. Without these reports, which cataloged what the futures traders were doing in the energy markets on a weekly basis, Newsome was once again allowing himself to fly blind.

Neither Nymex nor any of the other U.S. financial exchanges were given this type of no-action letter—a letter whose terms were upheld in the very same legislation from 2000 that had created the Enron loophole. Like the exemption, the beauty of the no-action letter was that it allowed Sprecher's ICE exchange to legally break the rules that others could not. Receiving an exemption or a no-action letter was, in fact, better than hiring a team of lawyers to get a law overturned. That was old hat. The new way of doing things was to ensure almost everyone had to follow the rules *except you*. That way, you advanced yourself while handicapping your opponents.

Suddenly, it was extremely important to be on good terms with your Washington regulator. The exchanges quickly realized that the CFTC chairman could make or break you. Tailor-made exemptions and no-action letters were solicited and crop-dusted across the energy-trading

---

* These were a series of maneuvers that, among other things, would create power shortages in different regions by taking supply off the market to drive prices up.

universe (some hedge funds even boasted of having a pile of them), adding to an already complex system of favorites and non-favorites in the market. Of course, the letters and exemptions, like almost everything else, went unaudited by any higher authority. It not only undermined the integrity and transparency of the nation's economy but squandered the hundreds of millions of dollars forked over by U.S. taxpayers every year for the CFTC to protect them.

Completely unaware of what was happening, the ordinary consumer went on blaming OPEC, Big Oil, and the Middle East for the rising price of oil.

 Newsome knew that Goldman Sachs and Morgan Stanley were investing billions in physical energy assets, which couldn't help but affect oil prices, but he didn't want to dwell on what they were doing with them. Instead, he decided to try going *outside* U.S. borders to address the problem. "At one point, I even raised the question with our general counsel's office and the CFTC enforcement division about whether we could take action against OPEC for trying to control oil prices by manipulating global supply," he says. "OPEC doesn't control the price directly, but by raising and lowering the amount of oil it is willing to pump, it impacts the market."

Newsome was told that no, he could not regulate the members of OPEC, because they were *sovereign countries*.

Unlike OPEC, the banks did not make any announcements about what they were up to. The full record of how much physical oil, gas, and fuel they owned or managed, on top of their outstanding bets in the physical and paper futures markets, was not known and remains completely unknown. Like OPEC, they are afforded similar privileges to sovereign countries. U.S. regulators are unable to review their holdings or know what is going on. All that's known is what the banks feel like telling them or reporting in their quarterly earnings statements, which is very little. "Goldman and Morgan own a lot of physical energy assets and do a lot of trading as physical energy players," says Newsome, who occasionally spoke to the banks in private. "But they also have a lot of other customers they deal with, which gives them more access to information in the energy market than even the Nymex traders get."

 In short, Goldman and Morgan Stanley had enough of an aerial view of the market to work all sides of the three-dimensional chessboard. As it was with Enron (renamed Enron Creditors Recovery Corp. after its bankruptcy), they now saw more of the big picture than anyone else. This was why the Nymex traders, who also thrived on heavy flows of inside information, disliked the competition of the energy banks so much.

Newsome was a burly, pink-skinned, cattleman-looking man. Growing up on a farm in Plant City, Florida, he had not been groomed for the Beltway, but was one of its purest creations. Eminently agreeable, he had a firm handshake and an easy manner. Socially, he was quick-witted and knew even before you did how you wanted to be treated. He had a special telepathy that way. Whenever he greeted me, he'd beam and say, "Hey, Sunshine!" He did this even in front of the other reporters, singling me out at press conferences. Had it been anyone else, it might have appeared overdone, but from Newsome it came across as genuinely hospitable. All the other journalists knew he was from the South. Members of the media working for the newspapers up north didn't know what to make of it. Was Newsome crossing a line by being so . . . *nice*? We weren't sure what the rules of engagement were south of the Mason-Dixon Line. He could get away with it. And he knew it.

Newsome was also quick-witted in that he knew when to speak and when to keep quiet. That usually meant he was keeping quiet, but he was always listening. He appeared grounded and emanated benevolence. Above all, he was highly adaptable. A man of illegible thoughts and intentions, he was affably impassive and could shape-shift to meet the constructs of almost any situation.

Being a quintessential man of the South, Newsome had a tendency to surround himself at the CFTC with other quintessential men of the South. The Nymex traders called them the "Mississippi Mafia." To this day, if you dial the CFTC's press office, more often than not you will hear a long Southern drawl at the other end of the phone. This is because the Senate and House agriculture committees are charged with regulating the nation's futures exchanges. ("You know, just because the futures market started with farming doesn't mean that farmers should keep on running it," Gary Lapayover points out. "The real money is in the financial futures and energy marketplaces. These agriculture committees were small fries before the major traders in Chicago and New York came in. Larger government committees tried to take their control away, but the agriculture guys were not about to let it go. They fought to keep it.")

Oddly enough, the "agriculture guys" who backed the Enron loophole and thought nothing of loosening the trading rules on the energy and financial markets, did *not* want their sector, the agricultural sector, to be treated the same way. They believed light regulation of farm products to be very dangerous. The regulation of agricultural products, such as futures on corn, wheat, and cattle, has always been treated with extreme care, says Newsome. The reason is that the farmers have traditionally been much quicker than the nation's energy consumers to assert themselves before Congress. "Philosophically, there's very little reason to regulate one market differently than another. But you have a long history of agricultural groups concerned about the role of trading on farming and prices. Because of their strong lobbying, Congress takes stricter oversight."

By contrast, when it came to energy and financial products, the lobbying was almost always spearheaded by banks, exchanges, and hedge funds emphasizing *less* oversight.

Newsome's career began with farm animals. Over the years, he'd had other interests, but farm animals were what impressed him most. Reared on a farm whose biggest export had been strawberries, he'd harbored cattle-ranching dreams. His farm had poultry and about two hundred head of cattle, but Newsome envisioned one day owning a much larger spread. The eldest of four boys whose parents met at church, he decided to go to college, but always planned to come back to run the family business. With cattle in mind, Newsome assiduously studied livestock production for two years at the Abraham Baldwin College in Tifton, Georgia. He then attended the University of Florida as a food resource and economics major, and graduated in 1982 while keeping up his high school hobby of competitively rating farm animals as a standout member of the Future Farmers of America livestock-judging team. Though scorned as redneck sport by the blue states, livestock-judging was serious business down South. Newsome soon became a pundit of its many finer points. (In an unguarded moment, he once observed that judging a woman's figure was not wholly unlike judging a prized sow.) His knack for assessing mammals was his first step toward earning his passkey to Washington. But the journey would be a circuitous one.

Newsome's livestock-judging talents caught the eye of one of his professors, Don Wakeman, an expert in the field of animal husbandry. He told Newsome about a graduate assistant position that had opened up at Mississippi State University. It included starting up and leading the

school's livestock-judging team. He promised Newsome he would rec-
ommend him for the job. Newsome, who'd just graduated with honors,
told him no thanks, he hadn't even thought about going to grad school.
He was heading back to the farm. "At that point, Professor Wakeman
took the liberty of calling my father," Newsome says. "The next thing I
knew, I was on a train bound for Starkville, Mississippi."

Newsome led Mississippi State's livestock-judging team to six years
of regional and national wins as its head coach, while earning a master's and a PhD in animal science and agricultural economics. It also
was there that he met his future wife, Mary Margaret Pomeroy of San
Francisco, heiress to the wealthy J. H. Pomeroy family, which built
San Francisco's Golden Gate Bridge and owned a large swath of the
Seychelles, an archipelago nation east of Africa. Pomeroy's late grandfather, William Pomeroy, fell in love with the islands and married a
beautiful Seychellois woman, Jenny, while traveling around the world
on his yacht. Mary Margaret Pomeroy, nicknamed Mei Mei (Mandarin
for "little sister") by her Asian au pair as a child, stood out not only for
being a stunning blonde but also one of the only female members of
Newsome's livestock-judging and animal-husbandry team.

Newsome ran the Mississippi Cattlemen's Association from 1989 to
1998 as executive vice president. While he and Mei Mei had come from
different parts of the country, they considered themselves to be naturalized Mississippians. Newsome made some of his most valuable contacts in Washington through his job at the cattle association, including
Mississippi Republican senators Thad Cochrane (whose chief of staff,
Mark Keenum, had been a friend of Newsome's at Mississippi State) and
Trent Lott, who took a shine to Newsome. "Lobbying on behalf of the
Mississippi Cattlemen's Association, I met a lot of senators and congressmen," Newsome says. "My meetings with Trent Lott were always very
positive, because the cattle industry is one of the few agricultural industries not subsidized by the U.S. government. He always liked that we
never asked for any money; we just wanted to be able to do business."
When one of the five commissioner positions was vacated at the CFTC,
Cochrane rang up Newsome to ask if he wanted it. President Clinton
made the nomination, and the day before Congress's August recess
in 1998, Lott rammed the vote through. Newsome had literally been
plucked from obscurity and appointed one of the nation's chief regulators of a multitrillion-dollar market.

Only eight months into the position, Newsome had his first brush with Mark Fisher. Fisher was still fighting the CFTC charges against him, notwithstanding the loss of certain hard evidence during the September 11 attacks. The administrative court assigned to his case had already heard his testimony and adjourned for deliberations. Fisher was asking for the case to be reopened to hear new testimony from a former CFTC official who was prepared to say that Fisher was being unfairly targeted for trading practices the agency had overlooked in the past. The CFTC was unsympathetic. Newsome ruled on the case in April 1999, alongside Brooksley Born and two other sitting CFTC commissioners, denying Fisher's motion. Fisher had already attacked the court's judge, George Painter (the same judge who'd handled Guttman's case), for being biased against pit traders and suggesting they had a propensity to steal, as evidenced by Painter's telling *Crain's Chicago Business*, "Why wouldn't you take a tick or two, if the opportunity is there? You'd have to be a potato-head not to do it." But Fisher had been met with resistance every step of the way in getting his charges dismissed. Much was at stake. He had one of the pits' biggest trading businesses.

When President Bush took office in 2001, he named Newsome the acting chairman of the CFTC. In contrast to Born, Newsome had established himself as a "pro-industry" commissioner, someone the exchanges could confide in and get along with. He also got on well with Bush, who must have genuinely preferred Newsome to the other candidates being floated. (Wendy Gramm at Enron had pushed hard for somebody else.) Bush, Newsome recalls, was "a sincere, relaxed, very hand-on-your-shoulder type of person and very much a man of the South. He always made himself available for conversations after meetings. There is no question in my mind he always tried to do the right thing. I think his rating was so low that he didn't make any of his decisions based on the polls. His feeling was, 'No one being polled has access to the same information I do.' So the polls, to him, for that reason, were worthless." Newsome was on the conference call with Bush on September 11 when the president told his key financial advisers, "We're gonna rip the guys who did this to us a new asshole."

In a confidential e-mail Wendy Gramm wrote to Steven Kean, Enron's chief of staff, in February 2001, she gave her honest assessment of Newsome. "Folks love Newsome and I think he's very nice and appears to be very free-market . . . but I have found that the farm reps on the commission may sound deregulatory, but are not and have been really troublesome without a good free-market person on board." Gramm said she would pull together a list of people she considered superior prospects to replace Newsome as the permanent chairman, but warned, "The CFTC is in awful shape. The quality of the staff is horrendous" and "many quality folks do not want the job as chairman because it's been such a backwater." Despite Gramm's efforts, Bush named Newsome permanent CFTC chairman later that year. But the message imparted to Newsome was clear: nobody wanted another regulator with the slash-and-burn style of Brooksley Born. If Newsome hoped to excel in his new position, he needed to be as laissez-faire as possible.

Before coming to the CFTC, the closest Newsome had ever been to fossil fuels was filling up his tank as a teenager at the mini–gas station on his parents' property. That had mainly been for farm vehicles. Newsome says he never talked with Bush about energy policy or his reasons for invading Iraq, despite being in charge of overseeing the global oil market. "I never had any policy discussions with the president or anyone in the administration about that," he says. "I am not naïve. I realize oil is probably the planet's most precious commodity. But my personal opinion on going to war with one of the world's top oil nations? It is above my pay grade."

At $145,600 a year, Newsome was painfully aware that many things were above his pay grade. Though much higher than the salary of the average American, it was well below the starting salary of an average top-tier university graduate on Wall Street. As a member of the president's Working Group on Financial Markets, which included the Federal Reserve chairman Alan Greenspan, the secretary of the Treasury, and the chairman of the SEC, Newsome wielded incalculable power but lacked the paycheck to match. Like most CFTC chairmen, he would not close out his five-year term before rectifying that.

War in Iraq, which held the world's second-largest pool of proven oil reserves next to Saudi Arabia, was now a foregone conclusion, and the Nymex traders were busily preparing for it. Each headline that flashed across the television and wire-service screens in the pits was tirelessly dissected. The traders hadn't forgotten that during the first Gulf War, every letter of every word in the zipper headlines had counted. "I'd been trading only six months when that war started," says Mark Lichtner. "The secretary of defense, James Baker, came out and said—I can still see his quote—'I see no Iraqi flexibility.' I was long in the oil market, and as soon as everyone saw the 'no' and the 'Iraqi' together, before the next word even hit, the market ticked up $2 a barrel. It probably wasn't the biggest one-day price move of the entire Gulf War, but I'm willing to bet it was the biggest in a fifteen-second time span, ever. When you're at war, all you can do is take it fifteen seconds at a time. I made $42,000 in that fifteen seconds. I remember thinking, right now, I better sell this shit. But, you know, that's a normal day for a lot of people."

On the opening day of the Gulf War's Shock and Awe campaign on March 21, 2003, all I heard through the telephone, my lifeline to the pits, were the traders bellowing Saddam's name as they raked in unprecedented oil bonanzas and Iraq burned to the ground. Until then, I'd never imagined that a war or a hurricane could elicit such childlike joy in hundreds of grown men, but it was not an uncommon occurrence, Lichtner told me. "It's kind of disgusting, because if you're a real human being, you don't want a war and you don't want a hurricane. But on the floor, everything is ass-backward. Good is bad. Bad is good. Death and destruction aren't necessarily terrible things. Just the opposite. Death and destruction most of the time mean that a lot of people are going to make a lot of money."

If the Nymex traders thought they were doing well before, the second Iraq War ushered in a period of effortless riches that put every other belle epoque to shame. Ben Kaufman, who was traveling through Asia at the time, rushed to an Internet café as soon as he heard about the invasion. "This was when we started seeing some of the first really big highs in oil prices. The highest highs I'd seen in my life. They were crazy days. I was glued to the screen. I suddenly didn't want to be on vacation anymore. I wanted to go back to the trading floor. That job was like an addiction. With prices going up like that, if you made a mistake, it was the end of your career. Messing up just cost too much."

The Iraq War became the triggering event that started oil prices on their five-year hot streak, ending with them above $147 a barrel and retail gasoline over $4 a gallon. But by the time they peaked in July 2008, no triggering event would be needed for the market to reach near-crisis levels. By that time, prices would overheat on hysteria alone.

The cheering on the first day of the war repeated itself when hurricanes ripped through the U.S. Gulf Coast, killing dozens of people and tearing offshore oil rigs and gas platforms asunder. Energy prices catapulted to record highs in 2004 after Hurricane Ivan and again in 2005, with the onset of Hurricanes Katrina and Rita, both of which were also killer storms. From the traders' perspective, the tragedies were viewed at a distance and in financial terms only. (As one British floor trader dryly observed: "Isn't it daft? We make millions off people buying fuel and burning it, creating the greenhouse gases that caused these hurricanes to happen, sending prices back up for us to make millions off again.") Nymex gas trader Steve Berkson became legendary for reaping an estimated $40 million at the market's opening bell the morning Hurricane Katrina made landfall. After that day, he was set for life. A father of five from Scarsdale, New York, Berkson gave generously to the hurricane charities before buying the house next door to his own so he could turn it into a full-scale sports complex for his athletic children. "I was there for Katrina. I was there the day it touched down," Kaufman says. "It was monumentally stressful. Everything was out of control. I was having the time of my life."

The traders were in an especially buoyant mood in May 2003 as they planned their annual trip to the Kentucky Derby. In what would be hailed as a new high-water mark for the kind of audacity for which they'd become known across Wall Street, several traders hired a private jet to take them to the races, stuffing it with Brazilian hookers. The prostitutes accompanied them to the derby events, even joining them at Nymex's trackside tent. Something the pit traders had learned to refine from their cohorts at Enron was the art of the "canned hunt," situations in which the women were paid in advance for their services, told to mingle with the traders and then pair off—like an ordinary romantic liaison, only the sex was guaranteed. It allowed for the appearance of propriety without all the unsavory exchanging of dollars and cents that made everyone feel so dirty. During Enron's glory days, one trader told me that a group of girls, also Brazilian, had been hired by the company for the evening, only to find out that there were too many girls and not enough traders. "We had to fly in some more traders from Houston to São Paulo to even it up. Wouldn't want a hooker going home alone, would we?"

One of the female Nymex executives attending the Kentucky Derby was thoroughly disgusted. "Our tent never looked like any of the other tents. You go to the Kentucky Derby and on the one end of the spectrum there are the Fortune 500 CEOs with their seersucker suits and straw hats, and on the other are the Nymex traders with their tattoos and hookers." Next to betting on energy prices, poker, and sports, betting on horse races was one of the traders' favorite pastimes. Some of them, such as senior energy trader Sanford Goldfarb, took it one step further and bought, sold, trained, and raced dozens of Thoroughbreds for millions of dollars. Trading champion horses was not quite the same as trading energy futures, but both were precious commodities and could be turned around at a steep profit.

Up in the executive suite, Vincent Viola was less concerned about the war with Iraq than the ongoing war with ICE. Deftly stepping into the void left by Enron, Sprecher was going after Nymex's business with a vengeance, taking the Nymex settlement prices and incorporating them into his ICE electronic-trading platform. Viola, who was trying to prepare Nymex for a public stock offering that would make him and the rest of the Nymex traders even richer, went on the offensive, suing ICE for trademark and copyright infringement. Though Nymex was a public market, the exchange's lawyers argued, that didn't mean its oil prices were up for grabs. Sprecher coolly countersued. The scuffle went on for years and could have overturned ICE, as it depended on the Nymex prices to bolster its legitimacy, but when Sprecher offered a generous settlement, Nymex refused. Again, if it had only listened to Sprecher, it would have made a fortune. But Nymex, being Nymex, went all in on the wrong bet.

In the end, Sprecher won the lawsuit and Nymex appealed. Sprecher won a second time. In the eyes of the law, Nymex's attempt to copyright its public settlement prices was rather like the phone company trying to copyright its public telephone numbers. The U.S. Copyright Office, which had turned down Nymex's request to copyright settlement prices back in 2002, filed a statement of interest with the court, more or less calling Nymex's case ludicrous. It noted "strong public-policy reasons against providing intellectual property protection to *what are essentially facts*." U.S. District Court judge John Koeltl agreed. He dismissed Nymex's suit and Sprecher's countersuit. Nymex's public prices, once its salvation, were now being used as the chief weapon against it.

Viola's next move was to try and buy ICE, but Sprecher wasn't in the mood to make deals anymore. He scoffed at Viola's offer of approximately $300 million, calling it "an insult." Viola tried to get the board to offer almost double that, but the directors wouldn't give in. He and

Sprecher, who got along fairly well under the circumstances, continued talking sub rosa. Viola didn't mind stepping down to let Sprecher run Nymex as chairman and, as it turned out, Collins didn't mind either. Neither of them cared very much about being chairman or president. But the pit traders did not want to join forces with the banks that were backing ICE, particularly Goldman. "We tried to achieve a merger of equals," Viola says. "I think we could have gotten a deal done, but the traders just hated the banks too much."

On the trading floor, another round of regulatory investigations was causing turmoil and instigating upheaval. Under tremendous pressure from Congress following the disintegration of Enron, the CFTC's head of enforcement, Greg Mocek, a lawyer from Lafayette, Louisiana, was stepping up the agency's investigations into energy market corruption. There had been unexplained price spikes in natural gas, and he intended to get to the bottom of it. With little recourse to address corruption in the over-the-counter market, where Enron had done the bulk of its damage, Mocek snowed Nymex with a blizzard of subpoenas, prompting the usual groans from the pit traders of being unfairly targeted.

"Because the government doesn't understand the energy market, they only go after the market they are *already regulating*," says a Nymex trader. "This, for some reason, is preferable to considering regulating the larger market that they are ignoring, *where all the shit is happening*."

Mocek had been warned by Wall Street not to lift the iron curtain. He'd repeatedly been told by over-the-counter heavyweights that he should be looking at the exchanges instead of them, because they were the hidden market and the exchanges set the global prices. But he found it an empty argument and he knew Nymex was just a stalking horse for the broader energy market. The latticework of the public market and the private market were hopelessly entangled. The only difference was that Mocek had power in one and not the other.

The CFTC officials never stopped being amazed at the lack of tools they were given to do their job. "I remember the commission would spend two years doing a wash-trading investigation and then finally settle for $30,000 and they thought that was a really big deal," says one former department head. "Or online trading or a boiler-room case. What we really wanted to do were high-profile cases with major frauds and manipulations. We wanted to include the big firms and hedge funds. But there were only, like, 12 people out of the 160 in enforcement who were capable of understanding what we needed to do, which was stupid, because, you know, we were *supposed* to be doing this stuff. The Democrats wanted prescriptive rules and regulations. The Republicans wanted fewer rules but more aggressive ways of going after the fraud. There had been no structural changes at the CFTC in a million years. It was total bureaucracy. We actually put up a board called the 'Why?' board. It literally had seventy-five things on it that made no fucking sense with all the things we'd always been doing because we'd always been doing it."

Starting in 2003, Mocek's enforcement staff fanned out, subpoenaing trading records and recording phone calls of the Nymex traders and their clients, including energy companies and hedge funds across the nation. Many of the investigations were top secret. The specifics of nearly all of them were never made public, and Mocek didn't give many details, except to say he'd subpoenaed roughly forty companies and interviewed or taken testimony from dozens of people. The agency settled about thirty cases as part of its post-Enron crackdown, and imposed fines of around $300 million in all. But it was just a drop in the bucket compared to the damage done. The largest, most invisible part of the market, the realm of over-the-counter energy trading, remained out of sight and out of reach when it came to stopping proven energy fraud.

Viola wasn't pleased with the timing of the investigations. Filling in the Enron abyss and beating back ICE would not be accomplished if Nymex was also being highlighted for its dirty laundry. A separate trading probe into the silver pit by the CFTC also was becoming a hassle. There were silver traders outside Nymex insisting that the New York silver ring be exposed as a den of thieves. Nymex couldn't afford to get sucked into another regulatory dragnet just as it was trying to clean itself up and go public. If it was going to defeat ICE, it had to look, as Guttman put it, "purer than Caesar's wife." Even if it wasn't.

The pit traders had always prided themselves on not caring about what Wall Street or Washington thought. Nymex's Washington office had been repeatedly opened and closed over the years in a state of confusion. But the image-conscious Viola cared very much about these things. While Nymex was successful, it did not get respect. It had the money, but it did not have the political power to match its riches. It had no organized lobby in Washington or well-placed senators championing it (though there had always been talk of "buying ourselves a few senators, like the Chicago exchanges," Lapayover says). No one on Wall Street genuflected to Nymex the way he or she did to Goldman, OPEC, or ICE, all of which relied on Nymex prices. In terms of political capital, the energy traders had hardly improved their station since the early days of Michel Marks. Rappaport had maintained convivial relations with the CFTC, but until Viola, no one was capable of taking it to the next level.

The convergence of Viola's "Finance Mafia" with Newsome's "Mississippi Mafia" was a delicate matter few cared to discuss after the fact. What is known is that Viola and Newsome gradually became close enough that there were concerns in both New York and Washington about their relationship. It was customary for the CFTC chairmen to speak regularly with exchange chairmen and meet with them periodically to stay on top of market issues. But the two chairmen and their underlings seemed to engage in an unusual amount of after-hours camaraderie, including at least one late-night cookout at Newsome's house in Washington, attended by Nymex president Bo Collins and high-ranking members of the CFTC's staff. A Nymex consultant who later visited Viola at the exchange noticed him chatting on the phone frequently with Newsome, whom Viola affectionately called "Jimmy Boy." The consultant also overheard Viola say to Newsome, "There'll be some tickets waiting for you at the Nets game tonight." According to one ex–CFTC official close to the situation, Newsome was known to have attended extravagant dinners paid for by Viola and Collins, where $400 bottles of wine were consumed. "At the CFTC, you're not supposed to take anything from anyone that's worth more than $25, including meals," he says. "Jim Newsome was the only person I ever heard of doing that."

When I asked Newsome about his perceived closeness with Viola and Collins, he denied the cookout at first, but, after further questioning, acknowledged it, downplaying it as a strictly professional gathering. "We would get dinner and we got along very well, but our families didn't get together. My family was out of town the night of the cookout. Vinnie and Bo were coming to D.C. and they were going to get in late and the restaurants were all going to be closed. So we got together at my place and grilled up some steaks. There was a number of other CFTC staff there. I felt good about it, because there was no doubt that Vinnie was paying for everything."

It is unclear what the CFTC press office thought of the barbecue (the head of media relations, Alan Sobba, was a staunch Newsome ally, as was Greg Mocek, the head of CFTC enforcement; Viola also later hired Sobba to work for one of his trading firms). The Nymex press office, however, was getting uncomfortable with the situation. By all accounts, the relationship was getting too tight. "What Nymex chairman and CFTC chairman get together for casual cookouts *in the middle of the night?* That is not a professional relationship," says a former Nymex executive. "We'd never seen anything like that before."

On March 24, 2004, Newsome signed an order dropping all charges in Mark Fisher's case. Despite having thrown up legal roadblocks against Fisher's battle with the CFTC in the past, he had suddenly reversed himself. After twelve years of the complaint holding firm, Newsome had a change of heart. In a forty-three-page dossier, he explained why he now saw things differently. His remarks chillingly echoed Guttman's complaints about how his own CFTC case had been handled by George Painter, the judge assigned to Fisher. In his new findings, Newsome touched on what he called a "deep-seated antagonism" displayed by Painter toward Fisher in court during his case and the possibility of a "denial of a fair hearing." Newsome said he agreed that Painter engaged in "an abuse of his discretion" in the "abrupt termination of the cross-examination" by Fisher's defense. Newsome also recognized Painter's ignorance of material flaws in the case against Fisher and a disturbing degree of selectivity in his handling of case facts.

Newsome acknowledged reports that the CFTC's enforcement division had attempted to "coach and threaten" some of the traders prosecuted in Fisher's group, while picking and choosing among the credible witnesses and their testimonies. He wrote that the traders who did settle with the CFTC in Fisher's case gave such contradictory and confusing information as to be "insufficiently reliable to merit significant weight." In analyzing the testimony of Fisher himself, as well as that of the other traders accused of conducting illegal trades with him, Newsome said it "tends to raise as many questions as it answers. . . . Their versions of the events at issue also lack fundamental reliability."

Still, that was no reason to find fault with Fisher, he said. Summing up his assessment of the trades in question, Newsome stated, "In this instance, we acknowledge that there are a great many suspicious circumstances disclosed on the record, but conclude that they don't fit together in a manner that produces a coherent, compelling picture." He dismissed the charges. Newsome's decision was signed by three other sitting CFTC commissioners.

What made Newsome's move even more unusual was that Painter had ruled on Fisher's case years ago, ordering him to pay $350,000, the largest fine of all the traders penalized in his group, and banning him from futures trading for five years. A trading ban was more than Fisher could bear. "When the charges against Fisher were dropped, I was shocked," says a longtime former Nymex executive. "Sometimes you see the CFTC chairmen come down *harder* on somebody, but we'd never seen a chairman be more lenient with anyone, especially since that meant having to go against the findings of his own staff." Newsome, according to Mocek, was on excellent terms with his enforcement staff. But Newsome was also head of the star chamber, and his staff duly abided.

Whether Guttman was right or Fisher was wrong faded in rapid relief against the more jarring reality: at the CFTC, justice was in the eye of the beholder—and where the beholder, in this case, was headed, he would soon need to be on excellent terms with Mark Fisher.

"I don't begrudge Mark Fisher one red cent," says Guttman. "But an agency of the government with such serious conflicts of interest is worse than no government agency at all."

Viola was getting still more blowback from Nymex members over the overlarge compensation package he'd given Collins. Viola also had promised Collins a cut of any merger deal he was able to pull together. The idea had originally been to do a deal with ICE, but when that didn't take, Collins hotly pursued other deals. The Nymex members objected. They were the owners of the exchange, and they didn't want Collins doing a deal just because he wanted to get paid. During a marina walk with Guttman, who'd sided with the members, Collins vented his frustrations. As a trader, he believed his talents were being wasted as an exchange executive. He also didn't think he was getting paid enough.

"If I can't get a deal done, then I am going to resign and start my own hedge fund," he told Guttman. With the war bolstering oil prices, Wall Street investors were shoveling billions of dollars into the energy sector. In such an environment a skilled fund manager could make tens of millions a year, if not more.

Guttman could only imagine what another shakeup would do to the oil market, but didn't try to dissuade Collins. Instead he looked out over the waterway.

"Be careful what you wish for," he said.

In 2004, Guttman got married. He was fifty-five, and it was his first and only time. Her name was Connie, a lovely blonde in her forties, an attorney for the city. On one of their first dates, Guttman asked her, very casually, if she'd ever heard of "controlling person liability," the legal wrinkle that the CFTC had used to nail him. She said she hadn't. He took that as a good sign. He started dating her two months after his mother died. He'd never considered marrying anyone before, but he'd changed his mind. "You know what makes a lifelong bachelor finally give in?" Guttman says. "When he loses his mother."

In the early months of 2004, Collins attempted to sell a minority stake in Nymex to a Boston private-equity firm, but a storm of protest from the members followed. They didn't want to be owned in whole or in part by a private-equity firm in Boston. What they did want was Collins's head on a plate. Collins was informed that his employment contract would be renewed, on the condition that he accept a shrunken compensation package. That was all he needed to hear. He left to start a hedge fund. He hadn't even gotten his foot out the door before Fisher began campaigning heavily for his choice of a new Nymex president. Somebody without an ax to grind or an ass to save. Somebody who, it turned out, Viola already knew very well.

LENNY WILLIAMS IS a semiretired widower in his early fifties and father of two, a teenage son and autistic daughter. In his spare time, he raises money for health charities and walks for cystic fibrosis. For most of his career, he worked on the New York trading floor, starting as a Comex clerk sleeping in the gold pit and doing tours of duty at most of the city's exchanges before settling down at Nymex. It was in the pits that he met his wife, Dawn, whom he speaks of reverently, and it was in the pits that a chance happening touched off a series of events that helped propel Nymex's new president into office.

During the heyday of Enron, Williams worked for a Stamford, Connecticut, over-the-counter brokerage firm called Traditional Financial Services, putting together trades in the Nymex natural-gas ring. Enron was one of the firm's most important clients, but Williams didn't relish its business because of the hard time he was getting from John Arnold, its top gas trader. When Arnold called down to the pits to place an order, he wanted Williams to tell him what the other traders were doing. Williams was aware that such inside information could help a trader manipulate the market, especially a trader with vast credit lines, like Arnold. But he also was aware that, if displeased, Arnold could take his business elsewhere, causing his firm to lose a major customer. So Williams hedged and said he didn't know what the other traders were doing. A colleague finally clued Arnold in: Williams had the information; he just wasn't sharing it. Arnold, a trader in his mid-twenties described as "scary-smart" by his colleagues and competitors, rang Williams back.

"You are a nobody and always will be," he told Williams. "*I* make the rules, not you. The rules were made for people like you, not me."

It may have been an uncharacteristic outburst from Arnold, or he might have meant it. In any case, the diatribe went on for several minutes. When he was through, Williams was visibly shaken. Not long ago, he'd accompanied Arnold on a ski trip to Breckenridge, Colorado, as part of a larger group of traders and brokers staying at the Beaver Run Resort. He didn't know Arnold very well, but he feared he might face severe repercussions if he didn't bend the rules for him and Enron. His firm, aware of the incident, didn't do anything to defend him. Feeling caught in the middle, Williams eventually resigned a few months later, in June 2001, accepting a job as a vice president under Richard Schaeffer, who was head of global energy futures for Dutch bank ABN Amro, in addition to being treasurer of Nymex.

In early 2002, Williams ran into an old acquaintance, a high-level executive at Nymex who'd been at the exchange for a long time. The executive asked why Williams had left his last job, as he'd been up for a partnership there. Williams hesitated. He didn't know what to say, so he just told the truth.

"I'd like to answer your question," he said. "But I can't do it here."

Williams returned to the executive's office hours later and shut the door. "I am saying this as a friend and not in any formal capacity," he said, "but I left my job because I got verbally attacked by John Arnold and no one backed me up. My own clerks were ratting me out about the orders I wasn't telling him about, and he threatened to take his business away. I've been on the floor for years. I don't play like that." The executive listened intently. He wasn't surprised to hear that such things were happening. He just couldn't believe Williams was telling *him*. Officially, the incident would have called for him to take immediate action, but because it had been divulged in confidence and they were friends, he tried to keep it to himself. He regretted it the day he opened up the *New York Times* in July 2002 and saw a picture of Arnold on the front page of the business section with a story about how he had singlehandedly made Enron $750 million just before the company went bankrupt. The executive went cold.

"I don't care how smart you are," he says. "Nobody makes that much money and does it honestly." He had a bad feeling about it.

After much deliberation, the executive decided to come forward and share Williams's story with Nymex's compliance department, which was supposed to ensure fair trading practices in the pits. The compliance department quickly came to the conclusion that the case was too serious for it to handle. It referred the matter to the CFTC, which was already overwhelmed by the other Enron-related investigations going on in the winter of 2002. (To be sure, Congress never saw fit to give the CFTC more than $150 million to regulate a $20 trillion swath of the market.) With great trepidation, the Nymex executive relayed to the CFTC Williams's account of being pressured to share inside information in the gas pits with Arnold. He wanted to protect Williams and keep his identity private, so he presented the story as useful information from an unnamed tipster.

In August 2002, John Arnold took the $8 million he'd made trading for Enron—the highest bonus paid to any Enron trader in the year of its bankruptcy—and started his own Houston hedge fund, Centaurus Energy Advisers. In just four years, the mild-mannered twenty-seven-year-old grew his fund to $1.5 billion. In two more years, he would double that amount. It was understood that Arnold's trading records were among those being sought by the CFTC during its crackdown, though the CFTC never confirmed the names of the firms or the people it had subpoenaed. Combing through the records, the CFTC found enough to make it want to continue with its probe. The agency's staff went back to the Nymex executive and pushed for him to give up the name of his tipster. They wanted to talk to Lenny Williams. The executive, knowing Williams didn't want to get involved, protested that the tip had been given in confidence, but the CFTC would not take no for an answer.

Williams wanted to stay out of it, but once his name was disclosed, he didn't have a choice. The CFTC interrogated him three times between March and August of 2003. The agency brought in a dozen other investigators and staffers from the FBI, the SEC, and the New Orleans task force assigned to troubleshoot the Enron debacle. (New Orleans had been pulled in because of its close proximity to the Henry Hub in Erath, Louisiana, where Nymex's natural gas was delivered.)

All of the interrogators were actively involved in the post-Enron investigations, but after the very first interview, half of them dropped out of the Williams grillings, because he could hardly remember any of his three-year-old conversations with Arnold.

The CFTC and FBI continued to work him over.

A person consistently attending the interrogations was Stephen Obie, head attorney for the CFTC's New York office. The Williams investigation was kept under wraps at every stage. Throughout the proceedings, Williams was never subpoenaed. He didn't receive notices of any kind. There was no paper trail. The CFTC simply contacted his lawyer, Gary Stump, referring to Lenny Williams as "Mr. X." The interrogations, which took place at the CFTC's new offices on Broadway, were arranged by phone between the CFTC and Stump. Williams didn't know if he had anything useful to offer but did his best to cooperate. Enron's implosion, followed by a spike in natural-gas prices, had put the authorities under the gun and Congress wanted heads to roll. Preferably trader heads.

Williams attempted to recall what he could, but with the interrogators threatening to find him in contempt if he got the details wrong, he feared he didn't have much that was definitive to say. The interrogators warned him that if he talked to anyone, they would charge him with obstruction of justice. It was clear that they not only wanted to nail Arnold but also to implicate the entire Nymex natural-gas pit. Williams balked when they presented him with what they termed the "facts" of the case. When he attempted to correct them, they didn't want to listen. They only wanted sworn statements that fit their facts. He began to think that the authorities didn't care about whom they hurt or if they found the wrong people guilty, so long as they nailed someone. The investigators instructed Williams to go back to his old job, wearing a recording device under his clothing so that he could spy on his coworkers. He refused. They responded by making more threats.

Throughout the course of the investigation, which cost Williams tens of thousands in legal bills, the traders ribbed him whenever he walked into the pits. "Hey, Lenny!" they shouted. "Johnny Arnold says hi!"

Since the 1980s, Williams, like many traders at Nymex, had heard troubling stories about people at the CFTC. The agency's "lifers" were known to be hardworking, overstretched, and underfunded. But the officials who were just passing through, the "oath-takers" or "tourists," had become a problem. Too often, their actions were guided more by their desire to ingratiate themselves with entrenched private interests—the big futures exchanges, law firms, or trading firms that they hoped would one day offer them a higher-paying job—than by their duties to regulate and protect the market and the public. Tales of the revolving door included CFTC officials saying they would make all the traders' problems go away if they could just get a job that would pay them $200,000 a year for the rest of their lives. While the traders believed that everyone was for sale at *some* price, it seemed to them the price of a CFTC official was prohibitively low.

"Traders steal hundreds, sometimes thousands of dollars per order in the pits," says an ex–Nymex staffer who apprehended dozens of thieves as a member of the compliance department. Some of the pit cards would say "No comp," meaning to not put the prices in the computer, because the trades were to be done in secret, and others would have little notes on them saying things like "Kill 'em!" meant for the traders doing the orders. "You should see the trading cards they pass in. They're atrocious. There's stuff written on them and crossed out and then rewritten to hide what they are doing. It's like kindergarten. But how much have government regulators and Congress cost us with things like the Enron loophole? Trillions. You know how much one trillion dollars is? If you stack a bunch of $1,000 bills, end to end, it would reach more than seventy miles into the sky."

No one asked Williams to testify against anybody, but when he declined to wear the tape-rigged outfit, his interrogators got meaner. The language they used grew coarser and their threats became more personal. They told Lenny if he didn't help them get *somebody*, they were going to go after him. While Christmas shopping that year with his son, he noticed a tail on him. *Three* tails, to be exact. As he went from store to store, the trio of men in plainclothes followed closely behind. He didn't know what to do. He couldn't call the police. When the law was out to get you, who was going to save you?

When the Nymex executives found out about the probe, they were not happy. Investigations into the trading pits appeared to be escalating. John Arnold of Centaurus, one of the exchange's most important clients, was being targeted in connection with the suspected collusion schemes in the natural-gas ring, one of the exchange's top-grossing markets. ICE was swiftly gaining on Nymex as a competitor. Too much was out of control. If Nymex was going to have a public stock offering on a respectable stock exchange, it needed a success story it could tell potential investors, and a respectable veneer.

When word of the trading probe reached Schaeffer, who was angling ✓ to become the next Nymex chairman, he moved quickly. Schaeffer was not one to fiddle while Rome burned. In late September 2003, after Williams's final CFTC interrogation, he asked Williams to take a leave of absence from ABN Amro until the matter could be resolved. That same week, the Nymex executive who'd revealed Williams's story to the CFTC was informed that the exchange would not be renewing his contract. The executive, who had recently been promoted, was suddenly being forced out, yet Nymex still saw fit to give him the largest severance package it had ever paid in its 130-year history, totaling in the millions. The executive didn't know what that was supposed to mean. Was the oil market trying to buy his silence? The last thing Schaeffer said to Williams was, "Keep your mouth shut and everything will be fine."

But everything was not fine.

On his forty-sixth birthday, two days before Christmas, Williams was fired for the first time in his life. He received the notification by mail, in a sterile form letter. ABN gave no explicit reason for the layoff, except to say, "We have no other recourse but to terminate your contract."

Meanwhile, the CFTC was poring over Williams's phone and trading records, looking for something incriminating. It would find something. It could always find something. It attempted to charge him with prearranged trading, but the charge didn't stick due to lack of evidence. After hitting a dead end, the agency told Williams to leave the trading pits and never come back. Williams didn't resent Schaeffer for letting him go. He knew how it was. But he was upset by the way he and his family had been terrorized by the authorities. When his wife was diagnosed with brain cancer a few months later, he was glad he could at least be there for her. He cared for her until she died in 2008. Getting fired allowed him to spend the last five years of his wife's life by her side and, for that, he was thankful. When Williams reapplied for his futures market registration after her death, he received it without contest. He continued to work in the futures industry, but he never again returned to the pits.

Led by Mocek, the CFTC pressed on in its aggressive trading probe into the gas market, but after pursuing Williams and leaning heavily on the Nymex executive to give up his name, it never once inquired about the abrupt dismissals of either. Evidently, the coordinated firings of two otherwise reputable people who'd spent decades working at the exchange before becoming reluctant whistleblowers didn't even warrant a phone call. "I helped the CFTC on some very large cases," the Nymex executive says. "During Lenny's case, I even spoke directly with Greg Mocek. I suddenly disappear off the face of the earth and not a single person at the CFTC even tries to find out *why*? My firing made headlines. There was no way he didn't know what was happening."

The public investigation into the Nymex gas pits vanished. To this day, the CFTC will not comment on it. Years later, when Mocek resigned, Obie, who had gone after Williams, was promoted from New York to Washington to replace him as head of enforcement.

Weeks after Newsome squelched the charges against Mark Fisher, the CFTC's probe into the New York silver market also mysteriously ground to a halt. In a lengthy letter, the agency reported finding no evidence of any market manipulation, despite handwritten complaints from more than five hundred silver investors begging it to look into what they believed to be deeply suspicious activity. Online chat rooms of silver traders erupted in righteous indignation. One silver speculator posted an open letter to the CFTC, reminding it that "According to the Coin Act of 1792, those who debased the currency, 'or otherwise with a fraudulent intent,' were to suffer the death penalty."

A month passed before the CFTC's next big announcement. Accepting a signing bonus of $400,000 and annual compensation of $896,154, Newsome, at forty-four, was leaving his job as chief regulator of Nymex to become Nymex's next president.

Part III

The Sellout

12

Raids, Maids, and Civil War

*Contrary to what people think, Nymex doesn't just draw in
people who are animals—it draws people from all walks of
life and makes them into animals. The money itself attracts
everybody, but the environment is self-selecting, and only by
being an animal can you survive. That's why a place like this is
dominated by extraordinary personalities, risk-takers, and egos.
Give me a civilized man and in seven days, I'll show you a beast.*

—DEEP THROAT

JIM NEWSOME'S FIRST month at Nymex coincided, as it happened,
with the summer's inaugural drug raid. It was not the sort of thing he
was used to dealing with at the CFTC.

On the second floor of the Nymex building, just below the trading
floor, was a handsome, wood-paneled locker room where the members
kept their gym clothes, trading jackets, and drugs. On any given day,
it was said, the locker room had more drugs in it than a small town in
Colombia. Knowing this, the Nymex executives periodically called in
teams of cops to conduct surprise raids and had given Newsome fair
warning. Sensing he might have good reason to fear a bust, Newsome
became uncharacteristically skittish in the days leading up to the search.
At a time when he'd expected to be taking firm command of the presi-
dency, he was instead nervously darting around the executive suite, waiting for what he assumed would be news of the inevitable. Given the
circumstances under which he'd taken office, he was more than aware

that a raft of high-profile drug busts would tarnish the promise of his meteoric rise.

But Newsome had overestimated his new employer.

The raid, which only the highest-level executives were supposed to know about, had been leaked to the pit traders weeks in advance. "Jim was totally freaked out. I didn't have the heart to tell him that everybody already knew," says one of the executives, who worked in the office of the president. "I only found out myself after walking through the locker room and seeing everybody packing up their stuff and tearing out. I asked one guy, 'What's going on?' He said, 'The police are coming! Everybody's getting their stash out of here.' You know who told them? Nymex security."

Ben Kaufman, clerking in the pits, remembers Nymex's security personnel being almost as well-off as some of the traders. "Security was on *our* side. You had to be in with them, though, which meant paying them. I would have to say the top security guys were probably very wealthy. They made out like bandits on the holidays. The traders were very generous. In return, the security guys would always give us a heads-up whenever there was going to be a raid."

It was unlikely that the executives cared if the traders found out or not. The only thing better than an orchestrated ambush that gave the oil market the appearance of propriety was one where no drugs were found.

In August 2004, the day of the drug-and-contraband raid, the traders arrived for work as usual and headed for the pits. The cops stood outside with their K-9 drug-detection teams. Trader after trader was caught red-handed while being screened, but there was no physical evidence of drugs on any of them, says the Nymex executive. "Almost every guy who walked past the police, from the lowly clerk to the high-volume trader, made those dogs go insane. The police didn't find anything, but the traders obviously had cocaine powder or whatever residue all over their jackets. The police couldn't figure out what was going on. They thought something was wrong with the dogs."

The locker room also yielded nothing, though there was the rumor of a near-miss. "I heard that a ring reporter was selling pot, but had removed it from his locker. A dog walked by and found it when it sniffed the locker, but there was nothing there, so the dog got fired. Now I don't know if that's true, but that's what I heard," says a gas trader. "It really is the age of specialization. Can you believe a dog can smell a bomb, then turn around and smell pot? That's a lot of training. Then again, I gotta tell you, my sense of smell is not much, but I can smell pot. You don't have to be a special dog for that."

Newsome's slow adjustment to Nymex in late 2004 was understandable. He had a hard time getting used to the traders and they had a hard time getting used to him. It didn't help that no one could fathom what Newsome was doing there. He had a Southern twang nobody from the Northeast could get comfortable with. He was placid and agreeable, not gruff and crotchety like the pit traders. His edges were soft where the traders' were hard. There wasn't the slightest thing in the world to dislike about him, but the traders just didn't want an ex-regulator hanging around their exchange. They never hired outsiders to be president or chairman for the express reason that no outsider was capable of understanding them. They only promoted their own. But they had underestimated Newsome.

"There was a longer than usual feeling-out period, because I was from the regulatory side," Newsome says. "All the Nymex members were involved in the exchange's management issues and projects, a lot of cooks in the kitchen, which, frankly, made it harder for us senior staff to do our jobs. Because the members had a direct stake in the business, they felt being involved was their right. Remember, these were traders looking out for their investments in the overall business. There was no such thing as a closed door at Nymex. The doors were always open and everybody burst in. It took a while to get used to that. You'd be on the phone and think you had privacy."

An observer from Wall Street who visited Nymex assessed Newsome thusly: "The problem is, in a crazy place like that, a person who might qualify as normal, *he* looks like the crazy guy. He certainly had interest in making money. I understood he had a wealthy wife and I think he was under some pressure to keep up with that lifestyle. I think that's probably why he was there. Otherwise, why would he have taken the job? It's not like this was a place with a great reputation. What Nymex was getting out of it was obvious. He put a good face on the place."

Guttman was perplexed. "Why do we need a big-name guy from Washington coming in with zero experience to run our business?" he asked one evening at dinner, banging his fist on the table. "What kind of message does this send to the world? That we are too much of a mess to clean ourselves up?" In his opinion, Newsome was hired by the exchange solely to protect it from the investigations and mudslinging that had been beleaguering it. "He's lending an umbrella to all the crap going on."

Other reshufflings had taken place around the time of Newsome's arrival. In March 2004, Vinnie Viola had turned the chairmanship over to his humble protégé, Mitchell Steinhause, a well-liked, long-standing member of the board chosen for the job precisely because he had no interest in becoming the kind of larger-than-life, messianic chairman Viola had been. Steinhause's loudest feature was his silence, and his most notable physical characteristic was his handlebar mustache. The traders weren't sure exactly what Viola was up to, but because he was the only chairman ever to leave Nymex willingly—that is, without being practically forced out—they decided to support his chosen heir. Steinhause was a milquetoast but he was a respected man of the pits, and when he ran for chairman with Viola's imprimatur, no one opposed.

Those closest to Viola knew why he had chosen to leave. A plan was taking shape at the highest echelons of Nymex to defend itself against ICE and go public on the NYSE, but it was going to entail an as-yet-undetermined amount of pain in the trading pits, and the pit traders were not ones to keep quiet when they were in pain. Being chairman for the next couple of years was not going to be a Friday windsurf. Also, Viola's entrepreneurial side was yearning to be free again. "Vinnie felt he could make more money doing other things, no matter how much the exchange paid him," says Guttman. When Viola realized he could leave his position without losing his paycheck, his means of escape became clear. By installing Steinhause, he would continue to receive monthly "consulting" checks amounting to almost $1 million a year, close to the amount of Newsome's salary. Viola had just transformed Nymex into another one of his many revenue streams. Steinhause declined to comment on what Viola was doing to earn his checks. This bothered the traders. "Vinnie's got his fingers in a lot of pies, doesn't he?" one griped.

Steinhause's sudden shift from vice chairman to chairman had another lesser but equally important purpose. Murmurs were starting up that Michel Marks was looking to retake the chairmanship. Once king, he had not found it easy to be one of many voices on an over-crowded board of twenty-five, for which he had little respect. Viola, on the contrary, had great respect for Marks, but many of the directors felt discomfited by him, because he would speak his mind without any regard for his audience. Notably, he was the only board member to object to appointing Newsome president. "I found Michel a huge asset to the board," Viola says. "He was the first to make the assessment that oil would be the most sought-after commodity in the world *for the next century*. It was a brilliant call. No matter what, he should be remembered for that." Nonetheless, he made Steinhause a placeholder to keep Marks from muscling in.

Richie Schaeffer also had his eye on the chairmanship, which some thought Viola, after opening a few more businesses, might try to resume. With Viola gone, Schaeffer went after it with singular purpose. He bonded with Newsome, who desperately needed allies, and swiftly amassed the kind of power nobody would be able to challenge. "At the CFTC," Newsome says, "I mostly worked with Vinnie, so my first time meeting Richie was just months earlier at my going-away reception in Washington. He came to town representing Nymex and met my mom and dad and my family." At this point, the only person left standing between Schaeffer and the chairmanship was Steinhause.

Within months, Schaeffer and Viola were tussling over Steinhause like a host body waiting to be possessed. "Steinhause was like an empty vessel with Vinnie and Richie fighting over him to run the exchange by proxy," Kaufman says. Steinhause seemed only to want to stay out of everybody's way. He had enough to deal with, grappling with his chairman's paycheck of $1.4 million. Although he'd been a trader for most of his career, he'd never earned more than a mediocre living and was suddenly getting a larger salary than he knew what to do with. "Right after becoming chairman, Mitchell came into my office, closed the door, and said, 'I have all this money now and I don't know what to do with it. Can you help me?'" says one Nymex executive. "This is a lifelong trader asking me, a staffer, how to invest his money!"

The faceoff between Viola and Schaeffer might have been a close match if not for the release in late 2004 of the new Pontiac GTO. Viola purchased the muscle car right out of production and drove it home to show off to his son. In the driveway, he put the car in drive instead of reverse. The vehicle plowed through the automatic garage door, totaling both car and door. Shocked, Viola got out and stood there a moment, surveying the wreckage. Then he did a strange thing. He doubled over in hysterics. With his son looking on, Viola was still laughing uncontrollably beneath the garage door when the last metal coil snapped.

The door and its high-tension cables came down on him, slicing through his jaw and maxilla.

Viola came within inches of losing his life. It took him six months to recover. Parts of his shattered jaw and face had to be reconstructed. He got a synthetic maxilla and a perfect set of new white teeth. "I heard he had, like, twenty operations to rebuild his face," says Kaufman. Others said Viola would never look the same again. It was inevitable the speculation would take on theatrical overtones. "The stories about Vinnie got so widespread, I was hearing about him from the guys over at Goldman," says one former Nymex executive. "Vinnie had become this iconic figure on Wall Street after leading the oil market out of 9/11. So I'm standing there, trying to keep a straight face, while some gap-toothed, blue-blood Etonian is telling me about how Vinnie rises like Lazarus, half his face hanging off, and calmly tells his wife to call the paramedics. While he's waiting, he bench-presses five hundred. That's roughly the kind of stuff I was hearing."

Many of the pit traders had trouble coming to grips with a man of Viola's stature being felled by something as ordinary as a garage door.

With Viola out of commission, Schaeffer assumed the chairman's role in all but title. Steinhause didn't put up a fight. He kept his titular standing and continued sending Viola his monthly checks, while making regular use of Nymex's field-level Yankee Stadium box seats. (The exchange also reserved season tickets for Mets and Knicks games.)

Schaeffer had long been a person of fascination to many of the Nymex traders. Over the years, they'd fallen into the habit of swapping Cartesian, "evil-genius" stories about him. Some said he first came to power as Danny Rappaport's hatchet man before turning against him and backing Viola as chairman. Few, however, were able to pinpoint exactly what made him seem so evil, or so ingenious, other than his one key evil-genius accoutrement: a secret safe behind a decoy picture on the left wall of his office filled with cash. No one seemed to know where the cash in the wall safe had come from or where it was going, but the traders did know that they weren't used to seeing exchange officials loading cash in and out of their walls. Schaeffer says the safe was for personal use and not related to his job as Nymex treasurer.

Yet Schaeffer's wickedness, in person, did not live up to its reputation. He was off-the-cuff, unguarded, and conveyed an almost charming insouciance that made even those who despised him roll over to do his bidding. "He has a very engaging personality," recalls Rosemary McFadden. "He started at the exchange around the same time I did and I thought he was smart, enthusiastic, and a very hard worker. He was there first thing in the morning and really wanted to be involved and was involved."

Schaeffer distinguished himself from the other high-ranking Nymex executives by appearing to have absolutely no interest in managing his image, as evidenced by his sudden outbursts in the boardroom and grand-mal fits of swearing. "There was always this notion of, we don't want to get Schaeffer in front of a microphone for too long, because we never know what he's going to say. But he was an unbelievable boardroom tactician. He knew everybody and always knew which chairmen to snuggle up to and which ones to stay away from," Guttman says. "He was able to sniff out whether a guy was popular or not. If the guy was not popular, he would go the other way."

Schaeffer, interestingly, credited much of his boardroom prowess to Guttman. "Most of what I learned about playing politics in the boardroom was from watching Lou," he told me. Like Newsome, Schaeffer was an experienced politico, able to swing whichever way the wind blew without ever seeming to be inconsistent. He made no promises to anybody, or any excuses. He did what he felt was best at the time and didn't worry too much about it afterward. "Schaeffer tested people for their limits. He had a way of pushing you and pushing you until you either screamed or were washing his underwear," says one Nymex executive. "If you screamed, he'd back off. But he'd come away knowing exactly where you drew the line, which was very useful to him."

Wherever Schaeffer went, colleagues whispered that he was a backstabber and piranha of the first order, just as likely to be one's friend as one's enemy. But the backbiting did nothing to slow his indefatigable rise, and the rumors only reinforced his status as a man to be feared. They also pervaded his romantic life, which seemed at all times to consist of a wife, an ex-wife, and a mistress. I'd never actually seen any of them, as Schaeffer always presented himself to me as a lone wolf, perpetually unlucky in love. "It's not going to work out," he sniffed one night dejectedly over his cocktail about a woman he was dating. "She doesn't have enough of a dark side." Possessing a dark side was important to him. The main women in Schaeffer's life were his mother, Irene, and his teenage daughter, Rachel.

Though best known for cheerfully crushing his opponents, Schaeffer was capable of great acts of kindness. Overhearing a temp crying in the hallway outside his office one afternoon while telling one of the exchange's secretaries she could no longer afford day care for her son, he anonymously sent her a large sum of money. He bailed out a horse farm on Quogue, Long Island, for his daughter—an accomplished equestrian—after the farm's owner fell on hard times, and let the owner continue living there for free. He gave money liberally to his friends and family members, and even gave ex–Nymex president Bo Collins a loan after his first hedge fund went under. "If you are a shark and Schaeffer wants to neutralize you, you're in for it," Collins says. "But if you're an underdog, he can be the most generous person in the world and he will come out harder than anyone, often to his own detriment."

Such was the paradox of Schaeffer. He thought nothing of cutting his enemies off at the knees, but couldn't bear to see people weaker than him suffer. Though he didn't show it, he was also suffering. He'd had two strokes since September 11 and was worried there might be more.

Deep Throat was dubious. "Do you give a guy credit for giving to the poor and vulnerable? I mean, isn't it sort of like Carnegie building libraries to buy his way out of hell?" He believed Schaeffer's real source of power came from the fact he "just didn't give a shit. Here's a guy who came from nothing, who has nothing to lose. How do you do battle with a guy like that? It's like trying to win Vietnam."

Schaeffer did not deny the secret of his success. "I always had people hating me or challenging me, because I had a lot of power. But then I always had the support too of at least half the board. It's pretty amazing how I survived every chairmanship. Why did I survive? Because I am a great chess player in the political arena. The chairmen embraced me, either because they liked me or because they were afraid not to. I've never lost an election, although some of them I only won by a little bit."

Unlike Viola, who had any number of cars, jobs, phones, office locations, and addresses, Schaeffer liked to avoid unnecessary complexity. His primary indulgence was sugary snacks, which he munched with increasing frequency—in particular, Jujubes, Twizzlers, and Chuckles. "Richie's a simple man," says a former potato trader. "Even when I go golfing with him, he uses three of the fourteen clubs." Rappaport also noticed parallels between Schaeffer and his golfing habits. "Yeah, that's Richie. He doesn't want to bother with all that. He just wants to hit the ball."

On the trading floor, crude-oil futures prices were leaping above $50 a barrel by late 2004. At the pump, retail gasoline prices had inched repeatedly past $2 a gallon. On a normal day, $15 billion worth of energy contracts were trading at Nymex. More than a year had passed since President Bush's "Mission Accomplished" speech, but the Iraq War had dragged on, punctuated by pipeline explosions in the southern part of the country, which wiped out oil exports by the hundreds of thousands of barrels a day. The United States had not counted on saboteurs repeatedly laying bombs under Iraq's pipelines. In a posting titled "If the Iraq War Is About Oil, Then How Much Are We Getting?" a blogger bemoaned how the United States was receiving less oil from Iraq than *before* the September 11 attacks, which, he noted, had always been less than 5 percent of Americans' total oil consumption. "Those who claim the Iraq War is only about oil make it sound like U.S. troops are extracting oil directly from the veins of Iraqi babies and pumping it into my car," he wrote. "If it were that simple, why did I just pay $38.85 to fill up my Honda Civic?"

In Michigan, a gas and electric company was urging people to buy energy gift certificates, worth up to $50, for family and friends for the holidays. "There's no gift more helpful," said its e-mail advertisement, "than the gift of a warm home." Venezuelan president Hugo Chavez, the ultra-leftist firebrand dictator, also was taking advantage. Thumbing his nose at Bush, whom he called "the devil," he began a charity drive of giving away hundreds of millions of dollars' worth of fuel to thousands of American poor who could no longer afford to pay full price for heating oil. Overnight, in the ghettoes of cities across twenty-three states, he became an unlikely folk hero.

Willie Nelson, the country singer, began selling his own brand of clean-burning gas called BioWillie, made from soybeans. He even ran his own tour buses on it. (After a trial run in Texas, California, South Carolina, and Georgia that year, BioWillie failed, because it was more expensive than the other, dirtier fuels.)

In Manchester, New Hampshire, Robert Falco, a Dow Jones reader, wrote to me in an e-mail about the extent to which he was willing to go to lower his energy costs. "Earlier this year, I traded my Acura that got 21 miles per gallon for a Ford Focus ZX4 ST, which is giving me 26 miles. So I am getting 5 extra miles. I also installed a wood-burning stove to use as supplemental heat to my oil-fired steam gravity system and expect to reduce my oil consumption there by 400 gallons this winter." A second source in San Francisco told me about how he personally knew somebody building a bunker in his backyard for his extended family and stockpiling it with food, guns, and *gold bars,* after losing all faith in the government's ability to put a lid on high energy prices and maintain national energy security.

Wartime oil prices also were being met with warnings from economists of another great reckoning in the form of a global recession. Yet more than a year later, no recession had materialized. OPEC, which tried to keep oil prices as high as possible (just shy of fomenting worldwide backlash), seized the moment in late 2004, announcing a *cut* in production of a million barrels a day. It knew full well the move would push prices up. Although the cartel had lost its grip on the oil market when it came to lowering prices, it found it could always raise them. OPEC would continue to complain now and then about the unchecked dominance of the market's speculators, but only when oil prices dipped. "OPEC, especially the Saudis, could raise oil to $200 a barrel tomorrow if they really wanted to," says one Nymex executive, "but they don't do it. Why? Because they are *rational.* They are a drug dealer providing us with a drug, and they want to keep us addicted to it. If the price gets too high, they know we'll quit. So they dole it out very carefully. *Everything they do is to keep us where they want us.* Their objective is to charge as much as the market will possibly bear. And it's going to stay that way until we either run out of oil or the public refuses to pay these prices anymore."

Other factors put a floor under prices. Oil refineries around the world were crumbling from old age and overuse, causing a commotion in the Dow Jones newsroom when the Netherlands' Pernis refinery caught fire and the headline writer mistakenly misspelled the name by omitting the *r.* Fears of terrorism were keeping traders on a hair trigger, especially in New York, where the memory of September 11 remained searingly fresh. Three years after the attacks, the Nymex trading floor still had American flags draped all over it. Though it was well known that oil prices had dropped, not risen, just after the World Trade Center collapsed, the traders were worried that Saudi terrorists might try to target energy facilities on their own soil in an attempt to destroy the U.S. economy. Asian demand for oil also was overheating and the dollar was plunging to an all-time low against the euro. A weaker U.S. currency meant that Americans would need more dollars to buy the same amount of oil and fuel as they had in the past.

The intersection of events suddenly put Nymex at the center of Wall Street's radar. Just as Marks had predicted, trading volumes in the pits shot to hundreds of thousands of contracts a day and kept rising, making Nymex one of the most heavily trafficked betting parlors on earth.

The sudden attention was drawing television networks like CNBC to the oil-trading pits, where Melissa Francis, a pert, blond anchorwoman, earnestly reported on Nymex as if it were the new NYSE. A former child actress who'd starred in hit television series such as *Little House on the Prairie* and *St. Elsewhere*, Francis had studied economics at Harvard and soon established herself on the trading floor as the "Empress of Energy." It was a better nickname than those given by the Nymex traders to the other women of the pits. They called one Chinese-Italian assistant "Wonton Parmesan" and dubbed an attractive Native-American woman "Poca-hot-ass." The Nymex executives, aware of the crudeness of its denizens, resisted the TV lamplight at first. They didn't even allow *Wall Street Journal* reporters into the pits, knowing full well Nymex wasn't ready for prime time. But vanity eventually got the better of them.

Nymex tried to dictate to the traders a strict dress code on the days the film crews came in. "They made us all wear ties with our trading jackets when they knew they'd be rolling," says Kaufman. "On TV days, I thought it was extremely important to take it to the next level. I would come in wearing a black suit, white shirt, and tie, have my hair slicked back, and wear a pair of wraparound aviator glasses. When the cameras came on, I'd be sure to walk around in front of them as much as possible. That was the only way you could handle being told what to do by a bunch of assholes. You would think they'd have had a problem with the more obscene things that happened down there, but you never heard a word about that. I would wear my jacket with the half-naked Hawaiian girls on it, or the one with the beer-bottle print."

Mark Lichtner was also nonplussed about being told how to dress. "They tell me to tuck my shirt in when I come in. I say, why don't you stop people from stealing? Stop worrying about my fucking *shirt*."

Jeff Sprecher, the chairman of ICE, hoped to take control of the fast-expanding betting parlor. But to do that, he'd have to take some cliffhanger risks. In London, the oil traders at the International Petroleum Exchange, which ICE bought over Nymex's protests, placed bets on a trading floor similar to the one at Nymex. And just like at Nymex, the traders greatly preferred the pits to the trading screen. The International Petroleum Exchange, located near London's Tower Bridge, was not as big as Nymex, but it was the world's second-largest energy market and Europe's most dominant. Sprecher realized his only chance of cracking the lucrative energy market was to find a way to get the London oil traders to move from the pits to the screen. He had persuaded the major energy banks and BP to be his allies. He'd outlived Enron and even purchased some of its operations in the post-bankruptcy fire sale. But getting the Rabelaisian pit traders of south and east London to join him would be his toughest challenge yet. The only way to win them over, he reasoned, would be to force their hand.

With little notice, Sprecher announced that he'd begin shutting down the London trading pits November 1, 2004. The process would not be complete until April 7, 2005, but he wouldn't tell anyone that. He planned on taking his time and he wanted to keep everyone— especially Nymex—in the dark about it. He was giving the London traders a choice: move to New York and trade at Nymex with the other pit traders, or stay in London and trade on the ICE screen. The British traders didn't want to do either.

The Nymex executives were caught flat-footed. They'd hardly begun to contemplate what Sprecher might do next to take away their business. They were still inflamed about the ICE lawsuit. That had been a colossal mistake. "Sprecher once told me a key plank of his strategy against Nymex was basically to wait for them to fuck up," says one ex–Nymex employee. "In this business, it is important to know what your constants are, the things you can always rely on. For Sprecher, Nymex fucking up was practically a fixed variable."

Nymex's executives sprang into damage-control mode. They'd been misled by press reports saying that the top hedge funds and banks were hooked up to ICE but not using it, because no one else seemed to be using it. This had made them overconfident. As Marks once explained, a market needed to reach a critical mass before people would flock to it. If Sprecher could push the London traders onto the screen, they would help him get there. The Nymex executives considered the fact that their business model had absolutely no global reach. It had always been anchored to the New York trading pits. ICE, on the other hand, had access to any trader with an Internet connection.

But that wasn't the worst of it. Sprecher had found a way for ICE to get around the U.S. trading rules by getting a no-action letter from the CFTC to be regulated not by the United States but by the *United Kingdom*. The United Kingdom, it so happened, had looser trading rules. Because Sprecher owned the London trading pits, he argued to the CFTC that his entire exchange should be regulated by the UK authorities. The CFTC, under Newsome, agreed, knowing perfectly well that Sprecher's company was headquartered in *Atlanta*. The result was what would henceforth be known as the "London loophole."

After looking into the British regulatory system, the CFTC had decided there was nothing to worry about, despite the fact that its head of enforcement, Greg Mocek, was not at all impressed with its track record. In fact, he couldn't find a single instance of the United Kingdom ever bringing a case against a commodities trader.

Sprecher prevailed. Kenneth Raisler, the brilliant and kindly ex–Enron lawyer widely credited with crafting the language behind the Enron loophole, was a member of his legal team. A partner at Sullivan & Cromwell, Raisler had once been general counsel for the CFTC and, oddly enough, had also done work for Nymex under Guttman as far back as the 1980s.

Like the Nymex silver traders who'd arbed silver coins against silver futures decades ago, the advent of the London loophole was a prime example of a game that industry insiders liked to call "regulatory arbitrage," the objective being to operate from the region with the fewest rules.

The Nymex executives suddenly felt outmaneuvered *and* hemispherically challenged. For years, they'd been toying with the idea of building an oil market in Dubai, maybe opening a few satellite exchanges in Singapore, Shanghai, Tokyo, Taiwan, or Budapest, but nothing had ever come to fruition. The oil market had been a monopoly for so long, they had gotten lazy. The traders in the pits hadn't wanted to branch out into other countries. They owned the market, they wanted it in New York, and they didn't want to share it with anybody.

Even with Sprecher at their throats, Steinhause and the board members were in a state of paralysis. They couldn't bring themselves to accept what was happening. They did, nonetheless, break out of their torpor just long enough to commission a cost-benefit analysis of opening their own London trading pit. If they could swoop in and scoop up all the orphaned British traders after Sprecher's trading pits closed, they might have a shot at stealing his business.

The results of the analysis were not what the Nymex executives had been expecting. In documents sent to me by Deep Throat, the estimated cost of opening a London trading pit came to at least $10 million the first year, and many millions more after that. The red tape would be considerable, with a long approvals process in London and daunting logistics. There also was the incontrovertible fact that *nobody in their right mind had opened a trading pit anywhere in the world for a decade.* Europe's exchanges had mostly gone electronic, and the CME was hurriedly mothballing its pits in favor of Melamed's Globex online trading screen. Around the world, traders were blaming Nymex for keeping the energy market mired in the dark ages by clinging to its bad old ways. "We would see an explosion in trading volumes if this could be a twenty-four-hour electronic-trading market," said Patrice Blanc, chairman of brokerage house Fimat Group in Paris, at the Boca Raton futures conference. "That is not the case now, because of Nymex."

The analysis was conclusive. If Nymex did open a trading pit in London, there would be guaranteed costs and no guaranteed benefits. But if it moved trading to the Internet, there would be guaranteed savings and guaranteed profits.

The Nymex board voted to open a London trading pit.

The executive presenting the analysis was flabbergasted.

"I don't understand," he said. "Did you not hear anything I said? Why are we doing this?"

"Why are we doing this?" one of the senior staffers asked, turning coldly to give him a withering look. "I'll tell you why. Because *fuck ICE!*"

The board applauded.

All except Michel Marks.

THE GLOVES HAD come off, but in the war that went unexpectedly global, nothing would go according to plan.

Nymex discovered London didn't care if Nymex wanted to open a trading pit. The executives had expected to get the red-carpet treatment, but they'd been sorely mistaken. A lot of businesses wanted to open in London, which stood at the center of the world's desirable time zones, with the United States to the west and Asia to the east, and Nymex would just have to wait its turn. The Nymex traders weren't used to waiting their turns. They were rather more partial to immediate gratification. Instead of allowing Sprecher to maroon the London traders, whom, a few months beforehand, Nymex couldn't have cared less about, the board voted to open its first foreign exchange in the only city that agreed to fast-track its demands: Dublin.

Raiding Dublin was not exactly taking the battlefront to ICE's door, but Nymex had been getting excellent mileage from unwise plans for over a century.

November 1, 2004, was, as everyone expected, a surreal day. The London pits closed for morning trading only and reopened in the afternoon, with Sprecher experimenting to see what the British traders would do. Some of them stayed in London and tried out the ICE screen. Dozens more, rather than tolerate being Sprecher's guinea pigs, flew to Dublin to trade at the new oil market called Nymex Europe. They didn't particularly like being Nymex's guinea pigs either, but at least they were being treated like classy guinea pigs. Nymex was paying for a jet.

Kevin McDonnell was the Nymex trader tapped to lead the Dublin charge. A skinny kid from the Bronx, he was of Irish descent, a member of the board, a heavy drinker, and a skilled, $15-million-a-year oil trader. He had been one of the chief proponents of the Nymex basketball futures market back in the 1990s, which proved he knew how to get an obscure market off the ground. Within confines no bigger than a spacious living room, forty or so traders kicked off Dublin's first "global" energy market with a piercing battle cry. The Dubliners weren't used to so much noise in their cramped environs. Prior to Nymex's arrival, their pit had been used by a few currency traders and half a dozen brokerage firms. After taking a three-day trading course offered by Nymex, the Irish currency traders were, for the first time, attempting to trade crude oil.

Mitchell Steinhause stood before ringing of the opening bell and gave a rousing speech. It was startling, because he almost never spoke. The traders clapped, then jumped in the ring, arms flailing. Trading started first thing in the morning and went until eight P.M., when the New York pits closed for the day. It was worth it for McDonnell, who received a $300,000 bonus for his efforts, but the rest of the traders were exhausted after putting in twelve-hour days. Many missed their families back in London. Resisting screen trading would take more stamina than they'd expected. Betty Brazil, the full-time maid in Dublin, shook her head at all the dirty coffee cups and trading tickets piling up from the British-American invasion. "It's messier, but we'll get used to it," she said. It would be nearly a year before Nymex would be able to open its trading pit in London. In the meantime, Dublin would be its defiant, if ill-fated, answer to the screen.

The stampede across the continents would not stop there. The Nymex board had decided to expedite its plan to open an exchange in the desert city of Dubai, a glamorous, tax-free oasis bordering the Persian Gulf in the United Arab Emirates. The goal, Newsome said, was to offer traders access to Nymex's "world-class" energy market across as many time zones as possible. For better or worse, Nymex was going to open trading pits, city by city, carving up the world to prove a point. It would act alone, resolute in its convictions, impervious to reason or logic. When a British journalist helpfully pointed out to Newsome at the first Dublin press conference that if Nymex really wanted to globalize, all it had to do was move energy trading to the screen, he was flatly ignored. Nymex had just shelled out millions for a splashy ad campaign featuring glossy photos of traders hard at work in the pits, with the motto: "Nymex, fitted with the latest technology—humans."

Raiding Dubai proved easier said than done. There were questions about what kind of crude oil to trade (Dubai, it seemed, had none), power struggles with the city's royalty (the government was wary of foreigners in general and Americans in particular), and resistance among the Nymex board members (especially from the Jewish contingent) to doing a deal with any Arabs. The first two problems would take months to address, but the latter one could be dealt with easily enough. The board put Gordon Rutledge, the only African American on the board, in charge of Dubai.

More immediately, the push into Dubai would be made difficult by the fact that the Nymex executives, infinitely well-versed with the rough social order of the pits, had no idea how to behave in polite society while conducting international business. At an upscale venue in London, an off-color joke told to the director general of the Dubai Development and Investment Authority (DDIA) nearly derailed the whole deal.

In a private, high-profile meeting on the ground floor of Nobu Berkeley, an expensive Mayfair restaurant reserved specifically for the occasion, Saeed Al Muntafiq, the conservative and urbane head of the

DDIA, came face-to-face with Richie Schaeffer. "It was a hugely important meeting for us, and negotiations were at a precarious stage," says one Nymex executive, who went with the board. "Al Muntafiq, an Ivy League–educated Iraqi, comes out wearing an $8,000 suit. Schaeffer comes out in his loafers from Men's Warehouse and some piece-of-shit Brooks Brothers suit. They sit down and Al Muntafiq says, 'So you want to start an exchange in Dubai?' Richie responds, 'You know, I think we might also want to consider launching a *camel* contract.' I swear to God he said it, he said 'camel contract.' Al Muntafiq kicks me under the table and then excuses himself. I meet him a couple minutes later in the men's room. He is washing his hands furiously at the sink. He locks his eyes with mine in the mirror and says, 'We are going to do this deal, because our children and our children's children will thank us for it. *But do not let that man near me again.*'"

Al Muntafiq eventually warmed to the oil traders, although not to Schaeffer. "He would tell us these stories about his grandmother," says the executive. "He told us about how his grandmother had been out to get water from the local well and a robber tried to attack her. She cut his arm off with an ax. She still got the water. He said he did not think America would do very well in the war with Iraq."

The board's first trip to Dubai did not go smoothly. After meetings with city officials and the DDIA executives, the Nymex directors were looking forward to a night out on the town. They were told that alcohol was hard to come by in a Muslim city, but they'd also been informed Dubai had an impressive selection of exotic prostitutes. "You know what the pecking order is for prostitutes in Dubai? Arab women are the most expensive, followed by the European and American women, then Asians, then Latinas, then, well, pretty much everyone else," says the Nymex staffer who was asked by the board to look into the rates of sex workers for the night (the exchange's budget, after all, did have a line item for "board entertainment"). About eighteen of the twenty board members on the trip, according to the staffer, wanted to go to the local brothels. "We were staying at the Emirates Towers. When I got back to the hotel that night, a board member was coming in who had *two* girls with him. At the hotel, you can sign in one hooker, but you have to pay a fee of $100. You can't sign in two hookers, because apparently *that* would be un-Islamic. The board member wanted me to sign in the second girl under my name, because I didn't have anyone with me. I didn't want a prostitute under my name, so I wrote another board member's name instead, and also his room number. Then I went to bed.

"Hours later, I get a panicked call from the front desk. They're telling me to come down, there's a big problem. I rush down to find the board member whose name I had written down, all five-foot-seven of him, with this six-foot-two Russian prostitute. He is screaming bloody murder because they're telling him he has already signed in a prostitute and he hasn't. I go over to the guy behind the desk and explain the situation. I give him $200. The guy behind the desk is happy. The board member is happy. I am happy because I am going back to bed. Then I get another call at dawn. A *third* board member is in trouble. He sounds very far away and he's scared to death. He's like, 'I woke up here in this shantytown and I don't know where I am!' He apparently went *home* with his hooker. Now he's somewhere in a slum on the outskirts of Dubai and his wallet's been stolen. I'm like, 'Forget your wallet! You're lucky you still have all your internal organs!'"

Back in London, Sprecher was dealing with his own, albeit less weird, growing pains. ICE had repeatedly experienced technical difficulties with the burst of trading activity it was getting from London. The British traders were beginning to try out the ICE screen, though many of them were still raw about having been made to do it. When they heard Sprecher planned to close the pits for good in April, they got even angrier. But since the ICE headquarters were hundreds of miles away in Atlanta, they had nobody to take it out on.

That is, until the Greenpeace protesters broke in.

With oil prices targeting $60 going into the winter of 2005—and the Kyoto Protocol, an international environmental treaty to reduce greenhouse gases, coming into force during London's annual Petroleum Week—the Greenpeace protesters thought it might be a good time to hold a rally denouncing the evils of Big Oil. They burst into a smattering of black-tie events across the city, attended by oil company and industry executives from around the world, unfurling banners across building after building that read: CLIMATE CHANGE KILLS, OIL INDUSTRY PARTIES.

The fateful day the Greenpeace protesters chose to raid the London pits was February 16, the day the Kyoto treaty took effect. When one trader left the floor to get lunch at two P.M., using a security swipe card, a Greenpeace volunteer dropped a fistful of coins on the ground to create a distraction. As he bent to pick them up, he put his boot in the door of the building, holding it open for thirty other protesters, who pulled up in vans and poured in. They startled the security guards, who were unable to stop them, and ambushed the pits, blowing whistles and releasing helium balloons tied to rape horns that floated to the ceiling, out of reach, drowning out the sound of the traders shouting buy and sell orders. The postprandial aggression of the traders, who had, as usual, spent lunch at the pub, was immediate.

The traders began kicking and punching male and female protesters indiscriminately, pounding them across the trading floor, out into the lobby, and onto the pavement. "Sod off, swampy!" one of them shrieked. The traders were at least as fierce as the Nymex traders would have been under the same circumstances. No protesters had ever broken into the Nymex trading pits but, that day, the exchange hastily tightened its security in case of a coordinated attack. The Greenpeace protesters were blown away by the fury of the London pit traders. "They were just cockney barrow boy spivs! Total thugs," one of them told the *Times* of London. "I took on a Texan SWAT team at Esso last year and they were angels compared with this lot," a second protester told the paper. An ICE executive watched the entire episode on TV. "We could see traders in ABN Amro and Man Financial jackets, some of the most prestigious trading firms in the world, just pummeling everybody."

The pit traders didn't care that the cameras were rolling. The London police arrested twenty-seven of the Greenpeace protesters. No traders were reported arrested. ICE took full advantage of the chance to advertise the benefits of the screen, issuing a statement saying, "Pit trading was suspended, but electronic trading carried on."

A few of the Greenpeace protesters fled in terror after being beaten up by a mob of incensed traders who tried to hold them down and push giant filing cabinets on top of them to crush them. "We thought we were going to die," one of the volunteers gasped over the phone. "I swear to God, we didn't know! If we'd only known they were this fucked off, we would have never come."

The reason for the bloodlust wasn't just about money. For many of the British traders, the closing of the trading pits signaled an end to their freewheeling way of life. Unable to work in an office environment, the vast majority of them went on to become drivers in London's fleet of black cabs.

When the pits closed in April 2005, traffic on the ICE trading screen took off like a shot. Trading volumes of its top-earning European oil futures contract jumped to 130,000 lots a day, matching the level of business typically done in the London pits. By May, it would surpass 170,000 contracts. Sprecher's experiment had worked. Meanwhile, Nymex European oil trading volumes in Dublin slunk along at 6,000 lots a day before falling to 2,000. The traders, who were still putting in long hours to keep it going, finally gave up. "It looks like the word processor has won out over the typewriter," one said with a sigh, pulling out.

But Sprecher had no intention of stopping at London. He announced he was taking ICE public. He would be issuing stock worth $115 million, making him a much richer foe. While Nymex generated more revenue than that in a year, it usually squandered most of it. "The stronger ICE's cash position, the greater its potential as a competitor," Newsome warned Steinhause and the rest of the board. Before ICE had existed, Nymex had wanted to go public. Now it was falling behind.

Sprecher was like a welterweight with fast hands. After more than a hundred years of just getting by, Nymex had suddenly become one of the world's hottest markets—only to be confronted by its own ineptitude.

Steinhause hired Merrill Lynch to advise the exchange on its "strategic options," which, on Wall Street, was a euphemistic way of admitting to not knowing what you were doing. "We repeatedly told Steinhause he needed to put together a kitchen cabinet to figure out the best way to proceed," Guttman says. "He resisted."

The Nymex members were getting twitchy. "We aren't hearing jack from Merrill," Marty Greenberg said. "I don't know what the heck they're doing." Behind the scenes, some traders said, Fisher was calling for Steinhause's ouster. Leo Melamed was watching the situation from Chicago with a great deal of interest. The CME had become the biggest futures market in the world, but it still didn't have a foothold in the highly desirable energy sector. Melamed made a few phone calls. Other potential buyers also were coming out of the woodwork. Nymex was making money hand over fist, but its hesitant chairman and slow-motion response to Sprecher's hyperaggressive assault made it seem like the weaker contender.

Before anyone knew it, the New York oil market was officially in play.

Mark Fisher was the first to call it like it was. He held a rare town-hall meeting in March 2005. He invited all the traders, Steinhause,

Schaeffer, Newsome, the board, and the rest of the executive suite. It was time, he said, to address the emerging crisis. Most of the traders who attended the closed-door meeting were completely bewildered. Nymex never had open discussions about its future. It only had gossip. They didn't know what to make of an organized meeting to address its business strategy.

As soon as they'd assembled, Fisher got straight to the point.

"I called this meeting, not Nymex. This is not a meeting to look in the rearview mirror and say what we haven't done that we should have done. The problem right now is we are not competitive, and we need to become competitive. If we don't move forward in a proactive manner, the only people we'll have to blame will be ourselves." He suggested the oil market had basked in its own ignorance for too long, even as it had grown to be worth hundreds of billions of dollars. (Over the counter, the commodities market was now measured in the trillions, only nobody knew how many trillions.) Few of the chairmen had bothered to build up Nymex's business, instead focusing on paying themselves large salaries and soaking up the perks of their office. The traders had repeatedly cried foul when the board had traveled to Dubai, or booked trips to the Kentucky Derby, on the exchange's dime. Both were defended by Steinhause as legitimate business trips. Sprecher had successfully exploited Nymex's weaknesses and now he was closing in. "Our corporate structure is too big and too costly and doesn't allow us to compete in a quick and rational market," Fisher said. "We need the expertise of a private-equity firm to streamline our board, affect corporate governance, and help us go public."

What Fisher meant was that *he* was talking to a private-equity firm to see if it wanted to buy Nymex and take it public.

A lone trader spoke up. He told Fisher he didn't think Nymex needed to sell itself or go public. Why couldn't they just replace the bad management instead?

Fisher cut him down.

"If you disagree, that's fine," he said. "You're a *short seller*, no problem."

He concluded his speech by reminding the traders that his own neck, more than anyone else's, was on the line. "I have as much to lose, or more, as anyone in this room."

There was a long and uncomfortable silence.

Instead of Fisher's speech being a call to arms that would unite the traders of Nymex in a common cause to fight off its competitors, it was as if he'd dropped a neutron bomb on them. The traders had only heard one thing: Fisher was trying to cut a deal with a private-equity firm to sell *their* exchange.

If Fisher, who'd never before held office or a seat on the board, was attempting to play deal-maker, then why not the rest of them?

The speech did not leave the traders with a shared sense of mission. Rather, it gave them an excuse to cobble together their own deals in a race against one another—deals they hoped might personally enrich and empower them. Their market was under siege, but they could not stop locking horns with each other over the biggest trade of all. While this mentality had always worked for them in the pits, they soon found it didn't translate very well in salvaging their business. After overcoming so many external threats—OPEC, Big Oil, Wall Street, even Washington—the one thing the traders could not survive was themselves.

Within the space of just a few months, the Nymex chairmen, past and present, would coalesce in a final showdown that would pit board member against board member, trader against trader, in a civil war that would threaten to rip the oil market apart at the seams.

It was a battle royal only one man could win.

After the meeting adjourned, Deep Throat called me to weigh in.

His assessment was grim.

"The inmates have taken over the asylum."

13

Age of Excess

Leo Melamed called me up and asked, "Who's in charge over there?" I said, "Nobody is."

—ZOLTAN LOUIS GUTTMAN

IN LATE 2004, Mark Fisher's daughter, Jessica, was dating Seth Cohen, a handsome, broad-shouldered junior associate from the Blackstone Group, the prestigious $90 billion New York private-equity firm run by Steven Schwarzman and Peter Petersen. The two men had founded the firm in 1985 with only $400,000 between them and one secretary. They had since become society-page darlings and, not coincidentally, billionaires.

While he was talking with Cohen about the messy travails of the oil market, it dawned on Fisher he had the perfect opportunity to do something about it. Like make a deal.

In early 2005, Richie Schaeffer also thought he had the perfect opportunity to make a deal. He'd started his own negotiations with multibillion-dollar private-equity firm General Atlantic of Greenwich, Connecticut. (Vinnie Viola, who realized Schaeffer's star was rising, had introduced him to Bill Ford, General Atlantic's CEO. Ford, like Viola, was a smooth-talking, good-looking businessman. Only he'd gone to Stanford.)

Fisher and Viola, for good measure, reached out to the CME, wondering if it too might be interested in a deal. Why not try to make deals with everybody?

The Nymex members objected to this. They didn't understand why

Viola, who was no longer chairman, and Fisher, who had, again, never held office, were initiating merger talks. But their protests fell on deaf ears.

Michel Marks, meanwhile, was entering into separate discussions with San Francisco private-equity firm Hellman & Friedman—without telling anybody.

Danny Rappaport wasn't making any deals, but he'd soon reenter the fray.

Mitchell Steinhause, woefully marginalized at this point by Schaeffer, was relegated to watching from the sidelines. He was still chairman, but his role had mostly been reduced to announcing the decisions that Schaeffer made. Disappointed by Steinhause's silence at being so easily railroaded, the pit traders began disparagingly referring to him as "Steakhouse." Bobby Sahn called me at the news desk at Dow Jones, worried that too many secret negotiations were going on without him or the other exchange members being let in on the details. He had expected better of Steinhause. "Mitchell is an empty suit! What's going on over there? It's like Tammany Hall." But an executive who'd recently left the exchange in disgust saw one small reason for hope. "Even half-assing is an improvement. They've been no-assing it up until now."

The traders were extremely suspicious of all the stealth deal-making. Rumors started making the rounds in the pits that the Nymex officials were allying themselves with different private-equity firms in exchange for kickbacks or side deals while competing with one another to lead the oil market into its next phase. Confused by the under-the-radar pussyfooting, Leo Melamed called up his former associate, Lou Guttman, to find out what was happening. Melamed was not ignorant of the fact that Nymex had put out feelers about doing a deal with the CME. But what he really wanted to know was how the world's leading oil market had fallen into such a state of anarchy at the very height of the Iraq War—and its riches.

"It's not a good state of affairs," Guttman agreed. "Prices are sky-high. No one is running the exchange. Everyone is rushing around making deals without any authority and nobody's talking to anybody."

"You guys are sitting on a *gold mine*," Melamed said. "And you don't even know what you are doing. It's an amazing thing."

The sheer number of bids and counterbids whizzing through the oil market was dizzying. The traders were not used to Wall Street deal-makers tripping all over their wingtips in pursuit of buying them. Kohlberg Kravis Roberts and Thomas H. Lee Partners, both big-name private-equity firms, stopped by to take a look. "Supposedly, KKR showed up last week," Sahn said. "But they were late, so no meeting took place." Only Nymex would have the hubris to turn away a white-shoe firm like KKR. Meanwhile, "Tommy Lee," as the traders liked to call the founder of the eponymous investment firm, had the irritating habit of correcting everyone's grammar. Lee also would have his hands full by autumn with his investment in Refco, the multibillion-dollar commodities brokerage house that would unexpectedly collapse after its British CEO, the Warhol-and-Ferrari-collecting Phillip Bennett, was caught trying to hide $430 million of debt and then lying about it. ("How about the Refco investors draw lots to see who gets to run him over in the Ferrari?" one blogger suggested in the aftermath.)

Stories about Nymex being bought out were making national and international news, as the price of oil rose above $60 a barrel. The pit traders soon found themselves in the unenviable position of trying to stay on top of the unfolding events of the Iraq War while keeping track of whether their trading floor was about to be sold out from underneath them. Guttman ramped up issues of the *Nymex Advocate* to keep them apprised. He'd built a giant Excel spreadsheet with all the exchange members' names, numbers, e-mails, and home addresses on it. It contained over six hundred people.

In Washington, Congress was finally reconsidering the more disturbing aspects of the Commodity Futures Modernization Act, which had opened the Enron loophole and the London loophole, and inexplicably barred the CFTC from prosecuting any cases of energy fraud in the over-the-counter market. Some legislators suspected that the legislation wasn't in the best interests of the U.S. taxpayer. "We need to make sure these markets are transparent, fair, and adequately protective of consumers," said Senator Tom Harkin, a Democrat from Iowa and ranking member of the House Agricultural Subcommittee on General Commodities and Risk Management.

Senator Saxby Chambliss, the chairman of the Senate Agriculture, Nutrition and Forestry Committee ("shaping the future of farm, food and rural policy in the United States"), decided it was time to hold some hearings on the subject. Hearings were supposed to show that Capitol Hill was taking something seriously. "We decided to bring everybody in who has a dog in this fight and have them tell us how they think things are working and whether or not changes need to be made," said Chambliss, a hard-nosed, tough-talking Republican from Georgia. In March 2005, executives from Wall Street and the futures exchanges paraded into Washington to argue against stricter oversight of the energy market. Strangely absent from the hearings were the energy consumer groups. No one knew whether anybody had invited them. Filing into the conference room with the other journalists, I noticed the legislators were shadowed by a gaggle of young women in tight, short skirts, waving accordion files. As the committee listened to the exchange chairmen get up and speak, the young women darted around like gazelles, bringing notes and coffee to the senators. The room strained to focus on the drier topics at hand. The legislators appeared distracted by the girls and bored by the testimony.

Then a Chicago exchange executive mentioned, in passing, the existence of weather futures.

The senators instantly perked up. Antifraud legistlation and Enron were not interesting. But weather futures sounded like something they could get excited about. Even after the dialogue had moved on, the legislators eagerly kept going back to the topic. "Thank you for that," one of the committee members said to an executive after a particularly lengthy presentation. "Not to digress, but just how do these weather futures work?" Another executive from the CME patiently explained that weather futures and options allowed traders to bet on the likelihood of things like seasonal temperature changes, precipitation, and hurricanes. They were financial instruments used by farmers, so that when the weather didn't go their way they could still get paid, or by professional baseball players who wanted payouts in case of rain dates, or by traders simply looking to speculate on the next category 5 hurricane.

To watch their reactions, this was the most marvelous thing the legislators had ever heard of. As they oohed and aahed over the miracle of betting on the weather, it became patently clear why Wall Street was so mortally terrified of any form of government regulation. *Congress had absolutely no idea what Wall Street was doing.*

The hearings led to neither the closing of the Enron loophole nor an end to blocking the CFTC from cracking down on energy fraud. Jim Newsome's successor, Sharon Brown-Hruska, the CFTC chairwoman, told Congress she didn't really think the agency needed any more authority to regulate markets. She believed the over-the-counter trading arena was run very safely by the banks and other "sophisticated users." If the CFTC did try to regulate it, she warned, it would be an exercise in futility. "Supervising such a huge market would be an enormous task, and what's the benefit? Even if you had all that data, all those transactions, how would you organize it?" Dealing with monumental responsibilities was not the CFTC's forte.

The same flood of investor money overwhelming the New York oil traders was flowing in even greater quantities to the over-the-counter energy market. Bo Collins, the ex–Nymex president whose new hedge fund would not disintegrate until autumn of 2006, found himself standing directly under the money spigot. After a few trips to Geneva and London, he was able to raise tens of millions of dollars in capital, hire a few partners, including an executive and a trader from Nymex, and open offices on Park Avenue by December 2005. He immediately dispatched one of the partners to his home state of Texas to begin building up business relationships there. The partner was told it was important for energy hedge funds to become friendly with the Texans in general and the over-the-counter market's brokers in particular (these were the ones with the Rolodexes, who worked from home in their underwear). A hedge fund was nothing without the goodwill of its brokers, who knew how to navigate the narrows of the off-exchange netherworld.

As the arbiters of multimillion- and billion-dollar deals between the banks, hedge funds, and energy companies, these brokers wielded absolute power. For their services, they were paid millions of dollars a year, sometimes by a single client. Best of all, they were completely unlicensed and uncertified, as their market was unregulated. In truth, they weren't even getting paid for their brokering skills. They were getting paid for access to their golden Rolodexes, which linked them to nearly every major energy powerhouse in the world, including banks like Morgan Stanley and Goldman Sachs. The more people on your broker's top-secret client list, the more opportunities you had as a trader to do big deals. And big deals meant big money. The brokers were the trusted gatekeepers of the underground, and in a cutthroat market where the traders trusted no one—least of all one another—they were the sentinels who would watch your back, provided you paid them well.

In the same way that oil was one of the most overtraded products in the world, the over-the-counter energy market was one of the most overbrokered. If you could get into it, though, you could practically write your own ticket.

Collins's partner flew to Houston to meet with representatives of Choice Energy, one of the better-known brokerage firms run by a former Columbia University football star. A swashbuckling millionaire in his early thirties, Javier Loya was a first-generation Mexican American from a large, overachieving family, who counted among his many accomplishments being the first minority owner of the NFL's Houston Texans. He was the kind of prototypical, impossibly handsome wheeler-dealer for which the over-the-counter market had become infamous. He also had a predilection for partying and sports gambling.

"I called Javier's guys up and they told me to come meet them at this place called Treasures," says Collins's former partner. "So I am thinking it's a bar, right? Wrong. I walk in, and it turns out that Treasures is a strip club. The manager comes over to me and says, 'Javy says I'm supposed to set you up real nice. He wants me to give you the *full treatment.*' I am like, 'Uh, that's okay.' This was my first meeting with Javier's firm as a potential client, so I'm surprised this is where they want to meet. Then I find out this is routine, that they do this not only to butter you up but, more important, to test you, to see if you'll take the bait." Taking the bait, naturally, gave your cohort instant insight into your moral character.

The indoctrination was only the beginning of the partner's down-the-rabbit-hole misadventures in the dark market. On Wall Street, banks, exchanges, and hedge funds often treated their clients to dinners at pricey restaurants, but they tried not to overspend, lest their customers think them careless with their expenses and perhaps overcharging them. Yet in the over-the-counter market, concerted displays of opulence were almost mandatory. Since everyone knew everyone else was being grossly overpaid, there was no reason to bother keeping up the illusion. On a business trip with a group of traders and brokers at Body English, an all-the-pretty-people nightclub at the Hard Rock Hotel in Las Vegas, the same partner watched as Loya competed with a wealthy Russian oil magnate over who could buy the most bottles of Cristal. "We had thirty women at one point opening and serving $1,000 bottles of champagne to everyone in the club, all paid for by Javier. He dropped well over six figures that night. He traveled with this huge entourage, and I am not talking a couple dozen people. I am talking about 80 to 120. If we needed more girls, he'd just go outside to the line and go 'shopping,' walking around with the bouncer and picking out the girls he wanted to let in. We'd all get flashlights, and if we didn't like anybody in the club, we could just point the light at them and the bouncer would automatically kick them out.

"When we arrived, Javier had a section cordoned off for us, but one table in front of the stage had been excluded. He asked the owner, 'Why do I not have that table?' The owner said, 'It's for Jon Bon Jovi. He's playing here tonight.' And sure enough, there's Bon Jovi sitting at the table, having a drink. Javier turns around and says to the owner, 'Why don't you go check your books and see how much fucking money Jon Bon Jovi spends every time he comes here and then come back and let me know who has that table?' Before we know it, they're asking Jon to *move to another table*. The club was deafening, but from a distance, we could see Bon Jovi mouthing the words 'What the fuck is going on?' He switched tables. Seemed like a decent guy. Stuff like that with Javy was par for the course."

At least half of his entourage that night was from Bon Jovi's home state of New Jersey, Loya recalls. "*We* were the rock stars. We did a lot of immature things like that back then. When you're young and making a lot of discretionary income, your emphasis is on the good times. And you spend a lot of money on things of little or no value. You're foolhardy. We once sent a guy we'd just hired out to Vegas with $5,000 in his pocket, to teach him what it was like to be a trader, the highs and lows of winning and losing. We told him he had to get off the plane, walk right in, and put all of his money on the roulette wheel. If he won, he'd get to keep the money and stay a week in Vegas and spend it whatever way he wanted. If he lost, he'd have to immediately get back on the plane to Houston. He lost. I don't know where he is today. I think he went into real estate."

The traders couldn't always keep up their game faces. Bo Collins's ex-partner recalls flying back to Houston from yet another extravagant junket in Las Vegas with a group of energy traders and brokers. The Citation jet they'd rented hit an air pocket. "We instantly dropped, like, fifty to a hundred feet and, all of a sudden, we go from being braggart assholes to screaming like a bunch of prepubescent girls at an 'N Sync concert. We were terrified. I was literally, *literally* crying. Then, the plane rights itself and we are all fine. We look around at each other like, '*Anyway* . . .'"

Behavior in the Nymex trading pits was getting alarmingly excessive. "Let's just say this: I was almost always plastered at work," says one trading assistant, who gave a full account of the floor's culture in 2005. "One of my biggest talents was sneaking in food and booze, which was technically off-limits but no one ever paid any attention to the rules. Not even security and the exchange officials, who, for some reason, were much pickier about food being on the floor than the drugs or the booze. I could never figure that one out. We had the members' dining room and a restaurant on the tenth floor, but some of us were so addicted to the Philly cheesesteaks at this one place across the river in Hoboken, New Jersey, that we would actually pay the delivery guy to get on a ferry and bring them to us. It didn't take that long, but you know, he was coming from another state. We would order between 50 and 150 of them at a time and just gorge ourselves. When it came to drinking, I went for the hard stuff. I would drink and do my drugs in my trading booth. My Quaalude guy was in the options pit. I would have my intern go over there and pick up my pills for me, the little druggie. Sometimes I would pass out in my booth. One time I literally tripped on the edge of the pit and fell in, I was so wasted. The pits always reeked of booze.

"In terms of the ethics of the trading pits, nothing was shocking. Most of the pay the clerks got was off the books. I got lots of cash tips, sometimes drugs. I got taken out all the time in the evenings and on weekends with everything paid for. Extra money often came from traders who would tip the clerks for letting them know about the big orders coming into the pit from their customers. If you got a lot of orders and agreed to hook a trader up for a day, you could make $500 or more. Or you might just get a big bag of weed—my favorite payment. The deal was, if you got a job at Nymex, you could choose *who* you shared inside information with, but you could never choose *not* to share it. At least that's how I saw it. If you tried to be honest down there, you could get fired. But they would usually weed you out long before that. Almost no one was willing to take an ideological stand when things had been done one way for so long.

"Those who worked the phones were often in a prime position to gather and sell information. One guy had a client—I don't know who— but I do know that no one, *no one*, was allowed to touch his phone, in case that client called. It was like he was sitting on a freaking pot of gold. There was this one guy, a clerk, who was the biggest guy in crude when it came to getting huge customer orders. At one time, he knew every hooker in New York City. He would talk to you about what you were looking for and then give you a phone number. I remember once joking about how I was going to get my brother a prostitute for his birthday and he was in earshot. He comes over and gives me a number and says, 'This one's good—only $100. Tell her I sent you.' I was like, 'Johnny, I was only kidding!'

"The traders liked to go to the Penthouse Executive Club and New York Dolls and this other one off Times Square. Also, any number of the local massage parlors, which were always getting busted and relocating. I can't tell you which ones, or else I might get them busted. The traders had very specific taste in women. They either had to be extraordinarily sleazy or extraordinarily hot. And the guys wouldn't just watch them. They would actually sleep with them. That's why they didn't like to go to the more upscale clubs, like Scores. It was too strict. And they weren't just having sex with strippers. A lot of them were friends with them. They would hang out with the strippers, take them to dinner. Most of the Nymex traders' wives were trophy wives with fake breasts. I don't know what they thought of all the whoring. Either they weren't aware of it, or they just didn't give a shit. One guy, an independent oil trader, didn't even refer to his family members by their names anymore, like he couldn't be bothered. He would just call them 'The Wife,' 'Kid No. 1,' and 'Kid No. 2.' His wife was smoking hot, but that didn't keep him from going out and sleeping with everybody.

"There were clerks who were more or less pimping women on the side. That was probably the most outrageous. Most of the time, they would just show photos of the girls, but sometimes they would actually sign them in and get them down on the trading floor. I don't know exactly how they got them past security—they would generally be dressed extremely slutty—but maybe the guards just thought they were new trading assistants or something? That was understandable, because sometimes a trader would wake up beside a prostitute and get a message on his BlackBerry that his clerk had called in sick, and bring her down to the trading floor to fill in. It was easy money for her, and usually all she'd have to do was take orders, get coffee, and answer the phones. I am sure there were women who started out there as prostitutes who eventually got real jobs that way."

BY EARLY 2005, gasoline prices at the pump were topping $2 a gallon. Across the country, gas stations were struggling, as mass gasoline thefts edged past $300 million. "This is the worst year I've seen," Linda Fulton of the E-Z Mart filling station in Wake Village, Texas, told me when I interviewed her for the *Wall Street Journal*. "I am $111 short this week, and it's all from drive-offs. Normally, I wouldn't lose this much in a month." The same year in Canada, Grant De Patie, a twenty-four-year-old gas station attendant in Maple Ridge, British Columbia, was dragged more than seven kilometers to his death after trying to stop a car from driving off with $12.30 worth of gas. The driver, seventeen-year-old Darnell Pratt, was sentenced to nine years in prison after telling witnesses he could hear De Patie's screams from beneath his car and yet kept driving.

The truth was, selling gas was a thankless business. Gas stations got their fuel from a nationwide network of tens of thousands of distributors, many that worked as freelancers and independent "jobbers." Big oil companies had increasingly abandoned that part of the business, because the money just wasn't big *enough*. They were happy to stick to the drilling and the charging of high market prices for oil, leaving the fuel-hauling to the small-time dealers. The jobbers would buy the fuel straight from the refineries at the rack and drive it in trucks to the various gas stations they made deals with, taking a sliver of the profit for themselves. The gas stations would try to get the best deal they could from the jobbers and also take a cut. With jobbers competing against other jobbers and gas stations competing against other gas stations, the price of gasoline diverged widely from station to station, with each trying to take as big a cut as possible. "Gas prices are like airline tickets," says one jobber. "Everyone is going to the same place, but they're all paying a different price." With profits being sliced so thinly among so many, everyone was eager to raise prices but slow to lower them. On days when Nymex prices were rising swiftly, the jobbers would race to get to the refinery to buy before the market's settlement, so they could get the lower price and charge a higher one. The industry had a saying about gas prices at the pump: "Up like a rocket, down like a feather."

In an extraordinary example of how far people would go to get around high gas prices, in June 2005, one man almost burned himself to death in an attempt to steal fuel. He pulled up to a station in Cottondale, Alabama, driving a trailer retrofitted to hold three hundred gallons of gas. Parking in front of the fueling station, he used a homemade pumping device hidden under the vehicle to suck hundreds of gallons of gas from the ground. Halfway into loading, the trailer blew up by accident, severely burning the driver. He was admitted to the hospital in critical condition. The same month, members of a gasoline-theft ring in Florida were arrested for using trucks that could siphon upward of a thousand gallons of fuel undetected.

For the first time since the 1970s, white-collar workers, sometimes with expensive cars, were being caught red-handed driving off without paying for their gas. The phenomenon had become so rampant that states like New York were proposing license suspensions for first-time offenders. The public blamed the stations for price-gouging, but in reality the stations made almost no profit selling gas. The stations wouldn't have bothered to sell gas at all if not for the fact that the customers who came into their stores to pay often bought groceries, which was how they made their real money. Gasoline was just the bait. "In most cases, gas stations are lucky to make even a penny or two a gallon," says Jeff Lenard of the National Association of Convenience Stores. "So when someone drives away with $30 of gas, it can take hundreds of fill-ups to make up for it." Gas stations were just as upset about the supply gaming as the customers. "Big Oil has been looked at with suspicion for years, because the prices don't always make sense with what we are seeing with supply and demand. You don't see that with many other commodities to the extent you do with oil. Think about it; when Florida has a freeze and the price of orange juice goes up, you don't hear everyone blaming Big Citrus."

In the spring of 2005, the bidding at Nymex had gotten feverish, with half a dozen private-equity firms lining up at the door. Nymex received its first formal offer in April, of $185 million for 20 percent of the exchange, from Blackstone and Battery Ventures, a Massachusetts private-equity firm. The two companies had teamed up in 2000 to purchase and resell the London International Financial Options and Futures Exchange for an obscene profit. They each earned about 300 percent on their original investment, which, taken together, approached hundreds of millions of dollars.

Realizing the competition had gotten stiff, in July 2005, Blackstone and Battery Ventures came back and raised their offer for 20 percent of Nymex to $200 million.

In August, General Atlantic topped that, offering $240 million for the 20 percent stake.

The pit traders panicked. They did not want to sell their oil market, and, even if they did, 20 percent of it was too much to lose. They did not want to relinquish control.

Newsome was tiring of the traders' constant moaning. Backed by Schaeffer and Fisher, he made the definitive case to the members. He had become the diplomat. "We need a private-equity firm with some skin in the game to help us. If we're going to do a public stock offering, we need someone to sell our story to Wall Street."

The members remained unconvinced. "I don't understand why we need someone to help take us public. Shoe companies go public. They don't know anything about it, but they manage to do it. Why can't we?" asked Charles Federbush, a member for thirty years.

Gary Glass abruptly emerged from retirement to call for a rebellion. "The current board is completely out of touch with its shareholders and it's time for them to go!"

The private-equity firms were, if anything, even more put off by the Nymex disequilibrium. They were hoping that doing a deal with the world's largest oil market would be worth all the trouble, but it was looking like a toss-up. For one, the Nymex traders seemed to have a deeply warped view of Wall Street, which had a lot to do with the fact that they had been stuck in a time warp for the past three decades. Just as they'd fumbled in trying to conduct international business, they were now alienating the very people they were trying to do deals with.

In the middle of the night, Mark Fisher called up the lead partner from Blackstone, Chinh Chu, who had just put his children to bed.

"Wire a million dollars to Las Vegas," he told Chu. "I've got my jet waiting."

"Who *is* this?" Chu asked.

Needless to say, Fisher's G-5 did not leave the landing strip with Chu in it.

Word eventually got around about the incident. Fisher denied that it happened but, when I spoke with him about it, he denied it *from* Las Vegas, where he was playing in the World Series of Poker. "You should see all the people competing in this thing," he told me. "It's a lot like Nymex: sane people, crazy people, rich guys, middle-class guys, and, you know, the bums."

While the Nymex traders were still stuffing Brazilian hookers into private jets, the rest of Wall Street had moved on, learning to hide its darker impulses. "People don't realize that this kind of stuff isn't institutionalized behavior anymore. We're no longer openly doing lines off the conference room tables," says one Wall Street executive well aware of the gap between the Nymex members and the rest of civilization. "That went out with the eighties. These days, there's just too much money at stake." By contrast, the conference room tables at Nymex still saw plenty of action. A board member had only recently been caught by one of the exchange's evening maids, mid-coitus, mistress splayed on the boardroom table with his pants down. "Nymex has always been like that," Guttman says. "You want to talk about the intrigue, the mystery, the corruption, the sex—the sex! It was off the charts in that place." Sheltered by the pits for decades, the Nymex traders hadn't realized they were truly the last bastion of Wall Street's no-holds-barred, lecherous Gilded Age.

The private-equity partners put up with the Nymex traders for one reason only: they were hoping to hit the jackpot. When Blackstone and Battery Ventures had cinched their landmark deal in London five years earlier, they'd triggered a gold rush of investments in financial exchanges on a global scale. Once seen as the lumbering, not-for-profit utilities of Wall Street, the value of exchanges worldwide had exploded by $100 billion. "There isn't an investment firm on the planet that wouldn't lie down in the gutter right now for even the smallest slice of Nymex," one bank analyst told me. "I mean, it's not just a global exchange, *it's the fucking oil market.*"

Still, no one could get through its doors without being hazed.

"It was definitely a unique experience. When you're dealing in the world of Nymex, it is run by a different set of rules. It's run by the rules of Nymex. The governance was almost nonexistent. It was frustrating to the point of comical. There was no sense of organization. The deal-making process was multiple standard deviations from what normal people would consider a process of integrity. When you are dealing at that level with what is *supposed to be a federally regulated institution,* you expect a certain amount of practicality," says a partner from one of the firms that entered into negotiations with Nymex. "We used to laugh, because whenever even a minor deal point changed, the next day it appeared in the *Wall Street Journal.* We never saw that kind of information leakage with any investment we'd ever done before.

"There were a lot of personal interests combined with the discussions, a great deal of chest-beating and wild egos. We put a lot of work into trying to understand the history and the people who made the oil market what it is today. When you're dealing with older guys who created something from nothing like that, they take a lot of pride in the fact. There was almost a dichotomy between the real, emotional connection they had with the exchange and their financial motives. There were some serious characters in that place, and their stories! The jet-full-of-Brazilian-hookers story, we heard that one. It was much beloved at the exchange. These guys would make an amazing movie. You got Mark Fisher, the guy with the intellectual horsepower. You got Richie Schaeffer and Jim Newsome, who were like Frick and Frack. Richie would do all the machinating and then he would go to Newsome and Newsome would make it look good, put the stamp of approval on it. You also got these psycho games of backgammon going on downstairs in the cafeteria, where a lot of big money is changing hands. You got Lou Guttman, the godfather of the exchange. Then you got Gary Glass, the other Jewish guy, who dresses up as Santa Claus for his daughter's Christmas play. Both great guys. And the other members just killed us. Stanley Meierfeld, the chicken man who always had a tan. He lived at the tanning salon. It was like he and Bobby Sahn never left St. Croix. Some of them were real crooks, you knew they were lying to you and they were just bad guys. You can throw a nickel into a group of them and hit half that have been charged by the CFTC. But most of them were lovable buffoons. And they told you stories, like your grandfather."

A second private-equity partner was stunned by the sheer number of Wall Street firms invited to the Nymex buyout party. "You think you're going to do a deal and then you find out everybody else thinks *they're* going to do a deal. All the private-equity firms and their dogs showed up looking for a shot, but it really came down to Richie Schaeffer versus Mark Fisher. Richie wanted a power grab and he saw this as an opportunity to take control. He was clearly the power broker, from the board's standpoint. He seemed to have a high-burn-rate lifestyle, a real thirst and lust for money and power. Fisher wanted to make Nymex more competitive, take it public, and, no matter what, keep the trading pits open. He was the biggest clearer of crude-oil contracts and one of the biggest dealers in natural gas, so the pits were absolutely sacrosanct to him. He was very nervous about having trading move to the screen instead of the floor. The dynamic between Richie and Fisher was not great. Mark didn't respect Richie. He respected people who could trade."

When it became patently obvious the members would not vote for a sale of 20 percent, the Nymex executives scrambled. They decided to try and sell 10 percent of the oil market instead. Blackstone and Battery Ventures, the firms led by Fisher, offered $130 million for the 10 percent stake. General Atlantic, led by Schaeffer, came under pressure to bid more. Marks was still trying to get his own bid together without letting any of the other executives know about it, but someone squealed and they forced him off the board. In his letter of resignation, Marks wrote nostalgically of his chairmanship and his ties to the oil market. He also advanced a portentous warning to the members: "We face the risk of losing this moment, losing this potential, and losing control of our destiny."

John Conheeney, the husband of novelist Mary Higgins Clark, quit.

When Guttman heard about the Marks rout, he was livid. He had specifically asked Marks if he planned on putting together a private-equity deal of his own, and Marks had not been up front with him.

"I ask you a direct question, are you going to bid on the Nymex or aren't you, and you lie through your teeth!" Guttman stormed.

Marks offered no apology. Guttman had good reason to feel betrayed. Earlier that spring, he and Marks had had a climactic conversation right after the Boca conference. Guttman was headed to the airport with his wife for a vacation getaway to the Bahamas when Marks rang him up.

"Until then, whenever we'd broached the topic of joining forces, Michel would just say 'I'll think about it,' like he always did. But this time, it seemed like he'd made up his mind," Guttman says. "He was ready."

They spoke for over a half hour. Marks and Guttman had never gotten along with each other, but this time was different. The future of the exchange was on the line. Each man had lost something he wanted to reclaim. Marks, the first oil chairman, hoped to be the last oil chairman. Guttman, still smarting from his ouster years earlier, hoped for a clean slate, a fresh start. He felt he deserved it. Legally, he could never be chairman again, but he had the backing of the membership, which he could persuade to throw its support behind Marks. Together they could do what separately each man could not. Under anyone else, both men knew the oil market would continue to degenerate until it was beyond fixing. It was like the potato market all over again, only with more terrifying, global proportions. This would be their last chance.

The Nymex board, for the most part, had been none the wiser. As it turned out, it didn't need to be. The two accidental chairmen who'd never understood each other still didn't understand each other. In the aftermath of the discussion, they clashed bitterly over how they would run the exchange if they could secure it, who would and wouldn't be invited to join their new team. Guttman, overwrought, asked Marks what he wanted to do next. Marks never got back to him.

Amid white-knuckle rounds of extraordinary board meetings to consider deal proposals—at one point, Nymex received four bids in one week—Newsome announced the cutoff date for all bids would be September 20, 2005. "We are *not* going to keep on taking bids forever!" he thundered.

By this time, it was universally known that Schaeffer and Newsome were a package deal. Newsome's alliance with Schaeffer had given him immense clout. He'd become Schaeffer's mouthpiece and willing executioner. He'd even fired people on behalf of Schaeffer, so that Schaeffer didn't have to get his hands dirty. Anyone who sized up Newsome as all hat, no cattle would have Schaeffer to deal with. "My and Richie's relationship is proof you don't need to have identical personalities to work closely with someone. Me, a farm kid from the South, and Richie, a hard-charging business guy from New York; me, being very reserved and calculated in what I do, and Richie, having everything on his sleeve; me, mapping out my moves in advance, and Richie, working very spur-of-the-moment in his decisions. What wasn't seen, what was outside of the limelight, were the long hours that we worked together, just the two of us. I think he was good at pushing me forward and I was good at holding him back. Because of his strong personality, I found it best to talk to him one-on-one behind closed doors and that's how we made our decisions, just talking things out by ourselves."

As Newsome acknowledged later, what they were talking about was that the oil market didn't actually need to sell itself to a private-equity firm for the reasons he'd shared with the traders. That had all been window dressing. What Nymex did need, by his and Schaeffer's estimation, was a catalyst, a game-changer that might be used as a distraction while the board hammered out a deal, rewrote the market's rules and bylaws, and then seized power. The members now controlled the exchange and they were about to run it into the ground. Schaeffer, Newsome, Fisher, and the board were finally coming to terms with the fact that the traders would rather see their oil market reduced to rubble than give up the pits for the screen.

Time was running out. The CME's CEO, Craig Donahue, had already begun publicly talking about opening an energy market to compete with Nymex and ICE. If that happened, it was going to be World War III.

Yet the traders still insisted they had more time. "A trader is a trader: he trades what he sees. He hears that the pits aren't long for this world, but then he's in them every day and he's seeing record trading volumes," says Marty Greenberg. "All we want is to just make enough to retire," a pit trader told me. "It's like blow my brains out in three years, not now." But that wasn't the whole truth. In a poll of Nymex members independently funded and conducted by Marks, 49 percent admitted they wanted to keep the floor open "indefinitely."

The executives had come to their conclusion reluctantly. As Sprecher had done with the London traders, they realized they were going to have to force the traders' hands. But first, they'd have to trick them. "Getting the traders to vote themselves out of power became a higher hurdle than anything else," Newsome says.

Marks could accept that Nymex needed to move pit trading to the screen. He'd been saying that for years. But he didn't trust Schaeffer and Newsome. He didn't trust anyone. He had yet to finish putting together his deal, even after being booted from the board, but continued sending out personal letters to hundreds of Nymex members. In a September 14 missive, the day before the private-equity firms made their final presentations to the executive suite, he told them, "If we keep doing business the same way, then Nymex won't be Nymex a few years from now. Do you think I am an alarmist? Do you think that pit trading will be here ten years from now?"

In a September 19 letter, the day before the board was set to vote on the deal, Marks wrote, "Since June, I have devoted my time to developing a plan, assembling a team, and seeking input and guidance from fellow shareholders to develop a vision of the exchange in the twenty-first century." He was insinuating he was still pursuing a deal, but he never put in a definitive bid. The members read the letters, but they weren't sure what to think. One of the floor clerks, whose father had been close with Marks, theorized that Marks just longed once more to be chairman. "I think one day he was at Nymex and looked at all those oil paintings of the chairmen on the wall and saw himself and said, 'I look good and powerful. I'd like to be that way again,'" he says. But the members didn't care who won, as long as they got paid. "Once you're in play like Nymex, the only thing that matters is the price," said one of the traders. "That's all we care about."

They did not have a personal connection to the oil market the way Marks did.

Schaeffer and Newsome kept the private-equity firms in a state of total confusion until the last moment. On bidding day, Schaeffer laid down the ground rules. He told each firm what he considered to be an acceptable price range for the oil market and took the bids by telephone, say two of the private-equity partners intimately familiar with the proceedings. The partners were extremely uneasy with Schaeffer giving such exact price guidance, as well as taking the bids personally, since they knew he wanted General Atlantic to win.

"Let me put it this way: it is highly unusual for one member of the board to just orchestrate who gets to bid on a deal and then literally *feed you the price*," one of them says. "I felt Richie might be trying to fuck us. That he might try and trap us into a lower number. The whole thing reeked of conflict of interest. I honestly did think about trying to fuck him back, put in a much higher bid and make sure we could definitely take the deal from General Atlantic. I told Richie I would only place my bids with his outside attorneys. I didn't trust him to communicate the proper amount, that's the level of distrust I had for him. Don't get me wrong, Richie was never an obstructionist to the negotiations. He always talked to us and gave us the time of day, but it was clear he and Newsome had an agenda that they were pursuing, and that was for General Atlantic to win."

The joint bid from Blackstone and Battery Ventures of $135 million for a 10 percent stake was the *exact* same amount as the final bid from General Atlantic. Schaeffer convened the board for an extraordinary session September 20, and gave it the news. "The board freaked out. They didn't buy that the two major bidders came in with the exact same bid. And, frankly, we didn't either," says the private-equity partner. "The board felt something fishy was going on, that they were getting nickel-and-dimed." Schaeffer had a solution. How about a three-way deal with *all* the firms, carving up the 10 percent stake among everybody? "That's when the board really went ballistic."

Schaeffer instructed Steinhause to call Blackstone and Battery Ventures and tell them they were out. Steinhause complied. Schaeffer pushed through the General Atlantic deal in a unanimous vote.

The Nymex members strenuously objected. As usual, they were ignored. Schaeffer had the backing of the board, while Fisher only had the backing of the pits.

Sahn, suspecting the wool had been pulled over their eyes, called one of the private-equity partners and let loose. "I was in a boardroom in Los Angeles and I was literally able to hold the cell phone at arm's length and hear him screaming, 'Richie Schaeffer, that fucking fuck, I'm gonna fuck his eyes!'" Another trader called me at the news desk, bellowing, "Richie Schaeffer's rigged the bids. Can you believe it? He's rigged the bids!"

A Nymex member speaking from his Florida retirement home had a more sober, if equally profane, assessment: "These guys could fuck up a rock fight."

The traders wanted to know why the board had rejected the other deals. One exchange executive confirmed Nymex had been approached by nearly a dozen firms in all. Marks also had let it be known that on the morning of the vote, he had placed a tentative bid of $140 million for a 10 percent stake of Nymex, which was a higher price than the General Atlantic bid. On September 23, Battery Ventures returned, this time on a solo mission, offering $75 million for a 5 percent stake, a higher valuation than anybody. On cue, an exchange seat sold that day for $2.8 million, a record high.

The final salvo came from the CME, which sent a letter to Nymex, expressing its interest in making a bid—and everyone knew it could out-bid everybody.

Schaeffer and Newsome didn't think twice. They declined them all.

"Did Richie give us the red-hot poker? Yeah, he gave us the red-hot poker," one of the private-equity partners says. "Richie was not multidimensional. He knew he wanted to be the chairman of the exchange and he did what he needed to do in order to get that. Newsome was going to benefit from any deal that got done, he knew that. So he just played the straight guy. That's what he did. And he did that very well. To this day, I believe the outcome of that bidding process came from the desire of certain people to seize control of the oil market."

Newsome's pat response to the blowback: "It is not unusual to be hearing that the people who did not win are complaining."

With Hurricanes Katrina and Rita ripping through the Gulf Coast in the summer and autumn of 2005, it was not the best time for the leadership of the global oil market to be in flux. The storms sent oil prices hurtling past $70 a barrel. Refco, the brokerage that once catered to Hillary Clinton, went under without warning in October, due to bad debts that traced back to the Asian financial crisis. Nymex, despite its growing realization that the trading pits were an anachronism, opened its trading floor in London anyway, burning through millions of dollars until its inglorious closing just months later. The executives had moved too late in trying to win over the British traders. The traders had already adapted to the screen or become cabbies. ICE's stock price soared more than 50 percent to nearly $40 a share when it went public in November, but it would be three months later that Sprecher would roll out his nuclear warhead: a copycat version of the Nymex crude-oil futures contract meant to completely cannibalize the New York trading pits. Not since the days of the Marks chairmanship had Nymex been so directly threatened.

True to form, the traders pretended to not notice. In the pits, they were making more money than they'd ever dreamed of. Somehow, word had gotten around that the world was running out of oil, though there was no proof of that. Still, there was no proof it wasn't running out either. Saudi Arabia kept its oil field data cloaked in a veil of secrecy, causing the rest of the world to wonder: if oil ever did run out, would anybody get a heads-up on it first? It seemed to be a question that nobody wanted to answer. Major oil-producing nations, such as Russia and Mexico, were well past their prime, while others, such as Indonesia, were seen as likely to get kicked out of OPEC soon for running low on reserves. The New York traders were smitten by the concept of a possible end of days for oil and the world's total lack of preparation for it. Some of them had even gotten biblical about it. "In the Book of Revelation, did you know that the Rapture takes place right after oil runs out?" one of the traders gushed. Others took a more analytical approach. "When people say prices are higher due to the hurricanes or other events, I think they're confusing the symptom with the cause," said Peter Thiel, a hedge fund manager in San Francisco, during an interview I did for Dow Jones. "The storms didn't *cause* oil markets to go higher. Oil markets were concerned about a storm *because* global supplies are really tight."

Little could be proven about oil supply itself, but it definitely was provable that oil supply was not rising as fast as global demand, and the two were approaching a dead heat. There was only about a million barrels of oil a day of wiggle room, which left the world's energy security hanging in the balance. "It's going to be really hard to keep up with demand, because there are fewer and fewer places to explore for oil, except really exotic places like Western Siberia, or *Chad*," Thiel said. "These places are really hot, really cold, or just politically dangerous. People are looking in the last corners of the earth." Henry Jarecki, the septuagenarian hedge fund trader who swore never to trade on Nymex but long ago relented, was more circumspect about the price swings. "What did Archimedes say? 'Give me a place to stand and I will move the earth.' Notwithstanding the fact the world is unpredictable, the market gives us an idea of what is happening and at least gives people a place to stand. Is it the best place to stand? I don't know about that. But it's the only place. The markets may not always be right, but they certainly do a good job of encapsulating man's confusion."

With prices whipsawing every time a refinery shut down or a pipeline exploded, the Nymex traders were in ecstasy. They could make tens of millions of dollars a year and still return from work before their kids got home from school.

But they didn't always go straight home. On Halloween, south of the World Trade Center pit, on Greenwich Street, I was looking for a cash machine. Cordato's Deli, right next to the Pussycat Lounge, had a neon sign for an ATM outside. I'd never been to the deli and, afterward, resolved never to go back. The place was full of hoary, bottom-feeder types, a dingy mustering ground for neighborhood alcoholics and junkies. It wasn't the best part of town either, especially after eight o'clock at night, which it was. Looking around, I didn't see a cash machine anywhere. The deli owner pointed toward the back and nodded. I kept walking. At the far end of the room, there was a vinyl mud-flap covering a doorway and what appeared to be a dimly lit pantry beyond. And then darkness.

I turned and looked at the deli owner. He kept bobbing his head. "Keep going."

There didn't seem to be much there. But I ventured into the belly of the building, finally entering a long hallway with a gray door in it. Past that, I heard a loud thumping sound. I opened the door to a blast of music and a room filled with girls giving lap dances to older men. I still did not see a cash machine. Making my way through the heavily costumed crowd, past a bar with the wildest selection of sugary liquors I'd ever seen (excepting a bottle of 100-proof Yukon Jack, which tastes like death) toward the bathrooms to a distant corner, I found, at last, the ATM. As I waited, I glanced up to see a Nymex trader not five feet from me, still wearing his trading jacket and slumped over on a bar stool, getting the most over-the-top lap dance I'd ever seen.

These girls did not phone it in. They were staggering into the bar from a dirt yard out back, apparently shared with the Pussycat Lounge, reserved for smoking and more licentious behaviors. Lined up in high heels at the jukebox, their mouths slashed with crimson, the strippers, taking a break from working next door, pumped in quarters to dance to their favorite songs. It was $5 a lap dance, but I heard one man talk a girl down to $2. I didn't recognize the trader, but I did recognize his gold Nymex trading badge. He seemed in a trance.

The girl straddling him on the stool had her ankles hooked into the chrome legs, arching backward, nearly upside-down. The ends of her hair just touched the floor. Her rib cage protruded grotesquely. He grabbed the spaghetti straps of her dress in his hand and snapped them off her like rubber bands.

I asked Deep Throat about it later. He said, "Yeah, a lot of the traders go down to that place. I don't know how many go anymore. They meet girls in the dirt yard out back at lunch. We used to call it 'takeout.'"

Soaring oil prices did nothing to dissuade the traders from other pastimes, especially for the cross-dressing-obsessed Mark Fisher. One staffer recalls how the traders became so reckless, they nearly forced the oil market to close one morning before it even opened:

I told you about Mark Fisher and the men in dresses, didn't I? No? It's my first week on the job, and the head of security comes up and says to me, "We've got a problem." We run downstairs and there are about ten clerks dressed in slutty women's clothing and high heels, trying to get onto the trading floor. Security won't let them in, because we have a dress code, but they have to let them [in], because, otherwise, the oil market won't open. There are practical reasons for this. Have you ever tried to run an order in high heels? Now think of a man trying to do it. Apparently, Mark got into an argument with an oil trader about whether he could beat one of the trader's younger clerks in a hundred-yard dash. The trader bet him, because his clerk was like one of those twenty-year-old all-American sports stars, but what he didn't know was that Mark happens to be very good at the hundred-yard dash. And Mark never makes a bet he doesn't know he can win. That's the mark of a good trader. So Mark agreed to take the trader and all ten of his clerks to the strip club Scores if he lost. But he won. So now we have all these clerks in dresses and Mark's screaming to let them in, and finally they decide to send five home to change and keep five on the floor. You can't believe what it looked like at the open, having the world's benchmark crude-oil contract being handled by clerks running around in cold weather, freezing their asses off in dresses, their unmentionables hanging out.

By October 2005, gasoline futures had risen 140 percent, tracking oil upward like they always did. Heating-oil prices leaped more than 30 percent. As traders rushed to Nymex to take advantage of the rally, the prices of seats at the exchange hit record highs half a dozen times. Just to *rent* a seat at Nymex for the privilege of trading there now cost $20,000 a month.

"I sent out an e-mail saying I want all you potato guys charging me $20,000 a month for a seat now to go fuck yourselves," Mark Lichtner says. "I don't know how many there are, but they are eating well. I'll tell you this, there are many of these guys, mostly over the age of sixty-five, who are going to die with either $10 million in their pocket or $11 million in their pocket, and they're sucking us dry for that extra million. They won't take $19,000 for a seat. No. They want $20,000. How much money are you going to die with in your pocket, sir? How much before it's enough? And they can say the same thing to us. The reason why they do this to us is because they *know* what's going on down on the trading floor, because they did it. They're the inventors of it. They're the guys who owned the exchange first. Nobody's an angel. If we were angels, we would be in fucking heaven. But there's a right way and a wrong way to do the wrong thing. And they know it, and that's why they have tunnel vision. They don't care about us. Be careful of the people you meet on the way up, because you're going to be meeting the same people on the way down. Some of them will be headed *way* down, I think, if you know what I mean."

Traders leasing seats would have bought a seat if they could have afforded it, but they'd jumped to $3.775 million each. Guttman, who owned three, could get $60,000 a month leasing his. Sahn, who owned nine between him and his ex-wife, got three times that. Nymex, despite having made the wrong choices at almost every turn, was now worth over $3 billion. That year, its value eclipsed the NYSE, making it the most expensive market on the face of the earth.

With 2005 coming to a close, Fisher and his friend Sandy Goldfarb, the horse trader, decided they would throw a decadent holiday bash. The war and the hurricanes and the terror fears had all combined to make them millions. The party would be immense in scope, bringing together the pit traders and a procession of Wall Street A-listers. Celebrities would also be in attendance, such as LL Cool J and lead actors from the HBO hit series *The Sopranos* (the Nymex traders were huge fans of mobsters and mobster humor). More than a thousand invitations were printed on silver aluminum plates with the words THE PARTY stamped neatly on them. They were mailed out in early December. One of them, in a long, custom-made envelope, was surreptitiously dropped on my desk.

DESCENDING INTO THE underground maze of Crobar, a cavernous nightclub located in a trendy part of downtown Manhattan, was nothing if not disorienting. The venue, which abutted Scores, the gentlemen's club the traders did not like because they could not have sex with the strippers, made clever use of light and darkness to stun and sublimate. At first, I couldn't see anything. And once I could see, it was as if I had stumbled into Caligula's den. A thick forest of bamboo and rubber trees led to a bar full of models and hangers-on. Beyond that, a circular, white-tiled subway passage led to a blinding light and a great noise.

The walkway opened into a hangar-like room filled with traders spraying champagne under a constellation of female trapeze artists swinging, half-naked, from the steel girders above. Sequined, six-foot-tall girls with columnar legs luxuriated on top of floor speakers the size of rocket engines, feeding hungry oil traders slabs of meat from large platters. Sparkles and confetti covered every conceivable surface. The floor was slick with bubbly. And at the center, cocooned by his adoring fans and acting as if he did this every day, was Mark Fisher. He and Sandy Goldfarb were footing the six-digit bill, but no one could argue that it wasn't really being paid for by the world's energy consumers.

It didn't take long for Fisher to make his way up to the stage at the front of the room to address the holiday revelers. He was in his element. He gave his welcome speech, engaged in a bit of the usual Fisher pedagogy, and flaunted his daughter like a shiny, blond accessory, without introducing her. His spirits were high. The traders' spirits were high. There would be no sacrificial lambs tonight.

No sooner did he step off the stage than Rihanna, the Top 40 R&B vocalist, wearing little more than Daisy Dukes and a skimpy tank top, shimmied onstage with her coterie of backup dancers to sing her hit song "Pon de Replay." The performance had been unbilled. On the three-thousand-capacity dance floor and the tiered balconies and mezzanines, the traders roared, stamped their feet, and banged their fists. The rocket-engine speakers blasted. And the building shook as if it might come down.

It was the biggest event anyone could remember having been thrown by the oil traders since Michel Marks had held his coming-out party more than twenty years earlier. Fisher's party would neatly bookend their halcyon days, marking the end of the market as they knew it.

But they did not know it yet.

I searched for Marks in the crowd. He was nowhere to be found.

14

Blood for Victory

I went from zero and two strokes just months apart to having
$40 million overnight.

—RICHARD SCHAEFFER

"RICHIE SCHAEFFER AND I had a very antagonistic history with each other over the years. He was on the board when I got pushed out and he took his pound of flesh out of me," Lou Guttman says. "To move up in rank, you have to kill the guy in front of you. Everybody attacked. He was not the only one. But times had changed and we required a different approach.

"After the first 150 days of Mitchell Steinhause, my attitude was, it was time for him to go. Looking around, there was only one guy left on the board who I felt was capable of moving us forward, and that was Schaeffer. He was fearless and he could get things done. The only thing was, a lot of people didn't trust him. He had screwed over a lot of people politically. We sat down and had a heart-to-heart. I said, 'I'm going to back you, but I'm telling you right now, no more monkey business. No giving your word and violating your word. If we do this, it's got to be done right.' And Richie said, 'Whatever you do, I gotta stay on the board. That's my life.'"

It was agreed, but they needed to move fast. Two battlefronts had opened up and neither one was going well for Nymex: the international war with ICE, and the brewing civil war between the New York trading floor and its executive suite. The first couldn't be dealt with until a definitive détente had been reached with the other.

The start of 2006 had been, objectively speaking, a disaster. Onslaughts by the executives against the membership had suddenly turned litigious. The floor and the executives had always crossed swords, but they'd always protected each other from external threats, ensuring the perpetuity of their oil monopoly while vouchsafing each other's fortunes. That would not be the case this time.

The special partnership between the trading floor and the boardroom had started to crumble, as the executives of the fifteenth floor, led by Schaeffer, determined that the only way to save the oil market's wealth was to defy the pit traders.

On the eve of Thanksgiving, the board dumped four hundred pages of legal documents on the members, linking complicated new rules for running the exchange to the proposed General Atlantic deal. It included plans for an initial public offering (IPO), which would grant the executives of Nymex millions of dollars of stock. More troubling, the fine print revealed that the intent of the new regulations for running the market was to strip the members of their power over the board, shifting supreme authority to the executive suite.

Outraged, the members threatened to kill the General Atlantic deal, which they knew could not go through without their vote. Leading the rebellion was Cataldo Capozza, a retired real-estate mogul whose father had reared him from a young age in the oil and gas business and who had been a member of the exchange for more than twenty years. Capozza's three Nymex seats had recently risen in value to more than $11 million, and he didn't have any intention of letting the board ruin it by converting it into stock and then taking half. He filed a lawsuit against the exchange in December 2005, alleging that "bid-rigging" and other untoward activities had unfairly allowed General Atlantic to win the vote of the Nymex board. Capozza demanded to see all the books, records, and paper trails associated with the proposed stake sale, and he wanted to know if Schaeffer had received any kind of payout or side deal from General Atlantic. "It looks to me like there is a very small number of seat holders and Nymex officials who are trying to seize control of the exchange," said Capozza's lawyer Mark Rifkin, a partner with Madison Avenue class-action law firm Wolf, Haldenstein, Alder, Freeman & Herz.

Schaeffer and Steinhause said nothing. Newsome shot back on behalf of the executives. "We make no apologies for the bidding process!" he said. He privately admitted later that he had no idea how a normal bidding process was supposed to work, as he had never been part of one before.

Of course, the Nymex executives *were* trying to seize control of the exchange. They didn't trust the members to make the right decisions at a time when the oil market needed a full-scale metamorphosis to stay alive. The floor traders, similarly, did not trust the board. They believed the executives to be greedy, intemperate, and in chronic disarray. "All these guys had traded with each other for years, so everybody had everybody else's number. The board was never seen as anything but a joke, and word was always getting out to the traders downstairs of all the crazy stuff that was going on upstairs," says a former executive, who attended most of the board meetings. "The board meetings were always sort of a freak show. We had a conference call with some major clients and had to patch in an elderly director who was traveling on business in Germany. He calls from his hotel, immediately falls asleep, and thens starts snoring. At first, it's very quiet and we try to ignore the noise. But then it gets louder and louder and Mitchell Steinhause asks the phone technician to disconnect the line. It turns out we can't disconnect the line without dropping everyone else off the call. So there we are, thousands of miles away from this guy, stuck with his snores blasting through the speakers above the boardroom table like the wrath of God coming down on us. Richie finally screams, 'Somebody call the fucking hotel and get someone to wake him up!' Somebody at Nymex calls the front desk and tells the hotel staff *he is having a heart attack.* I guess they wanted him to wake up in a hurry. Over the speakers, we hear the door hit the wall and a woman screeching in some German dialect we've never heard and the board member waking up terrified."

Another time, before Stuart Smith left after being caught taking a bribe, there was a boardroom discussion about the new soap dispensers in the men's room. "These were not ordinary soap dispensers," says the executive. "They were large and curved and looked very phallic. They were silver and had these motion sensors on them, so you had to wave your hands in front of them to get them to spit soap out. When they were installed, no one said anything. But a few weeks later, at the end of a board meeting, the chairman asks, 'Did anyone else have anything to add before we adjourn?' Stu, the head of operations, goes, 'Yeah, I just wanted to let everyone know I finally managed to remove all you guys' teeth marks from the soap dispensers.' The room just exploded. We were pounding on the tables. We were laughing so hard we were crying."

At the Dow Jones news desk, I was assaulted by dozens of calls from Nymex seat holders insisting that Schaeffer, Newsome, and the entire board were chipping away at their control over the oil market. They insisted that something be done about what was happening to them. They wanted an article in the *Wall Street Journal* about Schaeffer and Newsome taking over the exchange as oil prices hit a record $70 a barrel. They felt their market was being stolen. They even believed the members of the executive suite wanted to take the oil market public for the sole purpose of enriching themselves. This was feasible, they said, because when ICE went public in November 2005 and when the CME went public in 2002, the executives at both exchanges made tens of millions of dollars. "It's the biggest sellout of a company in corporate history and nobody's doing anything about it!" yelled Bobby Sahn. "This has nothing to do with Steinhause. It's all Schaeffer. I swear to you, I swear on my children's eyes, there are guys who are going to be waiting *to lay him down.* They want him Grasso-ed.[*] They don't want him to be able to walk in the street in daylight hours."

The members did not approve of what was happening, but the board had always done what it wanted to do, and they felt powerless to stop it.

Gary Glass and a handful of other seat holders controlling a sizable portion of the votes were ready to revolt. But the members couldn't get themselves organized. They could only squabble. "Bobby Sahn is a loose cannon!" one seat holder bellyached. Another took to excoriating Glass. "Let me tell you something, if you're ever near him, hold on to your wallet. You're walking down the street and he's looking for nickels stuck in the tire treads. You go to his house in Florida and the patio umbrella out on the back deck doubles as a satellite receiver for stealing cable."

It was beyond the patience, if not perhaps the natural abilities, of the Nymex traders to mobilize, let alone get a class-action suit together to follow Capozza's lead. As it was, many of them freely admitted to suffering from short attention spans, dyslexia, and attention deficit disorder. It

---

[*] Dick Grasso, the former chairman of the NYSE, was forced to step down in 2003 after it came to light that he was in line to receive nearly $200 million from his handpicked compensation committee—a situation the pit traders compared to the goings-on at Nymex.

also didn't help that they were as likely to call one another crooks as they were to call members of the board crooks. "How many fingers do I have up?" one trader asked during a lunch meeting. "Five. Between the seat holders and the executives, maybe there's this many honest people at the exchange. Or I should say, five fair ones, that's a better way to put it." A Wall Street analyst called me in January with a question. "Those guys over there at Nymex look as though they've got a great racket going. Don't they know they can't keep it if they have an IPO? I don't get it. Why would they ever want to go public?" The trading floor still didn't have surveillance cameras, and while landline calls of the pit traders were recorded, they could easily coordinate prearranged trades or any collusion schemes by cell phone.

A few days later, I received the most candid call of all. It was Schaeffer, who had yet to publicly comment on the oil market's civil war. Until he could push Steinhause out, he was staying in the background. Elections wouldn't be until spring. We'd spoken off the record in the past, but as of early 2006, we'd never met. He was deeply unhappy with Capozza's suit and made his unhappiness known by issuing a long stream of exotic expletives I had never heard strung together before.

At first, I did not know what to say.

"So does that mean I can quote you?" I asked.

"Yeah, try putting *that* in the *Wall Street Journal*."

Before hanging up, he had an afterthought. "I don't care. *This is how I really am.*"

Guttman had spoken with Capozza and supported his lawsuit, in theory. He also didn't feel comfortable with how the board had been handling the General Atlantic deal and the terms of the stock offering. He too had been disturbed by the Thanksgiving-eve document dump and worried that Schaeffer was already reneging on their "no monkey business" compact. But he was even more concerned about the breakneck speed with which Jeff Sprecher's electronic exchange seemed to be overtaking the trading pits. Nymex's attempt to thwart Sprecher by opening trading floors in the United Kingdom had been bungled terribly. The exchange had lost a small fortune and looked the worse for it. Sprecher had emerged the winner yet again and, through the ICE screen, now dominated most of Europe's oil market. "There's nothing to be done about it now," one of the retired London pit traders said ruefully. "The bald bloody American bastard won."

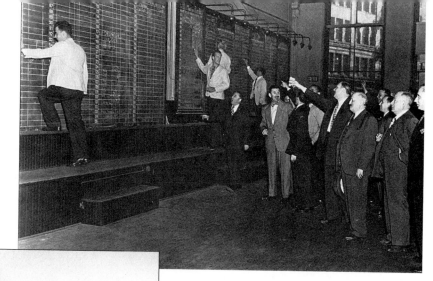

The board boys of the potato era could write down prices with either their right or left hands and were so familiar with the merchants' voices that they didn't have to turn around to know who was calling a trade.

The New York traders swore the mansion at 6 Harrison Street had millions of dollars of precious coins buried beneath it, but an excavation in leaner times turned up nothing.

The earliest trading rings resembled poker games.

Just weeks into the job, Michel Marks unexpectedly became the youngest chairman in the nation. A rare shot of him with his father, Francis.

Ever the lone wolf, Marks learned the ways of the trading pits slowly and "painfully."

Sherry Collins, the teenage sensation recruited by Marks to "ruffle feathers," posing in the exchange cafeteria during a quiet moment off the trading floor with Danny Rappaport (*right*), who would later become Nymex chairman.

The twenty-five-thousand-square-foot trading floor at the World Trade Center, shared by Nymex and three other exchanges, proved far too small to contain so many egos. Before and after shots of a typical trading day.

Spoofing the 1980s Ghostbusters logo, the oil traders celebrated their victory over OPEC. ("Isn't it amazing?" one exulted. "A bunch of Jewish guys beating the Arabs at their own game? The irony is so thick.")

Rosemary McFadden and
Zoltan Louis Guttman,
despite being fierce rivals,
frequently had to travel
together.

Guttman with New York City
mayor David Dinkins (*right*) the
morning he launched the natural-
gas contract that soon became
the thousand-dollar table at the
energy casino.

Wendy Gramm,
chairwoman of the
CFTC and wife of
Senator Phil Gramm,
seemed reluctant to
charge Guttman with
any wrongdoing, but
her successor was not.

The new Nymex building at the World Financial Center (*far left*) was designed to blend in with its surroundings along the marina. The architect, David Childs, wanted a modern statement building, but Rappaport objected to looking like "flashy asshole commodities traders." A recent photo with Richard Schaeffer's new yacht parked directly in front.

Rappaport (*middle*) and Schaeffer (*right*) enjoy a wine-soaked evening with Leo Melamed, the "Father of Financial Futures" and chairman emeritus of the Chicago Mercantile Exchange who, in the 1960s, would often sneak away to trade potatoes at Nymex.

Vincent Viola, charismatic gasoline trader, West Point graduate, and martial-arts fighter, struck fear in the hearts of the pit traders for his competitive streak and ferocity. Before and after his near-tragic accident.

When former race car driver and turbine salesman Jeffrey Sprecher strode into the Nymex boardroom in 2000, he didn't get any respect—until he started taking billions from the pockets of the proud oil traders. Outside the ICE headquarters in Atlanta.

The felling of the World Trade Center towers narrowly missed the oil market, whose immediate surroundings were gutted along with the rest of the World Financial Center. An aerial shot of Ground Zero, with the marina at the top, Nymex to its right, and Guttman's residence at Gateway Plaza to its left. *(NOAA)*

John Arnold, a self-made billionaire by the age of thirty-three, led the army of global screen traders to unprecedented dominance, wealth, and celebrity. Starting at Enron, he parlayed the $8 million bonus he received as the company went bankrupt into one of the world's largest energy hedge funds. *(Michael Stravato/The New York Times/Redux)*

Schaeffer (*right*), the oil market's last chairman, and James Newsome (*left*), its last president, were dubbed "the odd couple," but their financial interests were very much aligned. Standing with the chairman of the New York Stock Exchange, John Thain, on the day they became multimillionaires as Nymex went public.

Strip clubs were a popular pastime for the traders during lunch and after hours, including the nearby Pussycat Lounge (*right*) on Greenwich Street, which featured a champagne room, brimming with young, scantily clad girls, that one entered through a discreet door in the back of the neighboring deli (*left*).

The lonely country town of Cushing, Oklahoma, has long been the unlikely home of the world's top oil contract and secretive "tank farms" stretching as far as the eye can see.

The Saudi supertanker *Sirius Star* was turned into a pirate ship after being hijacked for its millions of dollars of oil. The crew, held hostage for months, wasn't released until a fat ransom was paid.

Traders and girls gather at Nymex's fully stocked bar, which continued to open religiously every morning above the trading pits, even after oil prices hit record highs. Scattered on the floor are the traders' castoff pit cards.

The oil market in its heyday, as prices rocketed toward $150 a barrel. The center ring was where tens of billions of dollars of crude-oil trades passed daily. Heating oil traded in a ring to the upper left of the pit, while gasoline traded in a ring to the upper right. To the far right, natural gas and options traded. *(Getty Images)*

Guttman today, standing on the tenth-floor terrace of the Nymex building. "Even in the good times, it was tough," he says. "But I do believe I am a better person for it." *(ianspanier.com)*

In February 2006, Sprecher was out to win again. He was staging his next attack on Nymex, only with a great deal more foresight and venom. This time, on American soil. He launched an exact replica of the Nymex crude-oil futures contract, retrofitted for the ICE screen. For ages, the New York traders had been insisting that the nation's energy speculators preferred to buy and sell oil through the Nymex pits. That had been a foolish assumption. In just three weeks, Sprecher swiped 10 percent of the U.S. oil market. At first, the Nymex traders couldn't believe it. Oil trading volumes in the New York pits didn't seem to be falling. They were still around 300,000 contracts a day, worth about $18 billion. To their knowledge, they hadn't lost any business. But on the ICE Web site, they could see Sprecher's oil trading volumes edging past 40,000 contracts a day. By March, they hit the 70,000 mark.

The oil traders decided Sprecher was lying. "They would literally look at the tally on the ICE screen, look at our tally, and flat-out deny it was happening," says Ben Kaufman, who still worked in the pits. "They would say that ICE was wrong, that it was miscounting the trades, whatever. They were overconfident and never questioned themselves, but that only gets you so far. They had a monumental inability to deal with reality."

What was happening was that the international sweep of the ICE screen was prodding the oil market into hyper-globalization. Having been bottled up unnaturally for so long in the Nymex pits, worldwide energy trading suddenly exploded. Electronic-trading "arcades" started cropping up in all the major financial cities—New York, Chicago, Houston, San Francisco, London, Paris, Geneva, Moscow, Dubai, Mumbai, Singapore, Hong Kong, Shanghai, Taipei, Tokyo, Johannesburg, Bermuda, São Paulo, even Gibraltar. Traders were having a field day arbitraging the energy prices between Nymex and ICE, working the gaps and pocketing millions. Oil prices on Nymex and ICE closely tracked each other, but there were always crevices between them just begging to be exploited. Sprecher, being Sprecher, opened an arcade at the World Financial Center only steps away from the Nymex pits.

With the rise of the screen, traders were suddenly playing the oil market exactly as if they were playing a video game, with the younger, more digitally agile traders trouncing the older, slower pit traders unaccustomed to screen action. There also was a David-and-Goliath effect: the scrawnier traders with the intellectual know-how, though perhaps not the athletic prowess that had once dominated the pits, were finally able to match wits against the brawnier traders, without fear of physical retribution. On Wall Street, the move to the screen was inciting a technological arms race among the banks and hedge funds, which began sinking millions of dollars into state-of-the-art automated trading systems that could move at near-lightning speeds, outpacing the floor traders, many of whom still traded with no more than paper and pencil.

The New York floor traders, whose brutality had once crushed the Marine Corps officers, were now getting a dose of their own medicine on their home turf—and they did not like it.

Bo Collins, the ex–Nymex president, rang up journalists from his hedge fund to tell them that ICE was beating Nymex. "ICE is definitely going to take over," he told Dow Jones. His energy hedge fund, which he'd named MotherRock (a geological reference to the mineral that makes hydrocarbons), was saving $12,500 an order by conducting trades on the ICE platform instead of going through the Nymex pits. Screen trading, he said, was more exacting than pit trading, where the orders were supposed to be executed at the best *possible* price, but frequently subject to price "slippage" by human hands. The screen was better at capturing specific price points without any foul-ups, he said. What Collins did not mention was that he owned several million dollars' worth of ICE stock, which meant that as he was extolling the company's virtues, he was also financially benefiting. In trader parlance, he was "talking his book." The price of ICE stock rose that day above $63. Even as Schaeffer and Viola invested in his new fund, Collins was literally making a buck off his old employer's misfortunes.

It got much uglier. Several high-level Nymex executives—including the one who'd shouted "Fuck ICE" at the board meeting a year earlier—were buying ICE stock. Though seemingly a conflict of interest, it was not technically illegal. "Hey, we're traders," the "Fuck ICE" executive told me. "We've gotta hedge!" In late February the checkmate everyone feared most finally arrived. Once the weaker market, ICE boldly made a bid to buy Nymex itself. Sprecher called up Steinhause, looking to head off General Atlantic at the pass. Steinhause gave him the same response Sprecher had given Viola two years before, when the situation had been reversed. A resounding no.

Outside Nymex, in the late-winter sun, the pit traders smoked and debated their future.

"How long do you think before the floor shuts down?" a young trader asked one of the old-timers.

Halfway through his cigarette, the older one stopped short, flicking the butt toward the Hudson River. It missed. He did not mince words.

"I give it six months."

The others nodded solemnly.

Deep Throat found the situation inconceivable. "If they wait any longer to act, they're going to be whistling as they're walking past the graveyard."

Michel Marks continued to earnestly write open letters to the Nymex members. He blasted the oil market's "cronyism, uncontested elections, and insider deals" and the "tens of millions wasted on technology and the London initiative." He wanted Nymex to get an experienced CEO and forge a deal with ICE. "Naïvely, I believed Nymex could be different from the rest of the corporate world. It isn't. Short-term money, profits, and self-interest reign supreme." It was hard to tell if Marks's letter, written that spring, was an appeal to the seat holders or an epitaph.

Guttman sent an open letter back to Marks, criticizing his criticisms. "You lament 'uncontested elections' and 'insider deals.' Michel, if I recall correctly, during your tenure you handpicked your board. The fact is that you were on the Nymex board and on the inside for the past five years. It's ironic that you now choose to bewail the miscues when, in fact, you had a front-seat view and were right in the middle of it all."

The oil market's two most powerful leaders, the chairmen most responsible for shaping it, were the only ones capable of fixing it. But they still could not get along.

The Capozza suit might have gained traction, but in the ninety days that had elapsed since the Thanksgiving-eve incident (some of the seat holders were now calling it the "Turkey Day paper caper"), the Nymex members had gone from being furious with the executives to running scared. Capozza was being pressured to settle his lawsuit, so the exchange could focus on the larger matter of saving itself from itself. Capozza was permitted to see the books and records he had demanded. But he was never allowed afterward to discuss the contents of the materials, which, under the terms of the settlement, were sealed from public view before being quietly destroyed. The traders finally came to a grudging accord with the executive suite. They did not like what the executives were up to, but if they were to be undercut, better it be by their own than ICE.

They met at a huge meeting hall inside the Embassy Suites, across the street from the pits, to determine how they might band together to defend themselves. Everyone was there, from the five chairmen and Newsome and Fisher to the seat holders to the traders leasing their seats to the CEO of General Atlantic, Bill Ford, who still wanted to buy a 10 percent stake of the energy market so badly he raised his offer from $135 million to $170 million.

The meeting was run by Steinhause, but throughout the proceedings, Schaeffer regularly interjected to tell certain louder members of the audience to sit down and shut up. The traders were told the game plan was to finalize the deal with General Atlantic, vote for a new board, offer around-the-clock electronic energy trading alongside daytime pit trading, and then execute a public stock offering, in that order. When asked if there were any questions or objections, some of the traders spoke up, but nobody had the gall to critique the master plan.

All eyes fell on Michel Marks.

Marks sat in the audience beside his younger brother Jan, the head of Paris Securities, staring straight ahead, his lower lip curled, wearing his thousand-mile stare.

He did not say a word.

SCHAEFFER GOT TO be chairman that spring, in the board election in which more than forty people competed but only fifteen prevailed. It had been decided ahead of time that a bloated, twenty-five-member board was no longer desirable. Besides, the fewer the people on the board, the easier it would be to control it. And the more each director would take from the pot at IPO time. David Greenberg, son of former Comex chairman Marty Greenberg, won one of the board seats, while Schaeffer persuaded Bobby Halper, the genius spread trader from the pits known for his honesty, to be his vice chairman. "Bobby didn't want to do it," Schaeffer told me, "but I guilt-tripped him into it. I told him since he'd made millions off the pits, it was time for him to give back." Danny Rappaport also ran for a seat and won. "I came back, because the exchange was finally doing everything I always wanted it to do, and I wanted to see it unfold." Bill Ford automatically got a seat on the board when the exchange members, not knowing what else to do, approved the General Atlantic deal by a vote of 580 to 30 in March 2006. In exchange for selling a 10 percent stake, the members received a dividend of nearly $200,000 for each seat they owned. When the deal went through, the price of the Nymex seats hit $3.9 million each, and seat bids shot to $4 million. Vanquished by Schaeffer, Steinhause returned to the pits. Viola continued to run his outside businesses. Fisher stayed far away from office but, as always, remained an unofficial adviser to the board, as was Guttman, who still lived across the marina at the Gateway Plaza.

Marks returned to self-exile.

Newsome was named CEO on top of his title as president. "I learned there's a long history of making threats by the members and lots of talk of 'there's gonna be blood on the floor,' but then they always vote over-whelmingly in favor of whatever it is the board wants to do," he said.

Schaeffer ran for chairman unopposed, though Steinhause had con-sidered running against him. Steinhause thought he might have enough support for a second term, despite Viola's having deserted him after he stopped sending him large consulting checks. "We were at the March futures conference in Boca, and Steinhause said he might run," Guttman said. "I told him go ahead, you know, but I don't think you'll make it." To Guttman, who could never reclaim the chairmanship, watching Steinhause passively manage the most expensive market in the world, as it once again flirted with extinction, had been painful in the extreme. "He had it all and he didn't do anything with it."

Heading into the spring elections, Schaeffer ramped up the intimi-dation tactics, signaling it was time for Steinhause to step aside. Their less-than-subtle dislike for each other boiled over during a boardroom session, when Steinhause had attempted to reprimand Schaeffer in front of the other directors.

"Sit down, Richie," he said, cutting short one of Schaeffer's rants.

"Yeah, let's pretend like you run this board instead of me!" Schaeffer retorted.

Nobody challenged him. And that had been that.

Other challenges had been trickier. The board members wanted to "professionalize" the exchange before its stock offering, so that Wall Street investors would think it was a well-run company. They decided to fire anyone who was getting a paycheck that seemed too big for their job. It turned out that was a lot more people than they thought. The lay-offs went on for months. They also installed surveillance cameras in the trading pits, which set off the traders. "It was a huge betrayal. It was like, how dare you do that?" says Ben Kaufman. "It wasn't about the insider trading, because we already knew how to get around that. Everyone knew exactly where all the blind spots were on the trading floor, by checking the live feeds—not to say that there weren't plenty of times when surveillance footage actually went missing or got stolen. People were mostly upset about the security cameras because it was harder to hide the drugs and the booze. But they got better at that. They'd keep booze and porn in the bathroom and sneak it into their booths."

The most horrendous of the trials had been trying to update the oil market's technology to compete with ICE. The board members thought they could salvage the trading platforms they'd developed over the years, slap them together, and use them to offer worldwide screen trading of the Nymex energy complex. An army of technology experts came in, took one look at the exchange's trading system, and pronounced it dead on arrival. There was no way it could support a global market of any kind, they said. For one thing, the system was on a *local* network.

The exchange's lack of twentieth-century wiring was staggering. The Nymex executives were told they wouldn't have enough time to build a new framework without risking the loss of their business. Sprecher, suspecting as much, chose that moment to announce he would launch Nymex look-alike gasoline and heating-oil contracts in April 2006.

The executives panicked. They needed a quick fix. They hastily signed a deal to offer electronic trading of the entire New York energy market on the CME's Globex trading platform, the largest trading screen in the world. It was a rash decision, but they didn't have a choice. They'd always been enemies with the CME, but they hated ICE more. "You know what? Nymex would have been dead in the water without that deal and Guttman should get the credit for it," says Leo Melamed, the CME's chairman emeritus. "At the CME, people were saying, 'Why the hell should we extend them a lifeline?' The Nymex technology was very unsophisticated. And it was understood by the wider investment community. There were those in Chicago who said, 'Let's just launch energy products by ourselves. We will beat everybody and win.' I didn't believe it and said I thought it would be difficult to wrest the product away from the established energy market. Another problem with talking to Nymex was that a lot of people in Chicago didn't know if they were serious. They did not have a good reputation."

Melamed knew he owed Guttman after backing out of the Globex deal they'd almost made two decades earlier. "When we met this time to do the deal, I heard somebody with the CME say, 'By the way, you guys, last time we really fucked Lou,'" says Guttman.

Newsome knew the stopgap measures would only work for a limited time. Nymex wouldn't be ready to roll out electronic trading until autumn, and by June, ICE had already captured more than 30 percent of the U.S. oil market. At a meeting of the board, Newsome railed against Sprecher's trick of launching a U.S. oil market through the more lenient trading rules of the United Kingdom, which was causing Nymex to lose business. Offering futures on a U.S. product from a foreign country had never been done before, he said. It was preposterous that Sprecher should run a U.S. market through *London* when ICE was based in *Atlanta*. The irony, of course, was that when Newsome was at the CFTC, he had signed numerous no-action letters allowing Sprecher to do just that. "I used to tease Jim after he'd made a long speech to the board about how the energy market needed a level playing field. I would say, 'Jim! *Jim!* That's what I was trying to tell you ten years ago, when I was testifying before Congress,'" Rappaport says. "I think when he joined Nymex, he got a dose of the real world. The lesson is, don't kid yourself while pulling strings at the CFTC."

At a Washington hearing later that June, Newsome tried and failed to convince the CFTC commissioners of the dangers of the so-called London loophole, arguing that Sprecher's electronic energy market shouldn't be considered a "foreign" exchange when it was, in fact, based in Atlanta. ICE had an unfair advantage over Nymex, as it didn't have to abide by the same U.S. trading rules as Nymex, he said. The CFTC commissioners listened but were unsympathetic. They seemed to remember Newsome feeling differently about it before being hired by Nymex as president and CEO. "I signed a lot of no-action letters and it worked out very well, until ICE decided to list U.S. energy contracts through a foreign exchange. That did not follow the intention of those letters," Newsome says. "Under that scenario, I think ICE should have been regulated by the CFTC. I think everyone dismissed it as a competitive argument between Nymex and ICE. Unfortunately, we couldn't get anybody to listen."

Realizing he wasn't going to make any headway, Newsome issued a veiled threat that would be hard to forget. He suggested that if Nymex had no choice but to offer its energy market through a foreign country, like ICE, to get around the U.S. trading rules, then that's what it would have to do. He was talking about entering the hazardous game of *regulatory arbitrage*.

Nobody batted an eye.

At a press conference that spring, Newsome announced Nymex would be opening an electronic exchange in Dubai. The most controversial thing about his announcement was that the Arab officials who'd traveled to New York from Dubai to meet the press proclaimed the venture would cost $300 million. In the United Arab Emirates, ventures with unaccountably high price tags were seen as impressive. In the United States, the opposite was true. Companies, even Nymex, were supposed to look like they were trying to save money. "The initiative is *not* for $300 million," Newsome insisted. "It will be for $50 million." The extra $250 million, it seemed, was simply the cultural version of a clerical error as the two sides struggled to iron out the kinks. The wealth of the oil market being what it was, it hardly mattered.

Bitter e-mails among the traders began to circulate that spring and summer over the impending doom of sharing their trading floor with the screen. In the past, the traders had competed only with one another, but now they would be competing with the best trading talent in the world. They also were upset about the General Atlantic deal and the Nymex stock offering, because the traders who leased their seats but did not own them would not be sharing in the riches. Some of them went so far as to ask the seat holders for a cut but were angrily rebuffed. The traders felt they deserved *something*, since they'd made the oil market as successful as anybody. They weren't sure what to expect from the screen, but they did know they didn't want to open up the floor to just anyone with a fat credit line and an Internet connection. Judging by what had happened to the NYSE when it went electronic, the screen would be their death sentence. The traders instinctively knew that if they let the world in, their world would suffer. A trader's mass e-mail, sent out in April, blamed and berated the seat holders:

> *A Nymex guy that made money early in his career "trading" potatoes is a trader in your ring when you first become a broker.*
>
> *He wears $9.99 Dockers. He trades ones and twos and can't make a living. So he goes to live at home and takes his seat, that he "earned" in potatoes, and leases it out for $4,000 a month.*

Now it's 2006. . . . He shows up every day in his new Armani suit to check to see where his seat is trading. He always asks for the high price when he leases his seat.

He loves the $4 million seat price.

HE IS THE GENIUS!!

He gets 20 Gs a month leasing his seat because of YOU.

He bought a seat, ergo, let him bask. Statute of limitations won't let us get him on the potato trading. We do not begrudge him that he owns a seat and should reap the benefits. But . . .

He feels you don't deserve shit.

No IPO, no nothing.

THE FLOOR IS OURS.

THEY ARE SELLING THE FLOOR!

We will get them if they do not agree to our proposal!

We can set certain prices too.

The press wants to know this story!

Or we go public and tell everyone about the cash deals and where to point the camera.

To the guy that never even threw out two lots and now owns his own "company"—and a seat—yup, you. . . . We keep notes!!

The Nymex executives didn't have the heart to shut down the pits for the screen, as ICE and the CME had done in the past, but they had decided to offer both and let free-market forces dictate the traders' fate. They could not protect the floor forever. "We always knew, even when I was chairman, that we needed to do this one day," Rappaport says. "We just could never bring ourselves to pull the trigger." Schaeffer was the only chairman capable of firing both barrels with impunity.

Tommy Ryan, a thirty-six-year-old who'd ditched his bartending job years earlier to trade in the pits, watched his floor business get sucked away by the screen as soon as Nymex went electronic on September 5, 2006. Within weeks, the pits began to die and the floor began to fill with computer screens as the traders attempted to learn a new set of skills for the digital world. Many of them went through depression and withdrawal symptoms as they logged on to their computers from home, finding it almost impossible to concentrate outside the pits. "I was in my home office and it was so weird. The sound of the dehumidifier was distracting," says one trader who'd worked on the floor since 1977. "I turned it off. But then it was too quiet, so I turned it back on again." The traders were inconsolable for months as they struggled with the transition. Many of their most faithful customers had stopped sending them orders. It seemed their clients had never trusted the Nymex traders or the pits. They'd only tolerated them.

"For fourteen years, I've traded in a ring," Ryan says. "Now I trade on a computer and things are a lot faster, especially with the banks' and hedge funds' trading systems. These days, it's machine trading against machine. It's tough. You feel like you're bringing a shoe to a gun fight. Traders are going down like lambs to the slaughter. I used to leave work all sweaty, hoarse, disgusting. I was shoulder to shoulder with guys all day. It's not that way anymore. You kind of miss that. Now I feel like I'm just burning my eyes out. We were those kind of guys. Put that many people in a pit where everybody has ADD and is thinking all the time, and then they stop it and you don't know what to do. Before, you would see which buyers or sellers were doing what, you would get a feel or at least a direction of what was happening. It's disorienting now. You're trading a lot more by the numbers and your charts. You know what you're really missing on the screen? It's the momentum. I mean, the market can drop, but there's no screaming and no yelling. You don't have a feel for it. It's nowhere what it used to be. The number of people on the floor is dropping; no order flow means no need for clerks, no need for brokers. Many of us are just trading for ourselves. A lot of the older guys who owned seats are leaving. They may trade at home, but they're no longer coming in every day grinding it out anymore.

"People down here, they were living a pretty great life—and when you take that away abruptly, it's hard. You went down to a place where you worked for yourself and that was what made it so great. That was the beauty of it. Now it's like working for a corporation. A year ago we would have been asked about extending our trading hours or raising our fees. Now decisions are just handed to us. The floor members used to have a say. Now they are just running us to raise the stock price."

Bing West, the ex–Reagan administration official and designer of war games for the Marine Corps, says that when U.S. soldiers were adjusting to screen combat in the 1990s, they experienced a similar loss of bearings. "In the wars we've fought since, there have been cases where it is straight digital, but a lot of people like having the radio on just to give you that immediate back-and-forth that keeps you in touch with what's happening on the ground. There's a phrase we often use, 'danger close,' when we're about to drop bombs on a spot where our own troops are nearby. When you are in a danger-close situation, you want all the supplemental information you can get, especially if you are approaching your own troops from overhead with a bomb at an attack angle. Having the sight, sound—the radio—and digital is preferable to just having digital, but it shouldn't be the difference between a good and bad outcome." For the pit traders, though, it made all the difference in the world.

West's earlier observations from playing war games with the Nymex traders on the *Intrepid* still held true, only now it had global ramifications. The traders wanted to win so badly, they were willing to kill off all their troops to meet their objectives. Once on the screen, the energy traders in arcades around the world became so intent on hitting their financial targets, they lost sight of the potential human repercussions. The screens had desensitized them to what was happening on the ground. Any harm done to energy consumers in the crossfire of their trading games was blithely categorized as collateral damage. Banks and hedge funds, whose automated trading systems bought and sold millions upon millions of energy contracts in just milliseconds, followed the same credo. Computer programmers were being hailed as the new gunslingers of Wall Street, fetching breathtaking salaries.

Veteran energy traders began reporting that some of the computerized trading systems were letting banks and funds trade on the screen in ways that would have been illegal in the pits. They pointed to what they called "phantom trading volume," "fake orders," and "quote-stuffing" that made oil prices appear to be headed one way when they were really headed another. It was a problem worth looking into, but with Washington's track record of understanding even the most basic financial instruments, like weather futures, it seemed unlikely it would be capable of troubleshooting advanced technology possibly being repurposed for the execution of illicit, high-speed trades.

The trader accused of spilling the most blood in the new battlefield of financial warfare emerged not in the trading pits but in the unregulated over-the-counter market and outside U.S. borders. Since Nymex had gone electronic, traders didn't need to be *in* the country anymore to game the U.S. energy market with the click of a mouse. Notably, the worst of the damage occurred just ten days after Nymex went to the screen.

Brian Hunter, a tall, sandy-haired, thirty-two-year-old Canadian, was working at a trading desk in Calgary when he was blamed for losing $6.6 *billion* in the natural-gas market and, according to the subsequent U.S. Senate investigation, driving up gas prices across the nation. Hunter, whose father poured concrete for a living, was a self-described "math geek," who previously had been fired from Deutsche Bank for, among other things, trading losses and a supposed lack of maturity. He had since become a vice president at Amaranth Advisors, a multibillion-dollar hedge fund based in Greenwich, Connecticut. But instead of making more than a billion for the fund, as he'd done in 2005 during Hurricanes Katrina and Rita, he sank the business and brought down MotherRock—Bo Collins's smaller, $400 million hedge fund—with it. MotherRock closed its doors the first week of August. Amaranth, whose wrong-way trades came to a head September 15, 2006, met with the same fate just days later.

Hunter had worked briefly on Wall Street after studying physics at the University of Alberta and soon became known as "one of the biggest wallets on the street," says a friend and former competitor. He was the quintessential commodities trader in that he had incandescent energy, was able to stay up all night and party for days while still coming into work early. He differed from most commodities traders, though, in that he was considered a budding genius. He and his wife, Carrie, arrived in New York just before the September 11 attacks, but didn't have much interest in staying afterward. He joined Amaranth after the fund told him it would allow him to move back to Calgary, an oil town where top banks like Goldman Sachs were setting up shop.

The game Hunter was accused of playing at his fund—and losing—was an old one. It had simply been updated for the screen. According to allegations made by the CFTC, which realized what was happening far too late to stop it, Hunter had tried to influence the settlement price of energy contracts on Nymex. It was the time-honored tradition the traders reverently called "slamming the close." When they first heard about it, the Wall Street bloggers spluttered to life. They had assumed the perpetrator had come from the Nymex trading pits. An anonymous poster on the Web site Dealbreaker.com condemned the widespread manipulation of the energy market. "This is energy trading. Manipulating the settlement prices is criminal. Take every bastard local from Nymex out in the street and shoot him!" A second poster: "Fuck that. You can't *manipulate* the Nymex. That's like exorcising a demon from Satan."

But the disturbance had come from the screen. What Hunter was being accused of was, in fact, a Godzilla-size version of what Bobby Sahn had described doing decades ago in the Nymex heating-oil ring. It seemed that Hunter's maneuver only differed from Sahn's in that, since the energy market had become exponentially larger, it now took an extraordinary amount of money to move the needle on prices.

Since Hunter had billions at his fingertips, that had not been a problem.

"Make sure we have lots of futures to sell MoC [market on close] tomorrow," he wrote a fellow trader in an online instant message February 23, 2006, several months before his spectacular flameout. On another day, he told a second trader to make sure the March contract got "smashed on settle, then day is done." After digging through more of Hunter's IMs, the CFTC unearthed a missive he'd written to a trader at a different firm on February 24 about how he planned to unload four thousand contracts at the market's close. It was expiration day for the March gas contract, a particularly delicate time for prices. Hunter called his plan an "experiment," but in terms of its effect on gas prices, it was akin to loading a herd of elephants into a rowboat. As a rule, the more contracts sold near the close, the better a trader's chances of influencing energy prices and moving the market where he wanted it to go.

A few minutes into the start of that day's close, which ended at two thirty P.M., the trader asked Hunter, "Aren't you done?" Hunter replied, "No . . . have a lot more to sell . . . waiting until two twenty." During the closing range, which lasted a few minutes, Hunter wrote one of his coworkers at Amaranth: "I am flexing here . . . today came together quite nicely."

The trader's response: "Looking preety [*sic*] bang on."

Hunter's correspondences were also peppered with what he believed other heavyweight traders were doing in the market, his chief obsession being John Arnold, the billionaire founder of the Houston energy hedge fund Centaurus. In an April IM that year, he discussed the likelihood of Arnold hammering the settlement with Amaranth's risk manager, David Chasman. Hunter fretted that Arnold was betting against him in the market, taking the other side of all his trades, and warning Chasman that "Arnold is the master of moving the close."

If Arnold *was* the master of moving the close, he was wise enough not to brag about it in an IM. He also was wise enough not to brag about collecting Picassos and de Koonings, which he did, unlike Hunter, who blabbed to *Fortune* magazine about his love of expensive cars and how impressed he was with the handling of his Bentley Arnage in the Calgary winters. Hunter also confided that he'd indulged in the purchase of a Ferrari F430 Spider.

Arnold, fellow traders said, was as discreet as he was gifted. His IMs consisted primarily of two things: lines of numbers that signified prices only traders of his caliber could fully grasp, and inside jokes about his coworkers, not excluding Bill Perkins, whom he called "Perky."

Pretending to offer a trade for Perkins, Arnold, a sports fanatic, wrote in the summer of 2008, "Perky for a bag of dried squid and a player to be named later."

Another trader proffered a counterbid. "*At two* bags of dried squid."

And that was roughly the extent of John Arnold's IMs.

Under the headline "Brian Hunter Is Unavailable Because He Is Playing a Computer Game That Takes Up His Whole Screen Called Losing Billions of Dollars," Bess Levin at Dealbreaker.com summed up his IMs thusly: "The job of a trader is a confluence of responsibilities, essentially limited to executing trades and IMing. Anyone who's ever interfaced with one of God's special creatures knows such an experience is a guided tour through copious spelling errors, homonym problems that suggest serious learning disabilities, response times that range from jackhammer to 3-hours-later-I'm-still-sitting-here, and cockiness as far as the eye can see (very occasionally justified, most often not)."

When Hunter began making his billion-dollar bets on natural gas, the Nymex compliance department didn't immediately notice, which spoke volumes about its vigilance as a self-regulatory organization. In August, it finally sent Hunter a letter asking what he was doing back in April, selling thousands of gas contracts into the close. Not satisfied with his answer, days before Hunter's self-immolation, Nymex forced him to offload his bets. But instead of getting rid of them, Hunter simply moved them to the over-the-counter market. "We got him off Nymex, but he just shifted his positions to ICE," Newsome says. "We took the risk out of *Nymex*, but not out of the *energy market* in general. This is the problem we have with some markets being regulated and others not." While Newsome had passed on his chance to do something about ICE while running the CFTC and his pleas had been ignored by the CFTC commissioners that past spring, he had been right.

David Greenberg, the only member of the Nymex board who dared defy Schaeffer by voting against letting the energy market go electronic, felt vindicated by the two hedge fund blowups just a week apart. "People don't understand that the energy market might be a global market, but it isn't big or versatile enough for trading at these insane levels," he says. "The amount of money going into it is more than it can handle. It's too much. And it's obviously distorting prices."

Greenberg was kicked off the board. Schaeffer did not like being overruled.

"What's the point of having a board if all the votes are always in your favor?" Greenberg asked him.

"Either you're with us or you're against us," Schaeffer retorted.

Brian Hunter and Bo Collins had actually been friendly before trading each other into oblivion. Across Wall Street, traders chalked up their downfall to the fact that their bets had been so bulky and obvious, they'd become easy targets for predators. Yet the dual implosions of their hedge funds against the backdrop of the increasingly unstable oil market did nothing to dissuade the Nymex executives from pushing forward with their IPO.

Schaeffer, by taking the market electronic, had recaptured most of the oil-trading business that had been lost to ICE, though a good portion of Nymex's gas business was gone for good. Nymex would never be the same, but only the pit traders really cared. In the first week of November, oil volumes on the screen doubled those of the pits, causing many of them to give up and retire. The shutdown by BP of the largest oil field in the nation, Alaska's Prudhoe Bay, after the discovery of sixteen miles of leaky pipelines, pushed oil prices to nearly $75 a barrel in late 2006. The extent of BP's corroded pipelines only came to light after the U.S. government had forced it to get tests done. Lax safety standards at BP's Texas City, Texas, refinery a year earlier had led to the gruesome deaths of fifteen people. In the years to follow, more would die in accidents there. While Goldman Sachs and Morgan Stanley have frequently been blamed for high energy prices, it's BP, says a prominent industry official, that is considered by industry officials to be "pure colonial evil."

Bill Ford from General Atlantic, surveying rising prices, urged Nymex to move quickly. He offered its members an extra $10 million to divvy up among themselves if they went public before the end of 2006.

Faced with that kind of temptation, the members, who always found a reason to object, had nothing to say.

MILTON FRIEDMAN, WHO won the Nobel Prize in Economics the same year that Nymex had its potato default, died the same week as Nymex's public stock offering. Friedman, an American economist, opposed the teachings of renowned British economist John Maynard Keynes, who believed that government should guide and stimulate economic growth. Friedman, who had long been friends with Leo Melamed, believed the government should simply supply the economy with money and get out of the way. The economist, who died at ninety-four, also spoke of the effects of "too many dollars chasing after too few goods." That had been his definition of inflation, but it could just as easily have been the definition of New York's overheating oil market.

After breakfasting in the gilt-edged boardroom of the NYSE, Richie Schaeffer, Jim Newsome, Vinnie Viola, Danny Rappaport, and a select group of Nymex members strolled down to the trading floor to watch their stock trade for the first time. They were met there by the NYSE's bespectacled chairman, John Thain, the ex-CFO of Goldman Sachs—the bank the Nymex traders had always hated. Being welcomed at the NYSE—the exchange whose traders had always hated them— was an oddly cathartic experience. Some of them had never set foot on Wall Street until that day. After being reviled for 134 years, Nymex was finally being embraced by the financial elite.

It was a brisk Friday, the week before Thanksgiving, November 18, 2006. Expectations were high, as the hype over oil had triggered a blood-thirsty competition among Wall Street's banks and hedge funds hoping to get in on the ground floor of the Nymex IPO.

Schaeffer, Newsome, and their retinue walked down to the famous, flag-draped balcony overlooking the NYSE trading floor. Just before the market opened at nine thirty A.M., Schaeffer mounted the podium and rang the opening bell with the press of a red button.

There was only silence.

The market had opened, but no one seemed to be buying Nymex stock.

"We were supposed to start trading at $59 a share," says Rappaport.

"We expected to see the price go up, but instead we are just standing and watching all these conversations going on down in the pit. The brokers are waiting, holding thousands and thousands of orders for our stock. But none of it is trading."

A small problem had come up. There were too many buyers of Nymex stock and *no* sellers. People wanted to buy the stock at $59 a share, but the banks that were holding the stock after underwriting the IPO didn't want to sell it at that amount. They thought they could sell it higher.

The trader appointed to handle the stock offering, Jeffrey Axelrad of SIG Specialists, called out the amounts the buyers were willing to pay against the amounts at which the sellers were willing to sell. It soon became clear that the two sides could not agree.

"Sixty, bid at $70," Axelrad shouted out.

No one was biting at $70 a share. The buyers remained stubborn. They were hoping the sellers would cave in. The sellers remained stubborn, hoping the buyers would give in. The older potato traders watched with growing amusement. They'd all seen this before.

"Seventy, bid at $80."

The buyers were now slowly filtering in at $70, but the sellers were pushing the envelope, jacking the price up.

"Eighty, bid at $90." Schaeffer sighed, visibly aggravated. The market was at a standstill. No one was budging.

Meanwhile, the clock was ticking. Thain was pacing and glowering at the trading floor. The Nymex executives began to sweat. The NYSE's live market feeds were going out, letting the world know that nothing was happening. The executives looked at one another. They should have known this would happen. At Nymex, the probable and improbable never failed to awkwardly collide.

At 9:58 A.M., after almost a half hour of the gridlock, bids for the Nymex stock bolted to $120—where, at long last, it traded.

The Nymex members and executives went from anxiety to shock. They had banked on getting $59 a share. With each seat counting for ninety thousand shares, that would have come to just over $5 million a seat. But not this. Their seats now were worth $10.8 million each. "When you're in shock like that, you don't scream. The only thought is that maybe this isn't really happening," says Charles Federbush.

Having seen his fortunes double, another member leaped into the air, shouting, "It's like I never got a divorce!" All the money he'd lost at the end of his marriage he'd just won back.

Schaeffer and Newsome instantly became fabulously rich. On top of Schaeffer's compensation of $6 million that year, he earned $32.4 million in the stock offering. Newsome, who would take home a paycheck of $5 million that year, watched the value of his stock soar to $21.6 million.

"None of us could believe it," says Rappaport, who owned two seats. "Here we are at the New York Stock Exchange and our initial public offering ends up being one of the most successful in a decade."

But that was not all. Exactly ten minutes later, the Nymex stock hit its all-time high of $150.01. The Nymex members, many of whom had never finished high school or college and had toiled in obscurity in the pits for years, were now rich beyond their wildest dreams.

In less than an hour, each had earned in excess of $13 million.

Traders like Bobby Sahn, who owned nine seats with his former wife, had just earned more than $120 million. The Nymex members, almost entirely by accident, had become New York's largest club of multimillionaires.

Marty Greenberg, who owned four seats, called it like it was. "Look, we were the oil market, we had the right product. We had how many hurricanes and wars? It was timing. The main story here is that we were a success in spite of ourselves. But we've always been that way, that's always been us. If you really want to look at it realistically, when you remove the rose-colored glasses, what have we really done?"

Heading back to the Nymex pits before lunch, the members came face-to-face with the traders who leased their seats but did not own any. They had missed out on their one shot at true wealth. "As you can imagine, it was a mixed feeling. There were the seat holders, who were ecstatic, and then there were the leasees, who were resentful, because they didn't make anything and, at the same time, they were losing business to the screen," says Rappaport. "We were the seat owners, capitalizing on what they felt had been their labor. I don't know everyone on the floor anymore, but that day you could tell as soon as you looked into someone's eyes if they were one of the haves or the have-nots." Federbush also felt sorry for them. "We always fought, but we were a family, and what happened, it really broke up the family. I am sure there are seat holders and leasees who are best friends now, living very different lifestyles. It's hard, because you have to walk on the floor and see them in the elevator. Some people decided to buy a house or have an $800 bottle of wine every night instead of buying a seat. But everyone made his own decision."

A hedge fund trader visiting the floor that day witnessed the opening of the oil market's socioeconomic schism. "It's such a strange situation. Half of them are super-millionaires and half of them have nothing. But that's trading for you."

Conspicuously absent from the Nymex contingent at the NYSE that day had been Michel Marks and Lou Guttman. Both had been invited and both had declined. I called each of them that morning, but only Guttman picked up. Marks kept odd hours and usually let his home answering machine take his messages.

"I can't talk now. I am at my mother's grave," Guttman said. "It's the anniversary of her death. I'll call you tomorrow."

15

The Man Who Traded $100 Oil

You ask a big-time CEO what he makes, and it's a huge number, but it's all tied up in stock and options. Traders get paid in cash. It's liquid, it's real. You can go, "Here, look," and slap someone across the face with it.

—BILL PERKINS

AS THE DUST cleared, a greatly altered oil market emerged. Richard Schaeffer, who'd once been a regular of the trading pits, now avoided them altogether, riding around in an armored black Cadillac Escalade SUV and traveling with personal bodyguards. He also hired Viola's kung fu master as his head of security. He was the victor in the showdown between the traders and the executive suite, but winning meant he had become a pariah in the pits.

With the Nymex shares worth far more than a barrel of oil in early 2007, the exchange members took up the new pastime of betting on the stock price instead of oil. They traded the Nymex stock obsessively. They traded options on the stock, they called each other on the phone to talk about the stock, and they analyzed Schaeffer's performance as chairman, wondering if he could get the stock above $200, making them even more millions. They did not believe such hopes were unrealistic. ICE's stock now traded over $120 a share, and Melamed's CME traded well past $500. Not a day went by when the retired Nymex members in Boca Raton didn't check on the prices of all three exchanges. Schaeffer was aware of the heightened scrutiny and found it, by and large, amusing.

"You know what? I'm getting the nicest letters I've ever received from Cataldo Capozza, that guy who sued us over the General Atlantic deal," he told me over breakfast at the downtown Ritz. "They say things like, 'Richie, I think you're doing a pretty good job, *however* . . .' For him, that's about as good as it gets."

In February 2007, I met with a group of traders who still leased their seats and had not made any money on the stock offering, but had managed to continue eking out a living in the pits. They didn't get much business anymore, but, like the potato traders of yesteryear, they planned on staying until the bitter end. We had lunch at the Grill Room, a seafood restaurant at the World Financial Center's Winter Garden, which had been rebuilt after September 11. I was introduced to one of the biggest remaining gasoline traders. In between discussing how the pits were a "ghost town," he catcalled at the pretty Asian waitress. He was in his thirties, balding, and dripping with Staten Island machismo. He whistled and clicked his tongue when he wanted the waitress's attention, which was often, criticized her promptness at taking our orders, and joked loudly for most of the meal about her relentless interest in his physical endowments. He also offhandedly referred to her as "half-breed." His explanation: "You can't be nice to them. You have to make them work for it." When I asked about what he and the other traders thought of the Nymex seat prices hitting an all-time high that month of $11.2 million, he conjured up his best impression of a retired Nymex millionaire at his Boca Raton ranch, clutching at his face and neck and breathing laboriously off a respirator at the mere mention of a waver in the Nymex stock price.

At the end of the meal, he ordered a cabernet for dessert, nixing the suggestion of port, telling the waitress to "stir it with your finger." When she brought ginger cookies sprinkled with confectioners' sugar, he shoved one across the table at me. "Don't be afraid of it," he glared, "just put it in your mouth."

As the traders went through the five stages of grief in rapid succession, their behavior became even more aggressive than it had been normally. Ranking high on the list of that year's offenses was what one Nymex staffer dubbed the "ball-punching incident of 2007." A minor scrape between two traders led to a 911 call when "one of them got down on the ground and literally punched up between the other guy's legs," the staffer says. The puncher was suspended from the trading floor for three months. The punchee passed out and had to be taken out on a gurney by EMTs.

The traders really wanted to attack Schaeffer, but it was nearly impossible to get at him, since he had bodyguards. When the chairman made a rare visit to the pits that spring with former New York City mayor Rudolph Giuliani, who was campaigning for the Republican presidential nomination, the traders booed Schaeffer wildly. By that time, more than 80 percent of energy trading had moved to the screen, with the major banks, hedge funds, and oil companies taking it over. In the staring contest between Nymex and Wall Street, Wall Street had won. The oil market was more profitable than ever but, against the more sophisticated players, the Nymex traders couldn't compete. Without being able to control the oil market from the pits, they'd lost their home team advantage. Gone were the days of thronging into the pits in thousand-strong packs to trade. The few Nymex traders left had been reduced to sitting on the steps of the pits, quietly punching away on electronic tablets like fifteen-year-olds at a video-gamers' convention.

Wall Street, which had despised Nymex for so long, had finally seized control, and revenge was sweet. In 2007 alone, U.S. banks and trading firms hired a record number of people to join their commodities-trading desks, offering traders $2 million signing bonuses. The demand was so great that, even as the housing market collapsed and Wall Street slid toward the worst financial crisis in almost a century, headhunters were still snapping up mortgage-bond salesmen who'd been fired from their jobs to fill up empty chairs. Energy hedge funds the world over quintupled. Perhaps most astounding, 90 percent of the big oil companies, according to the more in-the-know Nymex executives, were running dedicated trading desks specifically designed to bet on oil and fuels armed with heaps of exemptions. Energy traders were the new market wizards. Even an energy trader of mediocre ability could score a salary of half a million a year.

On his way out, Mark Lichtner, one of the many traders who'd booed Schaeffer that day in late March, was handed a memo along with everyone else. It was a directive from upstairs, titled "Decorum on the Trading Floor," and its contents created quite the stir. "Rule 60.6(E) states no member, nor any other person within jurisdiction of the exchange, shall engage in any conduct subversive to good order or decorum or which interferes with the personal comfort or safety of others or shall violate any rules, regulations or resolutions adopted by the board which relate to the conduct or attire of those on the premises of the exchange," the memo read, before going on to explain the range of punishments and fines it could impose on any violators. The exchange was not objecting to another incident of drug dealing, illegal trading, or ball-punching. On these matters, it was typically silent. But on the loud booing of its chairman, it was drawing the line.

Lichtner was a humble man, a self-described "scalper," who made small amounts of money on small trades, even in the boom times. He kept a modest home, had a girlfriend, and loved his cat. He was not an arrogant trader, but he also was in no mood to be scolded by the executives whom he considered to be just as corrupt as the worst of the pit traders. That night, he sent out an e-mail to his trading colleagues, defending the first man who started up the booing and decrying what the oil market had become:

> The man this memo is directed at spoke the truth . . . we all know that. You want some more truth? How about fining the people that steal? That will take the money out of your pockets. Firing phone clerks that take cash? Calling the media about all the shit they DO NOT KNOW? Especially about our board members who are supposed to set an example. . . . We all know who they are. Yet one guy speaks the truth today and a warning memo is sent out. Stop me when I am not telling the truth. . . . All you guys out there pull your fucking steal trump cards out of your ass. How big is your glass house? Most of you are hypocrites anyway. . . . Remember, the amount you make or made will never raise your IQs or make you a tough guy in the real world. If you can honestly say that every one of your trades is squeaky-clean, then God bless. If not, then shut the fuck up.

It was likely that the memo from upstairs was not Schaeffer's doing. He was too thick-skinned to care about getting booed. His loyalties were to the oil market's stockholders, not to its traders, and with the former camp making out like bandits in the IPO, he was enjoying an unusually calm period of peace and prosperity. He and Jim Newsome, according to people who worked with them, were renting jets and expensing them to the exchange, flying dozens of hours and reestablishing what Gary Lapayover once called the Nymex Hunt & Fish Club.

"Richie went everywhere by jet and was always offering it to his associates, 'Hey wanna use my jet?' He would take it down to the place he owned in Miami for the futures conferences and Boca Raton," says a former high-level staffer who worked in the executive suite. Schaeffer also kept a 110-foot Horizon yacht, the *Adriana III*, at the marina next to the exchange. Renting out at around $40,000 *a week*, the cabin cruiser had a sun deck, an outdoor barbecue, sun pads, and a deck Jacuzzi pool. The price did not include the cost of docking the *Adriana* at the World Financial Center, estimated to be one of the most expensive marinas in the world.

Newsome, though less ostentatious than Schaeffer, committed his own indiscretions, remaining dangerously chummy with top officials at the CFTC, including his former chief of staff and close friend, Scott Parsons, who started a Washington financial lobby to which Nymex proceeded to funnel hundreds of thousands of dollars under Newsome's watch. A member of Ducks Unlimited, Newsome also would go bird-hunting with Greg Mocek, the head of the CFTC's enforcement division. Mocek, a Southern man himself, thought his former boss was a good shot and admired the way Newsome's conversation veered easily from topics like rodeo and calving to exotic derivatives. They hunted pheasant. At the urging of Congress, Mocek would soon, in 2007, be launching a massive probe into the global oil market, but three years after putting five trial lawyers and some of his most senior prosecutors on the case, the CFTC would decline to say whether it had found anything amiss.

The Orthodox Jewish boy who had come down to the pits in the early 1980s and told to remove his yarmulke was now all grown up. He was married, had children, and bought seats at the exchange that would support his family for many generations. He could retire early, but he chose to work. Throughout the years, he'd prided himself on avoiding many of the temptations that had caused others in the pits to steal from one another and from their clients. He'd refrained from bad-mouthing exchange officials, even when he didn't agree with them, and he'd avoided talking to the press. But when he saw oil prices resuming their upward climb toward $80, he felt he had to speak up. In a lengthy interview, he sat down and spoke with me about what he and the other traders thought they were seeing from their vantage point in the pits. It was his belief that Washington either did not notice or did not want to notice. He understood there were worries about oil supplies, but he also feared the situation was being purposely exploited and ignored.

"In the past, when the market got ahead of itself, it would always snap back in place in a day or two. But after we went electronic, oil prices came off their hinges. They're no longer in touch with reality. We're seeing things we've never seen before in the way the futures prices move, the relationships between the months and the way the oil prices jump. Before, when we passed from one season to the next, the price relationships between the months would always move like clockwork and you could anticipate them, but not anymore. It's all unraveled. These days, nothing makes sense. I don't care what anybody says about it. I was there and I have been there from the very beginning, back when Michel and Francis Marks started it all, and since the oil market's gone to the screen, we've seen prices go up sometimes $5 to $10 a barrel *a day*. Even on the really crazy days in the past, you didn't see daily price moves of more than a couple dollars usually. I want to know, what is happening out there that is warranting a price change of that magnitude? Did an oil field blow up? Is there a new world war being fought somewhere? I think the biggest one-day move we'd ever seen in oil before was an $8 jump in 1991, at the start of the first Iraq War. The market's no longer reflecting supply and demand. It used to be fundamentally driven. There's no new war, no big supply disruptions, and suddenly oil is going through the roof? Right. But it's just a computer game now, isn't it? Just guys trading around the world in giant rooms they're calling *arcades*."

I had heard this many times in the previous year from the pit traders, but since I was a journalist and not a trader, I did not know what to think. All I had were the barest of facts. Ultimate truths remained elusive. I knew I didn't believe in conspiracy theories. (Wall Street, in particular, did not seem to be very good at keeping secrets.) I had noticed a reluctance on the part of Congress and the CFTC to referee all things financial, but I assumed it was because too many people were making too much money for lawmakers or policymakers to feel they could safely object without risking the loss of their jobs or the derailing of their careers.

That spring, something more definitive happened. I'd left my job as a special writer for Dow Jones the prior year and started freelancing for magazines and newspapers around London and New York. I usually didn't do work for trade publications, but when Will Acworth called me from the Futures Industry Association—the organization that held the Boca Raton futures conferences that all the Nymex chairmen attended—asking if I would write an investigative piece about Goldman Sachs and its trading activities in the energy market, I said yes. I was wondering what I would find.

On the surface, my assignment seemed like a rather unexciting one: to see whether something called the Goldman Sachs Commodities Index, a financial product that allowed ordinary people to invest in the energy futures market, was contributing to record-high oil prices. As I soon found out, the long answer to the question was very complex, but the short answer seemed to be *yes*. Surprisingly, it did not take much more than back-of-the-envelope math to make the case that (a) the oil futures market was worth just over $20 billion, while (b) the money tracking the Goldman Sachs Commodities Index and other similar indexes heavily invested in the oil market was closing in on *$100 billion*.

If Brian Hunter from Amaranth could bully the gas market with several billion dollars, it seemed highly unlikely the oil market wouldn't be bullied by a war chest *five times the size of its overall value*.

David Greenberg, the energy trader who'd argued with Schaeffer before being forced off the board, had been correct. The oil market was far too small to handle the amount of money being crammed into it. In the words of the economist Milton Friedman, it was a case of too many dollars chasing after too few goods—which, according to him, led to inordinately high prices.

Heather Shemilt, the spokeswoman-cum-salesgirl for the Goldman Sachs Commodities Index, an uncommonly attractive blond bombshell type, explained to me that the bank expected the amount of money tracking the commodities indexes to hit *$110 billion* in the next year after rising fivefold in the previous few years. She was talking about Goldman's expectations for 2008, the year that oil prices hit their all-time high. That year, Shemilt would also be named a partner at Goldman, one of the highest-status jobs on Wall Street and known for paying its partners tens of millions of dollars a year. By that time, Goldman had gotten rid of the index, selling it for an undisclosed sum to Standard & Poor's.

I wrote my feature for the Futures Industry Association's magazine and handed it in. A month later, Acworth called me to say he was terribly sorry but after showing the article to people around Washington, he had been pressured to drop the piece. He took full responsibility for the situation and paid me for the article, saying he did not realize the extent to which the hard numbers might be "politically explosive."

It appeared that some in Washington did not want Goldman to be blamed for high oil prices.

The irony was that the people investing in these commodities indexes were mostly middle-class Americans trying to save up for retirement—teachers, dentists, plumbers, literally the entire California Public Employees Retirement System—the same individuals who were suffering the most from sticker shock at the pump.

Newsome, after being asked to give testimony to Congress about soaring energy prices the next year, urged lawmakers not to limit the amount of money flowing into the oil market from Wall Street (and, by extension, into Nymex, which directly benefited him). "The case has not been made to support a finding that institutional investors are contributing to the high price of crude oil," he testified to the Committee on Homeland Security and Government Affairs. "It would be premature to adopt a legislative solution for an unproven or unsubstantiated problem." Yet it was easy enough to substantiate. The truth was, there were just too many people who didn't want it substantiated. Sprecher at ICE shared Newsome's views. "ICE continues to question the causal link between speculative activity in the futures markets and energy price levels," his exchange stated.

Newsome went on to subtly remind lawmakers they should refrain from meddling in complex financial affairs that they didn't understand, warning forebodingly of the dangers of "substituting the judgment of Congress for the judgment of trained financial investment professionals." Newsome, who'd navigated the narrows of Congress before, knew there was nothing that lawmakers hated more than being blamed for fighting a disease with a cure that was even worse.

In June 2007, lawmakers attempted to show that although they still weren't comfortable threatening Wall Street over potentially catastrophic affairs *while* they were happening, they were enthusiastic about releasing reports *after* the fact. In a 130-page treatise, the Senate Permanent Subcommittee on Investigations revealed the findings of its probe into the Brian Hunter debacle and the collapse of Amaranth. Hunter's trading activities, it said, helped by the Enron and London loopholes, had led to the disruption of the nation's energy market. There was "no sound rationale," it said, for the government to regulate some U.S. exchanges and not others, to say nothing of the total lack of regulation of the over-the-counter market, which Newsome now described as a near-mirror image of the futures market, only much bigger and completely hidden from view. The loopholes had specifically allowed Hunter to shift his trades from Nymex, the regulated market, to ICE, the unregulated market, the panel said.

"It's one thing when speculators gamble with their own money. It's another thing when they turn U.S. energy markets into a lottery where everybody is forced to gamble with them, betting on prices driven by aggressive trading practices," said subcommittee chairman Carl Levin, a Democrat senator from Michigan. "Current commodity laws are riddled with exemptions, exclusions, and limitations that make it virtually impossible for regulators to police U.S. energy markets, particularly the Enron loophole, which means regulators can apply excessive speculation limits to regulated markets like Nymex but not unregulated markets like ICE. We need to put the cop back on the beat in all U.S. energy markets, with stronger tools to stop price manipulation, excessive speculation, and trading abuses."

The Senate panel also announced it might be a good time to hold a hearing. "Number one and two on Washington's list of top stalling tactics: call for a study, hold another hearing!" Guttman was fond of saying.

The Enron twist didn't stop there. The Amaranth trader who'd hired Hunter in 2004, Harpreet "Harry" Arora, had come from Enron—and even *he* objected to Hunter's risky style of trading after a few months of watching him. Hunter was making Amaranth so much money, however, that instead of censuring him, the hedge fund actually promoted him, making him Arora's equal partner in running the fund's commodities trading desk and allowing Hunter to move from Amaranth's headquarters in Greenwich, Connecticut, to his hometown of Calgary, where he would be able to carry on unmolested. Shortly before Hunter left, Nymex granted him an exemption to let him trade *three times* more gas futures contracts than was normally allowed in the public energy market. It had done so because Amaranth had written the exchange a letter asking for the privilege, emphasizing it had "assigned a risk manager to sit among the energy traders" to make sure they didn't get too foolhardy. Nymex, which made more money by granting the exemption, granted the exemption. That was part of the beauty of being a self-regulatory organization.

Weeks later, Hunter left for Calgary, taking his trading team and his exemption with him—but not his risk manager. Nymex, which had taken Amaranth at its word, was none the wiser. Despite Newsome's congressional testimony, given two years *after* the events, it seemed as though trained financial professionals did not always inspire the utmost confidence.

"Amaranth senior management took a rather hands-off approach to overseeing Hunter's trading operation," concluded the Federal Energy Regulatory Commission, which investigated the fund's collapse alongside the Senate, the SEC, and the Federal Trade Commission. Where was the CFTC? It was also looking into the matter, but that didn't guarantee anything. The other agencies had been asked to pitch in at the behest of Congress, which wasn't really sure it could trust the CFTC to do its job anymore.

The reason for the repeat problems, says a high-level exchange official, has been the rampant incestuousness pervading the business. "I think it's all right for traders who need to hedge their price risks on the *physical* energy assets to get an exemption, as long as they stick to the program, which nine times out of ten they don't. It is the purely speculative traders who are only in the market to place bets that I have a problem with. I don't think Amaranth owned a bunch of gas pipelines or oil fields they needed to hedge. They were just gambling. They blew the market up, because they were let loose in a candy store. Bo Collins at MotherRock shouldn't have had his fistful of exemptions either, but what did you expect? He used to be president of the market giving them out! You have Collins, the former president of Nymex, running a hedge fund, starting it up from Richie Schaeffer's office, who's also funding it, who's also about to become Nymex chairman. What do you think's going to happen?"

Hunter had been guilty of engaging in what the traders jokingly referred to as a "Texas hedge." This was a salute to the wildcat oilmen of the past century, who gambled without fear, regardless of consequences. To put on a Texas hedge was not to hedge at all, but to double down, multiplying the amount of money you placed on your bet. Hunter may not have been fearful enough of the market's wiles, but it turned out he'd been right to fear John Arnold. The billionaire ex–Enron trader had profited hugely off Amaranth's demise. That year, Arnold's Houston hedge fund, Centaurus, reported a record *317 percent* return, while Arnold himself earned an estimated *$2 billion*. Arnold's second in command, Mike Maggi, a trader from New Jersey who'd grown up in the Nymex pits and graduated to Enron, earned almost as much as Arnold. The figures were appalling, even in a business known for producing some of the world's largest piles of lucre. Most hedge funds were happy to make just 15 percent a year. At Centaurus, returns had never fallen below 178 percent. The bulk of the winnings weren't coming from

Nymex though. They were coming from the over-the-counter market, now worth over *$600 trillion,* according to what the CFTC unjokingly called its "guesstimate."

Enron was dead, but its legacy lived on. One trader dismissed the hue and cry. "That's capitalism," he says. "Love it or get the fuck out of the free world."

When I spoke with Arnold, known for having mythic number-crunching abilities, he did not want to talk about his Amaranth-related trades, but fellow Centaurus trader, Bill Perkins, explained that they'd bet on energy prices dipping in late 2006, while Hunter bet that another busy hurricane season would push prices up. Hunter lost; they won. "We were bearish. When you have cab drivers quitting their jobs to search for oil and people drilling through their bathtubs in Piscataway, New Jersey, you know that prices are way too high."

Hunter, seen in Houston a couple weeks after his blowup, looked paler than usual but otherwise had on his best poker face. "He was shrugging it off like, 'Yeah, we lost $6 billion. I'm over it already,'" says a trader who had a drink with him. In truth, Hunter was getting tired of being pilloried. He was a low-key and private person who didn't appreciate the constant media attention or the U.S. regulators chasing him down while he was trying to revive his trading career. Unfortunately, in the process, he made a brash move that only reinforced his propensity for grabbing headlines and the media's enthusiasm for labeling him a rogue trader. The tattler-style Wall Street blogs and Canadian newspaper *Globe and Mail* had a field day when Hunter ducked out on interrogators from the Federal Energy Regulatory Commission in New York, mid-interview, after leaving them with the impression he'd be right back after lunch.

Instead, he caught a jet out of the country.

BY MID-2007, SCHAEFFER was jarred from his period of peace and prosperity by a breakdown in the oil market's delicate machinery. He was receiving word that the dirty secret about Texas oil was spreading, that the West Texas Intermediate crude tied to Nymex's cornerstone oil contract was running out.

Just as with the Maine potato three decades earlier, Texas oil production was falling behind. What the Maine farmers had called "the Curse of the Potato" was striking again. Once the United States led the world in oil production, but now Texas only produced about 500,000 barrels of oil a day. The Middle East, which held 60 percent of the world's oil reserves, produced 25 million barrels a day. (About 80 million barrels are consumed by the planet each day, one-fourth of which is downed by the United States.) Even as the colossus grew to epic proportions, attracting thousands of new oil traders, its foundation was drying up. "Texas crude was disappearing and we knew we were eventually going to need something else to hold the global oil market up," says Greenberg. "It's part of why we wanted the European oil contract in London to succeed so badly."

When Maine potato supplies ran low, Idaho had taken over. But the 1970s had been a simpler time. Potatoes hadn't been tangled up with the global stock markets or economic sentiment, as the oil market was today. Traders didn't bet on potatoes as a hedge against the dollar, as they were doing with oil now. In short, fixing the situation was going to be a nightmare. Schaeffer did not like nightmares.

It left the energy market in yet another cliffhanger, ushering in the same games of brinksmanship that had once plagued the potato market—only instead of farmers and traders sparring over railcars and potato inspections on a local level, it was monster banks, oil companies, and hedge funds sparring over oil tankers, pipelines, and oil fields on a global stage. Throughout 2007 and into 2008, the market brimmed with stories of traders hoarding oil in landlocked storage tanks or hiding it offshore on supertankers as a way of camouflaging how much supply was really available, to keep prices up and profits high. The U.S. Energy Information Administration, which required companies that stored oil to report their inventories each week, didn't count the tankers on the ocean, a loophole that was exploited by market participants with buccaneering games of hide-and-seek. One high-level bank trader told me that daily tanker rates had gone to more than $125,000 a day, with about 80 million barrels of oil being parked offshore, bound for nowhere. Economists scratched their heads, wondering why oil prices didn't fall when U.S. oil inventories appeared so high. The answer was that by spring of 2007, nobody wanted to sell it for less than $80 a barrel. One of the largest charterers of ships in the world, a powerful but low-profile Dutch-Swiss company called Vitol, came under scrutiny for using its oil tankers as "floating storage." The company also happened to be the largest independent physical oil trading company in the world, with a built-in hedge fund that it didn't like to talk about.

While outwardly projecting old-school conservatism, Vitol didn't have a reputation for keeping company with the most savory of characters. In 2007, its Swiss arm pleaded guilty to a criminal charge in New York for paying kickbacks to Saddam Hussein's regime for Iraqi oil contracts. Mike Loya, the president of Vitol's Americas division—and the older brother of Javier Loya, the over-the-counter energy broker who'd kicked Jon Bon Jovi out of his table at the nightclub in Las Vegas— defended his company's use of floating storage, telling the *Wall Street Journal*, "We sell oil when it is most economical to sell it." And that entailed holding on to it for as long as possible until it could be sold for top dollar. As Herschel Smith of Mars Hill, Maine, said after the potato default of 1976, it was "the same old game."

As part of the CFTC's probe into possible oil market corruption (which notably started the same month that Congress began asking other federal agencies *to help the CFTC do its job*), its regulators decided to investigate how floating storage might be used to influence prices, as well as look into suspicions of false oil-inventory reporting, which could similarly sway prices. Yet again, millions of dollars and three years later, the CFTC reported no findings.

"It is widely understood that the CFTC is an agency captured by private interests, and the only times it gets confused is when it has two vested interests fighting each other," says one of the few former CFTC officials who has not gone on to work for a major financial exchange or a private firm. "The futures industry is a tight, closed group, and if you do anything to get in the way of their financial objectives, they will burn you and you will never be able to get a decent job. Look at the case just a few years ago brought against Man Financial in Philadelphia, one of the biggest hedge funds in the world. You literally had the U.S. district court judge *begging* the CFTC officials to do their jobs and stop turning their backs on the people they were supposed to be protecting. The reach of the private sector at the CFTC is outrageous. The things that go on there are not to be believed. The only time anyone ever looks into it, let alone does anything about it, is when things become so dire it's a national outrage. When gasoline prices hit the roof, Congress is furious with the CFTC. But otherwise everyone's failed to manage the situation."

Cushing, Oklahoma, the tiny Indian town where Nymex delivered

Texas oil by pipeline against its crude contract, became ground zero for much of the supply gaming. I took a trip to Cushing in 2007 to see for myself. Traveling north on route I-35 from Dallas, I passed catfish farms, fried-pie stands, Piggly Wigglys, big-box churches, and the Will Rogers World Airport (or, as my driver liked to call it, the Will Rogers "Intergalactic" Airport). The most curious of the landscape's features, however, were the pump jacks drilling for oil in schoolyards, empty lots, churchyards, even *graveyards,* swinging their slow, mesmerizing limbs under sun-bleached skies. Many of them were operated by ordinary homeowners scraping for the last of the region's oil. They let the pump jacks lie dormant on the wells until oil prices got above $60 a barrel and then got them going again.

Over in Cushing, horses and cows grazed among the miles of "tank farms" stretching as far as the eye could see, holding much of the nation's oil supply. Just how many tanks were in Cushing was a closely guarded secret, but each held up to 575 barrels for a total capacity of around 30 million barrels. The companies running the tank farms wouldn't say how much oil they were carrying or for whom, but they were building additional tanks as fast as they could, estimating about one-third of their clientele consisted of Wall Street banks and financial firms. Goldman Sachs was rumored to be storing oil in enormous quantities, while the land records office in Cushing indicated that one of the biggest holders of oil in the town was Morgan Stanley, which paid zero tax, courtesy of yet another special loophole.

Situated on a stark and barren plain surrounded by muddy grass-lands, the place was not much to look at. Beneath the ground, oil pipe-lines crisscrossed from all over North America, harking back to the days when oil in Texas and Oklahoma flowed bountifully. But above ground, the streets were empty. By the time I got there, the town's Web site didn't even mention oil anymore. Cushing had a deeply depressed econ-omy, a single movie theater, and a population of less than ten thousand. Its graveyards had more people in them than its homes. The boom time had come and gone, and what was left was grim. Talking to the residents, who mostly worked for the local hospital or prisons, I learned that few of them knew of their town's importance or its stranglehold on global oil prices. None of them knew that traders around the world were riveted by reports of their oil inventories, or that OPEC's oil ministers frequently remarked on the town's significance to the oil industry. "I knew that during the Cold War they used to say our town was one of Russia's big missile targets," one local told me. "But now we're so used to all the tank farms, we don't even notice them anymore."

Energy analysts, observing Wall Street's apparent interest in stowing away ever-greater amounts of oil in Cushing, fretted that the town was having an outsize and unreasonable effect on energy prices. They believed Cushing should no longer be the epicenter of the oil universe and that Texas crude had become a red herring. "The dynamics of the U.S. crude oil market have become increasingly bizarre in recent weeks and have now reached the point where the oil price mechanism itself has gotten stuck in a fairly vicious loop," wrote Paul Horsnell, head of commodities research at Barclay's Bank. "In terms of being a reflection of general market conditions, West Texas Intermediate has become about as useful as a *chocolate oven glove*."

But Schaeffer could breathe easy. The traders paid little attention to comments about chocolate oven gloves. They mostly just read the sports page. They were making a bonanza and the only way to keep the cash coming in was to keep on placing bets. With oil companies like ExxonMobil showing record profits while backsliding on their oil production levels, the traders were becoming even more convinced that oil might be running out. Oil-producing nations like Venezuela were getting more possessive of their crude reserves, insisting that companies like ExxonMobil pay more to drill on their lands or get out. China was madly stockpiling oil, and countries like Saudi Arabia, which had ten times more oil than Exxon, were getting even more secretive about how much was left.

By 2008, prognosticators at Goldman Sachs were hinting at the possibility of an oil "superspike" capable of sending prices shooting past $200 a barrel. Market bulls rejoiced. The market bears reminded everybody how Goldman Sachs might be predicting an oil price spike that it actually had a hand in creating. Either way, the heady talk was getting the Nymex traders riled up, and, as oil prices grazed $99.40, then $99.50 the day after New Year's, they couldn't take the suspense anymore. Diverging from prices on the screen and taking the lead in the pits, they traded oil at $99.90 on the floor while the price on the screen lagged by 40 cents.

The split between the screen and the pits caused mass hysteria as traders on both sides began furiously trying to close the price gap. Amid the wave of confusion, forty-three-year-old floor trader Richard Arens became the first man to quietly buy oil at $100 a barrel. Arens, a local trader who ran a small brokerage firm called ABS, purchased a single oil contract from another floor trader $600 *above* the market price, tucking it away as a souvenir for his grandchildren. It was just after noon on January 2, 2008.

Once the trade had been recorded, a second wave of confusion followed. Many traders believed the trade wasn't real. But it was.

When it was finally confirmed, newspapers from New York to London stampeded Arens. Not wishing to become the $100 oil poster child, he respectfully declined to comment.

In the executive suite, Schaeffer was facing a problem he'd never had before. He had all the money and the power he'd ever desired—but now what? He had spent his whole life trying to get to this place, but had never thought much about what he'd do once he'd arrived. Newsome was not having the same problem. He was busy promoting the Arab world's first energy exchange in Dubai, where Nymex would soon begin trading Middle East oil. It made sense, since the Middle East had most of the oil left. At a conference in London, a top executive from Bahrain was asked why the Middle East hadn't gotten its own oil market together, instead of letting New York do it. "What is the holdup?" the executive asked, leveling an imperious gaze on his audience. "I will tell you what is the holdup. We want what the West has, but we are still fighting over who gets it. Our problem is, *everyone wants to be Captain Kirk.*"

When Newsome launched the Dubai exchange, Jeff Sprecher immediately offered a Middle East oil futures contract on ICE, eliciting cries of "copycat" from the Nymex executives. Sprecher did not care. Similar to Schaeffer, he could more than handle being called whatever the Nymex traders wanted to call him. He'd been copying Nymex's contracts all along and it'd made him millions. What was one more? ICE trading screens now dotted the Nymex trading pits. The traders couldn't afford not to keep tabs on Sprecher's market, which affected theirs too. Sprecher was landing on top CEO lists across the nation and growing his business at a breakneck pace. He bought up other exchanges, indexes, and trading operations all over North America, glomming them onto his empire. He even beat Nymex in a bidding war for the New York Board of Trade, which leased a trading pit *at* Nymex. Once the deal had closed, he could just walk into the Nymex building and hobnob with its traders whenever he chose.

Schaeffer's problem was the same one every Nymex chairman had had since the mid-1990s. He wanted the status, the power, and the money that came with being the oil market's chairman—but he didn't really want to *be* chairman.

16

Meltdown

It was our own greed that got us our riches. And it was greed that screwed us in the end. But you know what? It was one of the great roller-coaster rides of the twentieth century.

—ROBERT IRA SAHN

"DIDN'T YOU KNOW? Ever since Richie took office, the word's been out that the New York Mercantile Exchange is up for sale to the highest bidder."

It was early 2008, and Lou Guttman was drinking black coffee at the Gatehouse diner where we sometimes met near his home at the Gateway Plaza. He'd heard about the private jets, the yacht, the pheasant hunting, and he found it all nauseating. He could see Schaeffer's yacht across the marina from his apartment.

"What happened to all the noble speeches about getting serious, about professionalizing the exchange?" he asked, shaking his head. "It's grotesque. These guys pretty much spent the last year and a half not trying to run a business. Everything they're doing is to keep the shareholders barefoot and pregnant and do a deal, take the money, and run off to a sunshine state."

"But didn't Nymex just get bought out two years ago?" I asked.

"Yeah, but they don't have any interest in running the market. They're looking for it to get bought out again. For good."

"Richie doesn't want to at least *try* giving it a shot?"

"Why would he want to do that? He's already made his IPO money.

The best he can do is sell the place and cash out. I'll bet he's already got it all lawyered up."

What Guttman was talking about was a golden parachute. A golden parachute was a large, typically multimillion-dollar payout that top executives got when their company was bought and they were pushed out following a takeover. It also was a good way to make a quick fortune if one happened to want out anyway.

Guttman reminded me that this wasn't outside the grand scheme of things. Many of the Nymex executives were traders. They didn't build things. They didn't run companies. They simply extracted value from things for the fattest possible profit. To them, the buying and selling of their own oil market wasn't much different from trading silver coins—and, like the silver coins, they were going to extract all the value they could and *melt Nymex down*.

There was another reason Schaeffer might have chosen this time to cash out. In the past year, he had tried to run the exchange, to do deals like Jeff Sprecher at ICE, but his deals hadn't panned out. He'd dispatched Newsome to do work on the Dubai exchange, which had been a qualified success, but found the deal-making terrain in the United States extremely treacherous. He'd run into serious patches of bad luck. Nymex was reporting record earnings, but the word on Wall Street was that Nymex was so highly valued as to be overvalued. Analysts were saying the stock was too expensive, and none of them was recommending investors buy it anymore. With the stock price no longer going straight up, the Nymex members had started getting restless again. If Schaeffer lost too much support, he knew that like so many other chairmen who'd come before him, he'd be forced out. "If the board sees you weakened," Guttman says, "that's it. They turn on you like a pack of hyenas."

Schaeffer knew the situation and he knew his politics. He didn't grovel or pout. He was, above all, a realist. "I am made of Teflon. I get dinged up a lot. And sometimes my feelings get hurt. But what can you do? Anyone might backstab you at any time. It's the nature of the beast. There were always people who liked and hated me, but the opinions started going from about 70-30 percent, my favor, to 50-50 or less, *not* my favor. And it stayed that way."

Schaeffer's first strike had been investing over $25 million of the exchange's money in a small, over-the-counter brokerage firm called Optionable. Just days after he inked the deal, its worth on the stock market went from $475 million to pennies. He instantly lost tens of millions of dollars on the investment and one of Optionable's top clients, the Bank of Montreal, claimed the brokerage firm had botched risky options trades, causing the bank to lose an estimated $400 million. It pulled its business and sued. That's when other troubling revelations started to crop up. It turned out Optionable's CEO not only had a prison record but had been found guilty of credit card fraud and tax evasion. It was also discovered that Optionable's chairman, Albert Helmig, was briefly vice chairman of Nymex and had stayed very friendly with the exchange's board. Optionable's former chairman, who founded the firm with the tax-evading CEO, had once been a Nymex member himself, and his father still owned seats on the exchange. Even the tax-evading CEO had once been a Nymex clerk. The harder everyone scrutinized it, the worse it looked. After installing a board and upper management that was supposed to be disproving Nymex's long-standing reputation for engaging in shady deals and tomfoolery, it appeared as if the oil market had merely been putting lipstick on the pig. "You could always remove those in power at Nymex and replace them," Guttman says. "But there would always be new guys doing an even worse version of the same thing behind them. There was no end to it. All of us members were thinking, if we don't have the CFTC breathing down our neck in short order, we'll *all* be surprised."

He was right. Within months, the CFTC had charged a handful of Optionable's senior executives and a trader with fraud and deception. But no one was charged at Nymex. "This is vintage CFTC," cracks a former CFTC official who once worked for Nymex. "It only loves to go after the little guys."

Bobby Halper, the spread trader whom Schaeffer persuaded to be his vice chairman, called for further investigation. Schaeffer shot the idea down. Halper resigned. The board immediately began a smear campaign portraying Halper as a compulsive pot smoker, which, considering the drug dependencies of the other members of the exchange, seemed tame by comparison. Guttman was beside himself. "After the Optionable mess, the board did nothing to deal with it. Jim Newsome did nothing! Rappaport did nothing! Halper was the only one who spoke up and he got fired for it. Oh my God, he inhaled! So what? He was the only one with any integrity."

Mark Lichtner, the pit trader who generally thought so little of

Nymex executives, came out in Halper's defense. "Fuck them for screwing Bobby. I don't know if he has an agenda. I have never seen an agenda. Bobby doesn't need an agenda; he is a genius." Bill Ford, the CEO of General Atlantic, who remained on the board, kept eerily silent. "Bill was in Schaeffer's pocket," says one board member. "Why else would Schaeffer have picked General Atlantic? He barely said anything, ever, and if he did, Richie would just wipe the walls with him, like, 'Shut the fuck up, Bill! You don't know what the fuck you're talking about, Bill!' And you know what? Bill would shut up."

Ford had his reasons for keeping quiet. He would soon be lauded on the Forbes Midas List for making seven times his initial investment on Nymex.

Schaeffer's second strike had been his attempt to get bought out by the NYSE, which looked like a match made in heaven—at least for Nymex. The NYSE was looking to expand into new markets, and with oil prices well above $100 a barrel, Nymex was a guaranteed money-maker. Schaeffer assiduously courted John Thain, the same NYSE CEO who had been there for Nymex's IPO, giving him tours of the exchange, introducing him to the traders, and inviting him to his palatial apartment in Tribeca with the oversize drawing room, gourmet kitchen, and floor-to-ceiling oil paintings. But the talks dragged on for months, and, in the meantime, the Nymex stock slid below $100 a share, giving extreme vertigo to members like Bobby Sahn, who traded every day from his home at the Hotel Plaza Athénée. "The stock has fallen into the $80s twice now. Let me tell you, watching it tank, I must have aged ten years in the past couple of months. I am not kidding. The Nymex stock is tanking and here Richie's already cashed out. It's a good thing I'm so fit or otherwise I would have a heart attack."

Thain, unbeknownst to Schaeffer, was also in talks to become the next CEO of Merrill Lynch. He was already planning his exit from the NYSE. When he called Schaeffer to tell him about taking the job in late 2007, Schaeffer was left grasping at air. The NYSE didn't seem to be interested in doing the deal anymore. And that was the end of Schaeffer's proposed $14 billion merger coup. Traders at Nymex whispered fitfully that the real reason the deal went south was because Schaeffer conditioned the merger on his being given a management position at the NYSE and was "laughed out of the room." Schaeffer says it fizzled because the NYSE was occupied with a major merger deal in Europe.

Thain himself would be left in a lurch only months later, when Merrill became yet another victim of the credit crisis that would soon begin felling banks across Wall Street.

When the CME finally got serious about buying Nymex in early 2008, Schaeffer knew he was looking at his last chance for doing something big. The CME was one of the only companies that could still afford Nymex, and Schaeffer was already contemplating the next phase of his career: becoming a restaurateur. He'd never been much of a trader, but he did know enough to sell at the top of a market. Nymex's stock might have been sinking, but oil was just reaching its peak.

The two sides came together, at first, grudgingly. The CME had always seen itself as superior to Nymex, and the Nymex traders had always resented Chicago for its superiority complex. Leo Melamed, the CME's chairman emeritus, had a soft spot for Nymex after trading potatoes and eating corned beef sandwiches in its pits in the 1960s. But Craig Donahue, the CME's young, well-educated, and polished CEO, did not suffer such pangs of nostalgia. He was not impressed by Schaeffer or the rest of the Nymex board, and shared no long history with them. While he couldn't ignore their riches, he was not about to act like he was doing anything other than *deigning* to do a deal with them. On the whole, he preferred to work with Newsome, who at least spoke his language and tucked his shirt in his pants.

The courtship process was awkward at best but progressed steadily. The executives jetted back and forth between New York and Chicago, hammering out their financial terms. Mark Fisher, being Mark Fisher, tried to get involved, but Donahue was having none of it. "Fish, who supported the deal, came to Chicago for one of the meetings, but they wouldn't let him in," Schaeffer says. "He came anyway. He said his piece and then they made him leave."

Schaeffer's timing, which had been terrible for the first two deals, could not have been better for this one. Wall Street's economists had often stated that when measured against past energy crises, the current price situation was not that bad. That all changed when the price of oil sped past $109 a barrel in early March 2008, drawing a new line in the sand. Oil had officially surpassed the previous inflation-adjusted high of $103.76 of April 1980. Market bulls rejoiced—again. But the last of the pit traders were starting to get worried. Why was the market acting this way? There was no major news to explain what was happening. The collapse of one of Wall Street's biggest banks, Bear Stearns, later that month did not seem to lend itself to bullishness. The market was looking increasingly shaky and they *were* the market, so if they didn't know what was going on, they didn't know who did.

It was around this time that Fox News commentator Bill O'Reilly interviewed market executive John D'Agostino about how consumers might combat rising energy prices. It was the show after which D'Agostino would receive hate mail and a death threat.

Bill O'Reilly: Now in the United States, Shell and ExxonMobil are making record profits, profits that nobody has ever seen before in any corporation in this country. All right? So they're prospering from the chaos in the market, correct?

John D'Agostino: They're prospering from the price of crude oil, correct.

O'Reilly: All right. So whenever the barrel of oil goes up, they correspondingly raise all of their prices to make as much money as humanly possible. I say the folks should be angry about that, should be angry, should cut back 10, 15 percent of their buying of all of these [*sic*] people. If we all did that, would that drive the price of American gasoline down?

D'Agostino: I don't think you're talking about a boycott. You're talking about general conservation, using less energy.

O'Reilly: Yes.

D'Agostino: Absolutely. The only thing we can do is start to use less energy.

O'Reilly: All right. So if every American who owned an automobile or air conditioner said, "I'm going to use 10 percent less, 15 percent less," prices then would fall?

D'Agostino: Yes. If we kept at it. Now what happens—what happens in this country—what happens all the time is there's a price spike. We react. We use less gasoline.

O'Reilly: Then we go back up.

D'Agostino: Then we go right back up. But that—we're good at reacting, not conserving.

O'Reilly: I think people now know—and they should—politicians can't do this. They can only do temporary fixes, like a gas tax holiday.

D'Agostino: Absolutely.

O'Reilly: But unless the folks get angry, that's it.

D'Agostino: Now there's one slight problem. It's like a diet, right? We have to be on a tough diet. We have to take our lumps. The problem is we also have cousins in China and India that need to go on a diet.

O'Reilly: They're not going to conserve.

D'Agostino: So it's a tough thing. But it's what we have to do. And we have to convince the rest of the world to do it as well.

O'Reilly: They're not going to do it.

D'Agostino: It's the only way.

O'Reilly: We can and we should. And we should all get mad, because we're getting hammered. It's going to be $6, you know. Six bucks. And it's going to destroy the American economy.

Even in the oil business, which specialized in surreal events, 2008 was a superlatively surreal year. Gary Milby, a self-proclaimed oilman from Campellsville, Kentucky, was tracked down by regulators (not the CFTC) after flaunting his riches on the popular MTV show *My Super Sweet 16*. Accused of defrauding hundreds of investors of millions of dollars by diverting their funds from his oil and gas ventures to offshore accounts and family trusts, Milby was filmed throwing his daughter, Ariel, an over-the-top sixteenth birthday party, flying her in by helicopter and escorting her guests into a castellated tent by horse-drawn carriage. On the show, he presented her with a brand-new BMW 325i. "I love oil. Oil means shoes and cars and purses," Ariel exulted as her father took her and the MTV camera crew on a journey through his oil fields. When the father pointed out a drilling site, explaining it pumped 120 barrels a day, the daughter asked, "How many Louis Vuittons is that, Daddy?" The father didn't hesitate. He said: "A bunch."

In Washington, the U.S. attorney general announced that international organized-crime syndicates were fanning out into the energy market, noting that criminals and agents of terrorism had modernized their tactics and "broadened the scope and depth of their illegal activities" to reach into financial exchanges. Issued in conjunction with the FBI, the Department of Homeland Security, and the Department of Justice, the attorney general's announcement warned, "As U.S. energy needs continue to grow, so too could the power of those who control energy resources."

The statement was distressingly unspecific about what was being seen or done.

The culture of heightened government vigilance did not extend to all government agencies. Employees at the Denver branch of the Minerals Management Service were being accused of having sex with energy industry officials and one another while accepting gifts from oil and gas executives and taking drugs at work. The Minerals Management Service, which was supposed to be collecting roughly $10 billion in royalties from the energy companies that drilled on public, taxpayer-owned lands, had been neglecting their duties while attending golf tournaments with oil industry executives and improperly taking fees for consulting gigs on the side, said the U.S. Department of Interior's inspector general. In a report to Congress, the inspector general went on to say that thirteen people had violated the public trust in what he called a "culture of ethical failure." The more popular name being given for it, touching on the imbroglio's sexual overtones, was "Lubrigate."

It involved the oil company Chevron, which the inspector general said had refused to cooperate with the investigation, in addition to the Gary Williams Energy Company and Shell. His twenty-seven-page report was an X-rated tour-de-force exposing how vile government indiscretions could get, not excluding a detailed account of how a high-ranking government official, Gregory W. Smith, badgered his secretary at the Minerals Management Service for cocaine, purchased crystal methamphetamine from her at home, and had oral sex with her after, according to the inspector general, "she watched him snort it off the toaster oven in her kitchen."

The oil-related upheaval wasn't limited to U.S. shores. It was also extending to distant locales, such as the Gulf of Aden, a major waterway between the Middle East and Africa, where Somali pirates hijacked a slow-moving Saudi supertanker, the *Sirius Star*. Just south of Yemen, the Gulf of Aden was the site of more than a hundred attacks on sea vessels in 2008. Demanding a large ransom in exchange for the release of crew members from Britain, Poland, Croatia, the Philippines, and Saudi Arabia, the pirates communicated their terms to the press through their pirate spokesman. "What we want for this ship is only $25 million, because we always charge according to the quality of the ship and the value of the product," the pirate spokesman said. It seemed that the pirates did not object to the taking of hostages but didn't want to be seen as over-charging. He asked that they be paid "soon." (Eventually, the pirates were talked down to a ransom of $3 million, parachuted from a plane onto the deck of the stolen ship. But the matter wasn't settled until 2009.)

In April 2008, Nymex had its own share of scandal when forty-eight-year-old Steven Karvellas, head of the exchange's compliance committee, which tracked instances of illegal trading, pleaded guilty to two felony counts of—of all things—illegal trading. Karvellas, who'd worked in the natural-gas pit since Guttman started that market back in 1990, had been taking advantage of the rules that let traders engage in dual trading, the practice by which traders could trade for their own accounts in addition to the accounts of their customers. He had been assigning himself the most profitable of the trades he was supposed to be doing for his clients, according to the plea agreement he struck with Manhattan district attorney Robert Morgenthau. Noting Karvellas's position, Morgenthau publicly denounced him as a "fox in the chicken house." Newsome also made a statement: "Nymex will not hesitate to work with law-enforcement authorities or take whatever steps are other-wise necessary to protect the integrity of our markets."

Karvellas had regularly raised funds for the New York Police Department, even joining the officers for a charity bike ride from the World Trade Center pit to the Pentagon in 2005 to mark the anniversary of the September 11 attacks. He was fined $850,000 and sentenced to five years at Rikers Island prison, a maximum-security lockup known for its violent gang population of Bloods, Crips, Latin Kings, and members of the murderous MS-13. The punishment was seen as unusually draconian for a commodities trader. "Steve begged the prosecutors to not send him there, saying he would pay them millions," says a Nymex trader who was his friend. "They would not spare him. Guess we can't all get the kid-glove treatment of Bernie Madoff." Karvellas was released in 2009, but he would not discuss his time in prison. "When Steve got out, I was like, 'How are you?' and he's like, 'Fine,' and starts talking about his family and other stuff. Then I stopped him and said, 'No, I mean, you were at *Rikers*. How *are* you?' He clammed up. His punishment was the worst any of us have ever seen or heard of," says the friend. "And it's all because of *that little shit*."

The "little shit" was Karvellas's former assistant, who, according to the Nymex traders, ratted him out to the district attorney after being caught dodging his taxes. "It's the kind of crazy story you only hear in this business," says one of the traders. "This kid, in his twenties, had worked for Karvellas for a couple years as a clerk and then just split. They had a good relationship. The kid apparently takes out a trading account under his dead grandmother's name and starts making hundreds of thousands of dollars. One day, the authorities knock on the door and say to his grandfather, 'We're here to see your wife. She owes about a half million dollars in back taxes to the IRS.' And he says, 'What are you talking about? My wife has been dead for years.' That's when they follow the money and trace everything back to this kid. They corner him and he says, 'You can take me, or I can get you somebody bigger.' And he throws Steve under the bus. From what I understand, they were trying to get Steve to roll over on somebody even higher up, but he wouldn't do it. He's no rat. That's how it is down there. We're old school. Lie and cheat and steal from your customers, but if you stool-pigeon your own, that's it, you're done. It's the only offense that's unforgivable."

Getting Brian Hunter, the hedge fund trader from Amaranth, to justice would prove much more difficult. While Karvellas had finished out his term at Rikers by early 2009, the CFTC and the Federal Energy Regulatory Commission were still arguing over the facts of the Hunter case. Or, more accurately, rather than assisting each other, they were locked in a territorial death match that was wearing out even Congress. At one point, a group of senators had to step in to deliver a firm scolding. In late 2009, the federal agencies finally agreed to a settlement with Amaranth, the hedge fund, but Hunter himself would remain at large and frustratingly out of reach. Just to make clear who was boss, he even slapped U.S. officials with a restraining order. Despite years passing and a stream of IMs chronicling his suspect trades, Hunter had yet to be punished for any wrongdoing. He steadfastly maintained it was because he was innocent. "Mr. Hunter has not agreed to the agencies' unreasonable demands, because he should not be penalized for something he did not do," said one of his lawyers. The size of the fine levied against Amaranth was laughably small: $7.5 million, less than one-tenth of Hunter's salary during a good year. Hunter went on to open his own hedge fund in Calgary, then work for Boston's Peak Ridge Capital, which let him build trading models from his home in Canada.

The Federal Trade Commission attempted to reassure the public that it would begin policing the energy market with renewed zeal, imposing stricter penalties on anyone caught manipulating prices, but the damage was done. Through a panoply of legal loopholes, exemptions, no-action letters, self-regulatory privileges, and a shocking lack of antifraud protections at the CFTC, the government had given away the brunt of its regulatory powers in a market overrun by its own energy traders. As Washington lawmakers began to realize the gravity of the situation, Wall Street hastily issued a warning: if anyone tried to meddle with the over-the-counter market in an attempt to regulate it, Wall Street would simply find a way to create a deeper, darker, more secretive market offshore that no one would ever be able to touch.

As 2008 wore on, Congress announced in June it had closed the Enron loophole, when, in fact, it had *not* closed the Enron loophole. It had merely written a farm bill offering a way for anyone who wanted to try and close certain parts of it to spend thousands of dollars and years in court fighting Wall Street to get an *individual* unregulated market regulated again. Lawmakers didn't want to take this burden on themselves, but they didn't object to anyone else doing it. The senators who signed off on the bill included Carl Levin, the lawmaker who'd promised "to put the cop back on the beat" and Senator Dianne Feinstein, the Democrat from California who'd been demanding market reform ever since Enron's traders ran roughshod over her state's energy prices in 2000. President Bush tried to veto the bill. After a congressional override, the lawmakers won. But what had they really won? They'd succeeded in making the world believe that the Enron loophole had been closed, when, at that very moment, it was contributing to the disintegration of the global financial system, resulting in millions of layoffs, the destruction of more than $14 trillion of personal wealth, the slaying of global banks across Wall Street, and stock market losses not seen since 1931.

While existing loopholes were not being closed, new ones were still being opened. As Congress introduced eight new pieces of legislation to combat mounting energy prices, sternly lecturing the executives of ExxonMobil, Chevron, ConocoPhillips, BP, and Shell—all of which were fighting to keep $18 billion in tax breaks—the loophole mania continued.

It was at that moment that Nymex unleashed its "Dubai loophole."

Making good on his threat to find a way to offer U.S. energy contracts through foreign lands if ICE was going to be allowed to do it, Newsome asked for and received a no-action letter from his former staff at the CFTC to offer U.S. oil futures through Nymex's new energy market in the United Arab Emirates. It was almost as if the CFTC couldn't be bothered to exercise any of its regulatory powers anymore. As retail gasoline prices rose above $4 a gallon across the nation, it had quietly opened the door to *outsourcing the nation's oil market to London and Dubai.*

A professor at Schaeffer's alma mater, the University of Maryland, had even started teaching a class that used the U.S. energy market as a case study for what happens when regulators stupendously fail, leading to widespread dysfunction in the broader economy and, as he put it, "needlessly high prices which energy consumers now pay because of the high probability of excessive speculation and illegal manipulation and fraud within those markets." Michael Greenberger wasn't just another professor. He'd run the CFTC's division of trading and markets in the 1990s and worked for the Department of Justice afterward. In testimony before the Senate in June 2008, he said he could scarcely believe Newsome had been permitted to run the U.S. oil market through Dubai, given Dubai's track record.

"It is self-evidently *absurd* that the American public can rest secure that the CFTC found that Dubai's regulatory scheme is comparable to that of the U.S.," he said. "The fact that the CFTC could conclude that Dubai's regulation is, in fact, comparable to that in the U.S. simply demonstrates *that there is not a foreign regulator in the world who would not satisfy the CFTC.*" He concluded, "I am sure that the American consumers will take little comfort from an explanation that they are being protected from manipulation and excessive speculation driving up gas prices, not by U.S. regulators but by Dubai's government. I do not envy any member of Congress explaining that proposition to his or her constituents."

Dubai's ruler, Sheikh Mohammed bin Rashid Al Maktoum, had realized oil was running out in the Middle East, where it was referred to as "the black blood of Allah," and was trying to beef up the city's tourism and financial sectors to safeguard its economy. But there had been serious issues involving market regulators and executives clashing with the city's royalty, who weren't used to following rules that were supposed to apply to everybody. Most concerning had been the ouster in 2004 of Phillip Thorpe, the British CEO of Dubai's futures market regulator that was to oversee the Nymex's first Middle East energy exchange. According to a Nymex executive who worked in Dubai, Thorpe was fired for nothing more than "doing his job, which involved going after some wealthy, well-connected Arab and stepping on a few toes he wasn't supposed to." Yet the CFTC had decreed Dubai's regulatory regime sound.

The Dubai loophole was hardly noticed amid the crush of other improbable events that followed in rapid succession. On June 5, 2008, with no finite or cataclysmic reason behind it, oil punched up $5 a barrel, marking the biggest one-day price move anyone had seen since the first Gulf War.

The following day, oil went up *$10*—again, on seemingly nothing.

Schaeffer and Newsome were aware of the price gyrations, but they had their hands full trying to finish up the CME merger. The Nymex members were also aware, but they were too busy publicly blasting the exchange's $8 billion purchase price, which was far below the $14 billion price tag they'd been led to believe the NYSE would have paid for them only months before. They blamed Schaeffer and Newsome for bungling the price of the deal by tying it to the value of the CME's stock, which was falling. "They could have collared the deal so *our* price wouldn't have suffered, but they chose not to do that, which is fucking unbelievable! If the CME deal is done at these levels, I swear, somebody will kill them," Sahn fumed. "They won't renege on this. Schaeffer doesn't care. He's been selling his Nymex stock all along. Newsome's as useless as tits on a bull. Shareholders who have nothing but the Nymex stock to support them for the rest of their lives are getting killed. Literally, millions have been woofed away."

The drama came to a head in July. No one was minding the store when the oil market topped out. On July 9, Newsome's hunting buddy and head of enforcement at the CFTC, Greg Mocek, gave notice that he would be leaving his job to join a private law practice in Washington, where he would earn $875 an hour for defending banks and hedge funds against regulators like him. Realizing having its head of enforcement jump ship to, as one CFTC staffer put it, "join the enemy" at a time when the CFTC was being accused of not policing the market enough, the agency went into damage-control mode. Though Mocek left in July, the CFTC only told the public he left in September.

Oil prices kept lunging higher, even as the credit crisis on Wall Street reached a critical mass and the banks foundered.

Less than forty-eight hours later, on July 11, oil prices shot to an all-time high of $147.27 a barrel in electronic trading. Behind the scenes and unknown to almost anyone, Newsome, diagnosed with cancer, was emerging from major surgery after having one of his kidneys removed.

At the same time, Schaeffer slipped into a diabetic coma.

Unlike when oil reached $100, no one in the trading pits was bragging about it now. When people asked who'd done the trade, nobody had an answer. Not even Newsome, who technically had access to all the market's confidential trading information. "I am sure our compliance department at Nymex was in touch with the necessary people," he says. A former head of the Nymex compliance department wasn't so sure about that. "I was never satisfied with the paper trail over there at Nymex, or the diligence, so I am willing to bet there wasn't much of an investigation into the $147. No one has ever even tried to explain what was going on with that, which seems odd, since it was happening right as we were being brought to the brink of financial Armageddon."

The pit traders had another theory. They thought the trade had come from Goldman Sachs.

The Orthodox Jewish trader, who was retiring with millions in his pocket, knew that climbing prices weren't about to hurt him or his family. But he felt a sense of outrage when he saw oil hit its high. He'd checked the U.S. oil inventories to see if they were running low. At 320 million barrels, an average level for that time of year, it was clear they were not. So why the high prices? It didn't make sense. "Goldman didn't just fuck America, they fucked the world. And still, nobody is doing anything about it. I heard Goldman thinks oil prices are going back up again. Yeah, I'll bet they do. And if they don't, I'm sure they'll give it some help. The trading floor is a wealth of information. That's what made it so efficient. Now, with no floor, we have no information. There's no accountability anymore. It is all smoke and mirrors on the trading screen. It's like trading in a black hole. Who knows what's going on in there? On the floor, we always knew what was going on: everyone had to state their bids and offers and everyone knew everybody and we knew all the players we were dealing with. All the news came through the floor, because everybody had to trade through us. If Goldman was trying to push prices up, we could tell if they were just messing around and could trade against them. We could circuit-break them, you know? And they could circuit-break us. Now you see somebody anonymously trying to take the price up on the screen and you don't even know why. You don't know for sure if World War III isn't happening somewhere out there.

Maybe Goldman and we hated each other, but you know what? We kept each other in check. Now there is nobody to keep anybody in check anymore."

After reading the third or fourth magazine article blaming Goldman for goosing oil prices above the $147 mark, I asked a good friend over dinner at Bouley what he thought about it. He'd traded energy for years at some of the biggest banks in the world and, being French, was not one to sugarcoat the facts.

He dodged the question.

"Have you tried the caviar?"

"Come on."

"It's really quite good."

"Give me a break."

He put the caviar down, winked, and said: "It's just business."

For Schaeffer and Newsome, who had their health to think about, none of it mattered anymore. "I didn't know I was diabetic," Schaeffer says. "But you know how much sugar I ate every day? All those Chuckles and Twizzlers and Jujubes. I lived off that stuff. I went into a coma, so of course we had to tell the Securities and Exchange Commission, because I was the chairman of the oil market. But we were worried it might fuck up the CME deal, so we didn't tell anyone else."

The Nymex members continued to protest the merger, writing vitriolic letters and issuing statements to the press vilifying Schaeffer and Newsome, but they knew they were too late.

At an impromptu breakfast meeting at Burger Heaven on Madison Avenue in August, two hedge fund executives huddled over a table—one formerly of Nymex and the other a major trader of the Nymex stock.

"What the fuck is going on with the Nymex prices?" the trader asked. "It's like somebody thinks this merger isn't going to happen."

"This always happens at Nymex," the ex–Nymex executive explained. "Everyone always screams and protests and pushes for more money until people start thinking that the deal won't pass. And then, because the members never have any Plan B, it always does."

"Are you sure?" the trader asked. He had a sizable bet on the merger vote.

"Are you kidding? There's only a 0.001 percent chance this isn't getting done. Think about it. Nymex doesn't know how to run itself and there are no other bidders. They are stuck. Craig Donahue, the Chicago

Mercantile Exchange's CEO, wants to tell Nymex to go fuck itself so badly it hurts. But he knows that the best way to tell them to go fuck themselves is to buy them."

But the CME would have to play Nymex's way. Donahue soon learned he couldn't finalize the deal without getting dragged to Nymex's level. Because the deal required at least a 75 percent "supermajority" vote in favor from the Nymex shareholders—including Bobby Sahn, who was against the merger and controlled a large chunk of the votes— Donahue found himself doing a very un-Donahue-like thing. Just before the ballots were cast, he took a helicopter to Sahn's private estate in the Hamptons to kiss his pinky ring. "It was one giant ego trip for Bobby. We knew we already had him, but we just wanted to make sure of it," Schaeffer says.

Sahn, once duly appeased, gave the merger his blessing. "It was probably the most exciting twenty-four hours in the exchange's whole history," he says. He meant it.

It was the smart move on Donahue's part. Less than a year after the merger, the Nymex oil market was worth $50 billion a day. Sometimes it paid to grovel.

As Schaeffer and Newsome signed on to the merger deal, CME officials wasted no time in storming the Nymex building, changing the locks, taking down Nymex signs and replacing them with CME signs, tightening the rules to enforce a stricter dress code (no jeans or open-toed shoes in the pits), and barring the traders from betting cash instead of chips in their feral cafeteria backgammon games.

Just days after Schaeffer and the Chicago executives boarded his yacht for a celebratory toast, they locked Schaeffer out of the chairman's office. When the private-equity executives he'd thwarted two years earlier heard about what happened, they couldn't help but chuckle over the behavior of the two exchanges. "The CME guys are like the Nymex guys, only slightly less knuckle-dragging. They know how to act sophisticated, but underneath it all, they are still thugs," says one. "You can take the trader out of the pits, but you can't take the pits out of the trader."

In the months to come, Chicago would even change the Nymex T-shirts at its gift shop to say CME, although they would keep the Nymex brand name for marketing purposes. The CME hurried to whitewash the exchange of all signs of its past, dismantling the Nymex museum on the first floor that displayed in words and pictures the birth of the oil market. The press office at the CME claimed that all Nymex rel-ics and paraphernalia had been carted to the Museum of Finance on Wall Street, but the Museum of Finance said that it had received no such items. The trading pits were left to languish, with most traders either retiring or working from home. The cafeteria closed early. Even the booths around the pits, once real estate worth fighting over, stood empty, the traders' handwritten quotes from *The Godfather* films still taped to the walls on scraps of paper. The only fixture that was respected by the CME was the traders' bar on the tenth floor, which was busier than ever. Ethan, the tall bartender, continued to arrive at eleven thirty A.M. each day to serve drinks.

All traces of what had once been Nymex would probably never be on display in any museum again. Everything, the traders suspected, had been packed up by their new owner and put into the storage closet on the seventh floor.

SCHAEFFER'S GOLDEN PARACHUTE came to $21.7 million. New-some received a $16.2 million payout. In addition, each of them received a $1 million consulting contract with the CME. According to Schaeffer, his contract, which paid him more than $19,000 a week for a year, did not require him to do anything. "All they want is for me to stay out of the way," he said, relaxing in his Escalade as his bodyguard, Ralph, drove him through SoHo. "It's go-away money."

Newsome was still doing work for the Chicago exchange, although his job had been greatly streamlined from what had originally been envi-sioned. "Jim was promised a three-year deal and an office at Nymex. Then they made it a one-year deal with no office," Schaeffer says.

Those who suspected Schaeffer brokered an arrangement with Bill Ford in exchange for allegedly rigging the bids in the General Atlantic deal felt their worst fears were realized when Schaeffer landed a *second* $1 million consulting contract with the private-equity firm. "I told Bill, I'll do whatever you want," Schaeffer says. "As long as it doesn't involve exchanges."

Danny Rappaport, who went back into retirement following the merger, was impressed. "I think Richie's brilliant. Of all the chairmen, he probably served the shortest time and made the most money."

Guttman, who believed the deal between Schaeffer and General

Atlantic was probably a payoff, was deeply disappointed with the outcome of the chairmanship. He felt Schaeffer had used him to gain the support of the membership and then backpedaled on his promise to keep things above-board. "The thing was, Lou was always behind the scenes working the angles and I never knew whether he was with me or he was gonna fuck me," Schaeffer says. He liked Guttman, but he didn't trust him. As the merger with the CME was cemented, the two had it out.

Guttman, like many of the members, thought Nymex should have taken the proposed $14 billion merger deal with the NYSE while it was on the table. He considered the $8 billion price tag of the CME merger a woeful consolation prize. And he'd told Newsome as much. Newsome told Schaeffer, and Schaeffer called Guttman. By that time, the goodwill between the two had all but disintegrated.

"I don't appreciate your going around saying what you're saying," Schaeffer said.

"Hold your appreciation," Guttman retorted. "Don't take me to the woodshed."

"Either you're on our side or you're not."

Guttman didn't understand the logic of that. "I am on the side of the shareholders, who you are ripping off."

"I guess you're not feeling very well today, Lou," Schaeffer said. "Call me back when you feel better."

"When hell freezes over!" Guttman said, slamming down the phone.

The last time they saw each other was the day of the CME vote, when 80 percent of the Nymex members voted in favor of the deal after protesting it. Guttman joined the board and the CME executives for the toast on the *Adriana*. He thought about not going, but what else was he going to do—watch from his apartment across the marina? In a way, he felt oddly relieved. It was finally over. "You should have seen the look on the CME executives' faces when they saw Richie's all-expenses-paid yacht. They were disgusted."

As he was leaving, Schaeffer told Guttman, "I'll talk to you."

Guttman never heard from him again.

Cataldo Capozza, the Nymex member who'd previously sued the exchange over the alleged bid-rigging in the General Atlantic deal, sued again. He was retired in Florida, but had decided to keep working through his New York lawyer, Mark Rifkin, who felt the Nymex shareholders had a legitimate claim against the oil market and its overly ambitious executive suite. "I've looked at merger deals for twenty-four years, and I have never seen a deal done the way this deal was done," Rifkin says. "You had men negotiating with boys, without any decent conversation about the financial terms. Maybe deals like this have taken place in recent times elsewhere on Wall Street, but I haven't seen it."

Yet from another standpoint, the merger timing had been impeccable. If Schaeffer and Newsome had waited a few more weeks, the deal might not have gotten done at all. Within less than thirty days of stitching it up, an avalanche of debt toppled Lehman Brothers, which went bankrupt, and Merrill Lynch, which had to be rescued by Bank of America in a shotgun-wedding buyout, as the stock market fell its farthest since the attacks of September 11. The Dow Jones Industrial Average plunged below ten thousand points, streaking to its worst annual loss in American history since the Great Depression. Wall Street's landscape had become unrecognizable.

Bill Perkins, the ex–Nymex trader at Centaurus, was aghast that the former head of Goldman Sachs, U.S. Treasury secretary Henry Paulson, was pumping hundreds of billions of taxpayer dollars into failing banks. "It's unbelievable. I mean, I never expected this of Paulson. It's like, 'By the way, I'm a socialist. Didn't you know that?' It's like finding out your best friend is gay.

"These failed institutions masqueraded as banks, but they were basically glorified hedge funds. The banks that are in trouble are the ones that turned from being banks into speculators. They were bad traders and now we are giving them another pile of money? We are literally transferring wealth from those who are productive, the taxpayers, to those who are not. They are selling out capitalism. It's a theft that is wrong on so many levels."

Believing that Paulson would never let Goldman fail, Perkins bought sixty thousand shares of the bank between $90 and $129 as the stock caved in September 16 and 17. He then sold the shares on September 19 between $122 and $132, as the stock rebounded on the bailout announcements, pocketing a tidy profit of $1.25 million. He used the four-day paycheck to take out advertisements in the *New York Times* and the *National Review* to excoriate Paulson, Federal Reserve chairman Ben Bernanke, and President Bush for endorsing what he saw as bank welfare. "I guess it's capitalism on the way up and socialism on the way down," he vented. He continued his ad rampage for months against "the movement of capital by fear and failure of leadership rather than by logic or reason," even denouncing the Treasury secretary and the Fed chief on television. When it became clear the government bailouts would persist, he gave up and sent the rest, $400,000, to Save the Children, remarking, "At least I know they'll use it for something defensible."

After barreling past $147, oil prices crashed to nearly $30 a barrel by the end of the year.

Again, there were no explanations.

U.S. voters were fed up. There was the distinct whiff of Washington not so much failing to look out for their interests as, quite possibly, working against them—or, at least, looking the other way. With the election of President Barack Obama at the end of 2008 came the promise of a grand reckoning, a cleaning up of Wall Street, a replenishing of jobs, and a return to some semblance of order.

Obama named a new person to head the CFTC. His name was Gary Gensler. He was a former banker who'd retired from Goldman Sachs at the age of thirty-nine. Incidentally, Goldman had been Obama's single biggest campaign donor. The bank was also resuming its dire warnings of a return to record-high oil prices. Why not? It had always been an easy way of making billions since the first round of energy crises in the 1970s. The story of oil running out never got old. And, one day, it might even be true.

The party line in Washington was that Gensler, a slight, thin-haired man, was going to lay down the law. The party line in New York among the oil traders was that he was a "nebbish." While working at the Treasury Department from 1997 to 2001, Gensler had strongly opposed stricter regulation of the energy market and the over-the-counter market, which had subsequently turned into a breeding ground for the failures of Enron and Amaranth and the banking sector on Wall Street. Gensler was now taking it all back. "I feel passionately that we must bring the over-the-counter derivatives marketplace under regulation," he said. "Looking back, there's no doubt that I think all of us should have done more to protect the American public, knowing what we know now."

He announced he planned to hold a series of hearings.

Obama also appointed a new secretary of energy, Steven Chu, a sixty-one-year-old scientist from Silicon Valley who became the first Nobel Prize winner to join a presidential cabinet. Originally from Long

Island, he'd never had the inclination to work on Wall Street. Instead, he'd spent much of his career in California's Bay Area as director of one of the most venerated labs at the University of California at Berkeley, where he'd earned his PhD.

A low-key academic, Chu was lauded by colleagues and friends as impatient and brilliant. He abhorred wearing suits. He disparaged OPEC. He wasn't interested in becoming anyone's golfing buddy or political game-player. And he stunned the nation when he began to speak frankly about the likelihood of "very, very scary" rises in the sea level, increasingly powerful hurricanes, and the decline of California's cities along with its agricultural resources as global warming took over. He implored Congress to start earmarking funds immediately for the development of clean energy technologies. "We must begin making these changes now," he told lawmakers. "We don't know how much time we have left."

When Chu told a group of students and professors at the Massachusetts Institute of Technology in May 2009 that the world had already passed its point of no return in the battle against climate change, they were near-speechless. When asked if there was still time to reduce pollution enough to avoid a global disaster, he did not mince his words. The atmosphere had 385 parts per million of carbon dioxide in it, he explained. Climate change experts had come to believe that once it hit 450, the oceans would boil, the polar ice caps would melt, and droughts of biblical proportions would ravage the earth. The question wasn't whether the world would survive. The world had always survived. The question was whether mankind would be able to survive itself.

Then Chu dropped his real bombshell.

"The fact is, we're not going to level out at 450 parts per million. *We're going to go over 450*," he said. Even his scientific-minded audience at MIT was not expecting that. Wasn't the head of the Energy Department supposed to be discouraged from doing things like terrifying the public?

Privately, Chu took it one step further. He told a *Rolling Stone* reporter, "I hope we hit 550 parts per million."

He did not speak idly. His only personal luxury was his $5,000 Colnago bike with a carbon-fiber frame. He didn't drive a car.

The first year of the Obama administration marked the 150th anniversary of the world's first major oil discovery in Titusville, Pennsylvania, by Colonel Edwin Laurentine Drake. The story of his life could be seen as a cautionary tale of what happens when one man ties his fate to oil. Drake had not been a colonel but a train conductor. He'd given himself the title for posterity's sake. During a chance meeting with an oil executive at a hotel in Titusville, he had been offered $1,000 a year to investigate oil seeps in the area. Drake's pioneering work along what would soon become known as Oil Creek, using a drilling technique he could have patented but didn't, touched off a series of black gold boomtowns that made many a rich man—but not him. His fleeting fame was never met by lasting fortune. He lost what little he made in oil speculation just a few years later and died penniless in 1880. Deep in the foothills of Pennsylvania, abandoned oil wells can still be found tangled in the forest trees, their rusty pump jacks obscured by the thick underbrush.

BEN KAUFMAN, THE trading clerk who had come to the Nymex pits in 2003, reflected on the situation: pirates taking over oil tankers, allegations of bid-rigging, games of hide-and-seek with oil supplies, felons and hookers on the trading floor, government regulators running the exchanges, bankers running the government, unexplained oil price spikes, trading arcades, confused congressmen, and "Lubrigate."

Since arriving at the start of the Iraq War, he had seen many things. It would've been nice to be able to say he had learned something. "I can't imagine what the oil market's going to become now with machines trading against machines," he says. "I don't think it's going to have a very happy ending."

In fact, Kaufman wasn't sure what, if anything, anyone had learned. There were no easy answers to why the United States had gone to war with Iraq, nor were there easy answers to the questions surrounding the world's oil supply, how much was left, and how long before it was gone. Oil demand was nearly impossible to calculate, and two of the biggest oil-consuming nations, China and India, had only hazy statistics. Even the United States, which consumed the most oil of any country, had only "implied demand" figures based on how much petroleum *seemed* to be disappearing from the nation's storage tanks. This also required the U.S. government to rely on oil industry workers, who didn't put filling out their weekly petroleum surveys at the top of their priority list. With oil and fuel being bought and sold through so many channels, keeping tabs on it was nearly impossible. The high degree of uncertainty made it irresistible to traders, who'd always been drawn to the markets that were plagued by corruption and bad record-keeping—although at this point it was fair to say much of the statistical failure was deliberate.

There also were no easy answers to what effect the switch from New York pit traders to global arcade players was having on the world's energy prices, especially when those prices were reliant on a grade of Texas crude oil hidden in a town of 8,372 people that was clearly running dry.

Judging by the price spikes already seen since the oil market had moved from the floor to the screen, technological advances did not seem to be putting an end to its long history of manipulation. There was even some evidence the screen was making it worse. In July 2009, federal authorities hunted down a Russian computer programmer who'd worked at Goldman Sachs developing top-secret trading software that could, according to Assistant U.S. Attorney Joseph Facciponti, "manipulate markets." Specifically, the commodities and stock markets.

But Goldman's possession of such software, oddly enough, was *not the chief concern*. The reason for the manhunt was the programmer's alleged theft of the software from Goldman, which Facciponti publicly stated was worth "millions upon millions" of dollars—the loss of which, he feared, would be "very substantial" to the bank.

Wall Street had long held that the screen would force traders to become more accountable, but so far that hadn't been the case. When it came to oil, the market's wildcat spirit never died; it just changed form. The screen showed the trades, but unlike in the trading pits, it did not show the traders behind them. Face-to-face interaction had, by and large, turned into shadowboxing. Instead of being able to isolate a single trading floor in downtown Manhattan as the root of all evil, tracking down perpetrators in the energy market now required enduring stamina and reach beyond one's own borders. That is, assuming regulators could even identify who it was they were going after and felt like going after them. Given that federal authorities struggled to charge even domestic offenders, chances were slim that they were prepared for international guerrilla warfare. As of 2010, U.S. authorities still had been unable to successfully wrest a settlement out of Brian Hunter, the hedge fund trader who IMed his way to infamy, continued to maintain his innocence, and was *Canadian*. Steven Karvellas, the Nymex pit trader who had been incarcerated at Rikers, had already finished his jail time for infractions discovered almost two years *after* Hunter had stood accused. It didn't make for the most persuasive argument of why screen traders should ever fear the law.

Kaufman had seen the market's limitations well before the pits cleared out. "I got a high on the dramatic days, but I wasn't obsessive about money and you get tired acting like an asshole all the time. I also quit because drinking and drugs in the trading world is a big, big thing. My interests never really matched anyone else's down there. They were into TV and sports. They would make fun of me about all the books I was reading and the fact that I traveled. They would say, when are you going to leave this place? You don't fit in. You're supposed to go to college and do smart things. And at some point, you seriously start craving a person around who can actually talk to you about something intelligent. After I left, I became an EMT, so it wasn't hard decompressing. I just went straight into an equally hellish job, dealing with trauma junkies. It wasn't much of a detoxification, but it wasn't as bad as you think. Then I became a professional photographer, which is what I am now. I was glad to go, but I'm also glad I did it. I doubt I'll ever see anyplace like that again—a place where there are positively no rules. Every time you thought it'd be the end of the line, it would somehow keep going. You would think, how can this exist and no one does anything about it? Or you'd hear someone recount an old story and you'd be like, 'Oh my God, we really did that.' And you'd know right then, down the road, people would one day tell you that you were making it up or exaggerating, but you'd know—and about two thousand other people in the world would know—that you weren't. Once we're all gone, though, no one will believe it."

Congress, at the dawn of 2010, still didn't know what to do about it. It was promising sweeping reforms, but the CFTC continued to have no antifraud powers, and the Enron, London, and Dubai loopholes remained wide open. Rather than close the loopholes and apply practical solutions, the lawmakers were advancing wild proposals to kick speculators out of the market or limit trading activities in ways that didn't take seriously the realities of Wall Street. If one thing could be known about the oil traders, it was that they would never stop trading. Blocking them from the market would only lead to the creation of new markets elsewhere—likely farther away and even harder to control. Imposing socialist policies on a capitalist nation was unworkable. But ceasing to give socialist breaks to Wall Street had yet to be considered.

Oil traders remained kings in their own castles. They were still allowed to place massive bets on a disappearing commodity with almost no money down, a circumstance that could have been prevented by Congress when it had the chance to vote on it in July 2008, just *a few days after* oil prices topped out. But instead it scuttled the measure. In the end, lawmakers were content to chastise Big Oil on TV. The truth of the matter was, when the power was in their hands, they could do nothing but waffle.

On Wall Street, the devastation of the banking crisis had not chastened anyone who hadn't lost their job. Traders, bankers, and lawyers were already walking around saying that nothing, in fact, had really happened. The meltdown, apparently, was only pro forma, a figment of everyone's imagination. And they were even starting to believe it. After all, appearance was truth.

"All this goes to show we are now entering the second phase of the world financial crisis," a reader wrote in the comments section of the *Wall Street Journal*'s Web site. "Despite the fact that the anti-social nature of banks has been found out, the corruption of the Fed and the finance committees in the Senate and House are now public, and the solutions to the problems are well known, we still do not possess the political will to carry them out. It is clear now that a larger problem now looms—the crooks are firmly in power and intend to stay there. . . . Americans are again ruled by a plutocracy that has no interest in them other than the money that can be made off them, the same as in 1776. . . . If we cannot kick these people out of power, we are no longer America. And most people sense that. We have become the pleading chickens our founding fathers would have despised."

Unable to pump enough oil to bring down high energy prices, OPEC, the world's dominant oil "cartel," had lost most of its power. Big Oil hadn't done much better. In 2008, the year oil companies stood to make the most ever on a single barrel of oil, they had only managed to increase production by approximately 3 percent. Believing that this might be evidence of a possible oil drought in the future, many nations had begun to aggressively stockpile petroleum supplies, which just pushed prices up further.

With the war in Iraq plodding on interminably, the credit crisis still smoldering, and an astronomical national deficit putting a drag on the U.S. dollar, oil itself was threatening to replace the greenback as the new global reserve currency—which, again, only increased energy prices. The dollar was hardly worth the paper it was printed on, some Wall Street traders were saying, but crude oil was something of intrinsic value.

The world's oil dependence had brought incalculable pain to the average consumer barely able to keep up with spiraling prices. And while it was troubling to think that traders or the government might be to blame, it was still more troubling to think it was because of an oil scarcity, as some believed. "For the first time in history, people are scared that there may be more demand for barrels of oil, every day, than can be produced. Reserves are going down, oil fields are producing less. That isn't changing. We're gradually reaching that scary equilibrium. And in July 2008, we were *there*. In the past, the supply problems were caused by passing events, like wars. Long term, this problem still hasn't been solved. What happened that summer means we have serious problems in the global energy sector. It is unfortunate that prices came down, because it will put off doing what we need to do," Newsome says. "Congress has been looking for an easy answer. The feeling is, let's take it out on the speculators. But that will only lead to what it used to be like before public oil trading. The oil companies would love to have everybody outside the oil market, so they can go back to dictating prices behind closed doors."

During the energy crises of the 1970s, the decade when the United States lost its ability to meet its own energy needs, Republican president Richard Nixon had imposed oil price controls on Wall Street. It was understood back then that the nation would need to develop cleaner, cheaper energy resources by the time it entered the twenty-first century—or risk ongoing war, more oil price spikes, and a long-term threat to its prosperity. Yet the United States has only fallen further behind and has become used to depending on oil-rich nations—many of which are not particularly friendly with the United States—to deal with its energy problems.

As the country turned a blind eye to its energy security, the failed potato traders of downtown Manhattan, without much forethought, assembled their own high-stakes casino, which became Nymex. "It was our very own Manhattan Project," one trader recalls. "And we sort of looked at it that way. You know how the real Manhattan Project scientists afterward were like, 'We didn't realize how big it would be, we didn't know what we were doing, and, come to think of it, maybe we shouldn't have done it?' It's kind of like that."

Thirty years and trillions of dollars of debt later, the new CFTC chairman Gensler was pledging to rein in the casino and its traders, along with forcing a regulatory structure on the over-the-counter market. But Wall Street's banks, amazingly, still believed that after putting the nation's economy into cardiac arrest, they might finagle a free pass. The banks were not used to losing turf wars, especially on their favorite turf—the dark market. Generating for the banks around $35 billion a year, the virtually lawless over-the-counter trading arena had become their most profitable playground. They'd come too far and were making too much money to relinquish it now.

On Capitol Hill, the next theater of battle was already opening up, but, as always, it would be fought quietly behind closed doors. The bloodiest political brawls were almost never televised. It was the banks, the traders, and the exchanges versus the last few politicians and regulators still willing to go head-to-head with them. About this, the public would know little to nothing, but if past was prologue, the outcome would not be hard to guess. The game had been played for years by the people who knew it best (read: not the regulators, taxpayers, or politicians), and the winners fully expected to keep on winning.

Looking over the charred and blackened landscape, the Nymex executive whose honesty under pressure had forced him to resign years earlier, during the John Arnold–Lenny Williams fiasco, was skeptical of all the talk in Washington about reform. He'd seen the pendulum swing back and forth too many times. All lip service, he thought.

He'd already run a couple of financial exchanges since leaving Nymex and, having once worked in Washington himself, knew how to read the tea leaves. I caught up with him over lunch to ask if he thought the regulators and lawmakers were serious this time. If taking hundreds of billions of dollars from taxpayers to bail out banks and watching oil drop from over $147 to nearly $30 in just days didn't sober up Congress, what would?

In between juggling calls from government officials and Wall Street CEOs, he issued his brutal critique. "How do I think Washington, the CFTC, and Congress will respond to the next round of hearings? Let me be frank.

"There is obviously a perception of a lack of integrity in the market and it doesn't help that when the oil companies and banks and exchanges and traders all go to Congress they make defenses that sound wooden and lawyerly and, well, not very convincing. What they're really afraid of is that a relatively small market, the energy market, could be made even more backward with rules that fuck it up even more. Which, given what we know of Congress and its track record, is well within the realm of possibility.

"I think Gensler over at the CFTC will be giving the market an Obama ass-thumping, but will anything change? I don't know. I doubt it. I even saw that he brought in John Arnold from Centaurus to tell him how *he* would run the markets if *he* were CFTC chairman. It's obviously all kabuki theater. There are any number of valves you can adjust to make things better, to make people more honest, but will any of those things bring down the price of oil? I don't know if anybody can answer that. I don't think there's any way of knowing what the true price of oil is. It hinges on so much: money supply and politics and consumer demand and available global oil reserves and the weather.

"The CFTC has its new chairman and now he's coming in with his big we're-going-to-take-scalps-and-name-names stick. Everyone has a short memory. We've seen this all before. Maybe he's going to clean things up, but so far all I see coming from Washington is a lot of bark and no bite.

"I have a dog. I like my dog, but he barks like crazy. You know what you do with a dog that barks like crazy and won't shut up? You walk over to him—and pet him."

Epilogue

The Edict of Noah Sweat

RICHIE SCHAEFFER NEEDED an expensive centerpiece for the dining room of his new SoHo restaurant, and, unlike many of the ex–Nymex chairmen, he was a profligate spender. With teak-encased walls and porthole windows, his restaurant's nautical lines mimicked the curved interiors of a racing yacht. He'd already spent a few million dollars on it.

When he saw the blown-glass chandeliers of Dale Chihuly, he bought one and had the installers affix it to the middle of the ceiling, which took days. It arrived in thousands of pieces, all very delicate, consisting of what looked like many colored-glass octopus arms. On the ceiling, it resembled a field of purple and red sea anemones.

Chihuly himself wore a pirate's patch over his left eye and could have passed for a Nymex trader. He'd stopped doing his own sculptures years earlier, after a series of accidents beginning with an automobile collision in England and ending with a bodysurfing injury that dislocated his shoulder permanently impairing his ability to hold the glass-blowing pipe. To make his sculptures these days, he directed young apprentices, such as the student who did Schaeffer's chandelier, Michael Ayoub.

For the Nymex traders, the opening of Schaeffer's seafood restaurant, Harbour Drive, in March 2009 was a strange and bittersweet reunion. Schaeffer, who was not in the best of health after surviving his coma, nonetheless looked tanned and fit. He was not drinking. After undergoing a couple of difficult cardiac ablation procedures, he was trying to reform his bad old ways. When I walked in, he was holding court in the dining room, excitedly talking about his new boat. After being forced to give up the *Adriana* when he left the chairmanship, he'd found a hundred-foot yacht that was slightly more compact than its predecessor, with a captain, chef, and crew. It rented at $35,000 a week. "I had to downgrade," he cracked. Schaeffer loved to make poor-rich-man jokes.

The new yacht's name: *The Insatiable*.

Inside the bar area, Nymex traders and executives mixed with celebrities, socialites, and models amid a scrum of photographers and the glare of flashbulbs. Bill Murray supposedly had come and gone. Rosie Perez was on her way. Members of the rock band the Strokes were settled into a corner table in the main dining room, wearing leopard-print vests and Panama hats, quaffing champagne under the Chihuly. I doubted they had any idea where their meal ticket was coming from.

Perched on a stool at the bar, talking with the traders, was Jim Newsome, a Maker's Mark sunburn risen up in his face. A sports coat was loosely thrown over his shoulders in a navy-and-white houndstooth pattern, and he wore a loud yellow tie. His bare feet were stuffed into pointy, wicker-weave shoes, the fashion choice of eccentric Southern gentlemen. In his late forties, he'd severed his Achilles tendon playing with his two daughters during the winter but had since healed. He'd come alone.

As a young woman in a short skirt walked by, he extended his cattle farmer's arm and squeezed her derrière in his sausage fingers like an overripe tomato.

Lou Guttman had received an invite to the party but demurred. "I couldn't allow myself to go to that thing after everything that happened. You work for years to build something and . . . it's terrible what's been done. We were sitting on a gold mine and we were mining the gold. Then people decided to stop mining and take what they could and get out. They lived off the fat of the land, and Schaeffer and Newsome picked up the pieces and made off with the rest of it. It should have been *us* buying the CME. How do you go wrong when you control the market for oil and gas? How do you go wrong trading silver and gold? For one brief, shining moment we had the world in our hands. That was Camelot. I did my best. But I was always working with both hands tied behind my back. This is Corporate America. You don't reward a person based on his capabilities. You kill him off *because* of his capabilities. I didn't know about that. I thought I got to be chairman because I was so great. Schaeffer just moved things along and basically took a cut of everything. When I think of his wall safe full of money, it makes me sick to my stomach. Newsome should be strung up. Another regulator who sold his soul. How refreshing! It took me two full months to detox after that merger. These days, I don't think about them. And I am happy not thinking about them.

"We survived by the hair of our chins. What kept us going was less about us and more about the power of the oil market. By the end of it, 90 percent of the trading floor was corrupt. They were thieves. And now they're thieves on screens. Most of them couldn't trade themselves out of a paper bag. It's been quite the cast of characters. They went beyond the pale of basic moral values. With all that money lying around, nobody could keep their hands out of the till. All those mistakes that were made, they just covered it up with more money."

In December 2008, Cataldo Capozza died of cancer at age sixty-five, but his lawsuits against Nymex continued from beyond the grave. Capozza had known the entire time his days were numbered. He'd left word with his lawyer to keep up the fight, even if posthumously.

Guttman was amazed at Capozza's tenacity. "It puzzles me why a guy knowing he's going to die of cancer would waste his precious time fighting. He was certainly a nudge, but he was a good guy and forced the board to be slightly more honest by staying on their backs and filing all those lawsuits." (A year after his death, Capozza's suit was dismissed.)

Schaeffer, who was considering suing the CME for slashing his and Newsome's final payout by almost a third just before the merger wrapped, was peeved by the Capozza suit. To him, it was beyond preposterous that he should be forced to contend with the allegations of a dead man.

At the Palm steakhouse in Tribeca, he told me about his new life—his boat trips, his divorce dilemmas, his struggles to control his sixteen-year-old daughter's monthly $10,000 credit card bills, and his plans to retrofit the veranda at his three-bedroom apartment on West Broadway to accommodate a swimming pool. He lived several stories up, but he thought a crane could be used to lift pool materials over the roof and lower them onto his private terrace in back. He was still looking into the logistics of it. He seemed happy and less stressed out than most of the other Nymex executives. While past chairmen had struggled with the cutthroat politics of the boardroom, Schaeffer had thrived on them. For him, it had been like breathing. After years of threats and squabbles, his face had not crinkled, his hair had not frayed.

Earlier, I'd visited Schaeffer's apartment, for which he paid $22,000 a month in rent. There was no food in the refrigerator or kitchen cabinets, because he always ate out. He said, "This is my dream home." But he missed his daughter, Rachel. He kept a bedroom for her for when she slept over, decked out in pink pretty-princess hues. "She only gets to stay here once a week, because most of the time she's uptown with her mother. I've got a three-thousand-square-foot apartment and no one in it. I love my daughter. I wish she thought of me as much as I think of her. She'll know how good she has it in about ten years."

We were getting ready to eat. I was having fish. He was having red meat.

"What do we toast?" I asked.

Schaeffer, still unable to drink, held up his clinking glass of ice water, a wicked gleam in his eye.

"Let's toast to the death of Cataldo Capozza."

There was no way of knowing whether he meant it. Half of the things Richie said were just to test your boundaries.

"You don't mean that."

"No . . . right."

We toasted to our health.

Deep down, I was pretty sure he meant it.

THE NEW YORK traders came away from the oil market mystified by the monster they'd unleashed and what it had become. They'd built it, but they couldn't control it. They'd seen what it could do to them, its ability to transform their lives or ruin them. The market was a mirror. It showed them who they were, their vices and their virtues. It all came out in the end. They still didn't understand how exactly it had happened, how the market had lasted for so long without them running it into the ground, or where it was heading next. Most of them had been too busy trading to wonder about it or notice. It made no difference. Events had overtaken them and it was out of their hands. Nymex had survived, but most of them had been pushed out or had moved on. The only heavyweight trader left was Mark Fisher, and he would probably never leave.

Some of them had gotten rich, some of them had been left with little more than they came with or worse. Nearly all of them felt like the last souls emerging from a car wreck from which there had been almost no survivors.

BOBBY SAHN

"Did we ever really think about the impact we were having on the outside world? No. It's take the trade, turn it around, take the profit. It's all paper to us. People have this romantic, menopausal idea about our market, that it's historic and we're rugged individualists. Forget about it. Most of us don't see it that way. I don't care about the exchange. Nobody does. We've never taken a step back and seen this as something bigger. We are traders. We only think in the short term. There's a line from the movie *Wall Street*—'Greed is good.' We were greedy. But here's the thing: Nymex is a microcosm of life. We're different ethnicities, from different backgrounds. We all have our own agendas. And we're all battling it out in one place, just trying to make it." Living at the Plaza in New York, Sahn still trades and keeps in touch with old friends like Mark Fisher, who owns a home near Sahn's in the Hamptons.

ORTHODOX JEWISH TRADER

"In the beginning, the average local was happy to make markets and bring home $100,000 to $300,000 a year. A lot of the first people who went down there went to make a living, not a killing. The outside world is looking at us as if we are controlling all the oil prices. But we are just the little guys carrying out the trades of the big oil companies and banks and hedge funds. With everything modernized, are we better off? I may be biased, but I think it was better with us, because the pit traders weren't capable of stealing as much as the big banks or the hedge funds. Those guys would have to go through us. Now they have direct access and can just beat up or manipulate the marketplace with their multimillion-dollar trading systems. You know what the screen looks like now? *Star Wars.* I am not even kidding. I am retired and a grandfather, so it's all over for me, but it's the truth. And anyone who drives a car that runs on gas is a sucker for it."

GARY GLASS

"About fifty to sixty of us traders ended up retired in Boca Raton and we meet up every year on March 15. You see all the guys you used to hate in the ring and you can laugh at them now that they look older. No one's mellowed out. Nah. Everyone's still talking about who's making the most, checking out each other's cars and clothing. What's that saying? Once a scorpion always a scorpion. Everyone's still a shark. We used to hate each other in the ring. In the ring, I would cut your heart out for a penny. But at the end of the day, if someone said, 'I need $1,000 for the local charity,' you'd give it to him. It was funny like that. Those days are over, but you know what? We would do it all again."

DAVID GREENBERG

"I have gone from being a trader to a teacher. I've been teaching about the transition of pit trading to screen trading at the Whitman School of Management at Syracuse University. I walk in there, no tie, shirt-sleeves rolled up, and say, 'I know you guys are used to just sitting there while somebody gives you a lecture. Listen, just try to follow this, because we're gonna be all over the fucking place. I'll be switching topics and we're just going to roll with it.' I tell them about the good old days. They're like, 'When were the good old days?' And I say, 'A couple years ago.' I tell the stories about the pit and how we got into fights and stuff that happened on the floor and at the end of the hour and a half, these kids are on the edge of their seats. It is amazing to be around people who have a thirst for knowledge rather than people who are just into their own shit, their own money, and all they're looking out for is their own wallet. The woman that heads up the program says, 'You know, you were really good.' I'm like, 'Thank you.' And she says, 'I have just one question. Did *you* ever go to class?' I look at her, and I go, 'You looked up my grades, didn't you?' And she says, 'Yes, I did. And I don't understand how the only A you ever got was in marriage and family and now you're divorced.' And I said, 'That's the only A I got because I slept with my marriage and family teacher. She was divorced too.' That was the end of *that* conversation. But it's true. I was nineteen, and my teacher told me, 'You know, if you ever need any extra help, I don't live that far away from you.' This was, like, twenty years ago. So I get to her house and say, 'Well, I had a question about what we were doing today.' And she says, 'Do you want a drink?' I'm like, 'A drink of Pepsi—a Coke? What do you have?' And she's like, 'Well, I got whiskey, I've got Johnny Walker, I've got McCallum's, and I've got Crown Royal.' So right there, I was like, obviously this is like one of those extra-help movies you see on the Internet."

LEO MELAMED

"What the Nymex lacked, they always lacked. They didn't have any rules to prevent all kinds of funny things going on. They were too lax and it just went on like that forever. The culture of Nymex has always been that if you were powerful enough, or clever enough, or had the right partners, you could do whatever. Whatever you did you did, you did. That was an image that, unfortunately, they suffered. Image is very hard to change and, even if it's wrong, it's an image you live with. And it began with the bad behavior of the potato era. When I came to this business in 1969, it was a Wild West attitude. I was a lawyer and believed in constitutional law. We had a constitutional convention over in Chicago and we rewrote the rules to bring them into the modern world. And I have a lot of arrows in my back for it. That never happened over at the Nymex. But did they ever have great ideas. It's very hard to get a market started. Before trying financial futures, I tried potatoes, turkey, even shrimp. Look at *them*. They started oil and gold." Melamed remains the chairman emeritus of the CME.

DEEP THROAT

"Despite everybody's best efforts to blow it up, Nymex succeeded. The energy traders lacked social skills, yes, they are animals, but that ferocity and incredible energy is also what made the whole place work. It's a rough, highly politicized, aggressive experiment in evolution. There is no polished Fortune 500 side, there is *only* the animal side. But it's out of this fire that a place like that could be born. Remember, Nymex wasn't just a story of the oil market and of New York. It was a uniquely American story, admittedly one with a very dark side, but that's part of the American dream too. It's just the part we don't like to talk about."

MARK LICHTNER

"Let me sum up Nymex for you. I will give you a symbolic story. I was dating a girl whose father served on the board, and I was at their house. I open the cabinet to get myself a cup of coffee and there's, like, two hundred mugs with Nymex logos on them. They get shit left and right that nobody else knows about, and that's just the mugs. This guy is a good family man, but just imagine what else he gets. Why didn't the brokers get a mug? Why does someone need to have two hundred? It isn't anger. I speak the truth. What will I do when the floor closes for good? Listen, I am going to get a taco stand somewhere in Puerto Rico and stand there and catch some color."

GARY LAPAYOVER

Lapayover received the news he was no longer welcome at Nymex in true Nymex fashion. Despite having been on the board for years and serving as vice chairman, he arrived at the exchange in 2005 to find that his security card no longer worked. Someone had mysteriously deactivated it. "Now Nymex is nothing but a four-letter word," he says. "I talked to a recruiter about doing something else for a living, but he was dubious. He said, 'You've been working for yourself since your early twenties. You're now in your fifties. Do you really think you can handle sitting at a desk all day and having some guy half your age telling you what to do? Do you think you can really cut Corporate America?' You'd think being the vice chairman of the world's biggest oil market would count for something, but I guess not. So I retired. Now I have a lot of season tickets to games and watch a lot of live sports."

VINNIE VIOLA

Still a trader, Viola runs a Madison Avenue market-making firm and is a well-known champion of the kind of high-speed trading blamed for the disastrous "flash crash" of May 2010, when the stock market inexplicably plummeted, bleeding hundreds of billions of dollars, before bouncing back in just twenty minutes. He has continued opening other trading shops and running his banks in Texas. It's a far cry from where he started, betting on gasoline in the pits with his boyhood friends from Brooklyn.

"I don't know what I think of my time at Nymex. I have gone on to do lots of other things. I guess I don't regret it. I was the only Nymex chairman to be named to the Futures Industry Association's Futures Hall of Fame. Don't forget to mention that." Of short-lived demands from Congress that oil speculators be forced out of the market, he is very critical. "Really, what's the difference between some oil guy trading physical oil and a speculator trading it? So what if the second guy's drinking Red Bull and watching CNBC and clicking a mouse all day? Do too many speculators ruin the market for everybody? You really want to go there? This is a conversation about de Tocqueville. Welcome to the postindustrial world!"

ROSEMARY MCFADDEN

McFadden, now the deputy mayor of Jersey City, New Jersey, was not part of the 2009 dragnet in which dozens of politicians, three mayors, and five rabbis were charged in a scandal involving money-laundering and the illegal sale of body parts in a crime ring that stretched from Israel to Switzerland. She says she was just as shocked as anybody when she saw her colleagues being led away in handcuffs after a two-year sting operation that caught some of them passing bribes around in, among other things, a box of Apple Jacks cereal with $97,000 crammed into it. Some of her former colleagues at Nymex were less surprised, observing the events with a sense of wry amusement. "You wonder how many times so many important people can be cut down around a single person like that and still call it a coincidence," says one executive who worked with McFadden. In New Jersey, a state widely known for being as embattled as Nymex itself, the stings never seemed to end. "We have an old joke here whenever we go out to dinner," says the New Jersey superior court judge who helped Michel Marks get his start and also knows McFadden. "We always say, 'Lean forward and *speak directly into the sugar bowl*,' because that's how bad it is with all the microphones and the wiretaps around."

JOHN D'AGOSTINO

"Oil traders are interchangeable. Who they are doesn't matter. They don't have any real power; they're just riding the wave of America's oil addiction. Other people will come in to replace them. And that goes for the rest of the colossus surrounding the oil market, from the politicians to the regulators on down. It won't stop unless we stop using so much oil. We're effectively on a desert island and the oil nations are in the corner with the shade and the one coconut tree. Trying to fix individual parts of it isn't going to work. Changing a few trading rules isn't going to work. It's like trying to put a Band-Aid on a severed head. The oil market is like a criminal: it's always evolving, always changing. We have yet to have a president who will actually get up and tell everyone the truth, say to the American people, 'We can't control this bad boy anymore.' If it's true that you can't have innovation without the Frankenstein, then Nymex *is* that Frankenstein." D'Agostino went on to work for a number of family offices and hedge funds across Manhattan and abroad.

THE "FUCK ICE" GUY

After receiving several million dollars from the CME merger, the executive who led Nymex's failed push into London went from being a pit trader to a screen trader. He now works from home. "You know, after I left Nymex, I started walking my kids to school, but then I noticed that the other parents were avoiding me. I couldn't figure out why. Then I realized it was because I was wearing old sweatshirts and jeans and letting my hair grow out and I had a huge beard. They didn't think I had a job. I didn't, actually. But they didn't think I had any money. They thought I was this crazy guy, like the Unabomber. . . . That's when I got a haircut and cleaned myself up."

MICHEL MARKS

"We could have kept this market. We could have made much more out of it. But the politics and people's self-interest always got in the way." Following the CME merger, which Marks opposed, he repaired to his hometown of Red Bank, New Jersey, where he opened up a painting studio. He also started a local arts collective he funded himself. He still likes wine. He still reads poetry. And more than anything, he does not want to hear any more about Nymex. He thinks maybe one day he'll write a book about it, but for now he wants nothing more than to be left alone. "I think it was Michel's iconoclasm that was probably what made him such a success," says a former close friend of the Marks family. "He built Nymex, but he was not *of* Nymex. He was always an outsider.

When he comes down to the trading floor, everyone knows who he is. He still gets the respect. But he is not one of us."

SHERRY COLLINS ZABEL

"Michel and I are still close. In fact, we recently went camping with my kids and his adopted kids in the Pine Barrens. Michel loves the outdoors, but I got the feeling he's never actually been overnight camping. As the trip got closer, he started asking a lot of questions about having enough supplies and all that. But he had a blast. Since I left Nymex, I've been waitressing and I also referee lacrosse. You can actually make some pretty good money as a lacrosse referee. I went back to the Nymex after the merger, to see it after all these years, and the CME had a security guard following me around everywhere. They acted like I was going to try and steal something. It was great seeing some of the guys again. I went to the tenth floor to look at the oil paintings of the chairmen and you know what I saw? Richie's painting. It was about three times as big as all the other chairmen's paintings. He even took down some of the older chairmen's paintings so his could fit. And he put his next to the smaller ones, you know, for contrast. I was like, 'Wow.' It was outrageous."

BO COLLINS

After his hedge fund, MotherRock, went under, Collins's marriage foundered and he started a number of other ventures but hadn't yet regained his footing as a trader. Living between New York and Texas, he recently started a brokerage firm with another Nymex trader. "For a long time, Bo wasn't returning my phone calls," one of his former partners says. "Then I walked into a bar and who do I see sitting there all alone but Bo in jeans and a cowboy hat. He's had it tough, but he wasn't always so good to everyone on the way up. I heard he was trying to get something started with Richie Schaeffer, selling risk-management software to traders. Can you believe that? After blowing up his hedge fund. That's like the Octomom trying to sell birth control."

LOU GUTTMAN

Still living at the Gateway Plaza, Guttman keeps two apartments—

one, his old home office, and the other an expanded residence for his growing family. In September 2007, he and his wife had twin daughters, Kimberly and Karin. He was fifty-eight. "I gotta tell you, these little girls really keep us on our toes," he says. "But they are amazing. I work and then I go upstairs and see them and the stress just melts away. I also have a secret: I do not change dirty diapers. We have someone for that. It makes all the difference." Guttman, still banned from trading futures, now trades stocks. "I make enough that I can support my family and my dad and have a little left over. I am not the young huckster I used to be, I've let some of those passions and anger go. Looking at it now, I think everyone met their fate. What goes around comes around. You can't escape divine Providence.

"It used to bother the hell out of me, but as I get older, it doesn't anymore. Did the system mistreat me? Yeah. But who *is* the government? People! Just like us, looking to make a name and reputation for themselves, sometimes on other people's backs. What do they know? The six years I was running the exchange, I didn't have a life. It was everything. I was exhausted, I was constantly embattled, constantly in the trenches. Constantly a bachelor. I had no plans to not keep on being one. If I'd kept going like that, I'd have never stopped. I wouldn't have been able to take care of my mother then, or my father now. I wouldn't have gotten married. I wouldn't have Connie, my beautiful wife. I wouldn't have my two beautiful daughters."

RICHIE SCHAEFFER

Schaeffer's restaurant closed nine months after it opened. "He had trouble keeping his staff," says a former colleague. "At the exchange, screaming swear words at people is how things got done, but in the real world it doesn't work that way. Richie lost his chef and it was downhill from there. I guess the chef doesn't speak Nymexian." Schaeffer was not put off. He was already putting the finishing touches on his next big idea: a hedge fund. "You know where my new favorite place to park my yacht is? In the marina right in front of the Nymex building, just to piss off the CME. It's kind of like my own very personal 'Fuck you.' My dad is nearby and I have my daughter and I'm gonna take care of them. [Schaeffer's mother, Irene, had died a few years earlier.] But I don't know about the rest of it. I know what people say about me. But you know what? They are just jealous. Everybody wanted to take the oil market public and I did it. That was every chairman's dream, but they could never get everyone to agree. I like money, but you know . . . I don't care about it that much. I don't know what I am going to do down the road. Probably retire to a tropical island, marry a black manicurist." (Less than a year later, his wife, Jill, whom he had not divorced, gave birth to twin boys, Matthew and Daniel.)

JIM NEWSOME

Underregulating the over-the-counter market that sank the U.S. economy "obviously, in hindsight, was a very bad decision," Newsome says. He regretted that. The Enron loophole also had been a bad idea. He regretted that too. Newsome still did not agree with the London loophole, but made no apologies for the opening of the Dubai loophole. In any case, he couldn't do anything about it now. While on the board of the CME, Newsome founded a Washington financial consultancy with Scott Parsons, the same person from the CFTC to whom Nymex had shelled out hundreds of thousands of dollars when Newsome had been the oil market's president and CEO. When not lobbying on behalf of clients such as the CME, which compensated Newsome and Parsons handsomely, Newsome continued to sit on a highly influential advisory panel of the CFTC entrusted with safeguarding the integrity of the nation's markets. Again, nobody batted an eye.

In the summer of 2009, the last time I spoke with him, he was visiting the lush, five-hundred-thousand-acre spread along the Serengeti desert that belonged to Paul Tudor Jones, the billionaire hedge fund manager who was friends with Mark Fisher. Newsome also considered Fisher, the trader he once threw the book at, his "dear friend." On the way, Newsome and his wife visited her well-to-do grandmother Jenny, who was still running the La Reserve resort in the Seychelles. "My wife and I had a wonderful time observing wildlife migratory patterns in Africa," Newsome says, referencing their shared interest in animal behavior. Since leaving Nymex, his colleagues said, Newsome had set aside a portion of his millions to buy up farmland across the United States. Having never fulfilled his dream of becoming a cattle farmer, he could at least join the ranks of the landed gentry.

The first time I met Newsome, he told me about the late Mississippi judge and legislator whom he'd greatly admired, by the name of Noah "Soggy" Sweat Jr.

Sweat, a lifelong bachelor known for his love of shock value and his flaming red hair, had given an infamous speech in 1952 about another commodity from which the United States had never broken its addiction. The speech, instantly hailed as a monument to political double-talk, was, fittingly, Newsome's favorite and just as ill-fated as the many speeches delivered over the years about oil. However, Sweat's elegant diatribe—known as the "Whiskey Speech"—was about alcohol.

Sweat, aside from being an orator, had also been a drinker.

My friends,

I had not intended to discuss this controversial subject at this particular time.

However, I want you to know that I do not shun controversy. On the contrary, I will take a stand on any issue at any time, regardless of how fraught with controversy it might be. You have asked me how I feel about whiskey. All right, here is how I feel about whiskey.

If when you say whiskey you mean the devil's brew, the poison scourge, the bloody monster that defiles innocence, dethrones reason, destroys the home, creates misery and poverty, yea, literally takes the bread from the mouths of little children; if you mean the evil drink that topples the Christian man and woman from the pinnacle of righteous, gracious living into the bottomless pit of degradation, and despair, and shame and helplessness, and hopelessness, then certainly I am against it.

But, if when you say whiskey you mean the oil of conversation, the philosophic wine, the ale that is consumed when good fellows get together, that puts a song in their hearts and laughter on their lips, and the warm glow of contentment in their eyes; if you mean Christmas cheer; if you mean the stimulating drink that puts the spring in the old gentleman's step on a frosty, crispy morning; if you mean the drink which enables a man to magnify his joy, and his happiness, and to forget, if only for a little while, life's great tragedies, and heartaches, and sorrows; if you mean that drink, the sale of which pours into our treasuries untold millions of dollars, which are used to provide tender care for our little crippled children, our blind, our deaf, our dumb, our pitiful aged and infirm; to build highways and hospitals and schools, then certainly I am for it.

This is my stand. I will not retreat from it. I will not compromise.

Glossary

analyst—A financial professional who conducts research, specializing in specific industries or sectors.

arbitrage—The purchase and sale of an asset or similar assets in order to profit from a difference in the price. (See *regulatory arbitrage*.)

broker (or *brokerage*)—An individual or firm that charges a fee or commission for executing buy and sell orders submitted by an investor.

bucketing—A situation where, in an attempt to make a short-term profit, a broker or trader confirms an order to a client without actually executing it. (See *front-running*.)

commercial—A term used to refer to any party or organization involved in producing, transporting, or merchandising a commodity.

commodity—Any good exchanged during commerce, which includes goods traded on a commodity exchange.

Commodity Futures Trading Commission (CFTC)—An independent federal agency created in 1974 by Congress and mandated to regulate commodity futures and option markets in the United States with the goal of protecting the public and market users from price manipulation and abusive practices.

credit-default swaps—The buyer of a credit swap receives credit protection. The seller of the swap guarantees the creditworthiness of a product. The default risk, as a result, is transferred from one party to another.

derivative—A financial product whose price is dependent on, or derived from, one or more different types of underlying assets. (For example, an oil futures contract represents a thousand barrels of oil—oil being the "underlying asset" to the paper contract.)

dual trading—The practice of a market participant trading both on behalf of himself and his customers, which can lead to conflicts of interest.

Dubai loophole—Nymex's evasion of federal trading rules on the U.S. crude-oil futures contract, created when the CFTC approved oil's offering through an exchange in Dubai.

Enron loophole—Enron's evasion of federal trading rules that governed its over-the-counter market, subsequently extended to the entire U.S. over-the-counter market by Congress as part of the Commodity Futures Modernization Act in 2000.

exchange—A place where commodities and related investments trade in the form of options, futures, and other financial instruments.

exemption—A written grant relieving a market participant from a rule or requirement.

expiration—The time and the day that a particular futures-contract month stops trading, settles at a final price, and enters into the delivery phase.

Federal Energy Regulatory Commission—A federal agency created in 1977, which specifically regulates and oversees U.S. energy industries. (Its predecessor agency was the Federal Power Commission, formed in 1920.)

Federal Trade Commission (FTC)—An independent federal agency, created in 1914, which seeks to protect consumers and ensure a competitive marketplace.

front-running—The unethical practice of a broker or trader buying or selling a financial product in front of another order, often for purposes of self-gain.

fundamentals—The qualitative and quantitative information that contributes to the financial valuation of a company, security, or currency.

future contract—A legally binding agreement, generally made on the trading floor of a futures exchange, to buy or sell a particular commodity or financial instrument at a predetermined price within a fixed, future time frame.

Goldman Sachs Commodity Index—A basket of commodities investments that engages only in buying, not selling, which has led to some speculation of it keeping prices—in particular oil prices—artificially high. (Renamed the S&P GSCI after the index was purchased by Standard & Poor's in 2007.)

greenmail—An oblique reference to blackmail, this is a situation where an unfriendly party buys up a large block of stock in a company, putting pressure on the company to buy it back at a (usually) obscene price or suffer the consequence—for instance, an unfriendly takeover.

hedge fund—An aggressively managed portfolio of investments that uses advanced investment strategies, long and short positions, complex financial instruments, and borrowed money to maximize profits for wealthy customers.

hedging (or *hedge*)—Making an investment in one asset to reduce the risk of adverse price moves in another. Normally, a hedge consists of taking an offsetting position in a related financial product, such as the buying of oil futures to offset a physical oil position.

index—Measures statistical changes through a point system in a given market. Technically, an index can be devised to follow almost anything, but typically follows financial products such as futures and stocks.

IPO (initial public offering)—The first sale of stock by a private company to the public.

leverage—Borrowed money used to finance various trades. The more money one has to bet with, the more money one can make or lose. (This is how traders can make and lose so much so fast.)

local—A colloquial term used to refer to independent pit traders or speculators who trade with their own money and often live in close proximity to the market they trade in.

London loophole—ICE's evasion of federal trading rules by offering U.S. oil futures and other energy products online through the United Kingdom.

long—The buying of a commodity, security, or financial product with the expectation that the asset's value will rise.

market maker—A market participant who makes a living by accommodating both buyers and sellers by filling their orders, facilitating the trades, and profiting off them.

no-action letter—A letter written by staff members of a government agency (such as the Commodity Futures Trading Commission) typically acknowledging that no enforcement action will be taken under certain circumstances, frequently at the request of the company or entity being given relief.

Nymex board of directors—The oil market's main governing body mostly consisting of representatives from the pits, such as independent traders, or "locals"; floor brokers; commercials; brokerages; seat holders; and a few public members. This group fluctuated between fifteen and twenty-five directors during the course of the exchange's history.

open interest—The total number of buy and sell orders outstanding in a market, frequently broken down by asset type.

option—A contract giving a trader the right, but not the obligation, to buy or sell a specific financial asset at a specific price for a limited time.

over-the-counter market (or *spot market*)—A multitrillion-dollar, largely unmonitored trading realm existing outside the regulated exchanges, immense in its scope (although the exact scope remains as yet undetermined). Over-the-counter trades are often conducted privately online, in person, by telephone, or via Internet instant-messaging.

regulatory arbitrage—The act of moving a business or market to a location where the legal rules applying to it are more relaxed and, thus, more favorable. When Wall Street threatens to take its businesses offshore, it is essentially engaging in regulatory arbitrage.

securities—Any contracts assigned a value that may be traded.

Securities and Exchange Commission (SEC)—A government body created by Congress during the Great Depression to regulate the securities markets and protect the investing community against fraudulent and manipulative practices.

self-regulatory organization (SRO)—A nongovernmental organization, such as an exchange, that has the power to create and enforce industry regulations and standards.

short—The selling of a commodity, security, or financial product with the expectation that the asset's value will fall.

speculator—A person who trades primarily for cash or liquid profit, taking on higher-than-average risks in exchange for the chance of winning higher-than-average returns.

volatility—The extent to which prices rise and fall swiftly in a financial product. Many traders like volatility, because it gives them the opportunity latch on to sharp price swings, which earn them more money than gradual ones.

volume—The number of contracts or shares traded in a market during a given time frame. Often used as a measure of an exchange or financial product's overall business activity.

wash trades—An illegal and manipulative trading practice in which the investor simultaneously buys *and* sells shares of a financial instrument, often creating the false impression of heightened market activity, increasing volumes and boosting prices.

Acknowledgments

This book, while written in ten months, followed several years of research and many transatlantic journeys. To those who encouraged me to undertake the monumental task of putting it together, I am deeply grateful. They are: John Cochrane Duncanson, Sara and Howard Brathwaite, Thomas and Kathy McGrath, Kathleen McGrath, Rebecca Jean Helms, Cassandra Rea Holloway, Cheri Carroll, Lauren McCracken, Dayna Kanary, Kara Brickman, Dr. Cael Keegan, Victoria Hart, Sioban Hickie, Stephanie Cochinos, Shayna Sebold, Christine Nuzum, Colleen Debaise, Paul Vigna, Leia Parker, Beth Heinsohn, Susan McIntosh, Tony Tassell, Adrian Harpham, Craig Haines, Michael Guido, Greg Perrault, Axel Bogetic, Mitchel Coffman, Sonwha Lee, Shane Finemore, Edward Robinson; Peter Mazurczyk, Dwayne Drexler, Daniel Masters, Beatriz Abella, Dr. Adam Kantor, Bullard Andrew Holmstrom Spence, Russell Andersson, RBS, and Kevin Morrison, my former competitor and continued confidant at the *Financial Times*.

Thank you to my patient and criminally skilled editor, Mauro DiPreta, along with his fastidious associate editor, Jennifer Schulkind, as well as my copy editor, Olga Gardner Galvin, and everyone at HarperCollins who helped make this book possible.

To those at the *Wall Street Journal* who provided me with much-needed advice and assistance—in particular Andrew Dowell, Michael Siconolfi, Eugene Colter, and Kathleen Seagriff—I cannot thank you enough.

A special thanks also to Jim Impoco, my former editor at *Condé Nast Portfolio*, for his guidance and stellar edits.

I am hugely indebted to Richard Blake (one of those rare, unaccountably humble writers whose talents are too great to list here) for passing on the art of breathing life into even the driest of topics, and Rachel Eve Pine for her boundless enthusiasm and expertise every time I take on a new project. My thanks also to her husband, Adam Johnson, who allowed me to stay at their home in London while I conducted research.

My sincere gratitude to Virginia Cochrane, whose desert ranch in Arizona gave me the remove I needed to begin writing, as well as to Sharon Sergeant, Boston University professor and forensic genealogist of uncommon gifts, for helping me verify the lineage of traders whose families died in the Holocaust. In addition, I would like to extend my heartfelt thanks to Ben Kaufman, John D'Agostino, Sharon Abramzon, and Deep Throat for their unstinting support, candor, and trust.

Pivotal to my research were the following individuals: Zoltan Louis and Connie Guttman, Michel Marks, Sherry Collins Zabel, and Richard Schaeffer. Thank you for repeatedly tolerating intrusive questions and allowing me unprecedented access to your personal records, photos, and memorabilia—not to mention sharing with me your memories, even when they were sometimes painful.

To the New York Public Library, the Social Security Death Index, the Federal Energy Regulatory Commission, OpenSecrets.org, the Freedom of Information Act, and the rest of it. Without these and many other resources, a reporter would be lost.

To the Nymex chairmen, presidents, and executives who may or may not like this book, it was a daunting task capturing on the page just how unforgettable you are. To know you was a privilege. To do you justice is nearly impossible. I did my level best. To the traders, brokers, and clerks in the pits and the lawyers, traders, and bankers on Wall Street who shared their experiences and confidences, I am, once more, enormously grateful. Your humor and sagacity transcend your extreme-capitalist alter egos.

To those who did not want their names mentioned in this book, your contributions were as substantial as your numbers. To the protesters on Wall Street whose chanting kept me awake at all hours, you stand for something many of us still hope for. To the boys at Leo's Bagels for their obligingly endless supply of coffee and hot chocolate, thanks and thanks. To my doorman Eddie and my super William, who cheerfully carried my stuff, turned away visitors, and put up with me while I languished in my book coma, I owe you lunch at Ulysses. Thanks also to my landlord, Edward Reiher, who never ceased to be understanding of my uncertain comings and goings.

Most of all, I'd like to thank my mentor extraordinaire, Dr. Denny Wilkins, "God editor." You took a chance on an upstart. You may yet regret it. Thanks for the Maserati.

Index